THOMAS WOLFE

Modern Critical Views

These and other titles in preparation

Modern Critical Views

THOMAS WOLFE

Edited and with an introduction by
Harold Bloom
Sterling Professor of the Humanities
Yale University

CHELSEA HOUSE PUBLISHERS ◇ 1987
New York ◇ New Haven ◇ Philadelphia

© 1987 by Chelsea House Publishers,
a division of Chelsea House Educational Communications, Inc.,
   95 Madison Avenue, New York, NY 10016
   345 Whitney Avenue, New Haven, CT 06511
   5014 West Chester Pike, Edgemont, PA 19028

Introduction © 1987 by Harold Bloom

Printed and bound in the United States of America

∞ The paper used in this publication meets the minimum
requirements of the American National Standard for
Permanence of Paper for Printed Library Materials,
Z39.48-1984.

Library of Congress Cataloging-in-Publication Data
Thomas Wolfe.
   (Modern critical views)
   Bibliography: p.
   Includes index.
   Contents: Symbolic patterns in You can't go home
again / Clyde C. Clements, Jr. — The hills beyond /
Leslie A. Field — The escapes of time and memory / Morris
Beja — [etc.]
   1. Wolfe, Thomas, 1900–1938—Criticism and
interpretation. [1. Wolfe, Thomas, 1900–1938—Criticism
and interpretation. 2. American literature—History
and criticism] I. Bloom, Harold. II. Series.
PS3545.0337Z8627 1987 813'.52   86-29952
ISBN 0-87754-638-X (alk. paper)

Contents

Editor's Note

This book gathers together what I consider to be the most useful criticism of Thomas Wolfe's fiction. The critical essays are reprinted in the chronological order of their original publication. I am grateful to Henry Finder for his erudition and judgment as a researcher.

My introduction meditates upon the relation between Wolfe's life and his work, as set forth by his definitive biographer, David Herbert Donald. Clyde C. Clements, Jr., begins the chronological sequence with a study of the symbolism of *You Can't Go Home Again*, after which Leslie A. Field studies the "folk novel" *The Hills Beyond*.

The epiphanies, or moments of self-revelation, in Wolfe are analyzed by Morris Beja, while the vexed issue of the genre of Wolfe's fiction is considered by Richard S. Kennedy. Leo Gurko's exegesis of *The Web and the Rock* is followed by C. Hugh Holman's meditation upon how Wolfe's work was haunted always by memories and visions of the South.

John Hagan gives informed readings of *Look Homeward, Angel* and *Of Time and the River*.

Introduction

Thomas Wolfe died in Baltimore on September 15, 1938, about two weeks before what would have been his thirty-eighth birthday. He is remembered for his novels, the first two severely edited by Maxwell Perkins of Scribner's, *Look Homeward, Angel* (1929) and *Of Time and the River* (1935). His two posthumously published novels, *The Web and the Rock* (1939) and *You Can't Go Home Again* (1940), were even more fully edited by Edward Aswell of Harper. Though many novelists have owed considerable literary debts to their editors, Wolfe is notoriously unique in this regard. It is rather clear that both editors greatly improved their author's manuscripts, and that Aswell, in particular, was a better writer than Wolfe, on a paragraph-to-paragraph basis. We have been threatened with scholarly publication of Wolfe's original manuscripts, and doubtless the threats will be fulfilled, but the originals are most unlikely to revive Wolfe's almost dead reputation as a novelist. Wolfe's definitive biographer, the distinguished historian of the Northern experience of our Civil War, David Herbert Donald of Harvard, seems to me rather harsh when he sums up his view of Aswell:

> But I believe that it is equally misleading to speak of Aswell's work on Wolfe's posthumous novels as simply that of an editor. From standardizing the names and the tenses of Wolfe's manuscript, Aswell moved on to modifying the rhythm of his prose, to altering his characterizations, and to cutting and shaping his chapters. Greatly exceeding the professional responsibility of an editor, Aswell took impermissible liberties with Wolfe's manuscript, and his interference seriously eroded the integrity of Wolfe's text. Far from deserving commendation, Aswell's editorial interference was, both from the standpoint of literature and of ethics, unacceptable.

1

I am not prepared to argue ethics with Donald (or with anyone else), but from "the standpoint of literature" just what is the "integrity" of bad writing? What are the literary values of the rhythm of Wolfe's prose, as compared with Aswell's? The sample contrasts provided by Donald in parallel columns indicate, to me, that Wolfe's Byronic blank verse (very blank) masking as prose, left pretty much unaltered by Maxwell Perkins, is less tiresomely obtrusive after being worked over by Aswell. But then Donald, an admirable biographer and skilled historian, ought to have avoided writing literary criticism of Wolfe. A valuable portrait of Wolfe, that adolescent titan whose only appeal may still be to adolescents (perpetual and otherwise), is marred only by too-frequent descents into what Donald intends to be aesthetic evaluation of his subject. Insisting as he does that "Wolfe's books must be judged as literature, not as history," Donald admits that Wolfe "wrote more bad prose than any other major writer I can think of," but then proceeds not only to admire the prose at its most abominable but to print choice chunks of it as verse, explaining cheerfully that "to stress the poetic quality of these passages I have presented them here in verse form." So, we are offered this:

> October is the richest of the seasons:
> The fields are cut, the granaries are full,
> The bins are loaded to the brim with fatness,
> And from the cider-press the rich brown oozings of—
>   the York Imperials run.
> The bee bores into the belly of the yellowed grape,
> The fly gets old and fat and blue,
> He buzzes loud, crawls slow, creeps heavily to death
>   on sill and ceiling,
> The sun goes down in blood and pollen
> Across the bronzed and mown fields of old October.

The echoes here of Keats's "To Autumn" are quite unfortunate, and one line in particular is a candidate for that great anthology, *The Stuffed Owl:* "The sun goes down in blood and pollen." Donald quotes this, and then declares his appreciation:

> There are dozens of these passages. Among my favorites are Wolfe's magnificent recreation of locomotives snaking their way north through the Southern mountains, his lament on the frigidity of New England ("Oh, bitterly, bitterly Boston, one time more"), and his evocation of the spine-tingling first sight of New

York, "far-shining, glorious, time-enchanted." These are not the work of a cautious writer or of a conventional writer, and they have their faults. But they help to explain why so many of Wolfe's contemporaries thought him a genius. Rereading them makes it clear that Wolfe deserves to rank among the very great American authors.

The line on Boston has its palpable claim upon *The Stuffed Owl* also, and I well may cry "far-shining, glorious, time-enchanted," when next a car bearing me turns into the Henry Hudson Drive. Donald's exuberant and generous attempt to convert Thomas Wolfe into Hart Crane will not benefit the most dubious of all reputations among modern American novelists. Faulkner, our best novelist since Henry James, once set Wolfe first among his contemporaries but based this judgment upon the magnitude of Wolfe's failure, that being Faulkner's sublimely perverse test for greatness.

What, if anything, can we do with Thomas Wolfe now, except to read his life story as composed by the devoted Donald? We cannot *read* Wolfe. I mean this literally, having just attempted *Look Homeward, Angel* for the first time in forty years. There is no possibility for critical dispute about Wolfe's literary merits; he has none whatsoever. Open him at any page, and that will suffice. Here is the conclusion of *Look Homeward, Angel*:

> "On coasts more strange than Cipango, in a place more far than Fez, I shall hunt him, the ghost and haunter of myself. I have lost the blood that fed me; I have died the hundred deaths that lead to life. By the slow thunder of the drums, the flare of dying cities, I have come to this dark place. And this is the true voyage, the good one, the best. And now prepare, my soul, for the beginning hunt. I will plumb seas stranger than those haunted by the Albatross."
>
> He stood naked and alone in darkness, far from the lost world of the streets and faces; he stood upon the ramparts of his soul, before the lost land of himself; heard inland murmurs of lost seas, the far interior music of the horns. The last voyage, the longest, the best.
>
> "O sudden and impalpable faun, lost in the thickets of myself, I will hunt you down until you cease to haunt my eyes with hunger. I heard your foot-falls in the desert, I saw your shadow in old buried cities, I heard your laughter running down a million streets, but I did not find you there. And no leaf hangs for me in the forest; I shall lift no stone upon the hills; I shall find no door

in any city. But in the city of myself, upon the continent of my soul, I shall find the forgotten language, the lost world, a door where I may enter, and music strange as any ever sounded; I shall haunt you, ghost, along the labyrinthine ways until—until? O Ben, my ghost, an answer?"

But as he spoke, the phantom years scrolled up their vision, and only the eyes of Ben burned terribly in darkness, without an answer.

And day came, and the song of waking birds, and the Square, bathed in the young pearl light of morning. And a wind stirred lightly in the Square, and, as he looked, Ben, like a fume of smoke, was melted into dawn.

And the angels on Gant's porch were frozen in hard marble silence, and at a distance life awoke, and there was a rattle of lean wheels, a slow clangor of shod hoofs. And he heard the whistle wail along the river.

Yet, as he stood for the last time by the angels of his father's porch, it seemed as if the Square already were far and lost; or, I should say, he was like a man who stands upon a hill above the town he has left, yet does not say "The town is near," but turns his eyes upon the distant soaring ranges.

THE END

It is difficult to believe that this is not a parody by S. J. Perelman, or even some lesser practitioner, but indeed it *is* the thing itself, Thomas Wolfe at his most Wolfean. Donald tells us that he was "even more surprised to find that Wolfe was an experimental writer," and places Wolfe in the company of Pound and Eliot, Gertrude Stein and Joyce and Faulkner. But I will not go on beating a dead woodchuck. If you can read Wolfe, then God bless you, but you will not interest many among us unless your reading is animated by social and cultural history, since clearly Wolfe matters a great deal more as an American phenomenon than he possibly could matter as an American writer. How could a writer as hopelessly mawkish as this, however shrewdly edited, ever have achieved so major a reputation, even for a time? Donald hardly sets out to ask or answer that question, but I think the largest value of his work is that he provides material for an answer.

Donald quotes Alfred Kazin's judgment that Wolfe was an alert analyst of depression America, an estimate that I can understand if "analyst" means chronicler, both voluntary and involuntary. Kazin would thus be confirming Faulkner's remark:

> Among his and my contemporaries, I rated Wolfe first because we had all failed, but Wolfe had made the best failure because he had tried hardest to say the most.

Trying hardest to say the most need not be accompanied by any authentic literary talent and would not in itself make you into a good novelist, but your strong will might have made you into a very full chronicler of the cultural and social sorrows of that bad American decade, 1928–1938. Though he thinks that Wolfe was a great novelist, Donald is actually persuasive in showing us Wolfe rather as a cultural and social journalist, a passionate beholder of America in trouble. Whether Wolfe possessed any analytical understanding of the economic and social crisis is disputable, but his intense love for his own region, however ambivalent the love may have been, and for what must be called the idea of his country, gave him a curious kind of apprehension, neither cognitive nor aesthetic, that remains of human value in understanding his era.

Human, all too human, however, poor Wolfe was hardly a sage or even a particularly rational person. Donald does not try to defend Wolfe's ghastly case of anti-Semitism, which was augmented by his long and bitter love affair with the theatrical designer Aline Bernstein. As Donald says, Jews in Wolfe's fiction are marked by "arrogance and aggressiveness, extravagance and sensuality," this being a vision of them "so much more flattering than his own personal assessment of Jews" that "he was both angered and baffled by critics who found his novels anti-Semitic."

Donald shrewdly traces the ambivalent relationship between Wolfe and the Southern Agrarians (John Crowe Ransom, Allen Tate, Robert Penn Warren, among others). An apolitical man, neither of the Left nor the Right, Wolfe was scarcely more acceptable to the Agrarians than he was to literary Marxists. His Byronic prose and general formlessness were of little appeal to the disciples of T. S. Eliot. Warren, now our leading poet, with a Sublime voice wholly his own, was in the 1930s a follower of Eliot in both verse and critical prose and condemned *Of Time and the River* in colorful terms that were accurate then and seem quite definitive now:

> Chaos that steams and bubbles in rhetoric and apocalyptic apostrophe, sometimes grand and sometimes febrile and empty; . . . a maelstrom, perhaps artificially generated . . . [with] the flotsam

and jetsam and dead wood spewed up; iridescent or soggy as the case may be.

Wolfe's lack of affiliations with any literary, social, or political camp may have helped him as an observer of his contemporary American scene. New York City in the 1930s comes through in his writings with a squalid vividness, reported as though Wolfe were on Mars or on the moon. One of the few moments in Wolfe that I can remember is his vision of Brooklyn: "cunningly contrived, compacted, and composed of eighty-seven separate several putrefactions . . . deceased, decaying cats . . . rotten cabbage, prehistoric eggs, and old tomatoes."

Donald is an unwearied chronicler of Wolfe's endless disasters in New York City and in his seven European trips, particularly boisterous in Germany. Perhaps any good biographer has to grow fond of his or her subject, and a touching care and concern for Wolfe increasingly permeates Donald's pages. He is able to invest even the scene of Wolfe dictating a novel to a secretary with a memorable pathos. What he cannot do is to make Wolfe very likable, though he certainly helps us to understand why Wolfe became a really difficult and unpleasant personality. The son of a Pennsylvania tombstone cutter and a Blue Ridge Mountains boardinghouse keeper in Asheville, North Carolina, Wolfe suffered his parents' bad and violent marriage. The youngest of seven surviving children, he seems to have absorbed the horrors of his own family romance with a particular receptivity. Educated at Chapel Hill and at Harvard, living in New York City and in Europe from 1924 until 1938, Wolfe famously never left home. His tormented relationship with Aline Bernstein was an overdetermined nightmare; she was twenty years older than Wolfe, married, with two children, half Wolfe's size, and Jew to his anti-Semite. Loving Wolfe, she remarked many years later, was like a "Japanese maiden's self-immolating leap into a volcano."

A six-and-a-half-foot, hard-drinking monomaniac who believes himself to be the Great American Writer would appear to be fiction rather than fact, but Donald's Wolfe is very real. He is something like a parody of Nietzsche— not the Nietzsche of *The Genealogy of Morals* but of *Ecce Homo*. Some of Donald's chapter titles, drawn from Wolfe, approximate Nietzsche's: "By God, I Have Genius," "I Shall Conquer the World," "I Must Spin Out My Entrails." Though Donald keeps telling us that Wolfe got along amiably enough with the writers who were his contemporaries, none of them became his friends, and his only literary relationships were with his editors and his agent. But Wolfe seems to have had no real friends anyway. Donald depicts a man marked by violence, jealousy, paranoid mood shifts, sudden lusts quickly satiated, and a remorseless necessity to be his own worst enemy.

If there were a single indisputable achievement by Wolfe, I would be pleased to end with the High Romantic note that perfection of the work had replaced perfection of the life, a Yeatsian formulation that makes Wolfe's fate seem more unhappy even than it may have been. But Wolfe, as Donald vividly presents him, was a human disaster, and his books, despite Donald's enthusiasm, are all of them aesthetic disasters. I do not think that we can even say anymore that Wolfe is the novelist for adolescents, the Salinger of the 1930s, as it were. Perhaps some adolescents still read Wolfe, but I do not encounter them. The most significant sentence in Donald's biography comes in the preface: "Later, as an adolescent, I really read *Look Homeward, Angel* and was certain that Thomas Wolfe had told my life story." Growing up in rural Mississippi, the young David Herbert Donald fell in love with Wolfe's novels, lost that love in the 1950s, and found it again later on. It was, he observes, not uncommon for an adolescent in the 1940s to be deeply affected by Wolfe, but the return of such enthusiasm is rare.

Wolfe's credo was the famous: "I believe that we are lost here in America, but I believe we shall be found." Whatever that metaphor of being lost in America meant to Wolfe, it is not at all clear what he could have meant by "We shall be found." By whom? By what? Donald, remarkable historian as he is, cannot be expected to answer such questions. Wolfe evidently got lost in childhood, and never quite found himself again by or through writing.

CLYDE C. CLEMENTS, JR.

Symbolic Patterns in
You Can't Go Home Again

In *You Can't Go Home Again* Thomas Wolfe rendered his lifetime experience and reflection into a meaningful art form, a message made more universal by certain symbolic patterns in the novel. It is hoped that definition and explication of these symbolic patterns will assist in a reevaluation of Wolfe as a literary artist. All too often Wolfe has been pictured by scholars and even by sympathetic commentators as a protean writer of great energies whose later work revealed little form and artistry except that which his editors imposed upon it. Indeed, the problem has its basis not in the incoherence of Wolfe's imagination but in his extreme frankness and naiveté in laying before the public his literary as well as personal problems.

Richard S. Kennedy in his scholarly work *The Window of Memory: The Literary Career of Thomas Wolfe* does little to dispel this general impression of formlessness in his thoroughgoing account of the gestation process of Wolfe's works, saying "although all Wolfe's books since *Look Homeward, Angel* lack cohesiveness, *You Can't Go Home Again* seems more choppy than any others." This is curious in light of his earlier assertion that Edward Aswell neatly edited the book "like George Kaufman's doctoring of a faulty script for the stage." Certainly, Kennedy's book is invaluable for a detailed history of the writing of the manuscript that became *You Can't Go Home Again* and an account of the editorial relationship, but it still leaves the reader wondering about the most important question: is there a total and significant meaning to the work itself beyond that of a skillful fictional biography?

From *Modern Fiction Studies* 11, no. 3 (Autumn 1965). © 1965 by the Purdue Research Foundation, West Lafayette, Indiana.

My contention is that partly because Wolfe was working steadily on one elaborate manuscript in his later life (from 1931–34 with a large section taken out for *Of Time and the River* and from 1936–37 in a later stretch) he created symbolic patterns which inform and structure his work. This patternation of the artistic endeavor, best known to artists themselves, is pointed out by D. H. Lawrence when he says, "Symbols are the artist's means of creating patterns of thought and emotion which did not previously exist and of communicating what had previously been ineffable." And E. K. Brown has said in his stimulating article, "Thomas Wolfe: Realist and Symbolist," that Wolfe "joined with the perceptive and devouring eye of the master realist, the imaginative symbolist's regard for relationships, occult and profound."

Plainly Wolfe meant *You Can't Go Home Again* to embody a symbolic complex of meaning, but these patterns, which inform the meaning, are not readily apparent from the seven book divisions set up by Edward Aswell or by the explication in the bridge between the forty-fourth and forty-fifth chapters:

> *The phrase had many implications for him. You can't go back home to your family, back home to your childhood, back home to romantic love, back home to a young man's dreams of glory and of fame, back home to exile, to escape to Europe and some foreign land, back home to lyricism, to singing just for singing's sake, back home to aestheticism, to one's youthful idea of "the artist" and the all-sufficiency of "art" and beauty and love, back home to the ivory tower, back home to places in the country, to the cottage in Bermuda, away from all the strife and conflict of the world, back home to the father you have lost and have been looking for, back home to someone who can help you, save you, ease the burden for you, back home to the old forms and systems of things which once seemed everlasting, but which are changing all the time—back home to the escapes of Time and Memory.*

Rather the line of development of the novel must be scrutinized to find "patterns of thought and emotion" that structure the symbolic complex of "you can't go home again." For example, while in Europe Webber meets Lloyd McHarg, a portrayal of a world-renowned American writer, modeled after Sinclair Lewis; for Webber he is clearly symbolic, abstract fame embodied. *"For when Mr. Lloyd McHarg swept like a cyclone through his life, George knew that he was having his first encounter in the flesh with that fair Medusa, Fame herself."*

Moreover, the idea of fame is inextricably linked with Webber's own notion of finding recognition in exile, just as many famous American writers are first tapped with the wand of importance abroad, James, Eliot, Frost, to name a few; and with Webber's triumphant reception in Germany in 1936, where he is hailed as "the great American epic writer." His attraction to the idea of fame as all-sufficient, then subsequent disillusionment with Lloyd McHarg, and with his own "fame" in a Germany taken over by Nazi excesses, suggest the whole symbolic pattern of "Fame in Exile." The symbolic pattern, described briefly here, follows the usual sequence: attraction, enlightenment, and severance.

The rejection of "Fame in Exile" points toward the real concern of the novel, the development of the protagonist, George Webber, who is a conscientious artist struggling with his life material to find a philosophic purpose, that is, where he can go spiritually with his allegiances. The process of rejecting personal and social illusions as he matures is essential to the ultimate veracity of his vision. Thus Wolfe's book lies in a literary tradition with the short stories of Hawthorne and James, which trace the development of the artistic credo.

These syndromes in the artist-philosopher's search are structured by symbolic patterns; in each case Webber feels attraction, undergoes enlightenment and then forces severance of an illusion which he had held to be all-sufficient. The symbolic patterns fall into three groupings, Reminiscence, Progression, and Projection, reflecting stages in his search. I have identified the following symbolic patterns in *You Can't Go Home Again:*

> *Symbolic Patterns of Reminiscence*
> The Pattern of the Family
> The Pattern of the Hometown
> *Symbolic Patterns of Progression*
> The Pattern of the Business Ethic
> The Pattern of Love and Art
> *Symbolic Patterns of Projection*
> The Pattern of Fame in Exile
> The Pattern of the Father

PATTERN OF THE FAMILY

Although the novel starts out with George Webber in the city, the first significant action occurs when he is summoned home for the funeral of Aunt Maw. Webber feels the pull of a powerful sense of family ties: "Ever since his mother had died when he was only eight years old, Aunt Maw had been the most solid and permanent fixture in his boy's universe." "As far back as he could remember, Aunt Maw had seemed to him an ageless crone, as old as God."

Thus Aunt Maw had become a symbol of his blood ties with the mountain clan. From her fantastic memory she had told stories of their family history, demonstrating their psychic and enduring powers, instilling in the young boy's impressionable consciousness an idea of mythical qualities in the Joyners. In the cemetery Webber encounters Delia Flood, an old friend of the family, who reminds him: " 'Your Aunt Maw always hoped you'd come home again. And you *will!*' she said. 'There's no better or more beautiful place on earth than in these mountains—and some day you'll come home again to stay.' "

But the young writer rejects the entreaty to return to the family, for George Webber is *not* Eugene Gant, nor is Aunt Maw an eternal mother symbol like Eliza Gant whom the son will always feel drawn back to. When Wolfe changed the history of his protagonist, he replaced the fecund Eliza with Aunt Maw, a virgin who regards any interest in the flesh with suspicion, and substituted John Webber, a shadowy figure who ran away from his responsibilities as a father, for the monumental W. O. Gant. With his foster mother dead and his father gone, Webber painfully realizes that there can be no lasting relationship between an educated writer who moved in fashionable New York society and his half-mad mountain kin. Thus the illusion of the family which seemed to represent security, understanding, and everlasting ties is not sufficient, and Webber has experienced attraction, enlightenment, and severance in this symbolic pattern.

PATTERN OF THE HOMETOWN

If Webber feels a lost security in his family, he anticipates in the familiar rural landmarks of his hometown, a symbol of permanence in a life of mutability, "But why had he always felt so strongly the magnetic pull of home . . . if this little town, and the immortal hills around it, was not the only home he had on earth?" Yet no sooner does he board the train for Libya Hill than Webber hears talk of burgeoning real estate developments, of remaking his hometown into something bigger and better. Wolfe has drawn portraits in the social satire mold of Sinclair Lewis of the corrupt townsmen who relate the "progress" in Libya Hill—Jarvis Riggs, who runs the fastest growing bank in the state by manipulating the funds of the town, with the assistance of the amiable Mayor Baxtor Kennedy and the politician "Parson" Flack. However, the changes in his hometown are scored upon

Webber's consciousness by his encounter with three symbolic characters: Nebraska Crane, J. Timothy Wagner and Judge Rumford Bland.

Nebraska Crane, a character of pure invention, the Cherokee Indian who was a boyhood friend of Webber, has become a famous baseball star, wealthy and able to retire wherever he wants. On the train, when Wolfe asks him if he will be bored by life back on a farm in Zebulon, he reveals an attitude directly opposite to the corrupt town leaders. Crane is the only one of Webber's hometown acquaintances who conceives of land as a place to live and work on.

Still another meaning is evident in J. Timothy Wagner, "the high priest and prophet of this insanity of waste," a symbol of the complete derangement of values of the town; for an understanding of the changed values of the town is gained by seeing their new attitude toward J. Timothy Wagner. Webber recalls from his childhood memories a picture of Wagner as a local Bacchus, an extravagant young man who had run through two fortunes before he was twenty-five, turned into a drunk, and was regarded by the town with disgust. Since the start of the real estate speculation, J. Timothy Wagner had been apotheosized: "Tim Wagner had now become the supreme embodiment of the town's extravagant folly . . . so the people of the town now listened prayerfully to every word Tim Wagner uttered. They sought his opinion in all their speculations, and acted instantly on his suggestions." Even Wagner's habit of sleeping in a discarded hearse has morbid overtones for the town in which forty people committed suicide when their god of speculation failed.

If the townspeople flung paper fortunes away on the whim of a false prophet, they failed to heed another local prophet, Judge Rumford Bland. In a short number of pages, Wolfe has created a symbolic figure of the proportions of the Gant family. Bland is a mixture of good and evil, "a fallen angel" who has tasted the fruits of forbidden knowledge. Blind now, an unmistakable parallel to Tiresias, he had started with all the advantages of a distinguished family, a lawyer's education, and a good record in the southern community. Yet for some reason Bland's reputation soon became stained; his marriage ended in a quick divorce, and he gave up law for the practice of usury on hapless Negroes. He was as callous in his dealings with his debtors as he was with the prostitutes who gave him syphilis. Wolfe writes, "He was stained with evil. There was something genuinely old and corrupt at the sources of his life and spirit. It had got into his blood, his bone, his flesh."

Yet this same Bland exposes the corruptness of the local politicians on the train within Webber's hearing. They are "afraid of him because his blind eyes saw straight through them." Like the Greek prophet, Bland brings the truth no one wants to hear, " 'Do I remember now the broken fragments of a town that waits and fears and schemes to put off the day of its impending ruin?' " Reminding them that he will *see* them again, the full twist of irony comes when it is Bland who first discovers the dead mayor's body in the public washroom. It is also Bland who asks the nervous Webber the question that structures his future work, " 'I mean, do you think you can really go *home* again?' "

Sensing the inner honesty of the man, Webber thought that the terrible and cynical release of Bland's abilities had occurred because "there had once been a warmth and an energy that had sought for an enhancement of the town's cold values, and for a joy and a beauty that were not there, but that lived in himself alone." The tragedy of Judge Bland, a potentially great man who had ruined himself, was symbolic of the basically honest and rural Libya Hill, a town that had ruined itself. Webber has learned that the hometown of his spirit has changed radically in form and values, and he cannot go back to any certainty there.

PATTERN OF THE BUSINESS ETHIC

Disappointed in his philosophic search in reminiscence, Webber, an activist, turns to the present for answers—to the values of the new "American way" of the 1920s, the business ethic. The symbolic pattern of the business ethic goes beyond "the city" as a stronghold of dishonest privilege, being a folly of all America from Libya Hill to New York City, eventually bringing economic and moral collapse.

Webber perceives in the company man, Randy Shepperton, a new kind of evil masking as "sound business." For Randy the Federal Weight, Scales, and Computing Company, a nationwide organization of salesmen, is "the Company," a plainly marked symbol of the way to success. The company president had swept away the old business ethic based on fulfilling need and substituted a creed of creating a desire for his product. Represented by Merritt, a suggestively named, glad-handing boss, the Company seems paternalistic until business declines and Webber overhears him threatening to dismiss the faithful employee, Shepperton. Thus the company ethic is based on the naturalistic principle, survival of the fittest. Webber recalls a picture of slave labor building the pyramids, the only reward a lashing, as an image of the company structure. Shepperton is unable to comprehend his own dismissal because he has become a disciple of the magic of salesmanship, "that commercial brand of special pleading—that devoted servant of self-

interest—that sworn enemy of truth." Meanwhile, in Libya Hill the financial and moral terror that followed the closing of the municipal bank and
the mayor's suicide was the last legacy of land speculation.

In New York City Webber feels the same attraction to the world of
society, supported by the business ethic, before he senses enlightenment
about its values and forces severance. The wealthy Mr. Jack and his friends
delight in the animal-like struggle of laissez-faire, convinced that their professional hardness and amorality selects them for privilege: "When they
looked about them and saw everywhere nothing but the myriad shapes of
privilege, dishonesty, and self-interest, they were convinced that this was
inevitably 'the way things are.' "

Wolfe uses the party at Jack's, which ends in a climactic fire, as a
symbolic device to represent both the privilege and the disintegration of
society based on the business ethic. He juxtaposes the events at the party
just one week before the stock market crash, which ushered in the depression. The figures from the world of finance, the theatrical, literary, and
international set are superficial, jaded with power, or perverse. Their phony
liberalism is exposed by such business practices as child labor and strike
breaking.

The eventual failure of the business ethic is foreshadowed by the acci-
dental fire in the apartment building, which reveals the impotence of their
wealth, and the leveling of social classes in the depression, as all types and
classes seek refuge and mingle in the sidewalk below. Ironically, and to the
point, the only persons killed in the fire are two working men, Enborg and
Anderson. Corrosion of moral values becomes more apparent in the attitude
of the management, concerned only with protecting their wealthy tenants
from unpleasant news.

After the party Webber rejects the world of the business ethic, noting
the sordid conditions of tramps in the depression year 1932. He concludes
that the predicament in America has come about because of "catch phrases
like 'prosperity' and 'rugged individualism' and 'the American way.' "
America would not be able to go home again to any easy way of success, for
the future "would not be built on business as we know it."

PATTERN OF LOVE AND ART

Love and art function closely as a single symbolic pattern in *You Can't
Go Home Again*. Webber has a selfish and self-justifying attitude toward
love, and toward art for the sake of art; these are tied up with his sexual
relationship to Mrs. Jack. He is the young provincial who comes to the city

to find fulfillment: "From his early childhood, when he is living like an orphan with his Joyner relatives back in Libya Hill, he had dreamed that one day he would go to New York and there find love and fame and fortune."

As the novel opens, Webber returns to New York, finding Esther Jack and feeling again their tremendous pull of love. (Although their tumultuous affair had been the primary development of *The Web and the Rock,* Webber still believes that love can be the one fulfilling life action, if the lovers will use reason in their demands on each other.) "April had come back again" for them.

As symbolic device, the party at Jack's functions to show him that personal bonds of love are wrong because they bind him to a world with twisted values about life and art. The characters at the party treat love as an experiment or as a purchasable commodity. The beautiful Lily Mandell's aversion toward the wealthy Mr. Hirsch is calculated to raise the price of her eventual seduction. Even the extravagant critical acclaim given to Piggy Logan's circus cannot blunt the inanity of this tedious spectacle. The *pièce de résistance* of Logan's circus, an act in which he persists in pressing a pin down the doll's throat until the stuffed entrails spill out, suggests the hollowness of the society approving this spectacle. Piggy Logan's circus, which has been held up as the ultimate measure of sensibility and culture, is a symbol of the inner emptiness of Esther's society. Since the illusion of love means condoning the twisted values of Esther Jack's society, Wolfe writes "The fire was over," ambiguously suggesting the extinguishment of Webber's love as well as the apartment conflagration.

After his break with Esther Jack, Webber is free to reevaluate his artistic credo—his pained reaction to hometown disapproval has been to assume the role of the artist, sensitive and misunderstood: "George began to talk now about 'the artist,' . . . a kind of fabulous, rare, and special creature who lived on 'beauty' and 'truth' and had thoughts so subtle that the average man could comprehend them no more than a mongrel could understand the moon he bayed at." Under Randy Shepperton's questioning he begins to realize that his arrogant posture may have marred his art, " 'The failure comes from the false personal. There's the guilt. That's where the young genius business gets in—the young artist business, what you called a while ago the wounded faun business. It gets in and it twists the vision.' "

From now on, Webber resolves to be as objective about himself as he would be about any material for fiction. In rejecting the illusions of the young provincial, he finds he "can't go home again" to art for the sake of art, or to love for the sake of love. The rejection of these values within this symbolic pattern helps to prepare Webber for a broader vision.

PATTERN OF FAME IN EXILE

Failing to find a purpose in reminiscence or progression, Webber seeks in a projection, the idea of fame in exile, an answer to his quest. Since the main outline of this symbolic pattern is given in the introduction, a few corroborative details will be presented. Bound for Europe, Webber seeks renewal in a search for fame, *"And by his side was that stern friend, the only one to whom he spoke what in his secret heart he most desired. To Loneliness he whispered, 'Fame!' "* [italics added]. His projection assumes grandiose proportions, Milton and Goethe are cited as authority, and even the American dream becomes the chance for anyone to achieve fame.

But his trip through the English countryside with the embodiment of fame, McHarg, is a fiasco, compared to the Walpurgis Night of *Faust,* and Webber perceives fame has given his idol no security or peace. Nevertheless, he cannot resist fame in Germany where he received adulation and praise for his work, although he becomes uneasy at the Olympic Games of 1936, which seem to be chosen as "a symbol of the new collective might." The fear, suspicion, and tyranny of the Nazis are concretized in the abduction of the Jewish banker on Webber's train. His fellow passengers felt, "they were saying farewell, not to a man, but to humanity." Wolfe seems to use traditional Christian symbolism to emphasize the inner torment Webber experiences as he conceals the money the banker had given him to hide: "Turning half away, he thrust his hands into his pockets—and drew them out as though his fingers had been burned. The man's money—he still had it! . . . felt the five two-mark pieces. The coins seemed greasy, as if they were covered with sweat." There can be no return to the illusory place that promised identity and purpose for the writer.

PATTERN OF THE FATHER

When Webber leaves Germany, one illusion still binds him to a pattern of return: that of the symbolic father. In *The Story of a Novel* Wolfe makes the following assertion: ". . . the deepest search in life, it seemed to me, the thing that in one way or another was central to all living was man's search to find a father . . . the image of strength and wisdom external to his need and superior to his hunger, to which the belief and power of his own life could be united." In *You Can't Go Home Again* Webber's editor, Foxhall

Edwards, assumes this role. "Little by little it seemed to George that he had found in Fox the father he had lost and had long been looking for. And so it was that Fox became a second father to him—the father of his spirit." Wolfe also provides a suitable fictional background by giving Webber a most indistinct father and making Edwards a father without a son.

But after this attraction, the emotional Webber begins to tire of Edwards's rationalistic fatalism. Edwards's intelligence is described in animal imagery usually reserved for unsympathetic characters like Piggy Logan. The temperamental differences between the two are illustrated by their attitudes toward C. Green, an unidentified middle-aged American who jumped to his death out of the Admiral Drake Hotel. To Edwards this C. Green is a statistic of the American death rate, a cipher in an industrial society, a poor contrast to Admiral Drake. However, Webber refuses to admit Green's suicide was meaningless. Instead he considers Green's death as his distinguishing act from conformity, a symbolic redemption of his type, for the blood of C. Green brings his salvation.

In his letter of resignation to Edwards's publishing house, Webber rejects the editor's fatalistic attitude, which he equates with Ecclesiasticus, for a philosophy of activism: "You and the Preacher may be right for all eternity, but we Men-Alive, dear Fox, are right for Now. And it is for Now, and for us the living, that we must speak, and speak the truth, as much of it as we can see and know." Webber realizes that the search for the symbolic father is over; there exists no magical "someone who can help you, save you, ease the burden for you." Again Webber's reaction to the father figure has been in the customary form: attraction, enlightenment, and severance.

LESLIE A. FIELD

The Hills Beyond:
A Folk Novel of America

For most students of Thomas Wolfe, *The Hills Beyond* is a postscript to his total work. Ironically, the plan for this book appears first as an *actual* postscript to a letter which Wolfe wrote his mother in 1934. In the postscript Wolfe asks his mother to "jot down" a brief history of her family. He would like, he says,

> to get a list of the twenty children or more that your grandfather had by his two marriages and what happened to them and where they settled and what parts of the country they moved to, and so forth. . . .
>
> I'm asking you to do this because some day after I get through with these books I'm working on now, I may wind the whole thing up with a book that will try to tell through the hundreds of members of one family the whole story of America.

Wolfe did go on with his plan, but he died leaving behind only ten chapters of his fragmentary novel—a novel which has thus far received little critical attention. Although incomplete, *The Hills Beyond* is a significant sample of Wolfe's writing in that it does an extraordinary job of fusing autobiographical fiction, objectivity, and American folklore. It may very well be that in this novel Wolfe had departed completely from his *Look Homeward, Angel* approach to writing and was now pointing in an entirely new direction. Surprisingly, most Wolfe critics, including the folklorists, have failed to examine this new direction.

From *Thomas Wolfe: Three Decades of Criticism,* edited by Leslie A. Field. © 1968 by New York University. New York University Press, 1968.

This study, therefore, will attempt to show that in *The Hills Beyond* Wolfe did draw heavily on folklore material for the purpose of writing his fictional history of America. Moreover, Wolfe's fictional America will be seen emerging from two strong folklore strains: the frontiersman and the Yankee. We have, of course, Constance Rourke's *American Humor* to thank for its pioneering success in detailing and demonstrating a fusion of these traditions in American culture. But Wolfe adds a third dimension: the American utilitarian scholar. Perhaps it would be more in keeping with Wolfe's actual use of this third dimension to label it simply "practical book learning."

By and large Wolfe's critics do agree that Wolfe is steeped in a native American tradition. But they hasten to add that Wolfe's work is flavored by non-American myths. Furthermore, most students of Wolfe recognize his heavy dependence upon autobiography in his fiction. His work, to be sure, is deeply personal. As a result of this last element in his work, Wolfe has been praised by a few and damned by many.

Again, most agree that Wolfe was tending towards more objective, less autobiographical writing as he returned to his native tradition. That *The Hills Beyond* is the culmination of this movement cannot be easily refuted. Perhaps then it may be rewarding to see what it is that Wolfe has taken from his native tradition for use in *The Hills Beyond* and how the folk material acted as a controlling image for his "great new plan."

Wolfe's tentative plan we already have in his letter to his mother. But in its more complete form it goes as follows: Now that he has written four large "novels," the last two published posthumously, dealing with his own family history from about the turn of the century, he wants to backtrack to trace his ancestry as it relates to the American pioneer. William (Bear) Joyner, who lived about 1800, is to be the father of America—an American Moses.

In ten chapters of *The Hills Beyond* Wolfe traces the careers of Bear and those of eight of his children. The children are the offspring of Bear's two marriages. Wolfe does not get around to dealing with the twenty or so children and hundreds of grandchildren and great-grandchildren that his original plan calls for. The children he does develop, in their various occupations—lawyer, politician, teacher, businessman—represent the occupational face of America. They stand as prototypes of myriad rural and urban occupations. In the chapter entitled "The Great Schism," as a matter of fact, Bear's huge family does split up, some staying on the farm and others going to the city. In effect, these people are the beginnings of the American heritage as Wolfe sees it in his projected novel.

But just what is their source? What makes their heritage American rather than, say, Pakistanian? Their source is the grand old man who fathers this new race of fictional Americans. He is none other than William (Bear) Joyner, the man who fuses the two most powerful strains of American folk tradition, the frontiersman and the Yankee, and the third strain which Wolfe saw as a necessary addition. This last strain is the American practical or utilitarian scholar, the new American who learns to read so that he can rise above his fellow man, so that he can add to the Crockett-Bunyan type of hero another dimension—book learning. Not only does the content of Wolfe's tales bear a striking resemblance to general American folktales, but the manner in which they are told is often far too similar to admit coincidence.

It is doubtful that Wolfe drew upon purely regional North Carolina folklore. In *North Carolina Folklore* by Frank C. Brown and the Hendrick's collection of "tar heel tales," for example, little resemblance seems to appear between North Carolina lore and Wolfe's material. More probable sources, however, are Professor Frederick Koch's and Paul Green's works in the folklore area. Wolfe and Green were fellow students in Koch's folk-play class at Chapel Hill. Furthermore, Wolfe wrote two folk plays, *The Return of Buck Gavin* and *Third Night*. He also acted in several folk plays at the University [of North Carolina]. Thus in his undergraduate years Wolfe could not escape the influence of American folklore as interpreted by Professor Koch. Still another source for Wolfe's folklore material derives quite naturally from oral transmission filtered through his own immediate family. Wolfe's family, a family of irrepressible talkers, loved to "tell tales." Wolfe's mother, for instance, could, in folklore jargon, be termed a fairly good "informant," as demonstrated in Hayden Norwood's *The Marble Man's Wife.*

Again we may ask this question, how specifically does Bear Joyner, our American Moses, relate to folklore? Thanks to the monumental fieldwork done by an army of folklorists, we are able to compare actual folklore tales with the portrait Wolfe paints of Bear Joyner.

Wolfe tells the following of Bear's fighting prowess:

> The stories of his great physical strength, for example, were prodigious, and yet apparently were founded in substantial fact.
>
> He was said to have been, particularly in his earlier years, a man of hot temper, who liked a fight. There is a story of his fight with a big blacksmith: a quarrel having broken out between them over the shoeing of a horse, the blacksmith brained him

with an iron shoe and knocked him flat. As William started to get up again, bleeding and half conscious, the blacksmith came at him again, and Joyner hit him while still resting on one knee. The blow broke the blacksmith's ribs and caved in his side as one would crack a shell.

Bear's powers in and relish for hand-to-hand combat calls to mind another fighter—Mike Fink. Fink's love of fighting and excellence as a fighter are legendary, of course. In Emerson Bennett's version of Mike Fink, the hero roars:

I can lick five times my own weight in wildcats. I can use Injens by the cord. I can swallow niggers whole, raw or cooked. I can out-run, out-dance, out-jump, out-dive, out-holler, and out-lick any white things in the shape o' human that's ever put foot within two thousand miles of the big Missassip. . . . Oh, for a fight! . . . O for a fight, boys, to stretch these here limbs, and get the jints to working easy!

A. B. Longstreet has a spectator report the aftermath of a frontier Georgia fight in this way:

I looked, and saw that Bob had entirely lost his left ear and a large piece from his left cheek. His right eye was a little discolored, and the blood flowed profusely from his wounds. . . . Bill presented a hideous spectacle. About a third of his nose, at the lower extremity, was bit off, and his face was so swelled and bruised that it was difficult to discover in it anything of the human visage.

And in Paulding's *The Lion of the West,* Nimrod Wildfire says, "My father can whip the best man in old Kaintuck, and I can whip my father." The depiction of Bear Joyner as a strong man, a fighter, the gory details of hand-to-hand combat, and the actual "frame" in which the Bear Joyner story is told all point to more than coincidental parallels with the stock fighting characters and their stories in American folklore.

One of the most important folklore episodes concerning William (Bear) Joyner is the one in which he acquired his nickname.

He was known in his own day to be a mighty hunter; and old men who remembered him used to tell of the time he "chased the dogs the whole way over into Tennessee, and was gone four days and nights, and never knowed how fer from home he was."

There is also the story of his fight with a grizzly bear: the bear charged him at close quarters and there was nothing left for him to do but fight. A searching party found him two days later, more dead than living—as they told it, "all chawed up," but with the carcass of the bear: "and in the fight he had bit the nose off that big b'ar and chawed off both his years, and that b'ar was so tored up hit was a caution."

Professor Dorson comments about the frontier folk: "Legion were the stories that described fierce brushes, grapples, and encounters between a woodsman and a bear." In "A Bear Hunt in Vermont," for instance, there is the following account of a Vermonter's hand-to-hand encounter with a bear:

> "There he was, rolling round on the ground grappling with the fierce animal which was at least four times his weight, and not a weapon about him. . . . Presently he got one hand in the bear's mouth and grappled his tongue. The bear writhed like a serpent, and chawed away on his arm as if it had been a stick. . . . There he was floundering in the mud with a great bear and nothing but his hands to help him." Then the hunter almost effortlessly drowns the bear in a slough of mud and emerges victorious, but "winding his handkerchief round his arm which was horribly mangled."

In a similar vein—hand-to-antler combat—Mike Fink subdues a monstrous moose.

Note that in all three fights—Vermont bear hunt, Mike Fink and the moose, and Bear Joyner's encounter—the hunters were attacked at close quarters and could make use of no weapons, or for some reason their weapons failed to function so that they had to proceed with the fight in a primitive fashion. This approach to telling the story in each case adds a spark of folk realism.

Perhaps one of the most famous frontier stories concerning a bear fight appears at the end of Thorpe's "The Big Bear of Arkansas." This bear hunt differs from Joyner's, of course, in that our Arkansas hero felled his game with a rifle.

Paul Bunyan's superhuman hunting prowess is more closely allied to Joyner's, however:

> There are three [Bunyan] hunting stories; in one, Paul grabs the Timber Wolf by the ears, hollers, and the wolf dies of fright. In

another, Paul confronts a Polar Bear; having no railroad spikes
for his gun, he rams it full of icicles and kills the bear with them.
In the third, he grabs one mountain lion by the tail, and used it
to club two others to death.

Still another story is told of Bear Joyner in which he outwitted one of
his own kin, won a bet, and as a reward "walked off with enough leather
on his back to shoe a regiment." After a wager, Bear Joyner's relative, a
storekeeper, kept his part of the bargain:

> He pointed to the pile of leather in his store and told William he
> could take as much as he could carry. Joyner stood there while
> his companions heaped the leather on, and finally staggered out
> the door with eight hundred pounds of it on his shoulders.

And Professor Dorson comments on strong men:

> Fact and legend blended in tales of pioneer strong men. Home-
> making in the wilderness had stimulated physical performances
> that more tender generations recalled with awe and retold with
> relish. Most of these feats had to do with lifting great weights.
> Benjamin Tarr of Rockfort, Massachusetts, lifted an anchor
> weighing 800 pounds.

Dorson goes on to cite a number of other strong-men folktales, one
being of a man who effortlessly carries sixteen hundred pounds of boom
chains on his back. It should be noted that in all three strong men tales
depicted above we have the use of a seemingly magic weight, eight hundred
pounds, or some multiple thereof.

Throughout *The Hills Beyond* we have samples of the other folklore
strain in Bear Joyner's makeup. He was the shrewd trader, the keen Yankee
wit (even though he is a Southerner), the teller of tall tales, and the Yankee
with a wry sense of humor.

His ability to drive a hard bargain, acquire property, and then multiply
his holdings until the final accumulation of wealth from the deal completely
overshadowed his initial gain, would do justice to a nineteenth-century
Robber Baron.

Nor did Bear's offspring lack their parent's talents. One of Bear Joyner's
sons offered to sell a man some land for two hundred dollars. The man
refused, but later bemoans his folly: "And I was such a fool I didn't take it!
If I had, I'd have been a rich man today. You couldn't buy it now for a
million dollars." And Wolfe adds:

By the time the Civil War broke out the Joyners were accounted wealthy folk. It was "the big family" of the whole community. Even long before that their position was so generally acknowledged throughout the western mountains that when the boys began to "make their mark," it occasioned no surprise.

The traditional tales told of the Yankee often emphasized this very thriftiness, shrewdness, and parsimony which made Bear Joyner's people "wealthy folk." But the Yankee was more. He was a conglomeration, often depicted "as a sly and scheming knave . . . regional in projection and design [but a type that] . . . did not differ fundamentally from backward and backwater types throughout the land."

Even though Bear Joyner could hold his own in the realm of the tall tale and keen wit, it was really his son Zack Joyner who was "noted for his ready wit, his coarse humor, and his gift of repartee. People would come into the store 'just to hear Zack Joyner talk.' " The townspeople were proud of the "tincture of charlatanism and smooth dealing" in Zack. They told tales of his "superior adroitness and cunning, and men would wag their heads and laugh with envious approval, as though they wished they could do such things themselves, but knew, being merely average men, they could not make the grade."

As Dorson illustrates, the Yankee was a spinner of yarns. He told land stories, sea stories, fight stories, hunting and fishing stories, almost any kind of story—all tall tales. His repertoire, however, is inexhaustible. Not only did his story-telling display the Yankee's versatility and shrewdness, but his trickster nature also confirmed it. More often than not the trickster quirk in the Yankee was turned to profit. In short, Dorson continues, we have a practical joker who delighted in duping the country bumpkin, who twinkled as he passed off his glue-factory candidates for good, solid plow horses, and who luxuriated in the warm aura of his own yarn spinning.

In one respect we can contrast an army of unlettered folk heroes with Bear and Zack Joyner because Wolfe did add the third dimension. And he emphasized this dimension. "It is important, then, to know, [Wolfe points out] that William Joyner 'chawed the b'ar.' But it is even more important to know that William Joyner was a man who learned to read a book." And in the next few pages "learned to read a book" almost becomes a refrain. No unlettered Moses he, Wolfe insists. Our clan must be of the people, close to the land, but it must rise above the land through learning.

At a time when it was the convention for all men in the wilderness to be illiterate, in a place where the knowledge contained in

books was of no earthly use, nothing would suit old Bear Joyner
but that he must learn to read. . . .

For no one ever really knew where his father came from. And
it did not matter. Old Bear Joyner came from the same place, and
was of the same kind, as all the other people in the mountains.
But he was a man who learned to read. And there is the core of
the whole mystery.

If Bear Joyner was the Moses, the beginning of Wolfe's fictional tribe,
both his first and second wife shared part of the glory with him. And the
second wife especially, who effortlessly bore and reared some fourteen of
Bear's twenty children, has some of the frontier tall tale rub off on her.
Zack, for instance, has spoken of "the physical sharpness of her sense of
smell, which really was amazing, and which all of her children inherited (she
is said one time to have 'smelled burning leaves five miles away upon the
mountain, long before anyone else knowed there was a fire')."

And just as our American Moses had a more striking wife than was
Zipporah of the traditional biblical patriarch, so did he have in his son
Zachariah a man more marked than Gershom. Zack Joyner, one of the
oldest sons, is an extension of old Bear himself. Zack becomes a lawyer-
politician, a forerunner of the Willie Stark-Huey Long Southern dema-
gogue.

To the people of Catawba, Zack was

not only their native Lincoln—their backwoods son who marched
to glory by the log-rail route—he was their Crockett and Paul
Bunyan rolled in one. He was not alone their hero; he was their
legend and their myth. He was and has remained so to this day,
a kind of living prophecy of all that they themselves might wish
to be; a native divinity, shaped out of their own clay, and breath-
ing their own air; a tongue that spoke the words, a voice that
understood and spoke the language, they would have him speak.

Almost as if Wolfe were explaining the evolution of a folktale or a
myth, he goes on to discuss Zack:

They tell a thousand stories about him today. What does it
matter if many of the things which they describe never happened? They are true because they are the kind of things he
would have said, the kind of things that would have happened to
him. Thus, to what degree, and in what complex ways, he was
created so in their imaginations, no one can say. How much the

man shaped the myth, how much the myth shaped the man, how much Zack Joyner created his own folk, or how much his people created him—no one can know, and it does not matter.

And as Wolfe continues to describe Zack Joyner, the folk hero of the people, we hear echoes of the academic folklorist.

In examining the history of that great man, we have collected more than eight hundred stories, anecdotes, and jokes that are told of him, and of this number at least six hundred have the unmistakable ring—or *smack*—of truth. If they did not happen—they *should* have! They belong to him: they fit him like an old shoe.

Shades of Professor Koch's Chapel Hill folklore class!

"Did they happen?" . . . We are not wholly unprepared for these objections. . . . We have actually verified three hundred as authentic beyond the shadow of a doubt, and are ready to cite them by the book—place, time, occasion, evidence—to anyone who may inquire. In these stories there is a strength, a humor, a coarseness, and a native originality that belonged to the man and marked his every utterance. They come straight out of his own earth.

But back to the father, the American Moses himself. Is he merely Wolfe's transplant of the Bunyan-Crockett hero? Indeed not. Bear Joyner is at first very much the traditional American hero. He has no background, no parents, no tyrannical father; he overthrows no throne, is no prince in disguise; no one has cursed his birth or set him in the water. Thus he is no Oedipus, Heracles, Apollo, Zeus, Watu, Gunung, Nychang, Sigurd, or Arthur—at first. But from an almost one-dimensional American hero he is changed. The hero-bachelor takes a wife. And the wife begets children. And they beget. And so on.

So we have the patriarch who starts a clan. Perhaps we may say that we have in Bear Joyner a semitraditional American hero. Bear does not disappear after a series of picaresque-like superhuman episodes. He stays and becomes the patriarch—the Moses of the American family.

That Wolfe was conscious of his use of folklore in *The Hills Beyond* becomes a pedestrian statement in the light of the above evidence. How much "pure" folklore he would have brought to a complete version of *The Hills Beyond* is a matter for conjecture only. But there can remain very little doubt concerning Wolfe's overall literary plan, his controlling image. His four huge novels, as has already been mentioned, were autobiographical. In part, *The Hills Beyond* is also autobiographical. Wolfe's ancestry is so closely knit with the hill folk he discusses in *The Hills Beyond* that Wolfe becomes folk and folk becomes Wolfe. But his use of the various strains of folklore tradition does help him to objectify the personal elements in his characterizations.

Wolfe's novels document a pilgrimage—a pilgrimage which begins in the hills of North Carolina, moves to cosmopolitan New York and then Europe, and finally returns to old Catawba—the hills beyond—old North Carolina. Furthermore, the journey documents under various names the Joyner-Gant (Westall-Wolfe) life cycle. To be sure, the four novels, the vehicle for the "story," consisted of autobiography, myth, and folklore of a much more imaginative vein than we find in *The Hills Beyond*. But in this fragmentary novel, Wolfe was moving away from the first two elements and was attempting a story seeped in the last element—folklore.

The Hills Beyond may have provided an excellent folkloristic ancestry for the Wolfe tribe he had already depicted in his novels. *Look Homeward, Angel* and the other books, however, are complete. *The Hills Beyond* is a fragment. As such it must be judged. It has power, life, and color extracted from Wolfe's knowledge of the hills of North Carolina and of folklore in general—but it is shaped (albeit imperfectly) by Wolfe's own large imagination. As it stands, the story is rough, partmolded, incomplete. As a counterpoint it may be enough to conclude that *The Hills Beyond* encompasses far more than the traditional Bunyan-Crockett episode. But it may be even more important to end with this conjecture: Wolfe's fragmentary novel shows that he was approaching a most significant corner in his artistry. Had he lived long enough to turn the corner successfully, perhaps we would now have his "whole story of America" in addition to his "whole story" of Eugene Gant-George Webber.

MORRIS BEJA

The Escapes of Time and Memory

*I know there is nothing so commonplace, so dull, that is not touched
with nobility and dignity. And I intend to wreak out my soul on
paper and express it all. This is what my life means to me: I am at
the mercy of this thing and I will do it or die. I never forget; I have
never forgotten.*

—THOMAS WOLFE, *Letters to His Mother*

Moments of revelation are probably more frequent in the works of
Thomas Wolfe than in those of almost any other novelist. Saying that, as we
shall see, is by no means the same as saying that in him they are more
essential, or more functional, but it does indicate the important role epiphany plays in his novels. Many of the moments of intensity or illumination
that Wolfe included in his books were ones he himself had experienced—
and which he never forgot, had never forgotten: that, it turned out, was his
trouble. His passion for epiphany was akin to that of the other novelists I
discuss, but he had much more difficulty than they in controlling that passion and in curbing his urge to record in his art all his own sudden spiritual
manifestations. The problem became so acute that he ultimately wrote of his
determination to abandon them altogether. And so Wolfe is of special interest particularly because, among modern novelists who make extensive
use of epiphany, he was unique in eventually reacting against it. Or, rather,
against one type of epiphany, the autobiographical one that involves what
he came to consider were escapes from reality—the imprisoning escapes of
time and memory.

Wolfe's work is also notable for the fact that in few other writers can
the epiphanies be so appropriately divided into two basic groups: either they

From *Epiphany in the Modern Novel.* © 1971 by Morris Beja. Peter Owen Ltd.,
University of Washington Press, 1971.

stress an event in the past (an event which may now be recaptured, or one which may now be given a significance and meaning that went unperceived when the incident originally occurred), or they involve only the present. As in Proust, but in contrast to most novelists, present revelations are less frequent and less prominent in Wolfe than those that in one way or another center on the past; but in many instances they are his most effective epiphanies and are important enough to merit a separate discussion before I go on to consider the general development of his attitude toward the past and one's memories of it.

Though less central in Wolfe's work than those involving memory, epiphanies of the present are plentiful in their own right, and they produce such widely differing phenomena as the embarrassingly infantile awkwardness of George Webber's "squeal," which we are clearly but vainly meant to admire, and the childish beauty of Esther Jack's description to her father and his friend of her ability "to see a forest in a leaf, the whole earth in a single face"; but the most interesting examples are those arising from the experience of riding on a train, an experience Wolfe regarded as "one of the most wonderful things in the world."

Indeed, not a single image in all of Wolfe's novels has more meaning for him than that of the railroad. It pervades all his books, which describe train rides over the mountains of Old Catawba, under the streets of New York City, along the river in New York State, through the countryside in France, across the border from Germany. But by far the most important journey is the one between the southern and northern United States: "So relative are the qualities of space and time, and so complex and multiple their shifting images, that in the brief passage of this journey one may live a life, share instantly in 10,000,000 other ones, and see pass before his eyes the infinite panorama of shifting images that make a nation's history." This trip, for obvious biographical reasons, was immensely significant to Wolfe, and the excitement of it often produces for his heroes moments of vision greatly resembling those in Virginia Woolf that arise from brief contacts with other passengers in the same railway car. For example, when Eugene Gant goes "out into the world for the first time," riding the train from Altamont to Harvard, he experiences a "glorious moment" of "incredible knowledge" and "illimitable power" as he stares at the prosperous older men who, like him, are heading north.

Even more frequent are the mysterious and fascinating visions seen by Wolfe's characters out of the windows of the train. Such scenes, which recur till the very end of Wolfe's last novel, begin as early as Eugene's eleventh year, when he is traveling to and from Florida with his mother: "The picture of flashing field, of wood, and hill, stayed in his heart forever: lost in the dark land, he lay the night-long through within his berth, watching the shadowy and phantom South flash by . . . seeing, in pale dawn, the phantom woods, a rutted lane, a cow, a boy, a drab, dull-eyed against a cottage door, glimpsed, at this moment of rushing time, for which all life had been a plot . . . flash upon the window and be gone." And later, as he looks back upon his still young life, Eugene wonders at the fact that "so many of the sensations that returned to open haunting vistas of fantasy and imagining had been caught from a whirling landscape through the windows of the train."

We have already noticed passages in Virginia Woolf that parallel Wolfe's interest in trains and their ability to provide revelations; similar passages also figure importantly in Proust, Faulkner, William Styron, Michel Butor, and others. For as an interlude between two points of space and time, a journey structurally lends itself to being treated in fiction as a detached fragment of life, while the experience can, as well, be readily interpreted in terms of pervasive themes in twentieth-century literature—such as the modern urge for movement and speed, the relations of space and time, or each man's essential isolation.

The kind of epiphany that confines itself to what can be seen within a railway car itself is of course peculiar to trains or other vehicles that bring together people who have never seen each other before, and who will leave each other's lives within a very short time. The excitement connected with traveling and the stimulation of the sense of swift movement heighten one's sensibility, especially to the new faces about him; as Wolfe puts it in *You Can't Go Home Again*, "one observes all the other passengers with lively interest, and feels that he has known them forever . . . all are caught upon the wing and held for a moment in the peculiar intimacy of this pullman car which has become their common home for a night." There are also significant reasons for the frequency of the epiphany involving something glimpsed from the window of a moving vehicle. To begin with, the experience is necessarily both sudden and brief. If a train stops at a station or a siding, it will usually do so only for a short time; and when the train leaves, any envisioned scene will be lost not only in time, but also in space, as it is taken miles away from the spectator by his own rapid movement as a passenger or in the train. A still more fleeting vision occurs when one train passes a second one, and the riders in each gaze at each other, the relative movement of the two moving trains making the experience strangely impressive and a favorite one with Wolfe. Even briefer is the experience in which a passenger catches a glimpse of a stationary object as he dashes by it.

But a more fundamental basis for the persistence of both kinds of train epiphanies in Wolfe's fiction—as, in fact, in the fiction of the other novelists I have mentioned—lies in the general impression they give of separation, even of isolation, in the ease with which they can be regarded as manifestations of the inherent loneliness of all men. This is especially true of the train window type, in which the passenger is unavoidably separated from whatever he perceives and is being carried farther away from it every second. If he sees a person, he may, and in fact usually does, feel a momentary sense of union with him, but in Wolfe this feeling is almost always one-sided, with the person outside the train rarely so much as aware that he is being watched. Even when the sensation is shared by both figures, its fleeting quality only makes it serve the more to reveal their inevitable solitude.

On one of his trips in *Of Time and the River,* Eugene Gant's express catches up to a local and begins to pass it, while the passengers in each train smile at each other in friendly competition, and it seems to Eugene that he must have always known these people, that they will stay with him forever. But then, despite their smiles, he senses that they too feel sorrow and regret: "For, having lived together as strangers in the immense and swarming city, they now had met upon the everlasting earth, hurled past each other for a moment between two points in time upon the shining rails, never to meet, to speak, to know each other any more, and the briefness of their days, the destiny of man, was in that instant greeting and farewell." The idea that man is doomed to perpetual isolation is one of the central themes in Wolfe's work. From our mother's womb, he tells us in the epigraph to his first novel, we come naked and alone into exile. "Which of us," he asks, "is not forever a stranger and alone?" The theme is not at all limited to the image of the railroad (the crowded city, especially, seems to Wolfe a vast image of loneliness): manifestations of separateness dominated his books and, despite his occasional Whitmaniacal cries that he contained multitudes, gave his epiphanies an in-rooted and self-absorbed quality they did not begin to shed till his outlook underwent a number of significant changes late in his career.

The train epiphanies play varying roles in each of Wolfe's novels. In *Look Homeward, Angel,* they are especially associated with Eugene's growth and his increasing awareness of the changes brought about by time, as well as with all the other aspects of time in which Wolfe is so interested: the relations among time past, time present, and time immutable; the swiftness of its passage or the sensation that it has stopped; and the confusion between time and space ("time and movement")—all of which are manifested in "the weird combination of fixity and change, the terrible moment of immobility stamped with eternity in which, passing life at great speed, both the observer and the observed seem frozen in time."

But it is in *Of Time and the River,* more than any of Wolfe's other novels, that the train really comes into its own, and in fact a more appropriate title for the book might well have been *Of Time and the Railroad,* for the image of the river does not even approach in importance that of the train. I am not merely referring to the frequency with which railroad journeys appear in this novel, and I am thinking less of the large number of revelations involving trains than of the uses to which those revelations are put; for they lend to the book much of whatever unity it has, connecting all the sections of the novel, early, middle, or late, whether the action takes place in the South or in the North, in America or in Europe. Wolfe himself, when he tried to describe the "design" of the novel, did not refer to the continuous flow of a river, but was forced instead into the realization that he could "liken these chapters only to a row of lights which one sometimes sees at night from the windows of a speeding train."

Train epiphanies also help integrate *Of Time and the River* as a whole into the sequence of volumes that tell the life story of the Wolfe hero; but in none of the other novels do they play so large a role in providing a degree of internal coherence, limited as it may finally seem even here. Early in the novel, for example, the train taking Eugene toward Harvard stops at Maysville, the last town in Old Catawba; it is night, and as Eugene looks out from his berth onto the depressingly pretentious and artificial gaiety of a small southern town square, "in the wink of an eye, a moment's vision," he is filled with a "feeling of loneliness, instant familiarity, and departure." Under the pressure of the multitude of Eugene's impressions to which we are exposed, we might easily regard this incident as simply one of the many isolated passages that Wolfe so often seems to include in his novels for no other reason than that they interested him, and with no reference beyond themselves. But in this case we would be mistaken. The "familiarity" Eugene finds in the scene arises not only from its being typical of many that can be observed throughout the South, but also because it is an "image of ten thousand lonely little towns like this across the continent."

As a matter of fact, one night several years and hundreds of pages later, we do come across such a town in upstate New York. Eugene's train stops at one end of the station of a small factory town. Once more he looks out of his window, and this time he is able to see into a shabby bar, ornately decorated and containing a number of laughing men, a coarse but friendly-looking prostitute, and a portrait of Warren G. Harding. The train moves on to the other end of the station: "And again, from his dark berth, he could see without moving this whole immense and immediate theatre of human event, and again it gripped and held him with its dream-like magic, its unbelievable familiarity." The word "familiarity" reappears because in essence this northern town is Maysville, Altamont, and all the little towns he has ever known. So when he sees a boy on the street trying to get up the courage to approach a prostitute who is obviously waiting for him, we do not need to be told (though we are) that Eugene is witnessing an image of what he himself has been, of his own desire, indeed "of the desire of every youth that ever lived."

Trains are less important in *The Web and the Rock* than in most of Wolfe's work, though here their symbolic force is recognized by both Esther Jack and George Webber. As a child trying to explain to grown-ups what sort of things can teach you to see "a forest in a leaf, the whole earth in a single face," Esther cites as an example "the people in a train that passes the one you're in: you see all the people, you are close to them, but you cannot touch them, you say good-bye to them and it makes you feel sad." Later, we discover that one of the images that inexplicably persist in George's memory is "the face of a woman passing in another train, an atom hurled through time," just as Eugene, when it was his train that passed another, was especially struck by "a lovely girl, blonde-haired, with a red silk dress"—or just as Thomas Wolfe himself could never forget "a girl who looked and smiled from the window of the other train."

In *Of Time and the River,* some fifty-odd pages near the beginning of the novel were devoted to the train ride that took Eugene from Altamont to the North; in *You Can't Go Home Again,* some fifty-odd pages near the beginning of the novel are devoted to the train ride that takes George back south to Libya Hill. He is traveling on K-19 (the same pullman car that made the run between the North and Wolfe's own Asheville): "The moment he entered the pullman he was transported instantly from the vast allness of general humanity in the station into the familiar geography of his home town . . . it all came back again, his feet touched earth, and he was home." He is deceived, of course. You can't go home again. But George will not fully realize this until, years later, he experiences the train window epiphany that forms the climax of the novel—when he and his fellow passengers gaze at their former companion, the desperate little man whom the Nazis have caught trying to escape Germany. This passage is one of the most important in all Wolfe's fiction, and I shall later discuss some of its far-reaching implications.

In addition to revelations that concentrate upon present experiences, of which I have taken some involving trains as the chief examples in Wolfe, there are those that center on the past and one's present memories of it. And they, as I have already indicated, are far more important to one who, fascinated as he may be by what he sees around him here and now, is utterly obsessed with what has passed, with what is perhaps lost forever. Of course, it is not possible to distinguish completely between these two kinds of revelation, and neither one of them can be discussed without sooner or later bringing in the other, but the distinction is nevertheless generally useful, especially in regard to Wolfe. Much the same may be said of the division of the epiphany of memory itself into two further types, the "retrospective" epiphany and that of the past recaptured.

When one recaptures the past, if we are to believe modern novelists, he does not merely recall an event but actually lives through it again in all its original reality. During his privileged moments, consequently, it seems to Proust's Marcel that the past he relives fuses with the present and becomes contemporary with it, while Wolfe writes that once, when George noticed the first signs of spring, the color green so worked upon his memory that "the past became as real as the present, and he lived in the events of twenty years ago with as much intensity and as great a sense of actuality as if they had just occurred. He felt that there was no temporal past or present, no *now* more living than any reality of *then*." Eugene has the same experiences, and they always occur in an epiphany, suddenly: "always when that lost world would come back, it came at once, like a sword thrust through the entrails, in all its panoply of past time, living, whole, and magic as it had always been." Not everyone, however, is capable of recapturing the past; it would seem that one must have a virtually abnormal awareness of the sensations of the present in order to feel them again when they have gone, or at least when most people would say they have "gone." One needs the almost neurotic ultrasensibility of a Marcel—a quality already part of Eugene's make-up when he is "not quite six": "His sensory equipment was so complete that at the moment of perception of a single thing, the whole background of color, warmth, odor, sound, taste established itself, so that later, the breath of hot dandelion brought back the grass-warm banks of Spring, a day, a place, the rustling of young leaves, or the page of a book, the thin exotic smell of tangerine, the wintry bite of great apples."

Thomas Wolfe believed that he himself possessed such a sensibility and that his memory was characterized "in a more than ordinary degree by the intensity of its sense impressions." As an illustration, he describes in *The Story of a Novel* how one day he was sitting in a Paris café, when suddenly and for no apparent reason he remembered the iron railing on the board-walk at Atlantic City: "I could see it instantly just the way it was, the heavy iron pipe; its raw, galvanized look; the way the joints were fitted together.

It was all so vivid and concrete that I could feel my hand upon it and know
the exact dimensions, its size and weight and shape."

Wolfe asserts that this experience—and others like it, all of which also
took place, paradoxically, in Europe—enabled him to discover his America,
which he had begun to feel was lost to him. Both his fictional counterparts
also undergo the same discovery while in France: the incident that causes
Eugene to look homeward occurs toward the end of *Of Time and the River,*
when a church bell in Dijon brings him back to the bell in college at Pulpit
Hill, and then even further back to his childhood and "the lost America";
the incident that takes George home again occurs in Boulogne, as he enters
a hotel room for the first time yet "feels that he has been here before." All
the objects seem "like old, immensely familiar, and essential things, although an hour before he did not know of their existence." He is experiencing something very similar to what happens at the beginning of Proust's
privileged moments, though no special sensibility is needed to go this far,
and most people have had this feeling a number of times. While psychol-
ogists speak of it as *déjà vu,* it is known in the terminology of popular
song as the It-seems-we've-sat-and-talked-like-this-before-but-who-knows-
where-or-when phenomenon. George, however, hears a different song, as he
listens to the voices of a man and woman passing under his window:

> Suddenly, just as they pass, a low, rich burst of laughter, tender
> and voluptuous, wells up out of the woman's throat, and at that
> moment, by the magic of time, a light burns on a moment of his
> weaving, a shutter is lifted in the dark, a lost moment lives again
> with all its magic and terrible intensity, and the traveler is a child
> again, and he hears at night, beneath the leafy rustle of mid-
> Summer trees, the feet of the lovers passing by along the street of
> a little town in America when he was nine years old, and the
> song that they sang was "Love Me and the World is Mine."
>   Where?
> In the town of Libya Hill in Old Catawba twenty years ago.

Such a passage can leave no doubt that Wolfe's treatment of the past is
very similar to Proust's, but it would be quite another thing to say that
Proust influenced him. It does seem fairly certain that Wolfe was familiar
with Proust's work and greatly admired it, but his own tendency to emphasize the recapture of the past was so strong as to make any actual influence
by Proust probably superfluous.

Those epiphanies involving events that produce revelations only long
after the events themselves have occurred are so numerous in the novels of

Thomas Wolfe that it would be pointless to quote many examples here; they form the bulk of the long catalogues of Eugene's and George's memories that fill so many pages in Wolfe's books, and of which Wolfe wrote in terms that make it clear he regarded these memories as what I call retrospective epiphanies. *The Story of a Novel* describes how, when he began to work on the first book of an intended series, he compiled vast lists of almost every conceivable sort; some of them were put among sections of his manuscripts headed by the words "Where now?" and one of the incidents he uses as an example is the same one we have just seen recaptured by George Webber:

> Under such a heading as this, there would be brief notations of those thousands of things which all of us have seen for just a flash, a moment in our lives, which seem to be of no consequence whatever at the moment that we see them, and which live in our minds and hearts forever, which are somehow pregnant with all the joy and sorrow of the human destiny, and which we know, somehow, are therefore more important than many things of more apparent consequence. "Where now?" Some quiet steps that came and passed along a leafy night-time street in summer in a little town down South long years ago; a woman's voice, her sudden burst of low and tender laughter; then the voices and the footsteps going, silence, the leafy rustle of the trees. "Where now?"

Like his desire and apparent ability to recapture lost time, then, these manuscripts were the product of the general infatuation with the past that Wolfe brought to his art when he first began to write novels.

For a brief period before then, however, and despite the inclinations of his character, he did try to tone down his preoccupation with his own personal memories. In his writing, this attempt took the form of a number of plays that were not especially autobiographical. His major effort in a purely fictitious plot was *Mannerhouse,* a drama set during and after the Civil War. In the original version, according to a letter young Wolfe wrote to his mother in 1920 or 1921, at the end of the play the hero Eugene and his sweetheart Christine, "glorious forerunners of the New South," were to leave his family's mansion; because of the ruin brought upon Tradition by the War and the years that have followed it, the house is no longer his. "Take one last look at this room, 'Gene," Christine tells him, "and realize that this is past, that this was a fine life but a useless one. We are not living in the Memory of past greatness, but Now and Here. Are you ready to meet it?" As they are leaving, the house is being torn down to satisfy Crass Material Interests and "the inexorable call of Tomorrow. From the distance comes the deadly whirring buzz of the New and the Curtain Falls!" "Well," Wolfe concludes, "I have the stuff for a fine play here."

Be that as it may, within a few years he decided to change the ending, adapting it more suitably to the view of the past he then actually held, perhaps in spite of himself. He accomplished this by grafting onto the echoes of Chekhov's *The Cherry Orchard* the image of Samson destroying the Philistines. In the final version, which was not published until 1948, the Young Aristocrat rejects the present and the future, and embraces his past by pulling down a pillar—an act that brings down the house, crushing himself, the Southern Belle, the Poor White Trash who has come up in the world and bought the estate, and the Faithful Old Negro Tod. Clearly, the two endings reflect different attitudes toward the role of the historical past, as well as one's own. Around the same time, Wolfe changed his very art form to one that conformed to his views about the role of one's personal past in art—he began writing autobiographical novels. From then on, his work showed a great emphasis on his memories of his own life, a conscious and deliberate intention to utilize them in his work. He had the major requisite for doing so—a powerful memory that seemed capable of total recall—and he announced his full determination to rely upon it even before he actually gave up the dramatic form. In 1923, he wrote to his mother:

> I am at the mercy of this thing and I will do it or die. I never forget; I have never forgotten. I have tried to make myself conscious of the whole of my life since first the baby in the basket became conscious of the warm sunlight on the porch, and saw his sister go up the hill to the girl's school on the corner (the first thing I remember). Slowly out of the world of infant darkness things take shape, the big terrifying faces become familiar—I recognize my father by his bristly moustache. . . .
>
> This is why I think I'm going to be an artist. The things that really mattered sunk in and left their mark. Sometimes only a word—sometimes a peculiar smile—sometimes death—sometimes the smell of dandelions in Spring—once Love.

It was against the background of this obsession with time and memory that Wolfe wrote his first novel.

II

It would be pointless for me to trace the pattern of epiphanies in *Look Homeward, Angel,* or in any of Wolfe's novels, as I have in Joyce's and Virginia Woolf's, for the simple reason that there really is no pattern. Yet a chronological examination of his work does have value in suggesting how thoroughly moments of passionate illumination pervade it, how related they are to his basic notions of art and the artist, and especially in showing how his views toward the use of the epiphanies of his own past developed and changed.

Early in *Look Homeward, Angel*—as in *A Portrait of the Artist,* with its opening scene of Stephen creating a rhyme out of the demand that he "apologise"—we are given an epiphany that strongly hints at the hero's vocation as an artist. The incident occurs at school, where all the children have been able to learn how to write except Eugene, who draws only jagged lines and is unable even to see any difference. One day his friend Max looks at Eugene's sheet, and commenting that "That ain't writin'," scrawls a correct copy of the exercise on the paper; somehow this act suddenly causes Eugene to write out the words too—"in letters fairer and finer than his friend's"—and to go on hurriedly to copy the subsequent pages, as the two boys react "with that clear wonder by which children accept miracles."

> "That's writin' now," said Max. But they kept the mystery caged between them.
> Eugene thought of this event later; always he could feel the opening gates in him, the plunge of the tide, the escape; but it happened like this one day at once. Still midget-near the live pelt of the earth, he saw many things that he kept in fearful secret, knowing that revelation would be punished with ridicule.

Though this episode, like the one in the *Portrait,* may be regarded as revelatory primarily for the author and the reader, it does provide a mysterious new awareness for the two boys as well; and it is immediately followed by another revelation which they—"midget-near the live pelt of the earth," or trailing clouds of glory as it were—cannot communicate and so keep secret: but this time it is a vision of the hidden presence of evil in the world. Watching some workers repair a broken water main in one of the town streets, Eugene and Max are standing next to a fissure in the earth, a window that opens "on some dark subterranean passage," when they suddenly see gliding past them "an enormous serpent" which vanishes into the earth behind the working men, seen only by the terrified children and never revealed by them.

Such scenes appear throughout the novel, and many of them seem based on Wolfe's own memories; but art reflects the mind and world of its creator in more ways than one, so in *Look Homeward, Angel* a large number of the purely imaginary incidents, too, involve the recollection or recapture of lost time by various characters themselves. Olive Gant goes through such a moment when, to his dismay, the local madam buys his statue of an angel for a prostitute's grave. The importance to Gant of this angel has been prepared for by the first epiphany in the novel—one that also dealt with the discovery of artistic longings. Gant, fifteen years old, was walking along a street in Philadelphia when he saw a statue of an angel outside a stonecutter's shop, and it instilled a lifelong desire "to wreak something dark and unspeakable in him into cold stone," to "carve an angel's head," to "seek the great forgotten language, the lost lane-end into heaven." The angel purchased by the madam has been imported from Italy, but it is as close as Gant has ever come to carving his own angel and to finding the forgotten language. As he and the madam conclude their trans-action, their thoughts turning to the years that have gone by since their youth, they look out upon the town square, where everything seems sud-denly "frozen in a picture":

> And in that second the slow pulse of the fountain was suspended, life was held, like an arrested gesture, in photographic abeyance, and Gant felt himself alone move deathward in a world of seemings as, in 1910, a man might find himself again in a picture taken on the grounds of the Chicago Fair, when he was thirty and his mustache black, and, noting the bustled ladies and the derbied men fixed in the second's pullulation, remember the dead instant, seek beyond the borders for what was there.

"Where now?" Wolfe asks, "Where after? Where then?"

At the end of the novel, Gant's son Eugene sees in the same square a vision of his whole past life; in general radiance and significance, that final vision and the others I have cited are exceptions to most of the epiphanies in the book, which are plentiful and often individually very effective, but which too frequently have no real function in relation to the rest of the novel. They reveal a good deal about specific people, but little in regard to comprehensive themes, and sometimes they even seem like merely irrelevant intrusions. Occasionally, however, a moment of revelation will not only give us insight into Wolfe's characters, but also serve broader purposes of form by bringing together various themes or threads in the story—as with Eugene's climactic experience at the very end, the evening before he is to leave Altamont.

The vision of Ben concludes the novel with a forecast of the future, but it serves primarily as a summary of the past. The nature of that summary seems meant to illustrate Wolfe's assertion in his note to the reader that "we are the sum of all the moments of our lives"; gazing upon the town square, Eugene feels that he sees all his younger selves evoked before him:

> And for a moment all the silver space was printed with the thousand forms of himself and Ben. There, by the corner in from Academy Street, Eugene watched his own approach; there, by the City Hall, he strode with lifted knees; there, by the curb upon the step, he stood, peopling the night with the great lost legion of himself—the thousand forms that came, that passed, that wove and shifted in unending change, and that remained unchanging Him.
>
> And through the Square, unwoven from lost time, the fierce bright horde of Ben spun in and out its deathless loom. Ben, in a thousand moments, walked the Square: Ben of the lost years, the forgotten days, the unremembered hours. . . .
>
> And now the Square was thronging with their lost bright shapes, and all the minutes of lost time collected and stood still. Then, shot from them with projectile speed, the Square shrank down the rails of destiny, and was vanished with all things done, with all forgotten shapes of himself and Ben.

When the images of the past have disappeared, Eugene experiences another "moment of terrible vision," this time of "his foiled quest of himself," of the same hunger that has "darkened his father's eyes to impalpable desire for wrought stone and the head of an angel"; we are thus brought back to the first epiphany in the novel. Ben reveals in an "apexical summation" that what Eugene seeks must be found within himself ("*You* are your world"), and that the object of his quest—"the forgotten language, the lost world"— involves the past as much as the future. But it is forward that Eugene tries to look as he expresses in his final words his confidence that he will someday find what he desires, just as at the end of *The Story of a Novel* Wolfe himself is confident that we shall all "find the tongue, the language, and the conscience that as men and artists we have got to have." The last chapter of the novel has generally suggested the visions in Joyce's Nighttown episode in *Ulysses;* but it is Stephen's affirmation on the last page of the *Portrait*—that, as artificer, he will forge the uncreated conscience of his race—that is called to mind by the last page of *Look Homeward, Angel,* with the young artist's determination to attain what his father has sought but never found in the carved angel: "the forgotten language, the lost world."

We trace Eugene's progress toward the achievement of his goal in Wolfe's next novel, *Of Time and the River.* Through its portrait of the young artist and his attitude toward his work, we get a good picture of Wolfe's own views on art, and of his own goal. A central description of these views takes its departure from Eugene's feelings as he reads his play—which happens to be called *Mannerhouse*—to his friends Joel and Rosalind Pierce. Wolfe first deals with artistic genesis, citing Eugene's play as an illustration of the fact that the source of art lies in one's personal experiences—especially in one's moments of inspiration: "the flashes of blind but powerful intuition, which mark the artist's early life here in America." At any rate, they certainly seem to have marked Wolfe's life; if we can trust *The Story of a Novel,* indeed, one such sudden artistic inspiration, which took place in Paris, very much resembles the new self-awareness he attributes to Eugene at the end of *Look Homeward, Angel:* "I saw," he writes, "that I must find for myself the tongue to utter what I knew but could not say. And from the moment of that discovery, the line and purpose of my life was shaped." The words he uses in *Of Time and the River*—"flashes of blind but powerful intuition"—provide one example (we shall see others) of Wolfe's ability to point out both the strengths and weaknesses of his work, and to do so with something rare in his writing, a concise phrase.

Having commented on the origin of art, Wolfe goes on to describe its aims, which also turn out to involve moments of vision. First, he shares with other writers the belief that the artist's drive to create comes from the hope of recording epiphanies—what Joyce calls the attempt "to fix the most elusive of his moods." Wolfe, of course, greatly admired Joyce's work, but the important thing to notice here is that he did so largely because he felt that Joyce was able to do successfully what he himself longed to do—to record his evanescent moments with extreme care. Wolfe felt that in *Ulysses* "the effort to apprehend and to make live again a moment in lost time is so tremendous that . . . Joyce really did succeed, at least in places, in penetrating reality." In the passage in *Of Time and the River,* Wolfe refers to this compulsion as "the intolerable desire to fix eternally in the patterns of an indestructible form a single moment of man's living, a single moment of life's beauty, passion, and unutterable eloquence, that passes, flames and goes."

The artist need not be the only one to feel the flash of intuition, how-

ever; another of his aims is to impart it to his audience. As Eugene reads his
play aloud to his friends and realizes that they are powerfully affected by it,
he feels a tremendous sense of elation and learns "in one blaze of light, an
image of unutterable conviction, the reason why the artist works and lives
and has his being." It is, as we have seen it in other writers, to make his
reader experience a revelation, "to snare the spirits of mankind in nets of
magic . . . to wreak the vision of his life, the rude and painful substance of
his own experience, into the congruence of blazing and enchanted images
that are themselves the core of life, the essential pattern whence all other
things proceed, the kernel of eternity." The same purpose makes an artist
out of Eugene's alter ego George, who, as a boy, laments the inability of
people like his Aunt Meg to understand "the life of life, the joy of joy, the
grief of grief unutterable, the eternity of living in a moment" and therefore
longs for the power to "enlighten their enkitchened lives with a revealing
utterance."

His belief that the artist is characterized by an extreme propensity for
such experiences and an overwhelming need to depict and impart them to
others leads Wolfe to call him "life's hungry man, the glutton of eternity,
beauty's miser." This description may not fit most artists, but it does fit
Wolfe himself, and it shows how his interpretation of the role of the artist
as the recorder of epiphanies is very much related to his artistic tendencies—
including his faults. Wolfe sees the artist as the man who is hungry for all
experience, who has an insatiable craving to do all things and, unfortunately, to express them all. In Wolfe's own work, this aesthetic gluttony
leads to his most basic defects, a failure to control his material and a
consequent weakness in structure.

In regard to the structural use of epiphanies, the weaknesses of *Look
Homeward, Angel* are in one way alleviated in *Of Time and the River,*
where a measure of unity is provided by the many train epiphanies. But the
coherence thus achieved, though significant, is perhaps more than offset by
the very size of the book and the countless revelations of all types that run
through it, with little attempt at relating most of them to one another.
Wolfe's problems are further compounded by the novel's climax. *Look
Homeward, Angel* had at least ended with a powerful and unifying vision;
Of Time and the River ends with what is probably the chief example in
Wolfe of a nonfunctional and even harmful epiphany, one that seems com-
pletely out of place in the novel it is meant to conclude.

In the final scene, Eugene is leaving Europe and returning to America;
he is in a small boat with a number of other people, waiting to board
the ship that is to take them home. All the travelers feel the strange power

of the huge liner as it towers over them, but Wolfe gives special attention to
the effect of this "magic moment" on a woman named Esther, whom we
have never encountered before. We are then shown her own effect on Eugene,
as he turns toward her; from the moment he sees her, his spirit is "impaled
upon the knife of love." As if that were not bad enough, "at that instant"
he also loses the "wild integrity" and the "proud inviolability of youth."
Whereupon the novel ends. As the conclusion to an already ill-structured
book, this revelation, which should form the forceful climax to the entire
novel, succeeds only in leaving the reader hanging in the air. Eugene's loss
of his youth can hardly be regarded as a dramatic or convincing corollary of
what amounts to an epiphany of love at first sight. Besides, Wolfe's hero
instantaneously loses his youth forever very often, and in this case the
supposed loss is so unpersuasive as to be embarrassing. One would like to
be able to find some alternative thematic function served by this incident: to
regard it, say, as a culmination of the search for a mother—which, despite
Wolfe's claim that the controlling idea in *Of Time and the River* is "man's
search to find a father," often seems more central in his work than the father
theme. But the scene does not really fit this interpretation either, and, though
eventually Esther does in some degree become a mother figure, that role is
of course not evident until the George Webber novels. Indeed, no matter
how one looks at it, this scene is so unrelated to the context of the rest of
the novel that it can only be regarded as a passage that starts threads that
are entirely new. Strictly speaking, moreover, those threads were never
taken up and no sequel to the book was ever written, for Wolfe never
published another novel about Eugene Gant—though in the end, to be sure,
we must ignore Wolfe's switch from Eugene to George Webber.

One of the most frequently cited causes of the structural defects of *Of
Time and the River,* and of Wolfe's other novels as well, has been his
inability or unwillingess to control the flow of memories he so freely permitted himself to record in his fiction—so freely that the flow became a
deluge. Of course, Wolfe was correct in believing that there is much to be
said for what he called, in a famous letter to F. Scott Fitzgerald, the "putter-
inner" (as opposed to the "leaver-outer") approach to fiction. But this
approach also entails great dangers, and too often Wolfe's own work does
not overcome his obsession to be a putter-inner of everything. Yet is is an
oversimplification to say that Wolfe's "chief fault," in his own words, was
merely that he "wrote too much"; a lack of critical judgment was also
involved. He devoted so much space to autobiographical details which the
reader can only regard as at best unessential that his novels frequently give
the impression—valid or not—that he failed to understand that not every

moment personally important to him need also be artistically significant. To Wolfe, all the myriad experiences he gives his hero are important, even essential; all of them at least potentially involve revelations. And the ones explicitly described as revelations are so numerous as to appear in almost every scene. By itself, each might be fully credible—but not as simply one out of a massive crowd; under such conditions, they take on something of the character of a mere artistic "convention." Moreover, Wolfe aggravates his difficulties by treating every one of the illuminations as if it were of cosmic proportions. Instead of subordinating some of them in comparison with others, he uses the same superlative adjectives to describe what would seem to be relatively unimportant moments of insight as he uses in the accounts of those he obviously regards as vital or climactic, such as the ones that end all his novels. We are so frequently told that this or that moment will never be forgotten and produces a revelation completely changing the course of Eugene's life that each such passage loses much of its intended force, and after a while we begin to treat these statements with skepticism— worse, we may even cease to notice some of them.

After finishing *Of Time and the River*—or, rather, after Maxwell Perkins took it away from him when it looked as if he might never stop putting things in—Wolfe published in *The Story of a Novel* an account of how it had been written. No one who reads this account can help being struck by its almost masochistic eagerness to tell the truth, and by its perceptive recognition of the defects as well as the benefits of the methods Wolfe had thus far used in his fiction. Almost everything a reader of the novel is bound to suspect is shown here to have been true. Wolfe admits, for instance, that he "cannot really say the book was written"; rather, it "took hold" of him and "possessed" him, it came "pouring from its depth a torrential and ungovernable flood." When the resulting manuscript was finally deemed almost ready, it was Wolfe's task, with the help of his editor, to work on its mighty maze till it yielded a plan. Inevitably, considering how much easier Wolfe found it to add than to cut, their success was only partial.

The story of the composition of *Of Time and the River* also provides a review of that role that had thus far been played in Wolfe's novels by the memory of the past. He was, of course, much concerned with the whole problem of the representation of time in fiction. But systematic reasoning was not one of his strengths, and his discussion of the three elements of time that he discovered in his material—"actual present time," "past time," and "time immutable, the time of rivers, mountains, oceans, and the earth"—is after all neither profound, interesting, nor very enlightening in terms of his own work. The one time element that really monopolized his attention, as we have seen, was the past, together with one's memories of its individual moments. Although his preoccupation with it was closely related to a number of the other important themes he discusses here—notably the search for a father and the relationship between Europe and America—it towered above them all in significance. As Wolfe describes how he set about preparing to write his novel, and then how he actually wrote it, it is his "powers of memory"—which at that time "reached the greatest degree of sharpness that they had ever known"—that constantly take the forefront. We have already seen how they formed the impetus that made him compile the "Where now?" manuscripts which were in turn one of the bases for the finished book. In huge ledgers Wolfe listed retrospective epiphanies, writing down "not only the concrete, material record of man's ordered memory, but all the things he scarcely dares to think he has remembered; all the flicks and darts and haunting lights that flash across the mind of man that will return unbidden at an unexpected moment." Like so many modern writers, Wolfe strove to find in "material" details and fleeting trivia the sense of value and permanence for which he longed.

Where now? The phrase figures not only in the manuscripts described in *The Story of a Novel,* but in epiphanies recorded in the published versions of his novels as well. Yet, after his description of these manuscripts, Wolfe suddenly rejects both them and the uncontrolled use of memory they seem to imply. In an unexpected and disconcertingly brief passage, he writes:

> It may be objected, it has been objected already by certain critics, that in such research as I have here attempted to describe there is a quality of intemperate excess, an almost insane hunger to devour the entire body of human experience, to attempt to include more, experience more, than the measure of one life can hold, or than the limits of a single work of art can well define. I readily admit the validity of this criticism. I think I realize as well as any one the fatal dangers that are consequent to such a ravenous desire, the damage it may wreak upon one's life and on one's work. . . .
>
> . . . And now I really believe that so far as the artist is concerned, the unlimited extent of human experience is not so important for him as the depth and intensity with which he experiences things.

As here presented, Wolfe's new attitude is as yet vague and undefined, but it does suggest a stronger realization that his work has suffered from his lack of selectivity. It is of course inconceivable that Thomas Wolfe could ever

really have become a leaver-outer. But though the "Where now?" method
was inevitable and even justifiable for the early stages of his particular
career, he now sees that it must be modified to take into consideration the
quality of remembered experience as much as, or even more than, its quantity; not every event that had occurred to him is worthy of being recorded
in art as a retrospective epiphany. This new point of view indicates a degree
of reaction against the almost completely free play he had thus far given his
memory in the fictional chronicle of his life; and therefore, as far as it goes,
it is a sign of Wolfe's transition from the attitude we have seen in his
youthful letter to his mother—"I intend to wreak out my soul on paper and
express it all. . . . I never forget; I have never forgotten"—to his eventual
conviction that you can't go home again. I say "as far as it goes" because in
itself this passage is anything but a clear and emphatic statement, and its
context contains further qualifications. Nevertheless, it is one of the first
signs of a significant shift in his thinking.

There are a few less questionable signs in his next published volume,
though again only a few. *The Web and the Rock,* like *You Can't Go Home
Again* (Wolfe, of course, meant them to form a single novel), was never
corrected or even finished by Wolfe himself, and it had to be posthumously
edited by Edward C. Aswell. Much of it, moreover, was written as early as
Of Time and the River, and it is therefore doubly difficult to depend on it
in order to trace the development of Wolfe's tecniques and ideas. We know,
however, that except for a few passages, notably the ending, the last half
was written before the first, though he did rewrite "small portions of it"
before he died. This situation leads to some awkward discrepancies between
various viewpoints expressed within the novel itself, as well as with what
Wolfe had said elsewhere.

Conflicts are especially apparent in his comments on the role of memory in George Webber's art, and readers who have read *The Story of a
Novel* carefully, but who are unaware of the peculiarities in the chronology
of composition of *The Web and the Rock,* will be particularly struck by a
number of passages in the novel that contradict the position toward which
Wolfe had seemed to be groping. Thus, in the second (earlier) half of the
book, Wolfe occasionally speaks approvingly of George's great reliance
upon his powers of recollection, which make the past "as real as the present."
"The majestic powers of memory," we are told, "exerted a beneficent and
joyful dominion over his life, sharpening and making intensely vivid every
experience of each passing day," and enabling him to possess "a thousand
fleeting and indefinable things which he had seen for the flick of an eye in
some lost and dateless moment of the swarming past." Yet such remarks,

though published after Wolfe's death, are not indications of a late reversion
to the attitude that had produced the "Where now?" catalogues, but are
rather another early product of that attitude. The newly written sections of
the book, in contrast, reflect Wolfe's more recent concern about the perni-
cious effect on his work of his emphasis on memory.

When George begins to write his first novel, his memory is said to have
grown so "encyclopaedic" and preoccupied with the "minutest details" that
it impairs his art and becomes, "instead of a mighty weapon," "a gigantic,
fibrous million-rooted plant of time which spread and flowered like a cancerous growth." Eventually, as George begins to realize that he has been
trying "to pour the ocean in a sanitary drinking cup," he does attempt to set
down merely "a fractional part of his vision of the earth." However, he is
not really prepared to control the crushing power of his past, much less to
discard it, and in another year his modest effort has—and Wolfe repeats his
previous phrase—"spread and flowered like a cancerous growth": "From
his childhood he could remember all that people said or did, but as he tried
to set it down his memory opened up enormous vistas and associations,
going from depth to limitless depth, until the simplest incident conjured up
a buried continent of experience, and he was overwhelmed by a project of
discovery and revelation that would have broken the strength and used up
the lives of a regiment of men." We have here a description of essentially the
same power as the one that had previously been depicted as exerting over
George "a beneficent and joyful dominion," only now there is a marked
difference in outlook toward its desirability. The later Wolfe was coming to
suspect that—to adapt the terminology of the later Freud—the repetition
compulsion is nothing less than deathly. Nevertheless, though this and similar passages are significant, they are as yet isolated, infrequent, and coun-
terbalanced by the passages that sharply contradict them.

A more pronounced symptom of Wolfe's doubts about his reliance on
his own past in his fiction was his adoption of a new hero, to whom he gave
a childhood quite different from his own. This attempt to abandon strict
autobiography was, perhaps inevitably, abortive; but it did bring him face
to face with one of his most important failings—the almost complete absence from his work of objectivity. The novelist who works in the autobiographical form should not only be able to select the significant from the
inconsequential; he should also be able to look at himself with a certain
amount of perspective. And if he records his own epiphanies, as Joyce says
it is for the man of letters to do, he will be most successful if he can do so
with the impersonal self-analysis of a Proust, a Conrad, or of Joyce himself.
Wolfe's treatment of many of his epiphanies, on the other hand, is roman-

ticized and theatrical. It would be absurd to condemn his novels because they are autobiographical. But it would, I am afraid, be correct to accuse them of being *too* autobiographical, in the sense that he seems to have seen his hero first as a reflection of himself, and then as a character in a work of art: he usually—though by no means always—failed to achieve that unique blend of subjective interest and objective insight that Edward Bullough called Psychical Distance.

Extreme subjectivity controls not only Wolfe's own attitude toward his experiences, but also the attitudes of his heroes toward theirs. Far from attaining any true and balanced view of the world around them during their moments of revelation, at such times they frequently have a view that is if anything even more individual and distorted than usual. They can see neither themselves nor others in perspective: they are self-deluded as well as self-absorbed. To some degree, they may be looked upon as simply following in this trait the general emphasis of our time on the subjective quality of experience and revelation: young Eugene Gant realizes in so many words that everything he saw from the train had "no existence save that which I gave to it, became other than itself by being mixed with what I then was." But the egotism of Wolfe's characters is so excessive, and they are so incapable of looking at the world except through their own highly distorted glasses, that the credibility of their moments of supposed insight into the lives of other people is greatly affected. Thus, despite the many moments in which Eugene or George feels an overpowering communion with other people, one's general impression is that of a bitter man more capable of abhorrence than of sympathy. For every stranger in the streets of Boston or New York to whom he feels his heart go out, there is someone, barely an acquaintance perhaps, whom he knows and—consequently—hates, fears, and despises. As a result, the sudden insights during which he is said to fathom completely some person or object are frequently unconvincing, for we find ourself wondering if he is really capable of such insights. Generally, his abnormally self-centered relationships with other people, and his resulting inability to understand or communicate with them except on his own very peculiar terms and according to his own unusual needs, lessen the stature of the Wolfe hero as a human being; specifically, they lessen the seriousness with which we can react to some of his most important epiphanies, for we tend to regard his moments of compassion as more rhetorical than real.

The rhetoric of the epiphanies at the end of *The Web and the Rock*, when George confronts not someone else but his own reflection in a mirror, is an especially interesting example of some of Wolfe's major tendencies, including his inclination to view his hero too subjectively, and his technical handling of moments of revelation. George is in a hospital in Munich after having participated in a brawl at the October Fair. His face has been beaten into an awful sight, but as he looks at it in the mirror across from his bed he suddenly grins, and then laughs: "The battered mask laughed with him, and at last his soul was free. He was a man." After that last remark, we too are inclined to grin, and perhaps laugh. This is not the first of the spiritual *bar mitzvahs* Wolfe gives his heroes—nor is it the last, for that matter. But the embarrassingly mawkish today-I-am-a-man quality of this scene is particularly noticeable, largely because his treatment of it is so explicit, a trait we have noticed before in some of Wolfe's epiphanies: too often he spoils an excellent effect by pointing out the very things which, with the consummate art of all his undeniable genius, he has just dramatically shown or suggested.

For the final epiphany, the reflection even becomes vocal, and he and George have a dialogue—their talk, as might be expected, centering on the past: George lovingly describes to his image the memories of childhood, "the good time." "But," the reflection reveals in the last words of the novel, "you can't go home again." As a climactic epiphany, this scene is almost as inadequate as the end of *Of Time and the River*, and for essentially the same reasons. It is unprepared for and in its context even seems irrelevant. The revelation it produces seems artificially imposed and is not in the least convincing as the conclusion of all that has preceded it, much of which it in fact appears to contradict. One is therefore not surprised to learn that this scene was probably written much later than most of the last half of *The Web and the Rock*—which dates from the period of *Of Time and the River*, before Wolfe himself had actually come to believe that you can't go home again. Of course, Wolfe did not intend his manuscript to be split in two here, so he can hardly be blamed for the inappropriateness of this scene to its final position, though as the novel stands it is nonetheless inappropriate. It is also ineffectual and unsatisfactory in itself, despite the fact that Wolfe regarded the whole episode of the October Fair as one of the most central in all his work. At one time, he even planned to use *The October Fair* as the title of the novel dealing with the period of his life covered by both *Of Time and the River* and *The Web and the Rock*.

It is not until the end of *You Can't Go Home Again* that, for the first time since *Look Homeward, Angel*, we have an effective climactic epiphany in one of Wolfe's novels. George, having returned to his beloved Germany as a famous author, is now on a train leaving it once more. At Aachen, the last stop before the border, he and the other travelers in his compartment are shocked to see that one of their fellow passengers—a nervous little man, whom George has privately called Fuss-and-Fidget—has been seized by the authorities. The rumor circulates that he is a Jew who has been caught trying to escape with all his money. As the terrified little man tries to persuade the officers to let him go, since there must be some misunderstanding, he is led past his former traveling companions, his eyes glancing at them for just a moment. But he does not betray them by showing in any way that he knows them, and they board the train, leaving him behind on the platform.

> And the little man . . . paused once from his feverish effort to explain. As the car in which he had been riding slid by, he lifted his pasty face and terror-stricken eyes, and for a moment his lips were stilled of their anxious pleading. He looked once, directly and steadfastly, at his former companions, and they at him. And in that gaze there was all the unmeasured weight of man's mortal anguish. George and the others felt somehow naked and ashamed, and somehow guilty. They all felt that they were saying farewell, not to a man, but to humanity; not to some pathetic stranger, some chance acquaintance of the voyage, but to mankind; not to some nameless cipher out of life, but to the fading image of a brother's face.
>
> The train swept out and gathered speed—and so they lost him.

As so often before, Wolfe has used a scene envisioned from a train window to dramatize a symbolic isolation. But this time the person seen is not a complete stranger; he has had some sort of contact with George and the other passengers. Perhaps that is why their sense of union with him seems more real and of a more lasting nature than the union Wolfe's characters have thus far felt in similar situations. In the end, this isolated, helpless little man becomes an image less of solitude than of the unity of all mankind. He has achieved a bond—even an identity—with all men, but especially with the people in the train. He is not even aware of it, and it would be little comfort to him if he were. But it is apparently of the greatest importance to those who see him; and, paradoxically, he could never have attained this bond were he not isolated and manifestly doomed.

This episode is one of the best things Wolfe ever did. Its power relies not so much on the impassioned rhetoric so frequent in his work—though there is still some rhetoric, of the quieter sort—as on its relative calm, the frighteningly low key of its presentation. Even the discussion of the personal significance of this incident for George is treated concisely and with restraint. And the long letter to Foxhall Edwards that then closes the novel

discussing some of the broader ramifications of this experience is also handled relatively well; though it follows the climax, it does not really seem
anticlimactic. For we soon understand that this event does more than simply
reveal to George the true nature of Nazi Germany or even teach him about
humanity, though it does both these things; it goes much further and teaches
him about himself, enables him to see himself with an objectivity he has
never previously known. It thus prepares him for the evaluation of his entire
life and career that he undertakes in the letter to Fox. When we begin to see
the full significance of all he has learned, we realize that if this vision of a
brother may be compared in effectiveness to Eugene's vision of Ben at the
end of *Look Homeward, Angel,* it must be contrasted to it in theme. For
instead of involving the recapture of the past, it centers on the future. As
George's train takes him out of the Germany he has known and loved so
well, he realizes all that he has lost: but "he knew also the priceless measure
of his gain. For this was the way that henceforth would be forever closed to
him—the way of no return. He was 'out.' And, being 'out,' he began to see
another way, the way that lay before him. He saw now that you can't go
home again—not ever. There was no road back. . . . And there came to him
a vision of man's true home, beyond the ominous and cloud-engulfed ho-
rizon of the here and now, in the green and hopeful and still-virgin meadows
of the future." The little man's capture has been for George a catalytic agent
producing a violent reaction against much that he has taken for granted in
the past—and, even more important, against his great emphasis upon that
past itself. You can't go home again. This time the phrase is packed with
meaning, and the rest of this chapter is devoted to an examination of its
significance.

George's new discovery comes to him as a sudden shock despite the fact
that he has already supposedly learned in a moment of revelation that "you
can't go home again"; for the passage at the end of *The Web and the Rock*
is a careless addition, as well as a late one. It is completely inconsistent with
subsequent passages in *You Can't Go Home Again,* throughout which it is
clear that George has yet to discover the truth of this phrase, though he
occasionally comes close. Early in the novel, he is on a train heading toward
Libya Hill, when he meets his old friend Nebraska Crane. They indulge in
nostalgic reminiscences of their childhood, and George agrees with
Nebraska's comment that "it don't seem no time, does it? It all comes
back!" Yet shortly afterward, on the very same trip, he gets just the opposite
feeling, when he meets Judge Rumford Bland, a figure of evil but also of a
kind of dark wisdom. "And do you think," Bland asks him, "you can go
home again?" George's hesitant, "almost frightened" affirmative response

("Why—why yes! Why—") makes it clear that he has not yet had the new awareness attributed to him at the end of *The Web and the Rock*, that he still has much to learn, but that he is already beginning to be uncomfortable. He realizes that Bland's question refers not merely to the physical act of returning to the town of Libya Hill, and he is beginning to suspect—and this thought represents no less than a revolution in Wolfe's ideas—that lost time cannot be recaptured and that, contrary to Nebraska's words, perhaps it really doesn't all come back.

Indeed, this discovery is the one that George finally makes at the end of the novel. It is then stated, moreover, not simply as an inevitable fact, but also as a moral principle: you *ought* not to recapture the past, you *must* not go home again. The attempt to do so is not merely futile; it is wrong. George's new belief essentially amounts to a rejection of the most important epiphanies in the novels—those involving Wolfe's personal memories. They are rejected because they place an inordinate emphasis upon the recollection of the past. I do not mean to imply that Wolfe rejects the past itself; that would be absurd and useless. Nor does he repudiate his "home" when he sadly realizes that he cannot go there again. Rather, he rejects the idea that you can or should relive the past, that it can entirely control your life and art. The recognition of necessity is not completely sad, however, and if he has in one sense lost the past he has in another gained the present and the future. Thus, in a letter sent to Margaret Roberts a few months before his death, Wolfe wrote that after some initial terror and despair, his new conviction came to seem "triumphantly *hopeful*": "It was like death almost, because it meant saying farewell to so many things, to so many ideas and images and hopes and illusions that we think we can't live without. But the point is, I have come through it now, and I am not desolate or lost. On the contrary, I am more full of faith and hope and courage than I have been in years."

With his courage came a realization that until then he had been afraid, so afraid that he had always been running away—away from the present and the future and toward the refuge of some dream world of what used to be. Wolfe had once written to Julian Meade of his emphatic conviction that "in no sense of the word" could writing be considered "an escape from reality"; in fact, it is "an attempt to approach and penetrate reality." As an example of what he meant, he cited *Ulysses,* with its "effort to apprehend and to make live again a moment in lost time." But Joyce had been able to exercise strict control over this effort, while Wolfe, as he himself now saw, had made it almost his sole preoccupation. Consequently, he had so distorted its importance that it had become "an escape from reality" after all.

The means of escape were the things that make up the mysterious entity of one's past. Wolfe described the essence of his new knowledge in a letter written a few months before his fatal illness to Edward C. Aswell, who adapted Wolfe's words for the bridge between the German episode of the little man and George's letter to Fox:

> The whole book might almost be called "You Can't Go Home Again"—which means back home to one's family, back home to one's childhood, back home to the father one has lost, back home to romantic love, to a young man's dreams of glory and of fame, back home to exile, to escape to "Europe" and some foreign land, back home to lyricism, singing just for singing's sake, back home to aestheticism, to one's youthful ideas of the "artist," and the all-sufficiency of "art and beauty and love," back home to the ivory tower, back home to places in the country, the cottage in Bermuda away from all the strife and conflict of the world, back home to the father one is looking for—to someone who can help one, save one, ease the burden for one, back home to the old forms and systems of things that once seemed everlasting, but that are changing all the time—back home to the escapes of Time and Memory. . . . But the conclusion is not sad: this is a hopeful book—the conclusion is that although you can't go home again, the home of every one of us is in the future: there is no other way.

The "escapes of Time and Memory" comprehend all the others, and the radical nature of his departure from them, with all its personal, moral, and artistic implications, was not lost upon Wolfe—nor upon George, who admits to Edwards: "No man that I have known was ever more deeply rooted in the soil of Time and Memory . . . than was I."

As Wolfe indicates in his letter to Aswell, the escapes of Time and Memory had taken many forms, and his repudiation of them meant repudiating a great many of the things that he had always loved. George begins to realize just how much it entails as soon as the epiphany of the little man has ended, for one of the major lessons of this experience is that he must say good-bye to his beloved Germany. The reason he must leave is not that he has to go home, but rather that he must *not* go "back home to exile, to escape to 'Europe' and some foreign land." Europe and not America, paradoxically, symbolizes to George his own past, for it is more like the world of his childhood than is modern, ever changing America. In this sense, the Wolfe hero has long felt more "at home" in Europe, where there has been less progress, where there is more consciousness and preservation of the past, and where that past is more easily recaptured. Thus, in *Of Time and the River,* following his recapture of "the America of twenty years ago" at Dijon, Eugene Gant realizes that in this old French town he is "closer to his childhood and his father's life of power and magnificence than he could ever be again in savage new America." It is interesting that Europe should specifically bring back his father; it does so, of course, because both are associated with his past. So when the Wolfe hero rejects his general emphasis on that past, he also gives up his quest for his spiritual father: George announces his new attitude in the very same letter in which he announces his decision to break with Edwards, who has been for him an immensely important father figure.

This abandonment of what Wolfe had once called "the deepest search in life" and the consequent break with Edwards imply that George has achieved a new sense of independence; but this independence does not in itself mean that he becomes even more self-centered than ever. On the contrary, his new attitude to a large degree involves, in the broadest sense of the phrase, social consciousness—that is, a consciousness of others besides and beyond himself. One can easily see how such a vision as that of the little man caught by the Nazis could lead to this result, and while still on the train after that episode, George reflects: "There was no road back. Ended now for him, with the sharp and clean finality of the closing of a door, was the time when his dark roots, like those of a pot-bound plant, could be left to feed upon their own substance and nourish their own little self-absorbed designs. Henceforth they must spread outward—away from the hidden, secret, and unfathomed past that holds man's spirit prisoner—outward, outward toward the rich and life-giving soil of a new freedom in the wide world of all humanity."

This passage suggests that, had he lived, Wolfe might have tried in his subsequent works to tone down the stress on man's isolation and solitude that had so pervaded his previous novels, especially their epiphanies, and perhaps to increase the sense of the possibility of some sort of meeting with other people. In any case, the analogy between George's roots and those of a pot-bound plant feeding upon itself indicates the violence of his reversal in attitude, for, as we can see if we look once more at his confession to Fox, it seems to him that he had been "more deeply rooted in the soil of Time and Memory, the weather of his individual universe," than any other man he has ever known. But despite an increased concern with present as opposed to past evils, Wolfe had no intention of writing reform tracts. Rather, in his art his social awareness took the form of a new determination to avoid concentrating on himself or his own past experiences, simply for their own sake; he had now come to regard this practice as just as dangerous as the art for art's sake aestheticism he had long despised. To him, the notion that you can't go home again is both a moral and an artistic concept.

It applies to art in two principal ways: in its essentially moral statement that you can't use art itself as an escape from reality; and, more important for its complete reversal of Wolfe's former views, in its essentially aesthetic statement that you can't create worthwhile art through particular escapes of Time and Memory. In the latter respect, the end of *You Can't Go Home Again* effectually amounts to a substantial rejection of his reliance on his own recollected epiphanies, which till then had been one of the bases of his work. Wolfe is therefore unique among the novelists I am examining, in that he is the only one to react against the use of a major type of epiphany—in Wolfe's novels, indeed, the most important and prevalent type. His decision seems to arise from an increased understanding of his own peculiar tendencies and needs. He had already come to the realization that a novelist must be selective in his use of the past; perhaps because he has as yet been unable to put this realization into practice to his own satisfaction, he now suspects that one must not use the past at all, and his statements suggest a belief that the attempt to base one's art upon personal memories is *always* mistaken, even if carried out with the utmost selection and control: "He saw now that you can't go home again—not ever." He thus reacts against his former methods even more forcefully than reason might have dictated, though in his case such a fierce reaction is perhaps necessary. In the letter to Fox, George laughs at all the people who have spread rumors that he would never be able to start another novel. The ironic truth is that he has found it impossible to finish anything; his trouble, far from being an inability to begin, is an inability to stop recording all he remembers. His "huge inheritance" had become a "giant web" in which he had entrapped himself; in admitting this to Fox, George repeats the phrases that had become so familiar in Wolfe's novels: "forgotten memories exhumed . . . until I lived them in my dreams," "nothing that had ever been was lost," "I lived again through all times and weather I had known," "the forgotten moments and unnumbered hours came back." But though this language has appeared before, and despite George's obvious relish in reverting to it, there is now an unshrinking recognition that his "torrential recollectiveness" has been a burden, has brought about a distorted attitude toward life and art, and has produced a "million-fibered integument" which has bound him to the past and therefore stifled his creativity.

Wolfe's statements are not specific enough for us to be able to tell the extent to which he consciously intended his new position as a criticism of all that he himself had so far written, but it is natural that his readers look at the position in terms of the light it sheds upon Wolfe's accomplishments. One's attitude toward it necessarily involves an evaluation of Wolfe's entire career. In so far as one regards the view taken at the end of *You Can't Go Home Again* as valid, then so much lower must his estimate be of all of Wolfe's novels, for the new view rejects their very basis: the assumption that you can return to the past. But it is not a perfectly simple matter to judge the validity of Wolfe's notion that he had been wrong to try to go home again, for, though his memory produced some of the most glaring of his artistic defects, it often contributed much of the value and uniqueness his novels do have. It was at times his strength and at times his weakness.

One critic who believes that Wolfe would have been correct to discard his own past as a subject for fiction is Louis D. Rubin, Jr. Yet at the same time Rubin is convinced that at its strongest Wolfe's memory did produce his most powerful work, and that, because Wolfe's recollections of his childhood were his clearest and sharpest, and because the lapse of many years yielded a degree of perspective, *Look Homeward, Angel* is his greatest novel; when he begins to record his adult experiences his books "exhibit a sharp decline in the quality of the recall." Rubin's position boils down to a disagreement with Wolfe's phrase, "you can't go home again." Like the early Wolfe he admires most, Rubin seems to believe that you *can* go home again, though only to a limited extent and, perhaps, to certain periods of one's life; and Wolfe, so to speak, used up all his homecomings in *Look Homeward, Angel* and a few other accounts of his childhood. In other words, Rubin seems to say that you can go home only so many times. Wolfe, on the other hand, finally goes so far as to say that once you have left it you can *never* go back: "you can't go home again—not ever." Look to the future; there is no other way.

There is much to be said for Rubin's view as he presents it, but I think that in this instance it was Wolfe himself who recognized his problems most acutely. His main difficulty was not that he was too infrequently able to utilize his past, but that he was too exclusively concerned with it. He had allowed his obsession with his memory and its epiphanies to take over and run free, and they had thus impaired even his best work. Rubin feels that it was the poor quality of the memories in them that ruined the last three novels; but in fact those memories were in quality so intense that they could not be suppressed: the stronger Wolfe's recall, the weaker the art. The superiority of *Look Homeward, Angel* by no means shows that Wolfe was at his best when he gave his memory the freest play; on the contrary, it shows that he was at his best when he exerted the most restraint over it. Of all his novels *Look Homeward, Angel* is the one that least displays the defects of too much use of personal memories; shorter than his later books, it nevertheless covers the longest period of time, deals fully with the largest number of characters, and is thereby most selective in the choice of incidents that were powerful enough to be included.

Actually, it is doubtful whether Wolfe ever would or could have given up recapturing the past in autobiographical fiction; and it is at least questionable whether his future work would have been better if he had. One suspects he would have discovered that, like Orpheus, he had to look back whatever the cost. And if in the end Wolfe had found himself unable to write effectively about anything but the memorable moments out of his own past, regardless of all the dangers they entailed, he surely would have gone back to them with little hesitation—he was never one to be entrapped by a consistency, especially a foolish one. But his growing awareness of the dangers inherent in his use of such moments might have led him at last beyond a mere lip-service recognition of the need to control Time and Memory rather than to continue to let his art be controlled by them. He might have come to treat them as tools, not escapes—to create the great novel he never wrote, but which he had it in him to write.

RICHARD S. KENNEDY

Wolfe's Fiction: The Question of Genre

*I must create a System or be enslav'd by another Man's. I will not
Reason & Compare; my business is to create.*
—WILLIAM BLAKE, *Jerusalem*

Some years ago, after I had finished writing a book on Thomas Wolfe's
literary career, I finally found time to read through Northrop Frye's *Anatomy of Criticism*, a work I had hitherto known only through the reading of
scattered chunks. I realized then that many of the critical problems of Wolfe's
fiction and the whole question of his critical reception and of his subsequent
literary reputation lay in the area of genre. Frye's discussion of "confession"
and of "anatomy" opened the possibilities for a new view of Wolfe's work.
When I began to consider the problem with more care, however, I still found
difficulties. Wolfe's fiction is an amazing mixture and none of his longer
works fit easily into categories, even into ones as wide and welcoming as
those which Frye established. I saw that Wolfe's works were like novels in
that they dealt with human relationships in a recognizable and complex
society. Yet, as in romances, his characters were sometimes drawn to stylized heroic scale and his narratives even included supernatural episodes,
such as the conversation with the ghost which concludes *Look Homeward,
Angel* or the dialogue with the image in the mirror which concludes *The
Web and the Rock*. In another way his works were more like those that Frye
labeled confessions because they were fictional autobiography. Yet Wolfe's

From *Thomas Wolfe and the Glass of Time*, edited by Paschal Reeves. © 1971 by
the University of Georgia Press.

work also resembled the anatomy because of his characteristic habit of encyclopedic compilation and because of his unusual mixture of styles.

Frye has deliberately made his scheme very loose, and in order to avoid overly strict applications, he declared that "exclusive concentration in one form is rare and that hybrid forms of two or even three in combination will be found." Indeed, in dealing with Joyce's *Ulysses,* he declares that "all four forms are employed in it, all of practically equal importance, and all essential to one another." I was not sure that I could see that kind of proportion and that kind of integration in any of Wolfe's works. Moreover, I recognized that the acceptance of Frye's terminology in 1960 was a pretty uncertain business, nor was I eager to reconsider the critical conclusions of my completed book or to rewrite it, especially since I had been compelled for entirely different reasons to rewrite it once. So I merely added the following words near the end of my book: Wolfe "called his pieces of autobiographical fiction novels. Because literary criticism of prose narrative was (and still is) in a rudimentary stage, Wolfe encountered the charge that he was not writing novels at all, and he was profoundly disturbed by it. If now we turned to Northrop Frye's distinctions among novel, confession, romance, and anatomy, we could perhaps employ a cumbersome, hyphenated term that would apply more accurately than the word novel. But since editorial advice or arrangement pushed Wolfe's work toward the novel and since a set of usable critical terms has not been fully established, we should let the label 'novel' stick."

Although I had postponed it, I continued to think about the problem, and I was especially intrigued by the discussion of the form called anatomy. But I eventually concluded that the term anatomy would not do for Wolfe, for the term had been too restrictively defined and too closely tied to a larger design. If anatomy is characterized as "dealing less with people than with mental attitudes," Frye's emphasis on idea and intellectual play would rule out Wolfe's major works. In an admirable amplification of Frye's concept, Philip Stevick has taken a broader view of the term anatomy, for he suspected that it was just a catch-all term for prose works that Frye could not fit into his other categories. Stevick examines some works of this outcast sort to see what features they have in common. He finds not only the tendency to intellectualize, which throws all utopias into this bin, but also a tendency to run counter—both in theme and form—to established norms. Even with Stevick's amplification, the term anatomy will not accommodate Wolfe for two clear reasons. First, Wolfe seeks the center of the cultural values of his time. There is nothing subversive about him. He builds; he embraces; he does not tear down or reject. Even when he is satirical he is more likely to criticize those who deviate from traditional ways and beliefs rather than those who are too orthodox. The second reason: when Wolfe bursts the bounds of form he does not do so in order to overturn established forms—none of his works could be called an anti-novel. What he tries to do, rather, is to cram into his work materials that are too large, too unwieldy, or too unusual for the traditional novel and what is more, he tries to stuff too many of them in.

Frye's theory of genre is only a scheme imposed upon literary works in order to organize thought and discussion about them, and the chief value of his theory of fictional genre is in providing perspective on the great variety of fictional works and warning us not to judge all fiction according to the standards of the realistic novel. When Frye is vague and evasive with literary definitions, there is virtue in his not being absolute, for literary theories are best when they are not exact and demanding. We sometimes forget that we are dealing with art and not with science. Thus Robert Scholes, in his recent article on genre in fiction, has the wisdom to point out that a critic must be aware of genre before making literary judgments, but then he goes on into troubled theorizing: he is too exact and he reuses old terms in new and arbitrary ways.

I have come to be wary of criticism of this sort, for most genre criticism works from the outside. The genre critic approaches literary phenomena with bags and boxes of distinctive shapes and sizes, and he tries, then, like a packer from United Van Lines, to see which items fit, and how well, into the containers he has supplied. Analytical criticism, quite the opposite, works from the inside. Even when dealing with questions of genre, the analytical critic examines what elements constitute the work and make it what it is. If he finds no box or barrel which can contain the work satisfactorily, he tries to build one, using what knowledge he has about well-known and service able containers. This is what has to be done, it seems to me, whenever a critic encounters an unusual literary work. Many critics were simply unable to deal with such works as *The Waste Land* and *Ulysses* when they first appeared. Critics are more practiced now and they do better with such challenges as Nabokov's *Pale Fire* or Barth's *The Floating Opera*.

This special critical treatment has never been applied to Wolfe's fiction, although responses to it have continually reflected generic problems. Three decades ago reviewers had difficulty assessing his fictional work because they had in their heads a certain picture of the novel as a form. Even so astute a critic as Robert Penn Warren felt *Of Time and the River* was not a proper novel "but only a series of notes from which a great novel might be written." Later some critics who had more time for consideration of literary problems than the reviewers did still produced responses which showed their limitations whenever the techniques of analytical criticism were not applied empirically enough. Mark Schorer used Wolfe as one of his examples of failure in technique because Wolfe's works did not fulfill his generic expectations: they were, he said, not novelistic enough.

Let us approach Wolfe's work empirically to inquire about what elements make it up, about its structural principles, about the traditions it reflects, about its likeness and unlikeness to other works, about its characteristic features that seem to place it in one category or another, and finally to ask what evaluative criteria can be properly applied to works like Wolfe's which tend to be sui generis. To hold the paper within tolerable limits I am going to devote most of my remarks to Wolfe's middle period, from 1930 to 1935.

Let me go directly to a distinctive feature of Wolfe as a writer, the structural principle he followed in developing his fictional products. When we examine the way Wolfe worked, from the inception of *Look Homeward, Angel* until the end of his career, we find that he let his mind follow associations from one thought to the next, a method of development that is common to lyric poetry rather than prose narrative. Arnold's "Dover Beach," for example, moves from a view of a moonlit seascape, to a thought of the ebb and flow of the sea, to a memory of Sophocles' use of that image to stand for human misery, to an image of ebb tide suggesting the decline of religious faith, to a plea that the beloved one pledge the speaker her personal faith because of the moral chaos of modern life, which is like a confused battle. It is a splendid demonstration of what the shifts and developments of associative thought can bring about. Even when a poet projects his feeling upon a character and a setting in a lyric poem, this associative principle is the common method of development. In Edwin Arlington Robinson's "The Man Against the Sky" the speaker sees a human figure mount a hill at sunset and then disappear down the dark opposite side. But the poem then moves through three hundred lines of meditation on what kind of a man he was and what his future life was going to be, until the symbolic suggestion has built up an awareness that the meditation is really about mankind pacing out its future and considering whether that future life is worth living.

Fictional works which employ this associative principle I am going to call lyric fiction. I might digress to say that Wolfe is not unique among his contemporaries in having employed this method. It was a natural development in fictional technique as the modern fiction writers began to turn inward, and it became one of the common means of breaking with Victorian and Edwardian traditions in fiction. Joyce, Virginia Woolf, and Proust all used it skillfully in the 1920s. Beckett, Bellow, and Pynchon are still using it in the 1960s.

The associative principle began to operate as soon as Wolfe started the outline for his first book. He filled two good-sized writing tablets full of notes strung along in phrases as his mind jumped from one thought to another. For example, in the early pages we find:

> 1904 St. Louis—the Fair—I remember having to change and go up a flight of stairs at Cincinnatti—The house we lived in—the two little boys who rode tricycles up and down before the house— a large board fence around the house—the back yard—the fierce sun—the two cots which were there for airing—I eat a peach on which there is a fly—swallow the fly—Fred howls with laugh- ter—I become sick and vomit—The Inside Inn—Grover worked there. Grover and the pears. The ride with Effie through the rain before the Cascades. "Force." Mr. Lyerly and mama. The period of Grover's sickness. His death. That night—"the cooling board" Mable. Papa's arrival from home. The ride home. The stairs at Cincinnatti. Coming up the river from Knoxville[.] Home—the cry of Mrs. Perkinson—Asheville—the great dignity and author- ity of the familiar—"only one Asheville." Nora Israel in the parlour. The rest (Dear Brutus) is silence (Ben and Grover—what are twins like—Did Ben carry this strange doom with him—a brooding fatality, until his death.[)] The coffin in the parlour— we had just arrived. How did it get there? Had we waited at the station?
>
> 1905–1906—Max Israel—Charley Perkinson—the fire depart- ment—Christmas—the pony—the first compositions—Sept. 1906—I go off to school.

As he wrote his book, he would cross out those notations he used, thus *Look Homeward, Angel* as we have it now moves by means of these asso- ciative leaps. The association of ideas may provide a means of movement but it does not offer good opportunity for control. Lyric poems, we note, are usually short. If they are long, they tend to fall into a series of short units which make up the whole as in Whitman's *Song of Myself* or Tennyson's *In Memoriam*. Or perhaps the poet may use an autobiographical time scheme to impose control on his material. Thus Wordsworth in *The Prelude* re- hearses the development of his sensibilities over the years. Wolfe used the autobiographical device for a guide line to hold onto, and it became the one he turned to most naturally for the rest of his life. Therefore, in spite of its

lyric method, *Look Homeward, Angel* falls in the category of the bildungsroman very well, for the defining characteristic of the bildungsroman is the
movement of the central character through the struggles of growing up until
he reaches maturity, a point at which he has sufficient understanding of life
to bring his career somewhat under control, free from the mistakes of the
past.

But *Look Homeward, Angel* is an unusual example of this subcategory
of prose fiction. Most bildungsromans begin with a focus on the central
character's raising some question of his identity, like Dickens's Pip in *Great
Expectations:* "My father's name being Pirrip, and my Christian name Philip,
my infant tongue could make of both names nothing longer or more explicit
than Pip. So, I called myself Pip, and came to be called Pip." Or they begin
with the parentage as in Butler's *The Way of All Flesh,* which starts with a
look at old Mr. Pontifex, or as in Meredith's *The Ordeal of Richard Feverel,*
which takes a first look at Sir Austin Feverel and his book of aphorisms. But
Look Homeward, Angel begins with an incantation: ". . . a stone, a leaf, an
unfound door . . . of a stone, a leaf, a door. And of all the forgotten faces."
If we do not count that as the beginning, but take the opening of chapter
one, we still do not begin with a character or an ancestor but with the
cosmos and a meditation on the miracle of chance.

Another means besides autobiography for imposing an order on a long
lyric piece is the use of myth. This is what Eliot tried to do for *The Waste
Land* and what Joyce really did use to hold together the individual sections
of *Ulysses.* Wolfe employed myth very effectively in *Look Homeward, Angel*—two myths in fact, the Platonic myth of preexistence and the naturalistic myth of the universe governed by chance. In spite of these patterns
Look Homeward, Angel does not have a plot in the way a novel does. It
does not move from initial situation by means of probable incidents that
arise out of the interrelationship of the characters. It follows the method of
a long lyric poem.

When Wolfe prepared to write a second long work, he determined not
to use the autobiographical time scheme for control because too many
acquaintances, editorial friends, and reviewers had implied that this was the
mark of an apprentice. But as soon as he tried out other devices to govern
his material, he got into terrible trouble. He held to myth, however, attempting to use the story of Antaeus and Heracles, but it was inadequate for
his needs. He flailed about, writing meditations on time, home, love, ancestry. He worked on sequences about Americans in Europe, about a train
ride, about Aline Bernstein's childhood, about her father, about a teacher he
had known at New York University, and about the childhood of a monkey-

like boy who dreamed of running away with a circus. But he could not sustain anything for very long. Only when he began veering back toward the autobiographical scheme did he feel secure.

At last, when he was forced to publish something, he produced short works suitable for periodical publication, and he employed autobiography (with a first person narrator) to help hold those works together, and he began to try out some new devices within the autobiographical framework. "The Portrait of Bascom Hawke," his novella-length piece published in 1932, makes use of a character sketch interwoven with autobiographical reminiscence. "As for plot," he wrote to Maxwell Perkins, "there's not any, but there's an idea which I believe is pretty plain—I've always wanted to say something about *old men* and *young men,* and that's what I've tried to do here."

The next work, "The Web of Earth" (1932), is Wolfe's most successful grappling with his method of development by association. His speaker, Delia Hawke, begins telling about a mysterious voice she heard saying "Two, two. Twenty, twenty." Soon she has digressed into reminiscences of her childhood and memories of Sherman's troops coming to the farm and anecdotes of her grandparents and uncles and on to a story about two murderers escaped from the town jail. Each piece of the story reminds her of another story, which in turn leads her to another story, until, after several narratives have been introduced, Wolfe turns her around in the middle. She then moves backwards and winds up one narrative after another until she finally has disclosed the birth of her twins and the meaning of the ghostly whisperings. Meanwhile Wolfe has gathered a rich assembly of characters and accumulated symbolic associations around Delia Hawke as an earth mother and around her husband as a Dionysian harvest god.

But he never attempted this symmetrical interweaving of associations again—perhaps because it would have made his publications too much alike, but perhaps also because the work is so constantly digressive that it is hard to follow.

The next work is more autobiographical but it employs the associative principle in its overall organization in a new manner. "Death the Proud Brother" (1933) is arranged in a sequence of four reminiscences of death scenes which the narrator has witnessed. Nevertheless, the lyric quality predominates: the work begins with a meditation on night and moves to a consideration of Death, Loneliness, and Sleep, all personified as forces of the night. As the four death scenes are recounted, the narrator focuses not on an action that brought about death, but rather on the impact each death has upon the passing city-dwellers and upon himself. It ends with some pondering of the meaning of Death and an apostrophe to Death, Loneliness, and Sleep. This was a kind of structure Wolfe was to use a number of times thereafter—for example in "The Four Lost Men." When we note how much like the personal essay is the prose form most like the short lyric poem. Indeed, it is not surprising that the beginning of the nineteenth century which saw the development of the personal essay in the work of Lamb, De Quincey, and Hazlitt was the same period that saw the high achievement in lyric poetry by Wordsworth, Coleridge, Keats, and Shelley. Both are manifestations of a psychic turning-inward in literary expression. Wolfe's "Death the Proud Brother" with its lyric method is in the same genre as De Quincey's *Confessions of an English Opium Eater*.

The short fictional works I have been describing all seem to me to have grown and taken their shape rather naturally from the associative method of development. But the next work seems to have been more consciously constructed. "The Train and the City" is a short piece of fiction which follows the archetypal pattern of the Journey and Arrival of the Provincial in the City. We might say that Wolfe adopted myth again for structural unity. Since this attempt was for a short work only, he seems to have had success. But within that pattern are found four different organizational devices by which Wolfe exercises control over his lyric development. Each of them was to become an important means by which Wolfe learned to handle short units of his longer works. The first is the journey. It is a primitive form of narrative construction. It is just one step beyond the autobiographical scheme. If the autobiographical scheme provides movement in time (this happened, and then this, and then this, and so on), the journey combines movement in time and space (this happened in this place, this happened in the next, and so on). Byron used it in *Childe Harold's Pilgrimage* to organize a series of meditations. Picaresque novelists use the journey to tie together a series of episodes unrelated by probability. In "The Train and the City" the narrator has the adventure of participating in a race between two trains: he watches the engineer, the firemen, the porters, and the passengers in the diner of the passing train; he focuses like a Zen Buddhist in meditation on a vein in the back of an old man's hand and he experiences an unforgettable moment. He arrives, then, in the city to be astounded at the "tribal swarm of faces" and to be awed at the "enfabled rock . . . masted like a ship with its terrific towers"; he is amazed to be able to imagine the city as a living being which speaks with its own voice.

Since this is a very short piece, there is not much of a journey, but it is Wolfe's first published work that makes use of this kind of organization. The previous year Wolfe had worked out a short journey book called

"K-19," which Maxwell Perkins persuaded him not to publish. It was about a train journey home to the South with character sketches of various home folk who were passengers and with the narrator's discovery that he no longer felt in harmony with the people at home and their way of life. This narrative pattern is one that Wolfe tried over and over again to get published. He arranged it again in a story entitled "Boom Town," but magazine editors demanded ruinous cuts and changes. We recognize that it finally took shape as George Webber's journey south to Libya Hill in *You Can't Go Home Again*. But it was still just a device for pulling short disparate units together.

Now to return to "The Train and the City": the second organizing device is the catalogue. The young provincial brings a representative American's background of ancestry and experience with him to the city. Wolfe presents it in a Whitmanesque style, a series of statements which employ parallel constructions and accumulations of images in series. The effect is rhythmic pleasure combined with a sense of abundance as the fleeting images of the American scene are ticked off: trains pounding the rails, cities at dawn, towns silent at midnight, the dull red of boxcars, empty and lonely on sidings. This sequence is followed by a chant, a series of phrases that sum up the experience of his pioneer forbears settling the wilderness. The voices of the ancestors then speak, and within the catalogue we get a rhythmically-arranged epic boast from these dead warriors and builders, a boast of their vitality, their achievement, and even the superior richness of the earth which holds their buried bodies. This moves into a catalogue specifying and characterizing some of the ancestral dead and stressing the geographical range of their burial places, Oregon, Virginia, Pennsylvania, California, Old Catawba, and the presence of both Yankee and Confederate dead at Chancellorsville and Shiloh. To the effect of abundance and variety is added the sense of the presence of the past and the value of historical achievement.

Against the breadth and variety of the American landscape and the American past that he has just set forth, Wolfe places the modern, populous, seemingly chaotic density of the City. He brings order into the seeming chaos by means of his third device, collage. I label it thus because he has gone to his notebooks, culled out and revised notes of conversations he had overheard in restaurants, railway stations, subways, or on street corners. Out of all this he constructed his composite Voice of the City, which exhibits such tones as "pugnacious recollection," "epic brag," "ladylike refinement," "maternal tribulation," "outraged decency," stupefaction, and finally friendly and familiar exchange of amenities. Although the material is satirically handled, the effect is not only increased variety with some high contrast to the dignity of the ancestral voices but also fascination with the curious forms that human group behavior can bring into being.

Besides the three devices I spoke of a chant by ancestral voices. Not that it is a group of voices in chorus and that they are elders who are expressing the wisdom of their experience. Thus this portion of "The Train and the City" presents a prose version of the choral ode such as we find in Greek tragedy. I mention this first in connection with the ancestral voices in order to identify the generic origin of this literary feature, and I want to turn back to point out that Wolfe has been long developing this communal voice which speaks somewhat differently from the voice of an omniscient narrator. That higher strain is heard in the proem of *Look Homeward, Angel* and heard again in a few places of special emotional intensity in the book, such as the "Ubi sunt" passage addressed to Laura and in the dirge by the grave of Ben. The narrator falls into the communal "we" rather than other pronoun forms. But this device is not developed into full choral chants until Wolfe's middle period. The choral voice had emerged once in "The Portrait of Bascom Hawke" in an answer to Bascom Hawke's inability to communicate about the past and in a response to the young man's vision of the old people who have lost their vitality and cannot speak:

> The dry bones, the bitter dust? The living wilderness, the silent waste? The barren land?
>
> Have no lips trembled in the darkness? No eyes sought seaward from the rock's sharp edge for men returning home? Has no pulse beat more hot with love or hate upon the river's edge? Or where the old wheel and the rusted stock lie stogged in desert sand: by the horsehead a woman's skull. No love?
>
> No lonely footfalls in a million streets, no heart that beats its best and bloodiest cry out against the steel and stone, no aching brain, caught in its iron ring, groping among laybrinthine canyons? Naught in that immense and lonely land but incessant growth and ripeness and pollution, the emptiness of forests and deserts, the unhearted, harsh, and metal jangle of a million tongues, crying the belly cry for bread, or the great cat's snarl for meat and honey? All, then, all? Birth and the twenty thousand days of snarl and jangle—and no love, no love? Was no love crying in the wilderness?
>
> It was not true. The lovers lay below the lilac bush; the laurel leaves were trembling in the wood.

This is not the voice of the first person narrator speaking; it is as if the ancestral voices are speaking out and through him so that he becomes a kind of oracle and thus a group spokesman. These rhythmic imitations of the choral chants are one more device for organizing material.

Wolfe's next publication in 1933 was "No Door," his most important literary work since *Look Homeward, Angel*. (I am referring to the long version of "No Door" which appeared in the July issue of *Scribner's Magazine*). Here is an example of the other kind of organization that Wolfe came to adopt for his longer works besides the autobiography, the journey, and the personal essay. It is an assembly of several units which have thematic likeness, but little or no narrative connection. I know no literary term to describe it. If it were a musical composition, we could call it a tone poem. Since that is not a suitable term, I suggest we call it a thematic anthology.

"No Door" begins with a proem which introduces themes of contrasting aspects of life: of wandering and return home; of death and the recurrence of life in the cycle of nature; of loneliness and its cure in love. Wolfe then selected several units from the material he had been writing—his alter ego's travels, his meditations, his yearning for a father, and his jealousy of his mistress Esther. He changed his mind several times about what to include, and when he did select four fairly complex units, Perkins made him eliminate one long narrative portion in it. When we look at what we have, we long for more thematic coherence among the assembled units, but we do see a work of lyric fiction which employs several of the subsidiary organizing principles Wolfe had learned how to use.

The first unit is an essay on wealthy people who entertain a writer and exclaim with false envy about his rather grubby experiences in urban living, a device which draws together a series of anecdotes about the people in Brooklyn. The second unit combines two characteristically lyric expositions. One is a meditation on the fury of youth, depicting the young narrator in his attempt to read all the books in the Harvard library and in his zest to embrace all the simultaneous events in the city and to touch the life of all the people there. The other lyric presentation is a choral chant, which develops out of thoughts of home: "October has come again." A voice like that of the ancestral chorus urges the youth to return home but mingles the urging with images of harvest and autumn color all over America and with a picture of a train roaring southward. Note that, of the two lyric expressions, one is individual, involving human desire; the other, communal, invoking the natural scene and the expanse and variety of the national landscape.

The third unit records, in an essay full of anecdotes, some impressions of October in England. Its lyric quality is intensified by rhythmic, evocative language: "Smoke-gold by day, the numb exultant secrecies of fog, a fog-numb air filled with solemn joy of nameless and impending prophecy, an ancient yellow light, the old smoke-ochre of the morning, never coming to an open brightness—such was October in England that year." The development is similar to the collage of the City Voice, except that it extends beyond impressions of English speech to images of bony limbs and ugly facial features and to memories of tasteless food—nor is there any personification. It is a traveler's account of a way of life, and one sufficiently distinct that he feels excluded from it—it is a door he cannot enter.

The last unit is a summary of Esther's visits to the narrator's garret and an account of the trucking firm and its tough-tongued drivers which the lovers see from their window. It does not fit thematically with the other units except for its concluding portion, which presents another choral ode. Again, the choral speaker is an old man, seen unmoving at his desk in the next building. His solidity, his calm, sorrowful eyes invite the narrator's imagination until he hears a voice "that seemed to have all the earth in it . . . and in it were the blended tongues of all those men who have passed through the heat and fury of the day, and who now lean quietly upon the sills of the evening." It speaks as Ecclesiastes addressing modern urban man—"Life is many days," full of tumult and shifting fashions, but "some things will never change." The piece closes with imagistic assurances that the earth abides forever.

As we see, Wolfe was moving toward the solution of his problem of form that blocked his progress in producing a second book. This thematic anthology with is disjunctive shifts from scene to scene and with its mixture of personal essay, meditation, travelogue, and choral chant attempted to join together a series of visions and responses to modern life. As a total work it failed, for the individual units are not coherently related. But the individual units have their own integrity. It remained now for him, with the encouragement of Maxwell Perkins, to go back to the autobiographical sequence, which could join large numbers of units together and allow the variety of the material to find its own thematic connections.

The result was the publication in 1935 of *Of Time and the River,* preceded by that same proem, "of wandering forever and the earth again." This book was like nothing else that had ever appeared on the American literary scene—vast in scale, over 900 pages long, in scene ranging up and down the Atlantic coast of America and all over England and France, with more than a hundred characters passing before the observant eye of the narrator, who presents us with a shifting generic mixture. Gone is the first person narrator, to be replaced by an appropriately omniscient narrator once again, who follows Eugene Gant and turns away when necessary for oratorical apostrophe, bardic chant, or nostalgic essay.

What kind of work can we call it? It has the scope and encyclopedic variety that we associate with the term epic, but it has no consistently developed narrative structure. It has the heightened style and the superhuman central figure we associate with the epic, but it also drops down to the realistic dialogue of the novel and to the descriptive excesses of formal satire. Although it deals with a young man discovering life, it is no mere bildungsroman, for it reflects the national life, and it gives major space to developing formal lyric expressions of the great themes commonly found in the work of major poets.

Let us look closely once again at the first section. The book opens on a scene at the railway station where Eugene Gant's family is bidding him good-bye before he leaves for Boston. The treatment is almost a parody of a nineteenth-century novel—say, one by Henry James or Thomas Hardy. A specific time and place are recorded: "About fifteen years ago, at the end of the second decade of this century, four people were standing together on the platform of the railway station of a town in the hills of Western Catawba." An omniscient narrator proceeds in leisurely fashion to describe the scene— the kind of town, the appearance of the crowd. He approaches the characters with a nineteenth-century novelist's formality and hesitation: "It would have been evident to an observer that of the four people who were standing together at one end of the platform three—the two women and the boy— were connected by relationship of blood." The characters are not named for some time, but rather referred to as "the younger woman," "the mother," "the boy," "the older woman." The names emerge only when they begin to speak to other characters standing by and when extended expository dialogue acquaints the reader with information about Eugene's departure for Harvard, about the father's condition in the hospital, and other family matters. But we discover later that neither the bulk of the dialogue nor the identification of the friends and relatives in this scene points forward to further action or significance in the book. This work which opens like a novel does not continue to develop like a novel.

In the scene, however, there are a few hints of generic deviation from the usual novelistic development: in paragraph two the narrator mentions with authoritative inclusiveness that these people have come together to await the train, "an event which has always been of first interest in the lives of all Americans." One also notices exaggeration and stylization in the handling of the characters, especially Eugene, who groans miserably, shouts incoherently, and mutters darkly like a junior-grade King Lear: "Peace,

peace, peace, peace, peace. A moment's peace for all of us before we die."
We remember too that the section was entitled "Orestes: Flight before
Fury" and that it was preceded by the rhythmic haunting proem, "of wandering forever and the earth again." The departure from the conventions of
the novel form becomes even more evident after twenty pages when we
launch into an essay contrasting the North and the South, beginning as
Eugene's train arrives: "It was his train and it had come to take him to the
strange and secret heart of the great North that he had never known, but
whose austere and lonely image, whose frozen heat and glacial fire and dark
stern beauty had blazed in his vision since he was a child. For he had
dreamed and hungered for the proud unknown North with that wild ecstasy, that intolerable and wordless joy of longing and desire, which only a
Southerner can feel"—and it continues on in descriptive balance and contrast. It may be an essay, but its style places it with what De Quincey has
called "the literature of power," and its balanced syntax and its cadence (as
it accumulates its phrases in series) place it in the tradition of American
platform oratory.

    This stylistic intensification continues in the next chapter with the de-
scription of what a traveler sees as the train moves across the rugged terrain
of the American scene: "The great shapes of the hills, embrowned and
glowing with the molten hues of autumn, are all about him: the towering
summits, wild and lonely, full of joy and strangeness and their haunting
premonitions of oncoming winter soar above him, the gulches, gorges, gaps,
and wild ravines, fall sheer and suddenly away with a dizzying steepness,
and all the time the great train toils slowly down from the mountain summits with the sinuous turnings of an enormous snake." The traveler on this
train might be Byron's Manfred or the poet of Shelley's *Alastor;* it could
even be Thomas Gray writing a letter from the Alps: the American landscape is described in that romantic style that we associate with the term
picturesque, and as the passage continues we are aware that it is suitable for
conveying a sense of abundance, variety, and movement combined with
strangeness.

    This shifts into a choral chant: "Who has seen fury riding in the moun-
tains?" The tone, the images continue to reflect the romantic agony—indeed
Wolfe borrows some words from Byron about "the little tenement of bone,
blood, marrow, brain, and feeling" and places them very early in this six-
paragraph ode to fury before it dissolves into a memory of his father's vigor
on an April morning.

    The journey has begun, and this organizing device holds the rest of the
section together. We are aware now that the work is made up of short units

that melt one into another by means of the associative method and that shifts of style, tone, and generic expectations are going to be common.

As the next chapter opens the traveler's awareness is turned toward another aspect of the American scene—not mountainous heights and depths now but little towns silent at midnight that exhibit their loneliness briefly before they are swallowed up into the flow of darkness past the windows. Inside the train the boy listens to the conversation in the smoking car, which turns on two American subjects appropriate to autumn—baseball and elections. This is good talk now among the group of Altamont citizens, leisurely talk, of the sort that can set a scene and convey predominant attitudes in the opening scene of a play, before the major characters and their problems begin to emerge. In their drawling, joking way the men reveal their secret distaste for Woodrow Wilson and their reluctant support for Cox. There is a brutal quality of grab in their exchanges that runs counter to the generous American landscape. Mr. Flood, for example, sums it up in Babbitt's idiom:

> "We're tired of hearin' bunk that doesn't pay and we want to hear some bunk that does—an' we're going to vote for the crook that gives it to us. . . . Do you know what we all want—what we're lookin' for? . . . We want a piece of the breast with lots of gravy—an' the boy that promises us the most is the one we're for! . . . Cox! Hell! All of you know Cox has no more chance of getting in than a snowball in hell."

But when the question is put to Mr. Flood about whom he will vote for, the reply is "Who? Me? . . . Well, hell, you ought to know that without asking. Me—I'm a Democrat, ain't I?—don't I publish a Democratic newspaper? I'm going to vote for Cox, of course."

The men now turn to Eugene and question him about his family, and in this way Wolfe makes use of extensive expository dialogue to bring in characterizations of Mr. Gant, Luke Gant, and the dead brother Ben. But in the midst of the talk in which Eugene shyly, reluctantly answers questions, we have two interruptions, memories of his father and of Ben, that reveal the depth of feeling which Eugene cannot openly express. The images of the father are heroic in their vigor: Gant with his "earth-devouring stride" bringing meat home to the family; and the images are historic in their associations: Gant as a boy near the battlefield of Gettysburg, Gant awaiting his brother's return from the battle. In these visions Gant and Eugene are surrounded by the presence of America, and the past and present merge: "And the great stars of America blaze over them, the vast and lonely earth broods around them, then as now, with its secret and mysterious presences, and then as now, the million-noted ululation of the night throngs up from silence the song of all its savage, dark, and measureless fecundity."

The memory of Ben is different in form. It is a dramatic vignette: Eugene, aged twelve, visiting his brother at the newspaper office, is given a surprise birthday present, a gold watch and chain engraved with his name and the date. When Ben asks him if he knows what a watch is for, Eugene in his inarticulate gratitude replies, "To keep time with." As the scene in memory ends the choral voice moves forward intoning: "To keep time with! What is this dream of time, this strange and bitter miracle of living?" Gradually the chant becomes an elegy for Ben: "For now October has come back again, the strange and lonely month comes back again, and you will not return. Up on the mountain, down in the valley, deep, deep in the hill, Ben—cold, cold, cold."

The remainder of the train journey is taken up with some remarkable linguistic play that develops out of the situation of Eugene and two other young fellows getting drunk. I am inclined to call it montage because of the cinematographic quality of the spectacle and because it is made up of condensed, abruptly changing images and fragments of talk. The beginning of it assuredly has the film camera's cosmic vantage as it pans in toward the scene: "So here they are now, three atoms on the huge breast of the indifferent earth, three youths out of a little town walled far away within the great rim of the silent mountains, already a distant, lonely dot upon the immense and sleeping visage of the continent." As the sequence develops a number of elements are merged and, in particular, American motifs are inserted. We have the clickety-clack of the train, the drunken voices of the boys, the moonlight blazing down over Virginia, the voices of passengers at small towns bidding good-bye as they board the train, and the personifications of Death and Pity riding their horses to the beat of a Virgilian line: "Quadrupedante putrem sonitu quatit ungula campum." The drunken babble plays with language: with Elizabethan English, with the moonlight ("beaming, gleaming, seeming" and so on) in Virginia, with the Latin hoofbeats ("campum . . . campum . . . quadrupedante . . . putrem . . . putrem . . . putrem" and so on), and at one point a voice even imitates Mark Twain's raftsmen in a wild boast "I'm a belly-busting bastard from the state of old Catawba—a rootin' tootin' shootin' son of a bitch from Saw Tooth Gap in Buncombe," etc. The exuberance over the train journey leads into wishes to run the train into the west, the plains of Kansas or the fertile earth of Minnesota. Meanwhile counterpointing with silence, the moon is bathing a cinematographically viewed American continent—seacoast, mountain, desert, river, woodland—and sleep lies across the faces of the nation.

Only two more units remain in the opening section. The first is a five-paragraph chapter which describes daybreak and the steady progress of the train in the quiet of morning—an obvious allaying of the wild disorder of the previous chapter. The second brings Eugene to Baltimore to visit his father in the hospital—a unit made up of contrasting pictures of Gant—the man's youth and again the boyhood memory of the Confederate soldiers marching to Gettysburg, including his future wife's Uncle Bacchus; over against this, the withered, sick old man unable to communicate with his sons. Eugene leaves, knowing he will never see his father again, as the wandering motif is picked up by the whistle of the train: "Then he turned swiftly and went to meet it—and all the new lands, morning, and the shining city."

It is a remarkable mixture. *Of Time and the River* has done all the things a novel should do at its outset: it has introduced the principal characters whose presences (including the dead brother) are going to be important now and again in the book, and it has made clear the initial situation of the boy's escaping to the North. It has developed thematic motifs of wandering and home, the yearning for a father, the furious hunger of youth, and the puzzlement over time and mortality. At the same time the American geographical sweep, the regional contrasts, the place names, the politics and games have been worked into the scene, the talk, and the narrator's rhythmic assertions. The generic mixture is even more remarkable: novel, essay, choral ode, descriptive travelogue, oratorical discourse, dramatic vignette, cinematographic montage. The whole book continues this way for its 900 pages, whether the scene be Boston, New York City, the Hudson River Valley, Old Catawba, England, or France.

What we have been led to see is that Wolfe has no large-scale narrative gift. He does not write novels in the way that recent critical theorizing has begun to restrict that term. But he has extraordinary literary talents that are expressed in fiction, and what I have been moving toward is a simple generic theory of fiction that will accommodate Wolfe's work and associate it with other works of its kind.

The first distinction to make is between novelistic fiction and lyric fiction (and by fiction I mean an imaginative representation of life which is "made up" and in which the characters live by the special laws of that fictive world). The distinction is not based on characterization as in Frye's theory but rather on structure. Novelistic fiction develops by means of probability: one event causes the next to happen, which brings about the next, and so on. Lyric fiction develops by means of association: this is related to this, which is related to this, and so on.

But longer works of lyric fiction need to borrow from novelistic fiction some additional organizational schemes in order to contain the associations, otherwise the order of art would dissolve into the disorder of human mental activity. The simplest scheme of organization that it takes over is based on time, and segments of autobiography and biography are commonly used. The result is either the bildungsroman or something that used to be called the novel of character but is not really a novel—a word like MacKenzie's *The Man of Feeling*. A second organizational scheme is based on time and space: the journey. Familiar examples of this device in lyric fiction are the romantic wanderings of a hero in search of life—as in Goethe's *Wilhelm Meister*—or the adventures of the picaro when they are aimless—as in Melville's *Omoo*. Schemes based on space alone are not common in either kind of fiction because the reader absorbs the work in time, and it is difficult for him to adapt himself to an arrangement that implies: this happened at the time this was happening, while at the same time this was happening, and so on. But one finds occasional experiments in short sections of long works: the market scene in *Madame Bovary*, the wandering rocks episode in *Ulysses*, the party in *Point Counterpoint*. In fact, counterpoint has come to be the term usually applied to these spatial arrangements. If the material is brought together from parts of already existing units, I suggest the term collage. Dos Passos's "Newsreels" come first to mind as an example.

But if the principle of organization in a work of lyric fiction is an association of thoughts—which is to say: this thought suggests this, which jumps to this, and so on—then the stream of consciousness product results. The work may be a long sequence arising in a single mind like Dorothy Richardson's eight-volume work *Pilgrimage*, or it may present the thoughts of several minds like Faulkner's *The Sound and the Fury*. Additional strengthening of thought relationships may be introduced, such as thematic associations or more oblique governing schemes like myth. If the presentation of ideas is dialectic, then we are likely to have Utopian fictions, such as Bellamy's *Looking Backward* or B. F. Skinner's *Walden II*.

But these additional organizing schemes are more likely to be found in parts of fictional works or mixed together in the work as a whole. Thus a work may employ autobiography, myth, stream of consciousness passages, counterpointed materials, and so on—as does *Look Homeward, Angel*. At times even novelistic fiction may employ lyric sections, such as the interchapters of Steinbeck's *The Grapes of Wrath* or the time machine device of Mailer's *The Naked and the Dead*. The effect of these generic mixtures is to increase the scope of the work.

Lyric fiction, using the whimsical habits of human thought progression, strains at any bounds. Thus it is likely to wander away from fiction into other genre, or to absorb other genre into itself. As we implied earlier, the personal essay is a parallel form to lyric fiction—both use the associative method of development, although one addresses the reader directly whereas the other brings him into a fictional world. Because of this, lyric fiction is likely to drop from time to time into personal essay, as Wolfe's works do, or to push on the one side toward lyric poetry (as in Huxley's *Ape and Essence*) or on another side toward oratorical address (as in Dos Passos's peroration in *The Big Money,* "all right, we are two nations.")

We have seen all these manifestations in Wolfe's *Of Time and the River,* but we still need a term that would apply to a work of lyric fiction which displays complex organizational and stylistic variety, including the characteristic features of other genres. Earlier I used the term thematic anthology for "No Door," but this term implies both too much restriction (thematic) and too much looseness (anthology). At one time I likened *Of Time and the River* to the epic in many of its characteristics, but since the term epic is so generically opposed to the term lyric, we cannot make use of it. In my own searching about I have considered such terms as chrestomathy or miscellany but rejected them because of their connotations. I looked over German terms and seriously considered *Heldenleben,* but then put it aside. Finally I struck on the term thesaurus, which carries meanings of treasury, store house, repository, besides having associations with learning and with verbal abundance, and I decided to use it as the basis for a new literary term—fictional thesaurus. A fictional thesaurus is a long literary work made up of short units in prose or verse in which the parts are joined together by association of ideas rather than by probable and necessary development. It displays a mixture of styles and variations in mood but, taken together, presents a coherent thematic statement or view of life. It achieves unity by its association with the actions of a single character or a closely related group of characters and sometimes by the voice of a single narrator or spokesman. It may rise to epic dignity by an elevation of style and by a heroic stylization of character along with a thematic reflection of cultural or national customs, values, and beliefs.

Thus Wolfe's *Of Time and the River* can be placed in the same company with other works that have always caused generic difficulty, such as Waldo Frank's *City Block,* Joyce's *Ulysses,* Dos Passos's *U.S.A.,* Cummings's *Eimi,* Huxley's *Ape and Essence,* and Jean Toomer's *Cane.* Fictional thesaurus as a literary category is bounded on its sides by other works which strain at generic limitation. As fictional thesaurus extends toward narrative, it blends into large-scale novelistic works that have a few stylistic variations like *The Grapes of Wrath*. As it leans toward pure lyric, it merges into works like Whitman's *Song of Myself* or Norman O. Brown's *Love's Body*.

To make generic identification of a single work or a body of work is not to evaluate it. To be sure, scope and variety are literary virtues, but the critic should make other demands having to do with order, and thus he must consider coherence, proportion, density, appropriateness of part to part and part to whole when he approaches a fictional thesaurus. But the important consideration is to acknowledge that these demands will be met in different ways than novelistic fiction meets them. For instance, the very fact of generic mixture tends to place emphasis on part rather than whole, and this feature lends an anthology-like quality to most of the works I have just referred to and, in fact, it leads to the habit readers have of revisiting the works later for the reading of chosen parts. Critical discussion must take into account, then, that certain literary peculiarities will arise out of the genre itself.

We stopped our discussion of Wolfe's development as a literary artist with *Of Time and the River*. If we had traced it further, we would have observed the same procedure, the same experimenting, the same floundering until he had compiled another fictional thesaurus, *The Web and the Rock*, the huge work that Edward Aswell published in three separate volumes after Wolfe's death.

This last period had its gains and its losses. One of its losses is a serious one for American literature. No Wolfe scholar has ever looked at the Publisher's Note in *Of Time and the River* without a sigh of regret, for it promised four more volumes of the Eugene Gant thesaurus. Two of them, "The October Fair" and "The Hills Beyond Pentland," were announced as already written. When Wolfe decided to abandon his mammoth project, he left unfinished a great American work of heroic scale. We can see plainly that parts of it went into *The Web and the Rock* but we cannot grant that these altered parts are completely congruent with the first two volumes. If he had gone on to complete the projected series, some of the questions of genre that have troubled his literary position would have been resolved. As it is, we now have two incomplete heroic sequences. Bad editorial advice and a poor critical climate caused him to drop one; early death cut him off from work on the other. We as critics and readers can deal with this incompleteness best by being aware of Wolfe's procedures and by seeing the unfinished masterworks in a new generic perspective.

LEO GURKO

The Web and the Rock

At first glance, this third book seems to be *Look Homeward, Angel* all over again. Like Oliver Gant, the father—John Webber—comes down from the North to the South, marries a local girl with crowds of relatives, and the marriage doesn't work. Webber is a brickmaker, not so very different from Gant the stonecutter, and the town of Libya Hill looks like a duplicate of Altamont. But the resemblance is illusory. Wolfe goes all the way back to the beginning, to be sure, but only to run a different kind of race.

Where *Look Homeward, Angel* centers around the family, in *The Web and the Rock* George Webber is deliberately stripped of the usual family ties. His father goes off to live with another woman when he is still a small boy, and his mother dies soon after. An only child, he is brought up by an elderly aunt, and is in fact alone in the world, removed from father and mother, and devoid of siblings. The day-by-day, blow-by-blow growth of Eugene within the frame of a highly dramatic, intensely complicated, and incredibly noisy family situation is utterly absent here. George seems to grow up in a vacuum. Indeed he does not appear in the story at first hand until he is twelve years old.

The characteristic quality of Eugene's boyhood is din; of George's, silence. This is reflected in the prose. The first novel opens in ecstasy, with grandiloquent time sweeps and much palpitating rhetoric. The third begins soberly, with a quiet, restrained, almost documentary tone, as though a journalist rather than a novelist were at work. Factual sentences like these,

From *Thomas Wolfe: Beyond the Romantic Ego.* © 1975 by Leo Gurko. Harper & Row, 1975.

all but invisible in *Look Homeward, Angel,* bestrew the opening para-graphs: "In the main, those facts are correct." "Aside from that, it is worth noting that Mr. Webber had his friends." "The railroad was then being built and would soon be finished." "The bare anatomy of the story runs as follows."

Hitherto, the bare anatomy of anything was foreign to Wolfe. His energies ran to fleshing everything to the point of opulence. Now he strives for detachment, thinks of his present writing as "a genuine spiritual and artistic change," and even writes an Author's Note to tell us that this is so. In any event, the whole first chapter is as lean and terse as anything he ever wrote, almost as though he had gone through the regimen prescribed for him by Hemingway in *Green Hills of Africa:* "I wonder if it would make a writer of him, give him the necessary shock to cut the over-flow of words and give him a sense of proportion, if they sent Tom Wolfe to Siberia or to the Dry Tortugas."

It takes Eugene a couple of hundred pages to reach the age of twelve, by which time his growth and character have been minutely detailed. George gets there by page 13, at which point we know something about his family connections but about him hardly anything at all. In chapter 2, "Three O'Clock," we find George sprawled on the grass in front of his aunt's house at three in the afternoon, sunk in an extended daydream.

None of it has very much to do with himself. The chapter is a potpourri of thoughts and comments on a large number of subjects of great interest to Wolfe and only vaguely related to George: North Carolina as a better place than South Carolina; the odiousness of poor whites; the web as a metaphor for his mother's family, the rock for his father's; three o'clock on a golden afternoon, a peak of human existence from which one ought not to be roused by calls to trivial duty; the difference—among his boyhood com-panions—between adolescent clots like Ira, Dock, and Reese and the admi-rable and heroic Nebraska Crane.

George is primarily a device to get all these sketched in. As an observer he refracts very few of them on his own. Wolfe is proceeding inexorably on the path of using his fiction to paint states of mind, social landscapes, and ecological sprawls. George Webber, even more than the later Eugene, is the chief instrument to this end in the third and fourth novels, a much more adequate instrument because little energy is diverted to setting him up as an individual personality with complex requirements of his own and his own special ways of looking at things.

He is given a genealogy, a life history, an occupation as a writer when he grows up, a distinctive physical appearance—long-armed, simian, causing him to be nicknamed "Monk," Wolfe going to elaborate pains to make him look as different from Eugene as possible—and an ego of sorts that is later to erupt in quite inexplicable fits of fury. But aside from one extended love affair, he is given no private self, none of that stitchwork of individual traits that lead to the remembered character, very little even of the quirkiness and eccentricity that so often passes for characterization. George Webber is to become Wolfe's highly advanced tool, not for the writing of novels but for the recording of his feelings, images, and visions of life.

In *The Web and the Rock* such visions lean to the grotesque. George feels within himself a blood madness, which he attributes to a hereditary taint in his mother's family. These mountain people, the Joyners, isolated and inbred, hopelessly webbed in an unfathomable, slow-smoldering past, are sunk in a huge abyss of "drowning time," in "a sea of blind, dateless Joyner time," and have left him with an infection of the soul.

What all this means exactly is not wholly clear. What Wolfe is creating is less a rational structure than a state of mind, an intensely impressionistic sense of psychic sludge, suppuration, murkiness, out of which will rise, like a Grendel from the dark sea, outbursts of rage and violence. Much of this is beyond the range of coherent expression; once again Wolfe is pressing and forcing language to seize what is almost outside its power to do. Yet it is in this zone where the clear becomes translucent, and the translucent slopes off into the opaque, that Wolfe is most at home and achieves one of his resourceful triumphs as a writer.

The dark genealogical strain in George is matched, perhaps even signaled, by a series of grotesque episodes that begin on a small scale, then reach a plateau of pure horror. He is given to amusingly queer little superstitions, like doing everything in patterns and groupings of four or picking a different human organ to stare at one each day of the week—other people's noses one day, ears the second, mouths the third, and so on. This odd behavior soon leads into far more serious events, though they have nothing to do with George directly except that he witnesses them.

There is the incident of the two boys run over by an automobile, with brains and entrails scattered over the pavement and Wolfe pouncing, with sudden savagery, on the gruesome details. Nobody is actually killed in the next scene, which presents the butcher and his family, but its four members, the mastodonic, mind-crushing mother especially, are pathological monsters straight out of the naturalist bin of Zola and Maupassant. This whole sequence of exercises in the grotesque is climaxed by the stunningly executed chapter, "The Child by Tiger," in which Dick Prosser, a Negro ex-soldier, runs amok, and after killing a number of his pursuers with splendid military precision, is himself killed, badly mutilated, and finally immortalized in a thrilling requiem: "He came out of the heart of darkness, from the dark heart of the secret and undiscovered South. . . . He was night's child and partner . . . a symbol of man's evil innocence . . . a friend, a brother, and a mortal enemy."

If, as Thomas Mann asserted, the grotesque is the characteristic mode of twentieth-century art, then Wolfe is very much a writer of his time. To him the grotesque, however, is not something that lies on the visible surface of things, like graffiti covering the sides of trains on the New York subway. It is instead a force in nature, a current of energy hidden from view, erupting at irregular intervals and usually when least expected.

One goes along with the ordinary, the familiar, the normal, lulled into the conviction that this is the animating principle of the universe, when an explosion from within blows everything apart. The normal becomes abnormal; the ordinary, extraordinary; the rules of the commonplace and the routine suffer a severe internal convulsion and break into fragments. The grotesque is the disintegrative element hidden in the normal, the Mr. Hyde lurking within Dr. Jekyll's civilized appearance, as indigenous to the order of nature as the process of integration and wholeness in which, in fact, it is absurdly embedded as a prankish and malevolent twin.

So that as George is walking along the all too familiar main street of Libya Hill, there comes the rocketing smash of the two boys. As he enters the commonplace butcher shop on a routine errand, he hears the subhuman voice of the butcher's wife relating her frightful beating of her six-foot daughter to punish the girl for "sinning," followed without pause by the butcher's voice threatening to murder his embezzling and absconding son should he ever return.

And the bloody saga of Dick Prosser is prefaced by his normal conduct before he goes berserk: courteous, attentive, deeply religious, beautifully instructing the young white boys in making a fire, boxing, marksmanship, football, and all the manly arts. So that when, for obscure reasons, he goes mad, the terrible destruction that follows is all the more terrible because it flows organically out of its opposite principle. Wolfe manages and executes this theory and genre of the grotesque with great dexterity. This represents for him a reigning aspect of the world as constituted. To the very end, *The Web and the Rock* is the work in which it most forcefully operates, which supplies its most luminous illustrations.

George Webber's formative years pass very quickly, with himself not much in evidence. His uncle takes him on long walks in the mountains and douses him with lengthy folktales about the Joyners. Presently he is sixteen and in college, the same college Eugene and Wolfe began attending at the same age. The four college years are telescoped into a handful of special moments: a football hero whom the school worships; George's discovery of Dostoyevski; a lone professor who makes an impression on him; some casual satire on flaccid academic bromides about service to humanity while hardship and poverty on a mass scale go on undisturbed; enthusiasm for the First World War, and how all the young men longed to fight in it and hated to see it end. Again the focus is on the general rather than the particular, on commonly shared attitudes toward commonly shared experiences: war, sports, literature, suffering mankind, and the academic life. Any young man of reasonably open mind could have exchanged places with George in these pages, and the result would have been largely the same.

Eugene and George are the same personality types, young writers of explosive genius who are very full of themselves, but where Eugene is encouraged to express himself on his own terms, and in *Look Homeward, Angel* without restraints of any kind, George is kept in check, and through the first half of *The Web and the Rock* severely so. Wolfe is quite right in claiming in his Author's Note: "This novel marks not only a turning away from the books I have written in the past, but a genuine spiritual and artistic change. It is the most objective novel that I have written." The artistic change began taking place, as we have seen, in *Of Time and the River,* and is now in full operation. And what Wolfe means by "objective" is not quite what the reader senses. He is referring to created figures in the novel who are drawn directly from his own life. The reader sees Wolfe's "objectivity" less here than in his representation of the characteristically general rather than the uniquely particular.

With what for him is remarkable speed, Wolfe gets George through college in North Carolina and up to Manhattan, where he is finally launched as a writer. We learn even less of George in the act of writing than we did of Eugene. He seems always to be either about to write or to have just written.

While he is trying to get on as a writer, he earns his living as a teacher—as did Eugene. We at least witnessed Eugene in the act of teaching. He *was* in the classroom, with students before him of whose presence and race he was all too conscious. George is never seen teaching. His classes are off somewhere in the middle distance; they never appear onstage. About all that we get are some sneers at New York University. George dubs it the School for Utility Cultures, an educational factory manned by grubby, mean-spirited, sterile faculty members whose only aim is to get promoted, whose principal emotion is envy, and whose favorite weapon is backbiting. Thus his teaching, even more than his writing, turns out to be a cover for other matters, a formality to give George something to do while Wolfe grapples with subjects more vital to him.

One of these is New York or, as the sociological cant phrase puts it, the urban experience. If anything can be said to anchor Wolfe's imaginative energies, it is the great city. It is never far from his thoughts, fantasies, and longings, and keeps surfacing even when his mind is occupied with other business. New York is the enfabled rock, the only arena that can realize his dream of greatness, the shining tower of the North luring him from his remote birthplace in the South, the supreme climax of the country, pivotal to "the plantations of the earth." Upon it he lavishes some of his most voluptuous prose, not always in love and admiration, often in anger and disdain, but unfailingly with a compelled fascination that never slackens. *The Web and the Rock,* and after it *You Can't Go Home Again,* are primarily soul outbursts about the glittering American megalopolis.

As George approaches the city for the first time, Wolfe's epithets become as gracefully expressive as the Manhattan skyline itself. "That ship of life, that swarming, million-footed, tower-masted, and sky-soaring citadel . . . the gigantic tenement of Here Comes Everybody." The city is real, yet unreal. It holds forth the promise of fame, yet supplies a cloak of instant anonymity. "It offers all, and yet it offers nothing. It gives to every man a home, and it is the great No Home of the earth."

Wolfe is eloquent about the different seasons in New York, responds to the "green sorcery" of April, and rises to particular splendor with winter:

> On one of those nights of frozen silence when the cold is so intense that it numbs one's flesh, and the sky above the city flashes with one deep jewelry of cold stars, the whole city, no matter how ugly its parts may be . . . seems to soar up with an aspirant, vertical, glittering manificence to meet the stars. One hears the hoarse notes of the great ships in the river, and one remembers suddenly the princely girdle of proud, potent tides that bind the city, and suddenly New York blazes like a magnificent jewel in its fit setting of sea, and earth, and stars.

It even has its own special odors: "The odor of a dynamo . . . of electricity, . . . the odor of the cellar, of an old brick house or of a city building, closed, a little stale and dank, touched with a subtle, fresh, half-rotten smell of harbor."

Wolfe's special vantage point is that he is an outsider to the city, an entranced outsider to be sure, but an outsider to the last. He is never fully at home in it, never quite at ease. It is always a foreign country to be conquered. Among those novelists who grow up in the cities they write about, the city is always there, an intimate, familiar, and assumed presence. Dickens is frequently conscious of London but seldom self-conscious about it. Joyce does not have to rhapsodize about Dublin; it is too instinctive a part of him. There is no space between Dostoyevski and the St. Petersburg where young Raskolnikov commits his crimes and undergoes his fevered resurrection. Studs Lonigan and Chicago are one. The characters in Edward Lewis Wallant, perhaps the ultimate urban novelist in our literature, embody the New York slums and near slums which they inhabit; when they leave them for whatever reason, they seem like displaced persons.

By contrast, Wolfe is the eternal visitor, the perpetual, superalert tourist. He is forever grabbing Manhattan and Brooklyn (and to a lesser degree London, Paris, Berlin, and Munich) by the scruff of the neck and exclaiming to us, How marvelous! or, How awful! He is always *discovering* the city, colliding with it in quick ecstatic encounters, observing it as an exotic phenomenon. Wolfe has a great advantage in this over the native writer in terms of sheer level of awareness. He never takes the city for granted, never loses his sense of wonder, is always on the *qui vive*, his antennae bristlingly alive.

> The hoof and the wheel went by upon the street, as they had done forever, the manswarm milled and threaded in the stupefaction of the streets, and the high, immortal sound of time, murmurous and everlasting, brooded forever in the upper air above the fabulous walls and towers of the city.

Wolfe forces us, particularly those who have grown up in the city, to see it through eyes that are perpetually fresh because they are always foreign. When we return from travel abroad, our hometown seems shockingly new; for an interval, the familiar has become radically unfamiliar before it gradually lapses back into its original shape. What Wolfe does is to memorialize that interval, and compel us to see our habitat as though we were seeing it for the first time. One can extrapolate his outbursts about New York and present them as a sequence of highly intensified bas-reliefs, almost as an art form in themselves distinct from other elements in his books. In this instance, as in so many others, he fulfills the ancient role of the artist; he reveals the world in a transcendent light.

But Wolfe tackles the city not only in terms of epic impressionism. He also sees it as the source, the breeder, the nurturing ground of certain social types who by their very nature can flourish nowhere else. One of these is the

Jews, seen here not from below as in *Of Time and the River* where Eugene
was confronted in the classroom by the sons and daughters of struggling
East Side immigrants. They are observed from above, the wealthy Jews who
have made it to Park Avenue and arouse in George an admiration for their
energy, their opulence, their love of good food, and their refusal to put up
with the second rate. The fear of being dominated by them both spiritually
and sexually is still present in him but only as a quietly though persistently
throbbing undertone.

Another of Wolfe's urban categories is the rich. For them he reserves
some of his more ferocious condemnations. They throw their money around
like ostentatious grandees while the masses of people groan in squalor. They
"take up" and patronize artists and art, not out of any genuine feeling for
culture or the creative process but as ego gratification, as fads or toys to feed
their vanity and sense of power.

Yet he shares Fitzgerald's conviction that the rich are different from
other people: "Just as their garments are of the finest and richest textures,
so the texture of their flesh . . . and all their combining sinews, tissues, and
ligaments are fairer and finer than those of poorer people." Still, it is better
to know rich people than to be rich oneself, and "it is not wealth but the
thought of wealth that is wonderful." Some cautionary instinct kept Wolfe
from sliding into the abyss of money hunger in which the Fitzgeralds at last
drowned.

Yet another figure whose lot is tied to the city is the artist. The urban
sprawl generates all those complex forms of human experience which nourish his imagination. Within it there cluster the publishers, galleries, orchestras, museums that discover, display, and market his wares. It supplies the
patrons who sponsor his work, the flocks of aesthetes who feed off it, the
critics who from Wolfe's point of view exist only to attack and destroy it
like ticks bloating themselves on the blood of other organisms.

George Webber, in his role as aspiring writer, is always throwing himself at the city in an effort to swallow it and its secrets whole. At the same
time, almost in the same breath, he is defending himself against the hordes
of natural enemies whom he regards as conspiring to bring him down:
insensitive publishers (like the house of Rawng and Wright—one of Wolfe's
clumsier satirical contraptions), egotistical art patrons, celebrity-hunting
women, carnivorous book reviewers, self-important schools of critics, aesthetic dilettantes formulating fashionable attitudes, and all the fakers, po-
seurs, and would-be artists cluttering up the urban landscape. "He saw
them all—the enervate rhapsodists of jazz, the Wastelanders, Humanists,
Expressionists, Surrealists, Neo-primitives, and Literary Communists."

In such persistently dramatic terms, Wolfe conceives the struggle within the city for the soul of man and the integrity of the artist. As the source of experience and perhaps even ultimate wisdom, the city is the great rock. As the breeder of viruses dangerous to body and mind, it is the great web. Thus the metaphor embedded in the title of the book provides it with the positive and negative poles between which everything oscillates.

As another example of this polarized movement, and of Wolfe's fascinating if eccentric sociology, is his flat division of human beings into two spiritual groups: those who have richness and joy in them and those who have not. Among the first are prizefighters, policemen, racing drivers, locomotive engineers, steel workers, all the physical and active people. Among the second are those who rustle papers or tap keys, clerks, college instructors, people who eat lunch in drugstores, who live meagerly and in pale safety. After this, it would take a very bold reader indeed ever to allow himself to be caught eating lunch in a drugstore even if in his heart he believes that Wolfe's social categories are nonsensical.

Nonsensical or not, they are an attempt to cast light on the quality of life, on essential movements of the human spirit which in Wolfe's view are felt more forcefully in the city than elsewhere. In the end, his very images of good and evil are twined at the core of megalopolis. In language suggestive of Conrad describing the Congo winding its way to the heart of Africa or the telegraph wires in *Nostromo* coiling like tentacles through Costaguana, Wolfe describes the shocking impact of evil upon his hero.

He has come upon it abruptly in the midtown streets after the Dempsey-Firpo fight where milling thousands of vicious men, "the criminal visages of the night," snarled and screamed their raging disappointment. "Suddenly it seemed to Monk that a great snake lay coiled at the very heart and center of the city's life, that a malevolent and destructive energy was terribly alive and working there, and that he and the others who had come here from the little towns and from the country places, with such high passion and with so much hope, were confronted now with something evil and unknown at the heart of life, which they had not expected, and for which all of them were unprepared."

The Web and the Rock is Wolfe's ode to the city which brought his art, as it did his life, to its climax.

Wolfe's love-hate affair with New York is carried on simultaneously in George's affair with Mrs. Jack. She, like the Aline Bernstein of real life, is seen by her young lover as the embodiment of the urban spirit, and he is indeed drawn to her as much by that as by her personal charms. He has been lured out of his southern town by the promise of fame. He is attracted to

Esther Jack because she is already established, successful, and famous. She knows the city with the intimacy of a native, an intimacy George longs to acquire. She seems to know its special secrets, how the city works, how to manipulate the machinery of success, and as a part of their lovemaking, George pumps her without letup, seeking to shake all that she knows out of her in order that he may absorb it into himself.

When things are going well between them and their love thrives, he feels exhilarated about the city, loses his sense of impotence at being one human atom among millions, and is certain that he will triumph. At such times he regards Mrs. Jack as the incarnation of the city at its best:

> She was full of joy, tenderness, and lively humor, and she was immensely brave and gentle. He saw plainly that she was a product of the city. She had been born in the city, lived in it all her life, and she loved it; and yet she didn't have the harassed and driven look, the sallow complexion, the strident and metallic quality that many city people have. She was the natural growth of steel, stone, and masonry, yet she was as fresh, juicy, and rosy as if she had come out of the earth.

When things go badly between them, he blames not only her but the city, whose hostile and destructive side she now represents. Whatever the emotional climate, she is one in his eyes with the city from which she springs. In loving her and hating her, his real target is New York. Again it is characteristic of Wolfe's art—particularly the art of his growing maturity—that he sees the personal element in larger terms, that he transfers even the intimacy of a love affair to a frame of reference far greater than itself.

Like Virgil leading Dante into the circles of the Inferno, Mrs. Jack guides George Webber through the labyrinth of New York. As a set designer, she is privy to the secrets of the theatre. She takes him up front and backstage, while he devours hungrily all sides of this peculiarly urban phenomenon: its atmosphere, substance, tone, craft, everything that she exposes to his avid gaze. Her guided tour feeds his love for her; he is consumed with admiration for her at-homeness in all this glamour, and at the same time it feeds the black side of his nature by arousing in him clouds of jealousy over her "success" and a compulsive desire to expose the "phoniness" of these tinsel surroundings.

Wolfe is not interested in the theatre as such. Mrs. Jack is always designing sets for one play or another, but we never do get to see the plays unfolding or the actors playing or the scenes being rehearsed; for that matter, we do not even get to see the sets. Mrs. Jack is forever working over them in a little corner of George's room which she has transformed into a model of neatness and efficiency in contrast to the chaotic disarray of George's area. It is the artist *at* work rather than the artist's work which is the target. It is not the theater but the ambience and the feeling of the theater that are brought into focus. Again Wolfe is not after facts, he is after essences; and the facts are only the anteroom through which he must pass to get at his ultimate object.

Mrs. Jack is also a fashion designer for one of the elegant New York establishments, and when she is not working up sets for a new play, she is busy sketching the new styles. She thus has entrée to another of Manhattan's distinctive institutions, the garment industry, and along with it the great department stores and the merchandising world. George is greedy for all this special knowledge, which she willingly siphons into him in the most leisurely and abundant detail. The flow between them—her supplying and his receiving—is as much an act of love as their physical embrace, and it arouses both their natures to an absolute pitch. Her supreme pleasure is to give, just as his is to absorb, to swallow, and indeed to swallow up. So she offers up to him all her assembled experience, all her inside information, and this is the fuel that keeps their love affair rocketing along.

It is when he has emptied her of what she knows, when he has extracted from her all her secrets, pockets of intimacy, private revelations about New York, that their relationship begins to falter, stumble, and go downhill. In the end, when this essential supply of energy runs dry, he is to cast her aside like a squeezed-out lemon. Brutal certainly, with a shattering effect upon her, but logical, and on the emotional side, inevitable.

The conquest of Mrs. Jack, seen as the conquest of the great city, runs along a multitude of other lines. She and George are bound together by the very drama of the anonymous, teeming streets. They take long walks in which they swap heated impressions that literally radiate from them as they move. The massive assault upon the senses evoked by even a casual stroll through the city intoxicates them beyond measure, and they never feel closer together or love one another more than on such occasions when the communication of their instant, even instantaneous thoughts and feelings blends them into the same rush of experience and sensation. George at times has his fill of it; the city for him is more to be conquered than savored. But Mrs. Jack can never get enough: "She loved the unending crowds. . . . The city was her garden of delight, her magic island, in which always she could find some new joy, some new rich picture to feed her memory."

Mrs. Jack is also a great giver of parties, attended by many of her celebrity friends. As a convenience to her urban-mad lover, she introduces him to both of Manhattan's geographic spreads. When they first meet, she lives in a house on the West Side. After he has taken this in thoroughly, she moves to an apartment on Park Avenue where he thrashes about with hostile eagerness in the affluent surroundings of one of the world's most famous neighborhoods. Her parties are a showcase of the city, plainly designed to give George a quick opportunity to meet writers, bankers, business executives, publishers, lawyers, men and women from the representative arts, and an assortment of "interesting" personalities.

George, naturally, wants to get his novel published and become famous himself in the city which is the center and creator of fame. Wolfe's own intention is somewhat different: he wants to master the city as a phenomenon of life, and he quite ruthlessly uses George and Mrs. Jack to this end. He is only marginally interested in George's ambition and exploits that ambition for his own purpose, conceiving the love affair as a chance to get at the city, where the affair begins and flourishes, and where it finally expires in pain and tumult.

When the lovers are alone, when the city fades from view and they are in their own private space, it is not the love act but the love emotion that is at the core of their relationship. Sex is indeed curiously absent or reduced to a minor role. They are two people in love, rather than two people loving or making love. Their feelings for each other are expressed far more eloquently and certainly at far greater length even in the meals they eat than in any consummated passion made visible to us. Dinner, which Mrs. Jack prepares joyously and skillfully, is an amorous ritual in the best erotic tradition of Rabelais and Fielding. The act of eating is less a preliminary to the act of love than a metaphorical substitute for it, with the table rather than the bed as the focal point. Their joy in eating, like the joy they find in talking with one another and being in one another's company, is dwelt on more lingeringly and makes a much more lasting impression upon us than their physical union, a union which, it is suggested, takes place often but which is alluded to in only the vaguest terms.

Food is in any case a subject sure to arouse Wolfe at any time. He never recovered from the epic repasts served by his father, and the poetry of eating well—which to him meant not just eating good food but eating it in gargantuan quantities—appears in his writing from the start and recurs throughout. It would not be extravagant to say that Wolfe is the greatest exponent of and certainly the greatest ecstasizer on food in American literature. Not even Hemingway, another aficionado among trenchermen, devotes as much energy to it or treats it with as much artistry.

Neither George nor Mrs. Jack is in control of their feelings. He is given to irrational outbursts during which, while claiming to love her, he deluges her with torrents of abuse—berating her for being Jewish; for being older than himself, old enough to be his mother; for patronizing him and thus gratifying herself with the vanity of "discovering" and "bringing" him along; for having a husband and children whom she has no intention of giving up for his sake; for wanting to possess, dominate, and smother him.

On her side, in a quite different tone, with a good deal of wit that does not conceal her underlying anxiety, she mocks his pretensions, derides his conceit, scorns his anti-Semitism, and wishes him a life of tasteless meals served badly by a dried-up, meager Christian girl. Most of the time she does not openly express such thoughts, though they go on at length in her mind. Only under extreme provocation, when he has taunted her beyond endurance, do they burst forth. He of course never holds back anything. With George, to feel is to speak.

In love, Wolfe's heroes express themselves verbally rather than sexually. In standard Freudian terms, they, like Wolfe himself, are highly developed oral types. They eat and they talk. The mouth is their primary organ and certainly their most highly developed one. It takes in impressions, sensations, food and drink, and emits feelings and the raw material of art. Though Wolfe labored hard over his books and revised them extensively, they still sound like oral gushings and outpourings which, almost accidentally, happen to have been set down on paper.

The sense of freshness and improvisation this conveys is immeasurable. Southerners, the country's natural orators, have produced in Wolfe one of literature's great natural orators, and it is this irresistible flow of verbal fluency and energy, coming from some inexhaustible source within, that is one of his most arresting and distinguishing qualities. The mouth is the supreme conduit of his existence as man and artist.

Mrs. Jack conducts George not only through the urban space which she occupies so comfortably but through urban time. Her father had been a prominent actor and figure about town back in the nineties, supplying her childhood with the splash and glitter that emanated from New York during one of its brilliant periods. A true creature of Wolfe's imagination, she is endowed with his fervent, hyperactive memory which seems to have retained the subtlest vibrations of the past. She proceeds to pour out all her recollections to George's outstretched ears.

Never was there a more willing and attentive audience. He drinks in, listens, and hangs on to her every word, asks the most searching questions about the tiniest minutiae, as though what he is hearing is not only manna for his soul but the gruel of life itself. He feels invigorated and in some

profound way replenished by her outpourings. They are to work their way
into his books and thus nourish his career as an artist. They also supply him
with a rich source of accumulated human energy, the energy of her life going
back to its origins. He is Mrs. Jack's lover, but he is also her researcher,
pursuing to the last footnote the supreme object of his research, herself, and
through her the life span of the great city which, past and present, she
embodies. Seldom in literature has there been so complete a transfer of a
human table of contents from one person to another.

When this transfer, in both space and time, is complete, George is ready
to break off from Mrs. Jack. He finds her no less attractive than ever. There
has been no diminution in her warmth or vitality, and certainly none in her
attention to his wants. But since he is not primarily interested in her as a
woman, a mistress, or a cook, her unchanged condition along these lines is
of no avail.

The reason he gives himself for ending their relationship is that she is
too possessive, that he feels increasingly dominated and owned by her, and
must assert his own independence. But this is contrary to the obvious facts
of their case. She is in truth far more emotionally dependent on him than he
on her. The services she performs for him, the introductions she provides,
earn her as much abuse from him as gratitude. His real reason for rejecting
her, underlying the rationalized one, a reason that as a character in the book
he is only vaguely aware of, is that she is of no further use to him as a guide
to the world, and particularly to the world of the city. In this he discharges
once again his supreme function as agent of the author. As man and lover,
George has had no change of heart. As Wolfe's urban researcher, however,
his project, as it were, has come to an end.

When it is over, he bids farewell to Mrs. Jack and takes off for Germany where we see him, in the final chapter, convalescing in a Munich
hospital from a brawl at the Munich fair and, with his bruised face staring
at itself in a mirror, engaged in a lively debate between his body and soul.
For the historical record, the debate ends in a draw.

When Wolfe, in the Author's Note to *The Web and the Rock,* declares
it to be his most objective novel, he is of course defying the critics who had
accused him of being able to write only about himself. But he is doing more
than that. He is announcing an intention that goes far beyond the immediate
question of "subjective" and "objective," of whether he can create characters instead of just copying them down, of whether he is doomed by some
fatal defect of the imagination to the confining facts of his own biography.

That intention is to move from the particular to the general, from the
immediate to the permanent, from this moment in time and this point in

space to the representation of time and space themselves. So in George's love affair with Mrs. Jack, it is the emotion he is after, not the act; it is less their individual feelings for one another than the feeling of being in love, the element commonly present in love experienced by all men and women. If such a common element can be said to exist, that is what Wolfe is after.

He seeks to rescue feeling and sensation from the transient flux in which they live so vividly and briefly by seizing their enduring qualities, the qualities that are there whenever particular feelings and sensations appear and reappear in the endless occasions of the here and now. He is not primarily a describer or creator of men and women but a searcher after mankind. He is in fact no longer a writer of novels but a universal scene painter, and the needs of storytelling—credibility, orderliness, disciplined form—have been outrightly subordinated, if not actually submerged, to the needs of getting at humanity in the largest sense, in the sense of being alive inside the encompassing frame of the universe. One cannot get more "objective" than this. No writer who ever lived had a more "objective" object in view.

We have said that, among his contemporaries, the later Wolfe most closely resembles Dos Passos, in intention though not in texture or sensory detail. As he moves away from the grooves of familiar fiction—whether it be the experimental fiction of Joyce, whom he so consciously imitated in *Look Homeward, Angel,* or the traditional narrative of classic novelists like Henry Fielding and George Eliot—he begins to resemble, among the figures of the past, mutational novelists like Rabelais and Swift. Mutational in that neither was, strictly speaking, a novelist at all. Rabelais was a doctor who, aroused by the follies and depravities of his time, created the adventures of Gargantua and Pantagruel as a club to attack the corruptions of the day.

Swift was a parson equally incensed at human irrationality and folly, who wrote *Gulliver's Travels* as a mirror in which men could see themselves precisely reflected. It was Swift's hope that this might result in a reformation of their ways, though it was his gloomy and despairing conviction that mankind was probably beyond remedy. *Gulliver's Travels,* like the books of Rabelais, bears a surface resemblance to a novel, in places reads like one, yet it is not exactly a novel, and in the end is not one at all. Wolfe's later books move erratically yet powerfully in this general direction. *The Web and the Rock* is a distinctly clearer example of this movement than *Of Time and the River. You Can't Go Home Again* will be the clearest example yet.

Rabelais and Swift were both satirists. They used highly inventive forms of exaggeration to pump up their targets in order to make them as dramatically visible as possible. In the last paragraph of his Author's Note, Wolfe informs us that *The Web and the Rock* "has in it, from first to last, a strong element of satiric exaggeration: not only because it belongs to the nature of the story . . . but because satiric exaggeration also belongs to the nature of life, and particularly American life."

Exaggeration came naturally to Wolfe. He absorbed it from the tall tales native to the mountain region where he grew up. Southern speechmaking, dinned into his ears as a boy, was rich, ornate, and full of hyperbole—southern oratory was almost the last bastion of the baroque. Some of it came from his family, devoted as they were, young and old alike, to the unrestrained emotional life. It came also from the special circumstance of his being outsized, which meant a constant straining—as he poignantly describes in the short story "Gulliver"—either to shrink himself to the proportions of others or inflate them to match his own. The tendency to magnify is in his work from the start, as it was in his nature. Even a casual reading reveals dozens of instances, from the emotional outpourings and temperamental violence of his heroes to the vast sweeps over continental and planetary landscapes.

Less obvious but just as significant is his tendency to miniaturize, to reduce a large subject to single examples, and by concentrating on a single example, force it to yield the secrets of the whole to which it is attached. Both techniques are essential in satire, as Swift illustrated in his celebrated work. He applies reduction in Lilliput and magnification to Brobdingnag. In *The Web and the Rock,* Wolfe applies reduction in North Carolina and, for the most part, magnification in New York.

When Wolfe wishes to pinpoint time, he composes a 54-page chapter on three o'clock. When he deals with race relations, yet wants to avoid an essay on the subject, he reveals in the explosive episode of Dick Prosser the swing from servility to violence that marks the intimate connection between black and white. When he tries to get at beauty, it is not the Taj Mahal, the Isles of Greece, or Keats that he dwells on but "a spur of rusty boxcars on a siding, curving off somewhere into a flat of barren pine and clay." He gets at the idea of love by the sight of Mrs. Jack, delicately flushed, bending over the stove as she cooks dinner. And he manages to find in a melon or a roast of beef all the juiciness linked with sex.

Wolfe can take some small object, and work it over until it yields up its revelation, with the same élan with which he swoops over a mountain range or puffs up an emotion until it fills the world. He has his circuits of energy that magnetize him, with roughly equal frequency, in the directions of large and small. The cliché about his gigantism, his relentless impulse to inflate, must be corrected in the light of the countermovement in him to reduce, to deflate, and, keeping in mind the general proportion of his work, to concentrate on the head of a pin.

The ratio of impersonal to personal material is much greater in *The Web and the Rock* than in *Of Time and the River,* when the change in Wolfe visibly began. His third novel is devoted to two large subjects—the southern town and the northern city. It starts off with George Webber's boyhood in North Carolina which, in drastic contrast to Eugene's boyhood in the same area, is concerned not with the developing ego of the boy but with the ambience of the region. In fact, George as a boy is almost invisible. He does not emerge as himself. Wolfe deliberately keeps him under wraps so that he may more conveniently and detachedly play the role of observer.

Even observer is too strong a term. Focus would perhaps be more accurate. He is a focus or funnel through which Wolfe can conduct his real business, which is not to show the growth of a personality but to draw a graphic, highly impressionistic, terrifically energized portrait of the South. And in this portrait, like so many chunky tidbits in a fruitcake, there is scattered decisive information about southern landscape, weather, Negroes, violence, and football and football heroes, college life, provincial patriotism, and reverence for war as one of the supreme human experiences.

In New York, George does emerge. Not all at once and certainly not at first. At first he is only one of a cluster of young southerners who room together and roam about the city sharing more or less the same initial impressions, go out with girls, horse around, attend the Dempsey-Firpo fight, get tired of each other, quarrel, break up, and finally go their separate ways. Even when George begins teaching at the School of Utility Cultures, he remains nebulous—he issues a succession of sneers at the school but is never seen in the classroom. It is not until he is introduced to us as a writer and then meets Mrs. Jack that he becomes manifest for the first time as himself.

Unlike Eugene, his predecessor along the track of romantic youth, George's personality is only minimally developed. It seems to consist of only two impulses: a strain of mad violence inherited from his mother's family and a passion for order and discipline attributed to his father. "Two Worlds Discrete," one of the book's section titles, is Wolfe's description of this duality. Discrete is just the word for it: the two impulses are not only totally separate from one another but appear to be mutually exclusive. George experiences them one at a time, never both at once. At any given moment he is a simple or simplified organism. Wolfe's intention to present him that way is made evident when, as a child, George is abruptly severed from both his parents. His father goes off and his mother dies, so that we are never allowed to see him, as we do Eugene, growing up in the thick generative soil of a living family.

George is thus detached from the complexities of a fully realized character while continuing to give off its heat and energy. But the very element that makes him less convincing than Eugene on human grounds is what makes him the more useful to Wolfe as the agent of his new intentions. George has plenty of temperament but very little personality. He has a strong capacity to feel and react but no marked traits or even quirks of character. Psychologically he is fixed rather than mobile, and can be counted on to respond in much the same way to whatever he is involved in.

This is a great aid to Wolfe. He does not have to worry about his hero developing a streak of independence, becoming balky or recalcitrant, acquiring an autonomous existence, or refusing to obey his author's instructions. He is a perfect example of what E. M. Forster called a flat rather than a round character: i.e., a character whose attitude is predictable and who never surprises us by behaving unexpectedly. Wolfe has programmed him for another purpose: to move from personality to process, from fact to feeling, from action to emotion, from being the center of a particular story to being the catalyst of what lies beyond it, the catalyst of its permanent and recurring qualities that do not depend on immediate circumstance.

Like Plato, Wolfe wants to get at the essence of things. But unlike Plato, he does not want to transcend sense or escape time. He wants instead to root his essences in the loam of sense impressions, like a tree that can ascend toward heaven only because it is firmly planted in the earth. And far from longing to escape from time into the timeless, he wants to control time by forcing it to stand still. He emphatically does not want to get beyond it into Plato's firmament of ideas and disembodied thought.

It is tremendously important to him as an imaginative writer intensely attracted to the sensuous that time go on, for only the flow of ongoing time creates the new material and the new experience so vitally necessary to his imagination. But the act of memory that makes time stop is equally essential, and to this act Wolfe bends all his energies, straining, almost compelling the past by a supreme effort of the will to reappear in his mind with absolute fidelity. Eugene and George both go through agonies of recall, bellowing out their hunger to recapture everything, and by recapturing it create it all over again.

If the original experience is life, the re-created one is art, and Wolfe is fascinated by both in about equal measure. He wants to live and he also wants to write, gradually working himself to the point where the two become indistinguishable. Toward the end, it is not enough for him to live through an experience; it will not seem complete until he writes about it as well. When that happens, as it does in the later novels, the gap between George Webber experiencing something and cramming it into his book all but disappears. By the time we get to *You Can't Go Home Again*, he has been turned into a pure instrument of recall and re-creation.

The personal, biographical element is still present, though severely restrained, in the early stages of *The Web and the Rock*. This grows steadily more tenuous as Wolfe gets into the New York phase of the novel. Though George's affair with Mrs. Jack is marked by frenzied outbursts of temperament, these are only a gloss on his determined exploitation of her in pursuit of Wolfe's search for the soul of the city. The two lovers work out their love relationship at considerable length, but from the outset Wolfe is looking beyond them at the enfabled rock which he seeks to scale. Even to his seething ambition, this enterprise appears Himalayan in scope, a prospect that might discourage the rest of us but that only stimulates him to plunge ahead. It is this plunging ahead, past the characters and their particular lives, that carries Wolfe far beyond the familiar limits and conventional format of *Look Homeward, Angel*.

Read as a traditional novel, *The Web and The Rock* suffers by comparison with the earlier book. Read, as I believe it should be, as an intensely articulated mural, first of the provincial and then, climactically, of the urban landscape, it not only does not suffer by comparison with its famous predecessor, but is not to be compared with it at all.

It is in a category by itself. Taken on its own terms, *The Web and the Rock* is an extraordinarily interesting and highly original example of a work breaking out of the confines of its own genre. It is a triumph of Wolfe's newly directioned art, another stage in the saga of a novelist getting away from the novel.

C. HUGH HOLMAN

The Web of the South

When Thomas Wolfe went north after his graduation from the University of North Carolina, he went as a southerner, to write of southern subjects in George Pierce Baker's "47 Workshop" at Harvard, and to compose his first novel out of the southern scenes of his childhood with an autobiographical candor and an accuracy shocking to the residents of his native city. Yet Thomas Wolfe never returned for long to the South, once he had left it—indeed, he declared that "you can't go home again"—and some critics have believed, as Maxwell Geismar suggested, that Wolfe "was born in the South, but he shared with it little except the accident of his birth."

In his sprawling, loosely constructed tales and novels, he heaped a gargantuan scorn upon his native region, condemning what in *Look Homeward, Angel* he called the southerners' "hostile and murderous intrenchment against all new life . . . their cheap mythology, their legend of the charm of their manner, the aristocratic culture of their lives, the quaint sweetness of their drawl." In *The Web and the Rock,* betraying his mingled disgust and sense of shame, he expresses his anger at "the old, stricken, wounded 'Southness' of cruelty and lust," at men who "have a starved, stricken leanness in the loins," and at the lynchings that end with castrations. The southern intellectual fared little better in Wolfe's novels. He had contempt for the Agrarians whom he called in *The Web and the Rock* "the refined young gentlemen of the New Confederacy . . . [who] retired haughtily into the South, to the academic security of a teaching appointment at one of the universities, from which they could issue in quarterly installments very small

From *The Loneliness at the Core: Studies in Thomas Wolfe.* © 1975 by Louisiana State University Press.

and very precious magazines which celebrated the advantages of an agrarian society." And he wrote with feeling in the same novel of "the familiar rationalizing and self-defense of southern fear and southern failure: its fear of conflict and of competition in the greater world; its inability to meet or to adjust itself to the conditions, strifes, and ardors of a modern life; its old, sick, Appomattox-like retreat into the shades of folly and delusion, of prejudice and bigotry, of florid legend and defensive casuistry."

This South was feminine to him—what he called once "*the female principle*—the *earth* again . . . a home, fixity"—and in his thinking he opposed it to the father principle, which, in *The Story of a Novel,* he called "the image of a strength and wisdom external to his need and superior to his hunger, to which the belief and power of his own life could be united." From the maternal and subjective South, "the dark Helen of his blood," he turned to storm the male citadels of the North and to find in the "enfabled rock" of the northern city a defense against the web of the South. Yet this South beat in his brain and pounded in his veins. "Every young man from the South," he said in *The Web and the Rock,* "has felt this precise and formal geography of the spirit," in which South and North are sharply dichotomized autonomies; and the qualities in young southerners brought to the North "a warmth you lacked, a passion that God knows you needed, a belief and a devotion that was wanting in your life, an integrity of purpose that was rare in your own swarming hordes. They brought . . . some of the warmth, the depth and mystery. . . . They brought a warmth of earth, an exultant joy of youth, a burst of living laughter, a fullbodied warmth and living energy of humor." Wolfe could proudly boast in a letter to James Boyd, "I'm a Long Hunter from Bear Creek, and a rootin', tootin', shootin' son-of-a-gun from North Carolina"; and he could write Maxwell Perkins that "The people in North Carolina . . . are rich, juicy, deliberate, full of pungent and sardonic humor and honesty, conservative and cautious on top, but at bottom wild, savage, and full of the murderous innocence of the earth and the wilderness." What he said of his character George Webber is true of Wolfe himself: "He was a Southerner, and he knew that there was something wounded in the South. He knew that there was something twisted, dark, and full of pain which Southerners have known all their lives—something rooted in their souls beyond all contradiction." But all his knowledge of her darkness and damnation could not completely stifle his love for the lost and ruined and burning Helen in his blood.

That his vision of his native region was both obsessive and ambiguous was not surprising. Wolfe was born to a northern father and a southern mother, and the division of life into male and female, North and South, wanderer and homebound, was a simple extension of what he saw daily as a boy. He grew up in a southern mountain town, but at a time when it was changing into a resort city, flourishing in the shadow of the baronial estate of the Vanderbilts, the pseudo-French chateau "Biltmore," and literally mad for money. He went to college at Chapel Hill, a southern state university, but at the time when that school was beginning the pattern of liberalism that made it the symbol of New South progressivism, completely opposite to the agrarianism of Vanderbilt University. Ambiguous and contradictory though his views of his native region were, the South was a theme and a subject for much of Wolfe's work, and it existed for him in a sensuous, irrational, emotional state of mutual attraction and repulsion. And this contradiction and ambiguity, this coexisting intense love and passionate hatred are characteristic not only of Wolfe's attitudes toward the South but also of his total work.

Few American novelists have projected more ambitious programs or had more demanding plans for their novels. The motive force of his works seems to have been his desire to express the elements of a universal experience, and this universal experience was for him closely tied up with the national, the American experience. That the elements which made up his all-encompassing effort were woven from the filaments of his self and that that self was both woven and torn by his southern heritage should be beyond dispute; but in the interest of illuminating a little of both Wolfe and the literature of his region it may be worthwhile to point to some of the southern qualities in his work.

The urge to represent America, to embody it in a work of art, although by no means unique to the region, has been persistent in southern literature. The southerners of the antebellum period often raised their voices in support of a native literature and stood with the "Young America" group of critics in their intensely nationalistic demands for art in the 1840s and 1850s, despite the serious political differences between them and the New York critics. They distrusted the "internationalism" of New Englanders like Longfellow and of New Yorkers like the editors of the *Knickerbocker Magazine*. Yet these southerners were aware that the nation could better be represented by drawing its particularities than by picturing the whole. In 1856, for example, William Gilmore Simms, of South Carolina, had written: "To be *national* in literature, one must needs be *sectional*. No one mind can fully or fairly illustrate the characteristics of any great country; and he who shall depict *one section* faithfully, has made his proper and sufficient contribution to the great work of national literature." This view is not far from Wolfe's own, when he insists upon the representation of his unique self as the proper subject for a national art. Wolfe was like Thoreau, who said, "I should not talk so much about myself if there were any body else whom I knew as well. Unfortunately, I am confined to this theme by the narrowness of my experience." However, for Wolfe, the observation of his fellow men was a basic part of that experience, as it was not for Thoreau.

It is also typical of the southern writer that this epic portrayal of America should constitute a project of great magnitude and tremendous complexity. Wolfe's letters, *Notebooks,* and *The Story of a Novel* carry the evidence of the vastness of scope and the complexity of design of the "work in progress" on which he expended his days and hours and which he left incomplete. It is startling to one who has accepted the standard view of Wolfe's work as the spontaneous and unpremeditated overflow of the author's powerful feeling, recollected in abnormal intensity, to find him writing to Maxwell Perkins, "I think you may be a little inclined to underestimate the importance of arrangement and presentation, and may feel that the stories can go in any way, and that the order doesn't matter much." In the light of his efforts to get on paper the theme, the argument, the structure of the large work as he labored on its parts, such a statement—although it does not redeem his novels from formlessness—makes poignant and telling Wolfe's protests against the publication of *Of Time and the River* in the form in which Perkins sent it to press.

This large design would have traced the history of the Pentlands (or, later, the Joyners) from the Civil War to the present, emphasizing the southern roots of the generic hero. It would have included thousands of characters and episodes—the whole, Wolfe said, to be "seen *not by a definite personality,* but haunted throughout by a consciousness of *personality,*" and that personality was to be the perceptive "self" through whom the writer could know and express his America. Before a work of such magnitude as he projected, time became the great enemy. The scope of his ambitious plan—which was to be no less than the record of his nation and his people told through one representative man—merits in its magnitude comparison with the master projects of literary history, with those of Balzac, Zola, and Tolstoy. To embark upon such vast projects has also been typically, although by no means exclusively, southern, perhaps because the southerner tends to distrust abstraction and to doubt that one can see a "World in a Grain of Sand / And a Heaven in a Wild Flower." Whatever the reason, southern writers have tended to plan work of enormous scope, such as Simm's seven linked volumes of historical fiction on the Revolution; James Branch Cabell's many-volumed and incomplete record of Poictesme; Ellen Glasgow's fictional record in thirteen volumes of Virginia's social history from the Civil War to the 1940s (whether or not such a structure was her original intention or a design she imposed after a good portion of the fact); and William Faulkner's vast record of Yoknapatawpha County. Wolfe, like these other southerners, set himself a task that staggers the imagination and defies the reality of time. Little wonder that Faulkner considered him among the greatest of American writers because he dared the most.

Near the beginning of his first novel Wolfe wrote, "Subtract us into nakedness and night again, and you shall see begin in Crete four thousand years ago the love that ended yesterday in Texas. . . . Each moment is the fruit of forty thousand years." This concern with time grew more intense as his career developed. The artist's problem, he believed, is the resolution of a threefold consciousness of time into a single moment so that scenes can represent "characters as acting and as being acted upon by all the accumulated impact of man's experience so that each moment of their lives was conditioned not only by what they experienced in that moment, but by all that they had experienced up to that moment." Whether or not Wolfe is indebted to Proust and Bergson for these ideas, he certainly envisions his characters as set in a complete fabric of time, and their actions as having remote roots and immeasurable forward extensions. Louis D. Rubin, Jr., has noted that "The interplay of past and present, of the historical and the contemporaneous, causes all the modern Southern writers to be unusually sensitive to the nature and workings of time." This interplay is one of the basic materials of Wolfe's fiction.

Wolfe shares with many southern writers his concerns with the reality of the past in the present and with the nature of time. One can find examples of the southern writer's concern with time and his belief that it is not only fact or sequence, but, more important, a key to the nature of human experience, in Robert Penn Warren, particularly in *The Ballad of Billie Potts* and *World Enough and Time;* in Ellen Glasgow; in the elaborate dislocations of time sequence in many of Faulkner's narratives; in Allen Tate's "Ode to the Confederate Dead;" in the inverted structure of William Styron's *Lie Down in Darkness;* in Eudora Welty's *Losing Battles;* and in many other places. It is not surprising that one of Wolfe's best-known short stories should be "Chickamauga" and that the novel fragment on which he was working at the time of his death, *The Hills Beyond,* deals with his southern ancestors in the nineteenth century. Among twentieth-century American novelists only the southerners have with any frequency treated the past outside the pattern of romance and adventure. Faulkner, Warren, Glasgow, and Cabell have written extensively with a historical orientation.

The mixture of styles in which Wolfe wrote is also not uncommon in southern writing. On one level Wolfe illustrates with great effectiveness the concrete, the immediate, the sensuous. It is this quality in his work that gives many of his pages an intensity which almost approximates direct experience. This lyric aspect of his writing, in which the object is evoked with such power that it seems to be rubbed against the reader's exposed nerve ends, this ability to make "the world's body" vividly real, succeeds again and again in giving the reader new insights; in Wolfe's terms, in making "the utterly familiar, common thing . . . suddenly be revealed . . . with all the wonder with which we discover a thing which we have seen all our life and yet have never known before." A passage from *Of Time and the River* will illustrate the centrality of the concrete in Wolfe's writing. Eugene Gant is daydreaming and not worrying about where the money to fulfill his dreams is to come from.

> If he thought about it, it seemed to have no importance or reality whatever—he just dismissed it impatiently, or with a conviction that some old man would die and leave him a fortune, that he was going to pick up a purse containing hundreds of thousands of dollars while walking in the Fenway, and that the reward would be enough to keep him going, or that a beautiful and rich young widow, true-hearted, tender, loving, and voluptuous, who had carrot-colored hair, little freckles on her face, and a snub nose and luminous gray-green eyes with something wicked yet loving and faithful in them, and one gold filling in her solid little teeth, was going to fall in love with him.

Here, where he is mocking Eugene's stereotyped dreams, the rich young widow is made concrete and detailed, the lucky purse is found in a particular place. This use of the particular, this tendency to distrust the conceptual and abstract, is one of the most widely recognized characteristics of southern writing. As Robert Penn Warren has pointed out, the southerner lives in "the instinctive fear . . . that the massiveness of experience, the concreteness of life, will be violated . . . [in] the fear of abstraction." Virginia Rock has noted that the southern poet feels "not only a rage for order but also a rage for the concrete, a rage against the abstract." Even in criticism, southerners have concentrated their attention on particular works of art and have not formulated abstract systems. As Allen Tate put it, "There was no Southern criticism; merely a few Southern critics."

Closely associated with this concern for the concrete is Wolfe's delight in folk speech, dialect, and speech mannerisms. His works are full of accurate transcriptions of vivid speech. His characters seem sometimes to talk endlessly, but they always talk with vigor and with great distinctiveness of diction, syntax, and idiom. Yet the same writer who displays these startlingly effective qualities of lyric concreteness and accuracy of speech is also guilty of excesses in both quantity and quality of rhetoric perhaps unequaled by any other American novelist. With the power to evoke a particular object, scene, or character with remarkable clarity, he is unwilling to let these creations speak for themselves, but must try by sheer force of rhetoric to give expression to the peculiar meanings that they suggest, to define ineffable feelings, to formulate the inchoate longings and uncertain stirrings of spirit he feels all men share. These qualities are manifest in the following passage from *Of Time and the River,* where Wolfe is trying to define the "fury" that drives Gant toward the North and away from the South.

> It is to have the old unquiet mind, the famished heart, the restless soul; it is to lose hope, heart, and all joy utterly, and then to have them wake again, to have the old feeling return with overwhelming force that he is about to find the thing for which his life obscurely and desperately is groping—for which all men on this earth have sought—one face out of the million faces, a wall, a door, a place of certitude and peace and wandering no more. For what is it that we Americans are seeking always on this earth? Why is it we have crossed the stormy seas so many times alone, lain in a thousand alien rooms at night hearing the sounds of time, dark time, and thought until heart, brain, flesh, and spirit are sick and weary with the thought of it: "Where shall I go now? What shall I do?"

Set beside some of the apostrophes from *Look Homeward, Angel,* like the one to Laura James at the end of chapter 30, this passage seems restrained, yet it represents pretty clearly that rhetorical groping toward understanding and expression which is a large element in Wolfe's work. He is fascinated by language, enchanted by words, carried away by rhetorical devices. A kind of primitive logomania is in him: if the word can be found and uttered, vast forces are unleashed and great truths miraculously uncovered.

The drift toward rhetoric is the aspect of Wolfe's work most frequently called southern. Alfred Kazin observed of Wolfe and Faulkner: "It is their rhetoric, a mountainous verbal splendor, that holds these writers together . . . the extravagant and ornamental tradition of Southern rhetoric." Wilbur

J. Cash believed that it was their use of the rhetorical tradition that tied
Faulkner and Wolfe to earlier southern literary traditions, and Joseph Warren Beach felt that "Wolfe's inclination to extravagant and ornamental
writing" should be associated with "something in the tradition of Southern
culture." Certainly the passion for the sound of the word, the primitive
desire to give the name, the sense of the power present in the magic of
incantation, show up with alarming frequency in southern writing. The
particular linguistic combination that Wolfe used—the combination of concrete detail, accurate speech, and incantatory rhetorical extravagance—is
also present to a marked degree in the works of Faulkner, particularly since
1936, and in the novels of Robert Penn Warren.

Wolfe likewise shares the southerner's willingness to accept and find
delight in paradox. At the heart of the riddle of the South is a union of
opposites, a condition of instability, a paradox: a love of individualism
combined with a defense of slavery and segregation, a delight in polished
manners and at the same time a ready recourse to violence, the liberalism of
Thomas Jefferson coexisting with the conservatism of John C. Calhoun.
Such paradoxes bother southerners less than they would bother their northern neighbors, for while they hunger for order and are moved by a rage for
tradition, they can at the same time accept instability at a permanent aspect
of human existence and the unresolved contradiction as a part of man's
condition. Southern writers often value paradox as a primary element in art.
Cleanth Brooks, for example, finds the meaning in poetry in the paradoxes
that are to be found in word, image, and structure. The Fugitive poets,
notably John Crowe Ransom, find the full meaning of an incident in the
comprehension of its persistent ironies. Allen Tate sees the meaning of a
poem in the "tension" created by the conflict between its intension and
extension.

Wolfe saw his world and himself through an only semilogical application to life of the Hegelian dialectic. He seemed to need to define a thing's
opposite before he could comprehend the thing, and to have a naive faith
that somehow the meaning was manifest if the opposites were stated. Hence,
there is in his work on practically every level—sentence, paragraph, scene,
theme, large project—a structure of paradox.

But all these attributes of Wolfe's work individually are essentially
superficial qualities of his "southernness." So strong a combination of these
attributes as he displays does not often occur in America outside the South;
yet these qualities suggest rather than define a distinctively southern quality.
In certain other respects, however, Wolfe seems definitively southern. One
of these is his attitude toward capitalistic industrialism; another is his

sense of the tragic implications of experience; and a third is his deep-seated sense of human guilt.

That Wolfe had little patience with the group of southern writers known as the Agrarians is obvious from what has already been quoted. He regarded their intellectualism as false, their devotion to the life of the soil as pretentious and unreal, and he heaped scorn on them more than once, calling them by the opprobrious name "New Confederates." Yet one has the feeling that much of his contempt rested on ignorance of what the Agrarians were advocating, and that he would have been pretty much of their party if he had known what that party really was. However, he belonged loosely to the New South school, which saw in industrial progress the key to a new and better life and believed that the South must emerge from its retreat to the past into the reality of the modern world. In *The Web and the Rock* he wrote:

> There was an image in George Webber's mind that came to him in childhood and that resumed for him the whole dark picture of those decades of defeat and darkness. He saw an old house, set far back from the traveled highway, and many passed along that road, and the troops went by, the dust rose, and the war was over. And no one passed along that road again. He saw an old man go along the path, away from the road, into the house; and the path was overgrown with grass and weeds, with thorny tangle, and with underbrush until the path was lost. And no one ever used that path again. And the man who went into that house never came out of it again. And the house stayed on. It shone faintly through that tangled growth like its own ruined spectre, its doors and windows black as eyeless sockets. That was the South. That was the South for thirty years or more.
>
> That was the South, not of George Webber's life, nor the lives of his contemporaries—that was the South they did not know but that all of them somehow remembered. It came to them from God knows where, upon the rustling of a leaf at night, in quiet voices on a Southern porch, in a screen door slam and sudden silence, a whistle wailing down the midnight valleys to the East and the enchanted cities of the North, and Aunt Maw's droning voice and the memory of unheard voices, in the memory of the dark, ruined Helen in their blood, in something stricken, lost, and far, and long ago. They did not see it, the people of George's age and time, but they remembered it.

They had come out—another image now—into a kind of sun-
light of another century. They had come out upon the road
again. The road was being paved. More people came now. They
cut a pathway to the door again. Some of the weeds were clear.
Another house was built. They heard wheels coming and the
world was *in,* yet they were not yet wholly of that world.

Yet Wolfe was also keenly aware that industrial progress and the things
associated with it could have damaging effects on American and southern culture. Writing to his mother, in May 1923, he condemned "progress" and commerce in scathing terms: "What I shall try to get into their dusty little
pint-measure minds is that a full belly, a good automobile, paved streets, and
so on, do not make them one whit better or finer,—that there is beauty in
this world,—beauty even in this wilderness of ugliness and provincialism that
is at present our country, beauty and spirit which will make us men instead
of cheap Board of Trade Boosters, and blatant pamphleteers." He defined the
"essential tragedy of America" as "the magnificent, unrivaled, unequaled,
unbeatable, unshrinkable, supercolossal, 99-and-44-one-hundredths-per-
cent-pure, schoolgirl-complexion, covers-the-earth, I'd-walk-a-mile-for-it,
four-out-of-five-have-it, his-master's voice, ask-the-man-who-owns-one,
blueplate-special home of advertising, salesmanship, and special pleading in
all its many catchy and beguiling forms." Certainly for him, capitalistic industrial progress had as little appeal as it did for the Agrarians; for him, as
for the Twelve Southerners who wrote *I'll Take My Stand,* the modern industrial world had become a perversion of the American dream. The Twelve
Southerners declared, "If a community, or a section, or a race, or an age, is
groaning under industrialism, and well aware that it is an evil dispensation,
it must find the way to throw it off. To think that this cannot be done is pu-
sillanimous. And if the whole community, section, race, or age thinks it cannot be done, then it has simply lost its political genius and doomed itself to
impotence." George Webber shared these sentiments when he said, in *You
Can't Go Home Again:*

And the worst of it is the intellectual dishonesty which all this
corruption has bred. People are *afraid* to think straight—*afraid*
to face themselves—*afraid* to look at things and see them as they
are. We've become like a nation of advertising men, all hiding
behind catch phrases like "prosperity" and "rugged individualism" and "the American way." And the real things like freedom,
and equal opportunity, and the integrity and worth of the individual—things that have belonged to the American dream since

the beginning—they have become just words too. The substance
has gone out of them—they're not real any more.

Admittedly, this sounds more like Sidney Lanier's condemnation of "Trade"
than Donald Davidson's advocacy of the Agrarian way, yet the enemy that
all three faced was an enemy well known to the South and commonly
confronted by southerners.

Wolfe looked upon himself as a radical, even, as he once called himself,
a "Revolutionary," and he angrily expressed his hatred of the gross injustice
and inhumanity that the Depression produced. But to him the solution was
never material; indeed, the substitution of the material for the spiritual was
the cause for his belief "that we are lost here in America," and only his
confidence that ultimately America would put aside the material for the
spiritual made it possible for him to add, "but I believe we shall be found."

Wolfe is peculiarly southern, too, in the degree to which he sees the
darkness, pain, and evil in life, and yet does not succumb to the naturalistic
answer of despair. "The enemy," he tells us in *You Can't Go Home Again*,
"is old as Time, and evil as Hell, and he has been here with us from the
beginning. I think he stole our earth from us, destroyed our wealth, and
ravaged and despoiled our land. I think he took our people and enslaved
them, that he polluted the fountains of our life, took unto himself the rarest
treasures of our own possession, took our bread and left us with a crust."

Wolfe seemed to feel, as George Webber did, "the huge and nameless
death that waits around the corner for all men, to break their backs and
shatter instantly the blind and pitiful illusions of their hope." He was su-
premely the novelist of death in American literature, for the ending of life
was an obsessive theme with him. All his characters come to face the fact of
death; as he expressed it, "They knew that they would die and that the earth
would last forever. And with that feeling of joy, wonder, and sorrow in their
hearts, they knew that another day had gone, another day had come, and
they knew how brief and lonely are man's days." And the end, at least in its
physical sense, was ugly. In *Of Time and the River* he described it this way:
"This was the sickening and abominable end of flesh, which infected time
and all man's living memory of morning, youth, and magic with the death-
putrescence of its cancerous taint, and made us doubt that we had ever
lived, or had a father, known joy: this was the end, and the end was horrible
in ugliness. At the end it was not well." In *The Story of a Novel* Wolfe is
explicit about this darkness and evil in life. "Everywhere around me . . . I
saw the evidence of an incalculable ruin and suffering," he said, and enumerated the "suffering, violence, oppression, hunger, cold, and filth and

poverty" he saw, so that through "the suffering and labor of [his] own life" he shared the experience of people around him.

This sense of evil and suffering is more typical of southern writers than of other Americans, for a variety of reasons: the South's distrust of progress, its refusal to believe in perfectibility, its experience of compromise and paradox—all culminated in the defeat in the Civil War and its long and bitter aftermath. As C. Vann Woodward has cogently argued, the South is the only American region where the principles of progress and the concept of perfectibility are demonstrably false. "Nothing," he asserts, "about [its] history is conducive to the theory that the South was the darling of divine providence." This sense of defeat led Ellen Glasgow to say that she could never recall a time when "the pattern of society as well as the scheme of things in general, had not seemed to me false and even malignant," and the same feeling found expression in the dark damnation of Faulkner's world and the ambiguous calamities of Robert Penn Warren's.

When, however, the nation as a whole began to experience the cataclysms of the twentieth century and to react to scientific and philosophic views of man that were less optimistic, the American artist outside the South tended to turn to programs of Utopian reform or satiric correction or naturalistic despair. The southern writer on the other hand, older in the experience of calamity and defeat, saw the tragic grandeur of man, the magnificence of his will in the face of disaster, and the glory with which he maintained the integrity of his spirit in a world of material defeat. Southern writers have often used their history to make a tragic fable of man's lot in a hostile world, and to celebrate the triumph of the human spirit when challenged by an idea or a responsibility. As Ellen Glasgow asserts, "One may learn to live, one may even learn to live gallantly, without delight." And as Ike McCaslin says in Faulkner's "Delta Autumn," "There are good men everywhere, at all times. Most men are. Some are just unlucky, because most men are a little better than their circumstances give them a chance to be." This view of man changes defeat into tragic grandeur and touches the spectacle of suffering with the transforming sense of human dignity.

Thomas Wolfe's view of man and life had this tragic sense. In *The Story of a Novel* he expressed it very directly. "And from it all, there has come as the final deposit, a burning memory, a certain evidence of the fortitude of man, his ability to suffer and somehow to survive." At the conclusion of chapter 27 of *You Can't Go Home Again,* Wolfe states that man to him is "a foul, wretched, abominable creature . . . and it is impossible to say the worst of him . . . this moth of time, this dupe of brevity and numbered hours, this travesty of waste and sterile breath." Yet Wolfe stands in awe of man's accomplishments. "For there is one belief, one faith, that is man's glory, his triumph, his immortality—and that is his belief in life. . . . So this is man—the worst and best of him—this frail and petty thing who lives his days and dies like all the other animals and is forgotten. And yet, he is immortal, too, for both the good and evil that he does live after him."

The southern writer is often obsessed with a sense of guilt and the need for expiation. Robert Penn Warren calls this feeling by its theological name in his poem "Original Sin," and sees it as the inevitable result of our lost innocence; in Allen Tate's "The Wolves" it is a threatening evil to be faced always in the next room; in William Faulkner it may be symbolized by the vicariously shared guilt which Quentin Compson must assume and die to pay for in *The Sound and the Fury,* or the inheritance of the father's which Ike McCaslin vainly tries to repudiate in "The Bear." This sense of guilt may be the product of the pervasive Calvinism of the region; it may be the product of the poverty and suffering that the region has known; it is certainly in part the result of the guilt associated with slavery in the nineteenth century and the Negro's second-class citizenship in the twentieth—a guilt most thoughtful southerners have felt. In any case, it appears to be a hallmark of the serious twentieth-century southern writer. And it is a hallmark that Thomas Wolfe's work certainly bears. He states his sense of his own guilt explicitly in *The Story of a Novel.*

> And through the traffic of those thronging crowds—whose faces, whose whole united and divided life was now instantly and without an effort of the will, my *own*—there rose forever the sad unceasing murmurs of the body of this life, the vast recessive fadings of the shadow of man's death that breathes forever with its dirgelike sigh around the huge shores of the world.
>
> And *beyond*—forever *above, around, behind* the vast and tranquil consciousness of my spirit that now held the earth and all her elements in the huge clasp of its effortless subjection— there dwelt forever the fatal knowledge of my own inexpiable *guilt.*

In *You Can't Go Home Again* he explicitly links this sense of guilt with the South and in turn sees the South as a symbol and in a sense a scapegoat for the national hurt.

> Perhaps it came from their old war, and from the ruin of their great defeat and its degraded aftermath. Perhaps it came from causes yet more ancient—from the evil of man's slavery, and

the hurt and shame of human conscience in its struggle with the
fierce desire to own. It came, too, perhaps, from the lusts of the
hot South, tormented and repressed below the harsh and outward patterns of a bigot and intolerant theology. . . . And most
of all, perhaps, it came out of the very weather of their lives. . . .

But it was not only in the South that America was hurt. There
was another deeper, darker, and more nameless wound throughout the land. . . .

We must look at the heart of guilt that beats in each of us, for
there the cause lies. We must look, and with our own eyes see,
the central core of defeat and shame and failure.

Thomas Wolfe did not live to complete his representation of his America through the portrait of himself as generic man, and out of the novels,
short stories, and letters we piece out the pattern he was trying to follow and
we guess at the meanings and intentions. One thing seems clear: Wolfe was
a southerner, torn by the tensions and issues that thoughtful southerners
feel, oppressed as they tend to be with the tragic nature of life, and feeling
as they often do a sense of guilt that demands some kind of expiating action.
The work he completed had demonstrable southern qualities; the total work,
had he lived to complete it, would probably have had these qualities too.
The South did, indeed, burn in his blood and on his pages like a "ruined
Helen"—beautiful, passionate, and dark with violence and guilt.

But although Thomas Wolfe shared many of that combination of qualities of mind and spirit that in some arrangement or other we call "southern," he differed in significant ways from many of his fellow southerners,
who had different geographical and spiritual roots. For despite the fact that
the southern region has had a unique identity, the term "South" is too broad
an abstraction to be handled with very much precision by its historians or
critics. There are not one but many Souths; and these may fall, at the next
level of abstraction, into a three-part grouping made by geographical differences, major variations in social patterns, and various strains of race and
culture resulting from different kinds and times of migration, so that "the
South" is comprised of at least three distinct subregions with radical differences among themselves—differences almost as great as those between
the total region and the rest of the nation. These subregions certainly over-
lap at many points, and they share many common characteristics, so that,
except for the extreme forms of each of these subregions, they seem to shade
into each other almost imperceptibly, despite the fact that each maintains a
geographical distinctiveness.

Geographically the southeastern United States consists of a broad coastal plain rich in rivers and readily accessible to those who boarded frighteningly frail crafts and sailed them over unknown seas to Roanoke Island, into the James River, and into the Cooper and Ashley rivers at Charleston. At the edge of the Atlantic coastal plain is the "fall line," a geological formation which separates the plain from the rolling hills. This fall line passes through Richmond, Virginia; Raleigh, North Carolina; Columbia, South Carolina; and Milledgeville, Georgia. Behind it the gentle rise of the Piedmont stretches westward until it suddenly flings itself skyward to form the Southern Appalachian and Blue Ridge mountains. Westward from the first ranges of the Blue Ridge and the Appalachian mountains is the Great Valley. The entire southeastern region is bounded on the east and south by the Atlantic and Gulf coastal plains and is marked latitudinally by climate variations. Virginia, the Carolinas, Tennessee, and much of Georgia are in a humid, warm, temperate zone. Florida, Alabama, Mississippi, and Louisiana are in a humid, semitropical zone. Hence we can, with some accuracy, talk of a temperate coastal South—variously called the Tidewater and the Low Country—of a Piedmont South which extends into and includes the Appalachian and Blue Ridge mountains, and of a Deep South which is largely a semitropical Gulf Coast plain.

Both the southern seaboard and the Deep South were haunted by the dream of baronial splendor. As a powerful dream, it realized itself in a mannered but intense code of violence in the Gulf plain states. Whatever limited reality it had came from the seaboard planter world. But behind the Tidewater and the Low Country was a world of sturdy, egalitarian men who settled and dominated the westward sweep of continent beyond the "fall line." The Piedmont hills, the mountain ranges, and the mountain valleys were first colonized primarily not by the British with Cavalier pretensions, who entered through the southern Atlantic ports and then moved inward, but by those of Scotch-Irish, Scottish, and German origin who came through the middle Atlantic ports of Philadelphia, Chester, and New Castle, and moved westward through the Great Valley for about a hundred miles until the tall mountains raised barriers that deflected them south. They came down the broad cattle trails into the Piedmont South, settling in Virginia, the backcountry of the Carolinas, Tennessee, and Georgia. There they created a social world marked by the grim Calvinistic attitudes of the dour Scottish Presbyterians and took unto themselves the Piedmont and mountain regions stretching from what is now West Virginia to a point in central and south Georgia.

When the Great Migration of the Scotch-Irish began in 1717, few of the migrants questioned the propriety of social classes or the value of a society with stability based on a concept of upper, "middling," and "lower" orders. But in America, particularly in mountainous Virginia and the backcountry of the Carolinas, class lines were soon blurred almost beyond recognition, and traditional distinctions underwent massive erosion. These people of the Piedmont created a special and frequently grim way of life so radically different from the Tidewater culture, which was only a few hundred miles away, that they might almost have lived on different continents. In this grim social world of the frontier Piedmont, the Scotch-Irish were quick-tempered, impetuous, inclined to work by fits and starts, reckless, and given to too much drinking. Their pietistic, puritanic Calvinism as yoked to an intense acquisitiveness, so that they earned the claim that a "Scotch-Irishman is one who keeps the commandments of God and every other thing he can get his hands on." Thus they formed a harsh society marked by widespread crudity and high animal spirits. It was an egalitarian, individualistic, religiously dissenting world. To those who visited it from the coastal plain area, it appeared to be lawless and frightening. The Anglican itinerant minister Charles Woodmason, who tried to serve the South Carolina backcountry from 1766 to 1768, left in his journal a record of the dismay with which he viewed the region. He declared that these people's chief characteristics were lawlessness, vile manners, ignorance, slovenliness, and primitive emotionalism in religion.

Their pragmatic view of life, their folk-version Calvinism, and their anti-intellectual individualism created a special world favorable to egalitarian democracy and having little patience with and no respect for aristocratic pretensions. This cotton country and hill country, made up of small farms, small towns, and small cities spaced very far apart, maintains to this day many of its early characteristics.

It is very far removed from the melancholy great oaks and broad plantations of the Tidewater which is Thomas Nelson Page's and Ellen Glasgow's world and almost equally removed from the tropical lushness and richness of the Deep South, best represented by William Faulkner. Here in the decades immediately before the Revolution was the sharp cutting edge of the frontier. Although by 1790 the Scotch-Irish represented no more than a quarter of a million Americans, their strength of character shaped the conventions of the world in which they lived and made them the controlling force for awhile in the westward movement. It was and is a country at the mercy of the capriciousness of weather and the vicissitudes of the cotton market. In this century it has been a land racked by diseases peculiar to poverty, a harsh sharecropper system, and by low income and little education. It is no accident that this area has been a central target for a war on poverty and economic and social distress by a socially minded federal government from the early days of Franklin Roosevelt's presidency to the Appalachian programs of Lyndon Johnson.

There has not been a time since the eighteenth century when this Piedmont and mountain South has not had its chroniclers, and its recorders have had a remarkable unanimity of opinion and attitude toward its inhabitants. The most obvious characteristic of this body of writers, aside from their exaggerated tendency toward the grotesque, is an emphasis upon a disordered society, a sense that there is neither in social custom nor in religious belief an ordering principle which is acceptable to the writer. As early as 1728, William Byrd in his *A History of the Dividing Line* portrayed backcountry North Carolinians, whom he called the inhabitants of "lubberland," with an amused awareness that at least by his standards they were grotesques. Augustus Baldwin Longstreet described the people of the Georgia Piedmont in a series of sketches written in the 1830s and collected a book form in 1835 as *Georgia Scenes.* His is the detached view of a cultivated lawyer and judge seeing these people as cruel and unlearned denizens of a world remote from the social order which Judge Longstreet revered.

The early novels about the southern frontier described the same kinds of people and judged them against a concept of an aristocratic social order, notably in the case of William Gilmore Simms's "Border Romances" and most obviously in his *Guy Rivers* (1834), which is laid in frontier Georgia. In midcentury, George Washington Harris in his comic character Sut Lovingood created a kind of American *Til Eulenspiegel* in this region. During the local color movement writers like "Charles Egbert Craddock" (Mary N. Murfree) presented, with a summer visitor's condescension, a whimsical picture of the eccentricities of the mountain people of this region.

In the twentieth century the region has called forth notable novelistic efforts, among them the works of T. S. Stribling, particularly in *Teeftallow* and in his trilogy *The Forge, The Store,* and *Unfinished Cathedral;* Erskine Caldwell, in his earlier and more serious period when his Rabelaisian exaggeration was redeemed from vulgarity by his social concerns; Lillian Smith, in her tractarian novels and essays; and most recently Flannery O'Connor, whose two novels and two volumes of short stories may very well represent the best writing done by a southerner during the past quarter of a century.

The writers of this tradition used many different literary forms. They have, however, all sought in differing ways for some outside, some external control by which they can judge the value of the society which they discuss.

This society is in many ways more nearly American and less distinctively southern, except for its grotesquerie, than the societies of the Deep South or of the Tidewater and the Low Country; and the standard by which it is judged, whether it be that of social justice, of religious order, or of moral indignation, has always been an outer and different standard from that embraced by the local inhabitants. Ellen Glasgow, of the Tidewater, and William Faulkner, of the Deep South, on the other hand, have found the standards by which to judge their societies in the ideals of their citizens, however little these ideals found firm expression in either of the cultures.

Many of the writers who deal with the Piedmont South, including Thomas Wolfe, launch attacks upon its impoverished culture much like those made by the middle-western writers who participated in "the Revolt from the Village"—written like E. W. Howe, Joseph Kirkland, Hamlin Garland, and Sinclair Lewis, who was a major influence on Thomas Wolfe's work. Where Ellen Glasgow used the novel of manners and William Faulkner the symbolic romance to give their fictional representations of the South, Thomas Wolfe turned to a kind of fiction which was lyric rather than dramatic, which was characterized by autobiographical plots rather than by tight structures, and which dealt with the problem of the definition of the self in relation first to a middle-class Piedmont South and later to the great world outside the region. The South which Wolfe knew was consciously Roundhead in its political allegiance, strongly egalitarian and individualistic in its view of man, characterized by rough, coarse, crude, and graceless manners and conventions, and grimly Calvinistic in its religious orientation.

In this respect, Thomas Wolfe takes his place very clearly and plainly as a writer about a South that is significantly different from that which occupies the popular, romantic imagination. That Wolfe knew that his world was a different one from that of many other southerners he made very clear. In *The Web and the Rock*, he contrasts two sections of the South in terms of "Old Catawba" and South Carolina. In making this distinction, he echoes that old, old remark that North Carolina is a vale of humility between two mountains of conceit. He says:

> Old Catawba has the slants of evening and the mountain cool. You feel lonely in Old Catawba, but it is not the loneliness of South Carolina. In Old Catawba, the hill boy helps his father building fences and hears a soft Spring howling in the wind, and sees the wind snake through the bending waves of the coarse grasses of the mountain pastures. And far away he hears the whistle's cry wailed back, far-flung and faint along some moun-

tain valley, as a great train rushes towards the cities of the East.
And the heart of the hill boy will know joy because he knows, all
world-remote, lonely as he is, that some day he will meet the
world and know those cities too.

Against that sense of difference and of outward movement, Wolfe poses
a view of South Carolina that is far from complimentary:

These people are really lost. They cannot get away from South
Carolina, and if they get away they are no good. They drawl
beautifully. There is the most wonderful warmth, affection,
heartiness in their approach and greeting, but the people are
afraid. Their eyes are desperately afraid, filled with a kind of
tortured and envenomed terror of the old, stricken, wounded
'Southness' of cruelty and lust. Sometimes their women have the
honey skins, they are like gold and longing. They are filled with
the most luscious and seductive sweetness, tenderness, and gentle
mercy. But the men are stricken. They get fat about the bellies,
or they have a starved, stricken leanness in the loins.

Such a distinction Wolfe pushes beyond the limits of reality. The difference between South Carolina and North Carolina is far less than he
indicates it as being; but he sees all of North Carolina in terms of his own
mountain and Piedmont region and all of South Carolina in terms of the
Low Country society. He declares, "Old Catawba is a place inhabited by
humble people. There is no Charleston in Old Catawba, and not so many
people pretending to be what they are not. . . . Now their pretense is reduced to pretending that they amounted to so much formerly. And they
really amounted to very little." Yet Wolfe knows, too, that "Old Catawba"
is not of a piece. In *The Web and the Rock* he says:

Down in the East, in Old Catawba, they have some smack of
anciently. The East got settled first and there are a few old towns
down there, the remnants of plantations, a few fine old houses,
a lot of niggers, tobacco, turpentine, pine woods, and the mourn-
ful flat-lands of the coastal plain. The people in the East used to
think they were better than the people in the West because they
had been there a little longer. But they were not really better. In
the West, where the mountains sweep around them, the people
have utterly common, familiar, plain, Scotch-Irish faces, and
names like Weaver, Wilson, Gudger, Joyner, Alexander, and
Patton. The West is really better than the East. . . . The West is

really a region of good small people, a Scotch-Irish place, and
that, too, is undefined, save that it doesn't drawl so much, works
harder, doesn't loaf so much, and shoots a little straighter when
it has to. It is really just one of the common places of the earth,
a million or two people with nothing very extraordinary about
them.

Thus Wolfe's attitude toward his immediate region is also ambiguous; for,
while he is highly critical of the crass materialism of the Piedmont, he also
loves it and finds it better than the Tidewater.

Certainly Wolfe does not embrace the concept of the nobility of the Old
South. Even in his early plays, such as *The Mountains* and *Mannerhouse,*
Wolfe dealt in unfriendly and destructive ways with the legend of the aristocratic South. His second long play, *Welcome to Our City,* is an attack on
the social conventions and beliefs of his own region. This quality in Wolfe's
work led his Chapel Hill classmate, Jonathan Daniels, in reviewing *Look
Homeward, Angel* in the Raleigh, North Carolina, *News and Observer,* to
declare that in that book "North Carolina and the South are spat upon."
Such critical attitudes are not surprising about a writer in the tradition
within which Wolfe grew up. Freed from the deep emotional commitment
typical of the Tidewater and the Deep South, Wolfe could look calmly and
critically at his region, deplore its weaknesses, and love its strengths, without indulging in the emotional upheaval over this ambivalent attitude which
Quentin Compson suffers in Faulkner's *Absalom, Absalom!* The tendency
of Faulkner and writers like Ellen Glasgow is, in their different ways, to
have as a subject a social order which serves as a frame within which they
may describe their characters, so that the region and its history, the people
and their customs, ultimately work upon the individual characters in their
books at the same time that they are created by these characters. Thus a
complex and subtle interrelationship between character and region emerges
from their novels. On the other hand, for Wolfe no such firm structure of
society existed; and he turned, as Whitman had earlier turned, and as
Tocqueville had suggested that the American democratic artist must always
turn, from the egalitarian social world to the inner self for the true subject
of his work.

The South which Wolfe lived in as a boy and young man he saw as an
entangling web to be broken through in the effort toward self-realization.
The past makes few compulsive demands upon him, for Thomas Wolfe is
fleeing the hills relatively unencumbered by history, looking back at the past
not in love or pain but in anger, and finally turning, like Eugene Gant at the

end of *Look Homeward, Angel,* "like a man who stands upon a hill above the town he has left, yet does not say, 'The town is near,' but turns his eyes upon the distant soaring ranges." These ranges were not only geographically but spiritually to the north and west. Thus Wolfe becomes relatively free of his past—the first twentieth-century southern American writer of major stature who deserts his region to embrace a national and then an international identity. Though he has a firm sense of the social world he is leaving, the center of his books is not that social world but himself.

Look Homeward, Angel, Wolfe's first book, is the record of the growth of a child from his birth until his college education is completed. It places a very great premium upon the impact on its protagonist, Eugene Gant, of the physical world, the social structure, and the actions of individual friends and acquaintances. Wolfe traces here the experiences of a delicate boy struggling to know himself in "the limitless meadows of sensation." But this boy, by Wolfe's own definition, is unique only in the degree of his sensitivity, not in his basic nature. "Each of us," he declares in the opening of the book, "is all the sums he has not counted." It is in the spirit of this generic man that Wolfe defines the lonely search of his characters, the search for communion, the search for meaning, the search for the deepest nature of the self, the old Wordsworthian search backward into the individual's origins in order to find the nature and meaning of the self.

When Eugene Gant moves from Altamont, he moves outward into the great world; and though he takes with him many of the qualities which he sees as the virtues of the South, he consciously leaves his native region for what he believes to be a better world. In *The Web and the Rock* Wolfe's protagonist remembers "all the times when he had come out of the South and into the North, and always the feeling was the same—an exact, pointed, physical feeling marking the frontiers of his consciousness with a geographic precision. . . . It was a geographic division of the spirit that was sharply, physically exact, as if it had been cleanly severed by a sword. . . . He ducked his head a little as if he were passing through a web. He knew that he was leaving the South." Certainly Wolfe is not right in attributing to all southerners that sense of expansion and release which crossing the Potomac gives him. Indeed, that kind of release is something which neither Ellen Glasgow nor William Faulkner would have wanted or expressed.

Of Time and the River carries his protagonist from Altamont to Harvard, then to New York City, and finally to Europe. Eugene Gant experiences in this steadily outward movement an increasing necessity to describe and to define himself, not as a southerner but as an American, and to begin a roll call of names and places which includes the South as simply a part of the larger world but does not isolate it as a unique subject. Typically in his catalogues—close in content and cadence to those of Walt Whitman—are lists of names such as he gives in one place in *Of Time and the River* where he names "The Wilderness; and the names of Antietam, Chancellorsville, Shiloh, Bull Run, Fredericksburg, Cold Harbor ... Cowpens, Brandywine, and Saratoga; of Death Valley, Chickamauga, and the Cumberland Gap. The names of the Nantahalahs, the Bad Lands, the Painted Desert, the Yosemite, and the Little Big Horn; the names of Yancey and Cabarrus counties; and the terrible name of Hatteras." The significance of such a catalogue is its indiscriminate inclusiveness, just as his "continental thunder of the states" begins with "Montana, Texas, Arizona, Colorado, Michigan, Maryland, Virginia, and the two Dakotas." Such catalogues are recurrent in Wolfe—he lists the names of Indian tribes, of railways, of hoboes, of great rivers, and his listing does not end in America but goes on to the Tiber and the Thames. Wolfe's characters, through their absorption of great ranges of experience and their merging of myriad persons with themselves, become archetypes of the American.

In *The Web and the Rock* Wolfe repeats many of the incidents of the earlier work in recounting the experience of George Webber, whose record begins when he is a child in Libya Hill, another thin disguise for Asheville, and who moves on out into the larger world of the North and of Europe. In *You Can't Go Home Again*, George Webber returns briefly to the South, writes a novel, travels in England and on the continent, and experiences both directly and vicariously the "complex fate" of being an American. At the conclusion of the novel, Webber gives an emphatic expression to a nationally oriented sense of democracy and its promise.

In *You Can't Go Home Again*, Webber sees people and actions more frequently than he participates in events, and the forms in which he sees them are often virtually self-contained units of the length of tales and novellas. Indeed, as it did for Faulkner, experience very often came to Wolfe in actions which were friendly to representation in short stories and short novels. After *Look Homeward, Angel*, which is itself an uneven book, Wolfe did not again produce a work in which the individual episodes are not more impressive than the whole of which they are a part. Both Faulkner and Wolfe attempted to formulate large structures which adequately controlled and shaped the individual dramatic scenes and in which their works appear naturally to fall. Faulkner chose the historical and social history of his region and used it to reflect universal experience. Wolfe, on the other hand, had as his focus the realization of one generic American; thus his form was autobiographical. In his firmly democratic insistence on himself as representative of the equality of man, he, like Walt Whitman, attempted to sing America by celebrating himself and in the process of so doing created a new self who was that of representational America. The central search which Wolfe's characters are embarked upon is a search for what he once called "surety" and that he symbolically represented as "the search for the father"—that is, a search for a home in a homeless land, a search for communion in a lonely world, the endless and always unfruitful quest for the lost leaf, the stone, the unfound door which leads out of the self into the surrounding brotherhood of man.

JOHN HAGAN

Structure, Theme, and Metaphor
in Look Homeward, Angel

The tastemakers have long passed it by, and the fiftieth anniversary of its publication in October 1929 went almost without remark, except in the South. One of the main reasons for this comparative neglect, I believe, is the still prevailing notion that Wolfe's first novel, though undeniably powerful in some respects, is mere "formless autobiography," the product of a *naïf* who had no "ideas" and only a rudimentary technique. To be sure, Wolfe was hardly a flawless writer, and the pattern of his book is not of the tightest; its structure could never be called rigorously Jamesian. But organic unity, formal cohesion, and thematic control of a larger and looser kind— of a sort to be found, for instance, in *Moby-Dick, Bleak House,* and *War and Peace*—are demonstrably present. Accordingly, in this paper I should like to show how the novel's various themes, images, and symbols are integrated in a rich, complex, many-layered whole, and reach their appropriate culmination in the brilliant and extremely moving last chapter.

I

Drawing upon late nineteenth- and early twentieth-century concepts earlier embodied in fiction by writers like Zola, Hardy, and Dreiser, the narrator of *Look Homeward, Angel* boldly sketches in the famous opening three paragraphs an uncompromisingly deterministic picture of the human condition which becomes a leitmotif throughout. Wolfe's protagonist, Eugene Gant himself, shares these ideas. Lacking any firm, traditional religious beliefs, he becomes early in life a "fanatical zealot in the religion of

From *American Literature* 53, no. 2 (May 1981). © 1981 by Duke University Press.

Chance," the secular faith of the philosophical mechanist. Moreover, though there is, after all, good fortune as well as bad, the novel's conception of determinism, like that of the naturalists in general, tends to be bleakly pessimistic. At the time of the death by typhoid fever of his eldest son, Grover, at the St. Louis Fair in 1904, W. O. Gant feels the dreadful power of "the inexorable tides of Necessity." Later, a conspicuous and embarrasing skin irritation which Eugene has inherited from his mother's family convinces the young man that "there was no escape" from his biological heritage; he was "touched with the terrible destiny of his blood, caught in the trap of himself and the Pentlands, with the little flower of sin and darkness on his neck."

Heredity and other deterministic forces—variously called "destiny," "chance," "necessity," and "accident"—thus constitute a "trap" within which Eugene feels himself confined. At the same time, one of the very traits he has inherited from his father makes it impossible for him to resign himself to such a condition. This trait is his enormous, "Rabelaisian" lust for life and boundless exuberance, his surging energy and huge, "Faustian" hunger, under the compulsion of which he is ready to hurl himself against whatever constrains him from devouring experience to the utmost. The whole thrust of his life, therefore, becomes a heroic struggle for freedom, for if heredity and other deterministic forces themselves cannot be overcome, he never loses his faith that there are many other thwarting circumstances, analogous to them, which can be. His very first bid for liberation takes place only a few months after his second birthday when he slips away from his negligent baby-sitter into the driveway of a wealthy neighbor and is almost trampled by a horse drawing a grocery wagon. "It was his first escape," the narrator points out, and he "carried the mark of the centaur [on his forehead] for many years." The image of the centaur as a symbol of liberation also appears in chapter 29 in Eugene's "whinnying squeal—the centaur-cry of man or beast, trying to unburden its overladen heart in one blast of pain and joy and passion," and again in chapter 39 in the description of him as "a centaur, moon-eyed and wild of mane, torn apart with hunger for the golden world." Still other metaphors of his desire for physical and spiritual escape are among the novel's most pervasive tropes—that of trains (on which he and others travel or whose haunting whistles, bells, and rumbling wheels he hears from a distance); that of the "door"; and that of "journeys," "quests," and, above all, "voyages," of which the comic antithesis is the intellectual incompetence of his eccentric schoolteacher, John Dorsey Leonard, who "skirted Virgil because . . . [he] was a bad sailor—he was not at all sure of Virgilian navigation. He hated exploration. He distrusted voyages."

From one point of view, of course, the quest for liberation marks Eugene as a late avatar of the archetypal romantic rebel and outsider, individualist and man of feeling, metaphysical seeker and poet. Indeed, one of the paradoxical features of his consciousness is the way in which early nineteenth-century romanticism and late nineteenth-century pessimistic determinism meet in it and clash. The coexistence in the same character of these different kinds of sensibility—the romantic-poetic and the naturalistic-scientific—is one of the chief sources of the novel's dramatic tension. But it is not only the quest for liberation that links Eugene with the early romantics and their typical heroes and plots. He is a romantic in a more specific way, which we may loosely call "mystical," and which, as many recent critics have pointed out, is associated with the Platonic and Neoplatonic doctrine of "preexistence" as developed by Wordsworth in his great ode, "Intimations of Immortality." On one level at least, the "home" of the title toward which the angel is implored to look is the life before birth, where alone can be found the true home of the spirit. An even more obvious reference to this realm is the fourth paragraph of the famous lyrical prose poem which serves as an epigraph to Part One of the novel and supplies a recurrent refrain: "Remembering speechlessly we seek the great forgotten language, the lost lane-end into heaven, a stone, a leaf, an unfound door." The "door," which Wolfe often uses as a symbol of escape in general, here acquires the additional, fairy-tale-like meaning of an entrance specifically into the paradise of preexistence—an entrance whose location is also marked by the "stone" and the "leaf." Finally, Eugene's recollections of this paradise—of which there are several scattered throughout the book—are defined by two other important images, those of sound (voices, bells, or music) and water: "somewhere within or without his consciousness he heard a great bell ringing faintly, as if it sounded undersea, and as he listened, the ghost of memory walked through his mind, and for a moment he felt that he had almost recovered what he had lost."

Now, the point to be made about these mystical experiences is that, far from being merely "poetic" embellishments or merely exotic indicators of Eugene's "sensitivity," they provide every phase of the central story of his quest for liberation with a crucial frame of reference. In opposition to the bleak, deterministic prison-house of "destiny," "chance," "necessity," and "accident" in general and various other constricting circumstances in particular, they feed Eugene's passionate and, at bottom, religious yearning for transcendence, for escape into beauty and order, permanence and perfection—his desire, in a word, for an Earthly Paradise. For although *Look Homeward, Angel* is in many ways a naturalistic novel, its protagonist is an imaginative young man of torrential vitality and idealism for whom a naturalistic view of life can never be enough. His gargantuan hunger for this-worldly experience in all its manifestations coexists with a profound need to believe that such experience can be fabulous and enchanted, and provide a genuine "home" for his heart's desire. The other-worldly realm of preexistence and the ecstasy which recollection of it arouses become for him not only an image of paradise lost, but a model, an archetype, of the paradise which can be regained in the here and now. For no matter how often he is made aware of "the nightmare cruelty of life," Eugene remains to the end a "Mythmaker," a visionary, a romancer, an American Adam, who is always seeking to return to the paradise from which he feels he has been expelled.

Specifically, his efforts to preserve this poetic conception of experience in the face of circumstances that are always threatening to destroy it consist of various struggles—carried on more or less simultaneously in complex counterpoint—to achieve some measure of ideal existence by escaping from five major constraining conditions: loneliness, family, hometown, native region, and (taken together) time and death. The first four of these quests terminate in his decision at the end of the novel to go to Harvard, and the last in his discovery at the same point of his vocation as an artist, a discovery which resolves at the deepest level the other quests as well.

II

Eugene's sense of the lost paradise of preexistence is one of the main sources of the intense feelings of loneliness which he begins to have even as an infant. But his loneliness is also due to more ordinary causes, typical of many other bildungsromans. For both his temperament and his values effectively isolate him from everyone in his family (except his older brother, Ben) and from most of his fellows in school and college too. During his freshman year at the state university, in particular, he is so "desperately lonely" that "he saw himself in his clown's trappings and thought of his former vision of success and honor with a lacerating self-contempt." The clown image, in fact, is one of the novel's chief symbols of his loneliness in general, just as that of the centaur is of his quest for liberation. Terrified by the seemingly huge size of the family members bending over his crib, "he saw himself an inarticulate stranger, an amusing little clown, to be dandled and nursed by these enormous and remote figures." And many years later, when participating in a ludicrous Shakespeare tercentenary pageant, he is dressed by the Leonards in "a full baggy clown's suit, of green linen" that prostrates the spectators in "wild, earthshaking, thunder-cuffing" laughter.

His quests to escape from this loneliness take three main directions: for the knowledge and stimulus to his imagination which can be gained from books; for "life" itself, which is to be found only outside of books; and for self-acceptance and independence. In each of these kinds of experience he seeks a "door" that will admit him to that fabulous and ideal "home"—that paradise of preexistence regained on earth—for which he so painfully yearns, and in the possibility of which he never loses his faith.

One of his earliest desires is for the knowledge which can be acquired from speech and reading, for while he is still in his crib he realizes precociously that "his first escape must come through language." Books, he soon learns, can liberate him from his loneliness because they introduce his vivid imagination to a "vast, enchanting, but unperplexing world" outside the confines of his narrow, immediate surroundings. Great teachers partake of the same glow for him. His years at the Leonards' private school "bloomed like golden apples," because "the school had become the centre of his heart and life—Margaret Leonard his spiritual mother." To her "he turned his face up . . . as a prisoner who recovers light," convinced that "the way through the passage to India, that he had never been able to find, would now be charted for him."

Ever since childhood, Eugene's voracious reading in cheap fiction has also been providing him with another mode of escape from loneliness in self-flattering daydreams. Several of these fantasies are of high adventure or of grandiose achievements which win him acclaim or power. He rivals his mother's epic acquisitiveness in visions of princely wealth, and compensates for his clumsiness on the playing field by imagining himself performing "heroic game-saving" feats of athletic prowess. Especially comic are his fantasies of glory at the time of America's entrance into the First World War, in which he is debarred from participating because of his youth: "he longed for that subtle distinction, that air of having lived and suffered that could only be attained by a wooden leg, a rebuilt nose, or the seared scar of a bullet across his temple." Even after the war is over, delusions of grandeur of still other kinds afford him an escape from his loneliness—now become almost paranoid—when he revels in thoughts of himself as "Senator Gant, Governor Gant, President Gant . . . Jesus-of-Nazareth Gant," and the like.

Eugene's daydreams are also often highly erotic. For sex too can be an escape from loneliness into a kind of glory, provided, of course, that it is sanctified by "love" and the woman, however passionate, is "pure." Although Eugene's lust is strong, his romantic, idealistic temperament makes it impossible for him to be satisfied with "pagan love" alone. Building elaborate structures of wishful thinking on the basis of popular society novels and the silent movies, he imagines preposterously elegant men and women making love "in kid gloves, to the accompaniment of subtle repartee . . . beyond all the laws of nature . . . exquisitely and incorruptibly," and himself as "Bruce-Eugene" or "The Dixie-Ghost," the noble, unblemished hero who never fails to enjoy the delights of passion with the most beautiful and ardent yet virtuous women.

More importantly, his quest for liberation from loneliness eventually takes him from books into "life" itself, when he comes to believe that the marvelous can be found in "real" (as distinct from merely imaginary) experience too—that the Ideal and the Actual, Romance and Reality, are one. "Facts" which fail to conform to this belief simply cease to be "facts" at all for him. Even when he learns certain unpleasant truths about Mrs. Leonard and her relatives, for example, he flatly refuses to believe them: "all the facts that leveled Margaret down to life . . . were as unreal and horrible as a nightmare. . . . Eugene believed in the glory and the gold." In the same way, after he has lost faith in the bookish teachings of Vergil Weldon, his professor of philosophy at Pulpit Hill, he is sustained by his conviction that "the world was full of pleasant places, enchanted places, if he could only go and find them. . . . He always felt sure things would be better elsewhere." Thus, "he was devoured by a vast strange hunger for life"; "the world lay before him for his picking"—not, as for Adam and Eve, a world radically different from Eden, but an Eden itself, "full of opulent cities, golden vintages, glorious triumphs, lovely women, full of a thousand unmet and magnificent possibilities. Nothing was dull or tarnished. The strange enchanted coasts were unvisited. He was young and he could never die." By the end of the novel, to be sure, he has not given up his quest for formal learning, for he is about to leave for graduate study at Harvard. But Harvard has come to mean much more to him than books; it too is a part of fabulous, liberating "life": "it was not the name of a university—it was rich magic, wealth, elegance, joy. . . . And he felt somehow that it gave a reason, a goal of profit, to his wild ecstasy."

Meanwhile, during the summer following his first year at Pulpit Hill, his quest for a paradise in "real life" has also resulted in a romance with one of his mother's boarders, named Laura James. No less than his earlier erotic fantasies that were fed by books, the two main parts into which chapter 30, which records their brief love affair, is divided are dominated by imagery of enchantment. In the first, he and Laura declare their love for one another in what might be the preternatural, mythical realm of one of his favorite poets—that "chief prince of the moon and magic"—Coleridge. "The moonlight fell upon the earth like a magic unearthly dawn. It wiped away all rawness, it hid all sores. It gave all common and familiar things . . . a uniform bloom of wonder." As the pair embrace, Eugene's "limbs" are "numbed" by a "passion . . . governed by a religious ecstasy"; and, after they have parted for the night, he falls asleep to the sound of a cock's "distant elfin minstrelsy." Equally idyllic, though taking place in daylight, is the scene in the second part of the chapter, in which Eugene and Laura picnic on the following afternoon in a cove in the hills. The comparison of her body to a "Maenad's" which might "grow into the tree again" unmistakably links her to "the flitting wood-girls growing into bark" who have appeared earlier in one of Eugene's recollections of preexistence. The setting too is a counterpart of the prenatal realm—a landscape which combines features of pagan pastoral, the Biblical Paradise, and fairy tale. Here, forgetting the passage of time and the "pain and conflict" of the town, which "lay in another unthinkable world," the lovers "clung together in that bright moment of wonder . . . believing all they said."

Laura, of course, ultimately puts Eugene's trust to a severe test: in their Eden there is a "snake," both literal and figurative. The young girl betrays "the apple tree, the singing, and the gold," because she has been secretly engaged to someone else, and only a few days after leaving Altamont marries him. Eugene is crushed; having sought escape from loneliness in a "real life" paradise of love, he appears to have been left more lonely than before. Nevertheless, he soon recovers: his very loss of Laura, together with other experiences, teaches him that there is yet another way in which loneliness can be escaped—a way already suggested by his juvenile fantasies of demonic "isolation and dominance over sea and land . . . victorious dark all-seeing isolation" and of "opulent solitude" (reminiscent again of preexistence) in "kingdoms under the sea, on windy crags, and . . . [in] the deep elf kingdoms of the earth's core." For if there are many times when he finds his loneliness and the self-contempt it can breed an intolerable bondage, there are others when he eagerly embraces the proud self-acceptance which can be fostered by loneliness itself, and rejoices in his solitary state as a field for the development and display of heroic independence.

During his last year at the state university his hope of finding a "vast Utopia of . . . loneliness" reaches its climax. Although he is troubled at first by a repetition of the students' mockery, and driven almost mad with shame by the Pentland rash, which has appeared on his neck and made him absurdly conscious of all his other physical blemishes, he eventually begins "to take a terrible joy in his taint," because he has come to believe that the truly

great men of the world have also been "tainted"—"wasted and devoured by
the beautiful disease of thought and passion." By thus persuading himself of
his kinship with such "lords of the earth," "Eugene escaped forever from
the good and the pretty, into a dark land that is forbidden to the sterilized,"
wherein "he felt that . . .there was in him a health that was greater than they
could ever know." In more appealingly modest and comically self-ironic
moods, he even achieves enough objectivity to live comfortably with the
heretofore intolerable idea that he may not be the genius he has always liked
to think himself after all: "over that final hedge [of self-knowledge], he
thought, not death, as I once believed—but new life—and new lands." The
magic of one such "new land," Harvard, consists precisely in his faith that
there he will be able to cultivate his "proud loneliness" to the fullest.

III

In various ways, then, Eugene seeks to escape into some kind of Earthly
Paradise from the prisons of loneliness constituted by his exile from the
realm of preexistence, by his family, by school and college, and by Laura's
rejection. At the same time, his family, hometown, and native region spur
his quest for liberation because they are the sources of additional discon-
tents.

Eugene's attitude toward his family is by no means always simple. The
words that the narrator uses to describe the boy's feelings at the time of
Ben's death suggest his ambivalent reactions to them generally: "there was
no moment of hate that was not touched by a dozen shafts of pity: impo-
tently, he wanted to seize them, cuff them, shake them, as one might a trying
brat, and at the same time to caress them, love them, comfort them." For
this very reason, his relations with them are more painful than they would
have been otherwise, and his frustrations all the greater. The characteristic
image of home for him becomes that of entrapment. Prominent also is water
imagery, which, as I have remarked, can symbolize the very different "home"
of preexistence: the boardinghouse is "a smothering Sargasso," in which his
mother, Eliza, is " 'going to strangle and drown us all'," and a "deep pit"
of "death and darkness" in which Eugene's "soul plunged downward,
drowning . . . : he felt that he could never again escape from this smothering
flood of pain and ugliness." The sense of liberation he feels after delivering
his newspapers—a job which his parents have forced upon him—is like that
felt by "a sailor drowned within the hold, who gropes to life and morning
through a hatch" and by "a diver twined desperately in octopal feelers, who
cuts himself from death and mounts slowly from the sea-floor into light."

The phrase, "octopal feelers," in turn echoes an earlier reference to Eliza's extraordinary memory as "a great octopus." Moreover, Ben's "messy" death reminds Eugene of his childhood "hatred of the semi-private bathroom, his messy discomfort while he sat at stool and stared at the tub filled with dirty wash, sloppily puffed and ballooned by cold gray soapy water"; and Ben himself, succumbing to pneumonia, is, in the words of the doctor, " 'Drowning! Drowning!' "

But if there is no hope for Ben, Eugene refuses to give up hope for himself. Even as Ben lies dying, the key symbol of the door reappears when Eugene "paced restlessly up and down the hall or prowled through the house a-search for some entrance he had never found." Although his sister Helen's erratic oscillation between love and hatred in her treatment of him has always been extremely painful because it has plunged him "unexpectedly from Elfland into Hell," he never loses his faith that "each time . . . you die, you will be born again." And if Helen is transformed on such occasions from a "bountiful angel" into "a snake-haired fury," he can always turn to another angel: "Come lower, angel," he implores; "whisper in our ears. We are passing away in smoke and there is nothing today but weariness to pay us for yesterday's toil. How may we save ourselves?" This angel who can point the way to liberation is, on one level at least, the angel of the novel's title too, and the "home" in the direction of which it is exhorted to look is not only the other-worldly realm of preexistence, but the literal home of Eugene and his family.

Nor is it indifferent to his prayers: the way to his fullest escape from the family is opened at last with Ben's death and Eliza's sale of the original house on Woodson Street, for with these two events "the great wild pattern of the family had been broken forever" and its "final disintegration" assured. When the family berated Eugene earlier for getting drunk for the first time, he bitterly declared his seventeen-year " 'apprenticeship' " with them over; at the end of the novel he translates this into his adamant demand to be allowed to go to Harvard. Just as the glamorous university has symbolized for him liberation into knowledge, "life," and proud independence, it now symbolizes liberation from his crumbling family into " 'beauty' " and " 'order'," and "he waited for departure as a prisoner for release."

Of course, the university can arouse this euphoria in Eugene not only because it will free him from loneliness and his family. It is important because it is one of several experiences which also release him from the prison of Altamont. At the beginning of the novel, he is quite satisfied with the community; as he matures, however, he comes increasingly to see the mountains as an entrapment, the town itself as small, cramped, and ugly,

and himself as a Gulliver among the Lilliputians. Nor is it only the physical
ugliness of Altamont that offends and oppresses him. There is an intellectual
and moral ugliness in the place too, which is epitomized by the small-town
mentality of his slow-witted, insensitive teacher, John Dorsey Leonard. Although cowardice induces Eugene to participate in the "ugly and revolting"
persecution which Leonard conducts against a harmless, effeminate young
Jew, he does so not without a "piercing shame" that grows even more acute
with the passing years.

The process which eventually leads to his final rupture with Altamont
and its values consists of a series of journeys into various parts of the South,
each of which, in one degree or another, convinces him that the "land of
timeless and never-ending faery" lies only just beyond his native hills. These
journeys fall into two phases, the first consisting of those which he makes
between the ages of four and twelve with one or another of his parents, and
the second, and more decisive, those which he makes at the age of fifteen
and afterwards by himself. The climax of the latter journeys is his trip to
Virginia during the last summer of the First World War—a trip which not
only helps him develop his independence, but becomes an "initiation to the
voyage" of the rest of his life and "a prelude to exile." In fact, it is on this
occasion, for the first time since his love affair with Laura, that that ideality
of the actual, that romantic quality of "real life," in which Eugene so
passionately believes, fully manifests itself again. Travelling by train across
a landscape symbolically bathed in the same Coleridgean enchantment as
the lovers' nocturnal meeting, he stares "bewitched upon the great romantic
country clumped with dreaming woodlands and white as a weird dawn
beneath the blazing moonlight." Richmond, too, after this "lonely and
magnificent approach through the night," thrills him "by its very casual-
ness. All the little ticking sounds of a city beginning its day, the strange
familiarity of voices in an alien place, heard curiously after the thunder of
the wheels, seemed magical and unreal."

Eugene's adventures in Virginia, furthermore, are related to the important pattern of water symbolism which, as I have already noted, is frequently associated by Wolfe with both the other-worldly paradise of
preexistence and entrapment by the family. Beginning with his earliest travels with his mother, the image is also used to symbolize escape from
Altamont, for certain of the faraway places in the South which Eugene visits
are intimately connected with water and thus stimulate his hunger for "great
ships and cities" alike. The sound of the sea at Charleston, South Carolina,
for example, fills his mind with exotic images of "strange dusky faces, palm
frondage, and . . . the little tinkling sounds of Asia." While cruising out into

the Roads at Newport News, in particular, he experiences for the first time "a music and a glory in his heart" that he feels he will be able to sustain forever. And soon after, in a great romantic cry, he both identifies with the sea, and appeals to it as the Eternal Mother who "will bring me to the happy land . . . wash me to glory in bright ships."

As a result, then, of all these journeys to Virginia and elsewhere, Eugene is ready at the end of the novel to leave Altamont permanently. But in doing so, as the sea imagery implies, he will also be going away for the first time from the South as a whole. Indeed, he has come to believe more and more that, like his father, who is an "exiled" northerner, he is " 'a stranger in a strange land.' " Building on this feeling, Margaret Leonard evokes in him a fantasy of "faery London," and arouses his desire for the "Paradise" of Oxford. By the end of the book, though he has set very definite sights on a very definite place (Harvard), the rest of the world he hungers to explore has dissolved into a vast, romantic blur. As we have seen in discussing his quest for "life" as an escape from loneliness, myth and the reality of the lands beyond the South become indistinguishable, fusing into a seamless whole; reality, it seems to him, *is* mythic.

Physical liberation from the South thus becomes one of the main objects of Eugene's quests. At the same time—and as in the case of Altamont—the South threatens him with intellectual and moral imprisonment too. If he is fully to escape his region, the myth which he constructs of the world beyond the South must eventually replace another, more insidious kind of myth—the sentimental one of antebellum southern glory—constructed by the slave-owning aristocracy. During the time covered by the action of the novel, indeed, the latter myth, with its picture of "the romantic life of plantation and cornfields . . . moonlight . . . dancing darkies on the levee," and so forth, makes Eugene very much its prisoner. Unlike the other trammels in the novel, it is one from which he neither escapes nor from which he sees any need to escape until "years later." Yet that he does finally emancipate himself from it the narrator makes emphatic, the process (like that of the journeys from Altamont) occurring in two phases. First, after having lived for awhile in the North, Eugene reaches a time "when he could no longer think of the barren spiritual wilderness, the hostile and murderous intrenchment against all new life—when their [the Southerners'] cheap mythology, their legend of the charm of their manner, the aristocratic culture of their lives, the quaint sweetness of their drawl, made him writhe—when he could think of no return to their life and its swarming superstition without weariness and horror." At this stage, nevertheless, "so great was his fear of the legend, his fear of their antagonism, that he still pretended the most fanatic devotion to them, excusing his Northern residence on grounds of necessity rather than desire." The second phase is reached when he finally realizes that "these people had given him nothing, that neither their love nor their hatred could injure him, that he owed them nothing, and he determined that he would say so, and repay their insolence with a curse. And he did."

IV

The most inclusive trap from which Eugene's quest for an Earthly Paradise compels him to seek escape, of course, is that of time and death, the ultimate expression of those blind, remorseless laws of "destiny," "change," "accident," and "necessity" that govern the godless, naturalistic universe as a whole. Personal encounters with the agonizingly protracted dying of his father and the deaths of his brother Grover, his college roommate (Bob Sterling), Laura James, and especially his beloved Ben assure that a dread of mutability and mortality is never far from his mind. Indeed, his sensitivity to the brevity of human life, to the "lostness" and dreamlike strangeness of the past, and to the dizzying rush of himself and the world he has known to extinction and oblivion is shown in many ways throughout the novel to be extremely acute. It is a vital element in his insatiable energy and partakes of the same intensity, for life and joy are precious to him, as they were for Keats, precisely because he knows they are so fleeting. His loneliness, insofar as it springs from a sense of expulsion from the timeless paradise of preexistence into the temporal world, is directly related to the same awareness, and the latter encompasses and exacerbates his sense of entrapment by family, hometown, and native region as well. Furthermore, as I shall show, a complete resolution of his quests to escape from these other traps can come only when he is able to meet the supreme test of conquering time and death themselves.

This conquest is achieved when he discovers his vocation as an artist in the novel's last chapter—a discovery toward wich numerous signs (e.g., his precocious interest in language, his ravenous love of reading, his maturing critical powers and taste, his rich fantasy life, and his actual writings) have been steadily pointing the way. Before looking at the chapter in detail, however, we must consider for a moment how an earlier one prepares for it. This is the famous chapter 36 which describes Eugene and his brother Luke's visit to Horse Hines's mortuary, where they view Ben's corpse and make arrangements for his funeral, and which reaches its grotesque climax when the undertaker, regarding with great complacency the job of embalming he has done, decides that he needs to apply only one last touch to make his work of "art" perfect:

> "Just a moment!" said Horse Hines quickly, lifting a finger. Briskly he took a stick of rouge from his pocket, stepped forward, and deftly, swiftly, sketched upon the dead gray cheeks a ghastly rose-hued mockery of life and health.
>
> "There!" he said, with deep satisfaction; and, rough-stick in hand, head critically cocked, like a painter before his canvas, he stepped back into the terrible staring prison of their horror.
>
> "There are artists, boys, in every profession. . . . Did you ever see anything more natural in your life? . . . That's art, boys!"

At this point Eugene, unable to contain himself any longer, falls to the floor, almost strangling with laughter, and screams, " 'A-r-t! Yes! Yes! That's it!' " Needless to say, the episode is a masterpiece of macabre comedy—and an especially bold one at that, since it follows almost immediately the magnificent, extremely moving account of Ben's death. But it also makes a serious point, which can easily be missed, in relation to Eugene's discovery of his vocation. For when Hines attempts to give the appearance of "life and health" to Ben's corpse, he is only trying to perform, in however bizarre and parodic a way, that very function of triumphing over time and death which belongs to genuine art itself, and Eugene, in crying out hysterically as he does, seems to recognize this fact. The moment thus becomes for the young man an epiphany, completing his earlier recognitions of the power of Gant's stonecutting and of Homer's poetry to transcend flux, and leading directly to the resolution of his own quest for transcendence in chapter 40.

The action of this last chapter falls into four main parts, the first three recapitulating matters which the novel has considered earlier. Thus, the opening passage reminds us of Eugene's unusually powerful imagination by showing how, after arriving at his father's shop on the eve of his departure for Harvard, he conjures up Ben's "ghost" and imparts life and animation to Gant's stone angels. The second part of the chapter then dramatizes once more the power of Eugene's phenomenal memory, which calls forth into the Square "the thousand forms of himself and Ben" as they were in childhood, and for an instant holds in radiant stasis "all the minutes of lost time." Eugene also hints to the "ghost" of Ben how he has experienced faint memories of the even farther past of preexistence, and recalls having had such recollections as a child. In turn, this awareness of time, loss, and death leads immediately into the third part of the chapter where, in a "vision" of history which echoes Shelley's "Ozymandias," Eugene perceives again the

tragic ephemerality of mankind in general in contrast to the permanence of
the earth itself.

Finally, the fourth—and most difficult—part of the last chapter consists
almost entirely of a still more "terrible vision" of Eugene's own personal
future—a vision in which he sees that all of his quests for the Earthly
Paradise have ended only in frustration and defeat. He also sees himself as
turning at this same time to Ben for an answer: where are " 'an end to
hunger, and the happy land?' " " 'Where is the world' " he is seeking? Ben's
elliptical reply is that " 'There is no happy land. There is no end to hunger. . . . *You* are your world.' " That is, to find what he is searching for his
brother must explore himself, for this is the only reality which is accessible
and knowable to him. Apparently misunderstanding this advice, Eugene
resolves in despair to give up his quest entirely and simply wait for the final,
inevitable voyage into the " 'one land unvisited,' " death itself. But now Ben
reiterates what he has just said, and Eugene, at last grasping the point, is
marvelously revived. " 'Fool,' said Ben, *'this* is life. You have been nowhere!' " Besides death, " 'there is one voyage, the first, the last, the only
one' " still left—the voyage into himself—and Eugene immediately and ex-
ultantly vows to embark on it. How this journey will end he doesn't know,
for when he asks Ben the vision suddenly fades away. But no matter; Eugene
has been strengthened by his brother's counsel, and, as dawn comes and the
ghost of Ben disappears and the angels are once more frozen in their places,
he turns with bold, new confidence to his departure for Harvard and the
beginning of his great voyage of self-discovery.

The question to be asked, of course, is what this whole episode means
in relation to the quest pattern of the novel in general and the quest for
transcendence of time and death in particular. Most obviously, the chapter
is an allegory of education and hence a microcosm of the bildungsroman
pattern which governs the book as a whole: Eugene is the pupil and the
"ghost" of Ben is the teacher; whereas previously the former has learned
from experience, here he learns from his brother. But what he learns now is
that he must give his quests a vital new direction. Heretofore, looking
"homeward" has meant seeking for the Earthly Paradise in the world outside himself: as an escape from loneliness he has sought it in books, "life,"
and physical isolation; as an escape from his family, Altamont, and the
South, he has sought it in far and exotic places; and as an escape from time
and death he has sought it in consoling thoughts of Ben's liberation from
suffering, of his resurrection in the form of the flowers which grow above
his grave, and in scenes, like those glimpsed from the windows of speeding
trains, which create an illusion of timelessness. Now, however, under Ben's

tutelage, he understands that he must seek the Earthly Paradise—look for his spiritual "home"—somewhere else as well. For if death is in Arcadia (the traditional meaning of the Latin motto, *"Et ego in Arcadia,"* which crosses his mind at one point in his conversation with Ben's "ghost," in another sense Arcadia is a deathless place within himself, and there he must go to find it.

But what exactly does discovering himself mean? What is the nature of the self which we may presume Eugene will eventually find? The language which both he and the narrator use to describe "the lost land of himself" is practically identical with that which is used elsewhere in the novel to describe the paradisiacal realm of preexistence. Any full recovery of prenatal memories, however—not to mention a return to the prenatal life itself—is of course impossible, for these memories are, by their very nature, fleeting and elusive, and, according to Wordsworth, become progressively more so as the child grows into youth and adulthood. Like all his other quests, therefore, Eugene's quest for his hidden self can only be for some metaphorical equivalent of the prenatal paradise. What, then, is this something?

Although Wolfe does not explicitly tell us, the answer is clearly implied by the last chapter in its first three sections, which show how Eugene, who is painfully aware of the tragic ephemerality of man and his works, and longs to achieve the permanence, immutability, and timelessness symbolized by the enduring earth and the realm of preexistence, does actually triumph over time and death for a moment by the power of his imagination and memory, working together, to call back the past, raise the dead (Ben), and animate the lifeless angels. And what are imagination and memory for Wolfe if not the essential components of art itself, without which, indeed, the achievements of imagination and memory can only be fleeting? As memory immortalizes the past, so art must immortalize memory. Art, in fact, is doubly symbolized in the last chapter: first (and as elsewhere), by the angels themselves—those replicas of the angel which W. O. Gant, the artist *maniqué*, saw as a boy in Baltimore and has futilely longed all his life to carve—and then by the fact that Eugene's imagination brings those angels to life, making them *his* creations, *his* works of art, just as, in bringing to life on the same occasion his earlier self through memory, he has created "his son, his boy." By this symbolically dramatizing the power of art to triumph over the flux of life and render it timeless and beautiful, the first three sections of chapter 40 implicitly provide the reader with the answer to the question which, in the last section, Eugene fails to get from Ben: what he will ultimately discover as he pursues his "ghost along the labyrinthine ways" will be the enormous creative resources of his imagination and memory—in short, nothing less than his vocation as an artist. It is in the direction of this discovery that he has been moving throughout his story.

With the forthcoming discovery of his artistic vocation, then, Eugene will have achieved, in the only way possible for him, his quest for liberation from time and death. But, by the same token, this discovery will permit a resolution of all his other quests too, and is thus ultimately the controlling theme of the entire novel. For Eugene will be able to escape from the traps of loneliness, family, town, and region, and pursue his quest for the Earthly Paradise, not only in the ways we have already seen, but by making them the very subject of his art—by transcending them through a supreme act of re-creation. Heretofore, he has failed to understand this. Early in the novel, for example, when he tried to avoid facing the unpleasant truths which he had come to learn about Margaret Leonard and her relatives, and which he feared might plunge her "in the defiling stream of life," he believed mistakenly that "it was not truth that men life for—the creative men—but for falsehood," and at the time of Ben's death he regretted that he and his brother had spent their lives in the "mean cramped huddle of brick and stone" that is Altamont, instead of in more glamorous and exotic places like "Gath or Ispahan . . . Corinth or Byzantium." During his conversation with Ben's "ghost" in chapter 40 he makes this last point again, when he insists that stone angels should not walk in such an unremarkable place as Altamont's Square, but only " 'in Babylon! In Thebes! In all the other places.' " Beauty may be truth, and truth beauty, he is saying, but not here! Similarly, the name of Harvard appeals to him not only because the university it designates is far away, but because it is "enchanted" and sounds to him "like Cairo and Damascus." He has yet to learn what the narrator, paraphrasing romantics like Wordsworth, Coleridge, and Carlyle, has known from the beginning—that "it is the union of the ordinary and the miraculous that makes wonder." When he does discover that it is art which can effect this union, he will have come to know at the same time that the "door" to the Earthly Paradise can be found anywhere—even in ugly, humdrum Altamont—through the exercise of his creative power itself. Whereas Ben, who is "lost" and can find no "door" because he has felt neglected by his family, acquired no satisfying vocation, and failed to discover any meaning in life as a whole, willingly embraces death as an escape from his frustrations and torments, Eugene will both find himself and affirm life by recapturing the past—including Ben himself—in timeless artistic form. As he once suspected on his trip to Charleston, Eugene now knows that "his gateway to the lost world" really lies behind him in the experiences he has already had and those waiting to be shaped by his hand. Thus, although in the last paragraph of the novel, the town Square already seems "far and lost" to him, and he has become "like a man who . . . turns his eyes upon the distant soaring ranges," he and the angel of the title—which has now become his muse—will ultimately "look homeward" in the broadest sense of all, by immortalizing the family, the town, the region, and his own life there in art.

JOHN HAGAN

Of Time and the River:
The Quest for Transcendence

*In a system where things forever pass and decay, what is there fixed,
real, eternal? I search for an answer.*
— LETTER TO HORACE WILLIAMS, SEPTEMBER 9, 1921

Criticism today has left *Of Time and the River* largely ignored, Thomas
Wolfe's reputation—such as it is—resting almost exclusively on *Look
Homeward, Angel.* There are several reasons for this unfortunate situation.
In part, of course, it is simply the result of current taste and academic
fashion. But paramount among its deeper causes is the fact that ever since
its publication in 1935 Wolfe's second novel has been almost unanimously
assailed for its "formlessness." Some critics have even gone so far as to deny
that it is a novel at all. The latter view is obviously arbitrary and extreme,
but the first is so plausible that any attempt to question it might seem to be
perverse revisionism. Nevertheless, it may be that our detailed knowledge of
the extremely disorderly way in which the book was written and of the facts
of Wolfe's life on which it is heavily based has predisposed us to read *Of
Time and the River* in an inadequate way—to see it too much as raw,
undisciplined autobiography rather than as self-contained fiction. Because it
is a mixture of radically different rhetorical modes, we must be careful not
to assume that it lacks unity of theme or action. Above all, because it is not
a tightly constructed Flaubertian or Jamesian novel, we must not jump to

From *Thomas Wolfe: A Harvard Perspective,* edited by Richard S. Kennedy. © 1983
by Croissant and Company.

the conclusion that it is therefore chaotic. Between chaos and strict order there is a very broad spectrum of possibilities, ranging from those "loose, baggy monsters" like Thackeray's *The Newcomes* and Tolstoy's *War and Peace* that James stigmatized but that have turned out on subsequent analysis to be more satisfactorily structured than he realized, to novels like some by Scott and Cooper in which the coherent design is less pefectly achieved, but is nonetheless discernible and significant. It is in the latter category, I believe, that *Of Time and the River* belongs, and it is an outline of that kind of design that I should like to sketch in the present paper. Flawed Wolfe's book certainly is, but it can still offer the sympathetic reader a uniquely compelling, deeply moving experience. Essential to its appreciation, as I hope my discussion will suggest, is a recognition that although it is undeniably "realistic" in its overall method, there runs very deep in it a strain of the mythical, the parabolic, and the visionary.

I

As many commentators have noted, a basic constituent of *Of Time and the River* (as of all Wolfe's novels, for that matter) is the Quest. On whatever level we examine the work—its language, its action, its authorial commentary, or the psychology of its protagonist, Eugene Gant—the motif of questing is everywhere. But what are the objects of Eugene's quests? What is he looking for? The answer to this question lies in his obsession with time. In few major American novels of this century is time a more pervasive presence than in *Of Time and the River;* dramatic evocations of it appear on almost every page. Eugene's preoccupation with time, however, has little in common with the technical, abstract, and specialized interest of the professional metaphysicians. His concern is emotional rather than intellectual, and pertains to those familiar aspects of time that each of us immediately experiences in his ordinary, everyday life—in particular, loss of various kinds and especially the dreadful reality of death. Time is a source of some of Eugene's deepest anguish, because, having been profoundly affected by the unforgettably poignant deaths of his brother Ben and his father, he habitually regards it as a threat, an enemy, which destroys not only everything we value, but ultimately our very existence itself. Innumerable passages record his horror or extinction, his vision of "the bitter briefness of our days," of all things being swept up by time into the huge graveyard of the past. The theme of transiency is also richly developed by several recurring metaphors and symbols, such as smoke, dreams, the river, the sea, trains, a face glimpsed for a moment in passing and never seen again, and various places, especially Dixieland, Mrs. Gant's old boardinghouse, which for Eugene is almost literally haunted by the ghosts of all "the lost, the vanished people," including himself as a child, who have ever lived there. In fact, it is just at Eugene's age, Wolfe asserts, that "the knowledge of man's brevity first comes to us" and that "we first understand . . . that the moment of beauty carries in it the seeds of its own instant death, that love is gone almost before we have it, that youth is gone before we know it, and that, like every other man, we must grow old and die."

In the light of this theme, the incentives and objects of Eugene's quests become clear. For time, Eugene's preoccupation with it, and the profound anxiety it instills in him are not merely incidental features of the main action of the novel; they are its essential impetus. Between Eugene's sense of time and his quests there is a vital causal connection, in that the core of all his longing is his desire to transcend the limits of morality, his tireless will to believe that "he could never die," after all, or, as Wolfe succinctly put it in one of his notebooks, his yearning to "escape into life . . . that has no death in it." The epigraph of the novel (from Eccles. 3:21) points both to "the spirit of the beast that goeth downward to the earth," which in this context is a metaphor of various kinds of death, and to "the spirit of man that goeth upward," which serves as a metaphor of resurrection. Death and resurrection are also juxtaposed in the prose poem that precedes chapter 1: after "wandering forever," there comes "the earth again"—that is, the grave; but from the grave emerge "the big flowers, the rich flowers, the strange unknown flowers" of "immortal love," to which "we cried" and which will rescue us "from our loneliness." Moreover, the river and the sea, which, as I have just remarked, symbolize on one level the ephemerality of all things, can inspire the traveler with hope too, as in the magnificent passage at the end of the novel where the ship that Eugene boards both connotes man's tragic journey toward death, and is "alive with the supreme ecstasy of the modern world, which is the voyage to America." Another, more traditional way in which Wolfe depicts death and resurrection is by the cycle of the seasons. The month of October, in particular, is a microcosm of this cycle, because it is the season of both endings and beginnings, departures and returns, "sorrow and delight," "huge prophecies of death and life," the "sense of something lost and vanished, gone forever," and the "still impending prescience of something grand and wild to come." If his trip in October 1920 takes Eugene to the dying Gant in Baltimore, it also takes him to what he believes will be a thrilling new life in the North; and if, after his return to Altamont in October 1923, he laments the death of his father and the rejection of his play by a Broadway producer, he also hears the voice of a spirit that is both "a demon and a friend" assuring him that Ben and all the other dead young men will "walk and move again tonight . . . speaking to you their messages of flight, of triumph, and the all-exultant darkness, telling you that all will be again as it was once."

Such thematic patterns indicate that, although Eugene has no formal religion or even any discernible belief in God, his quests for some kind of deliverance from death spring essentially—albeit unconsciously and in a broad, elementary sense—from a powerful religious instinct, a desperate craving for a secular equivalent of transcendent religious faith. What Wolfe said in a letter about one of these quests definitively illuminates them all: "it comes, I think, from the deepest need in life, and all religiousness is in it." Eugene is an image of "modern man caught in the Faustian serpent-toils of modern life," who is always searching for a way back to Eden, a return to the lost Earthly Paradise, a "door" (one of the novel's key terms) through which he can pass from the harsh reality of pain and death into an idyllic realm of beatitude like that celebrated by Mignon's famous lyric in *Wilhelm Meister,* "Kennst du das Land," which prefaces *Of Time and the River,* book 1. He is seeking a "shining," "elfin," "glorious," and "fabulous" region of "enchantment" and "magic," where he can find "strength" and "love," "triumph" and "splendor," "exultancy" and "ecstasy." He is look-ing, in short, for a fusion of Actuality and Romance in a world so intense, vital, and magnificent that it is larger than life, ideal, "more true than truth, more real than . . . reality." The imagery of the novel is consistently polar-ized between this kind of paradisiacal vision, on the one hand, and various kinds of Wasteland or Hell, on the other.

Above all, the "religious" or "mythic" character of Eugene's quest for an Earthly Paradise is apparent in his hunger for permanence. Eugene is very much like one of Wolfe's favorite poets, Keats, in that, although he takes a lusty delight in all the pleasures of the senses, he also yearns for the change-less and eternal, as in the following typical passage, which describes the earliest and best phase of his relationship with Starwick:

> Now, with Starwick, and for the first time, he felt this magic constantly—this realization of a life forever good, forever warm and beautiful, forever flashing with the fires of passion, poetry, and joy, forever filled with the swelling and triumphant confi-dence of youth, its belief in new lands, morning, and a shining city, its hope of voyages, its conviction of a fortunate, good, and happy life—an imperishable happiness and joy—that was im-pending, that would be here at any moment.

Both contributing to and reflecting this insatiable desire for an immutable Earthly Paradise, and setting up an insistent countercurrent to his sense of flux, are numerous important occasions scattered throughout the book when Eugene experiences a certain radiant and visionary sensation of timelessness suggestive of "the calm and silence of eternity." These experiences are of several kinds. Again and again, he is aware, for example, that time, although it is the enemy that brings change and death, is itself changeless and deathless, in the sense that it is a feature of reality inherent in Being itself. Similarly, he repeatedly perceives the earth and the cosmos as a whole as "everlasting" and "eternal," in contrast to the fleeting lives of individual men. But Eugene's most significant experiences of timelessness are those that result from his recurring sense that the "lost" past is not really lost at all—that it survives somehow, somewhere, in defiance of death, and can be recaptured, made to "blaze instantly with all the warmth and radiance of life again." Such Proustian moments or Wordsworthian "spots of time" appear everywhere in the novel, especially in connection with Eugene's experiences of *déjà vu*—that strange, dreamlike sensation that something which has happened before, or seems to have happened before, is repeating itself. Thus, as Eugene makes his first visit to the estate of his friend, Joel Pierce, in Rhinekill on the Hudson, the whole scene seems "hauntingly familiar" to him, and he encounters it "without surprise, as one who for the first time comes into his father's country, finding it the same as he had always known it would be, and knowing always that it would be there." Other equally memorable experiences occur, as we might expect, on trains, which, when used as a symbol of time, powerfully heighten the *déjà vu* effect by contrast, as in the marvelously luminous passage on the town of Troy in upstate New York, which Eugene's train passes through in the middle of the night, and which, as he glimpses it through the window, seems to him "as familiar as a dream" and "like something he had known forever."

The most important means by which Eugene experiences the illusion of recapturing the past, however, is his phenomenal memory—a "memory that will not die"—which enables him to recall with extraordinary intensity not only major happenings and persons, but "the 'little' things of life—a face seen one time at a window, a voice that passed in darkness and was gone, the twisting of a leaf upon a bough." This power of almost total recall, this enormous retentiveness, is both a liability and an asset: a liability, because it makes Eugene agonizingly aware of time and death in the first place; but an asset too, because it permits him to transcend those limits by restoring the lost world to life again—making it "living, whole, and magic"—and thereby imparting to it a kind of immortality.

All these various, quasi-mystical experiences, then, help to develop in Eugene an unusually strong sense of timelessness, which in turn nourishes and mirrors his "religious" longing for an Earthly Paradise. But the principal roots of that longing predate all of these experiences and lie deep in Eugene's childhood. It was then that he heard "the sound of something lost and elfin and half-dreamed," and glimpsed a "half-captured vision of some magic country he has known . . . which haunts his days with strangeness and the sense of imminent, glorious re-discovery"—wonderful phrases that suggest those recollections of a Platonic and Wordsworthian prenatal "heaven" that played an even more conspicuous part in *Look Homeward, Angel*. Furthermore, partly because of these recollections, partly because of the reading of fairy tales and romantic literature that stimulated his boyhood's imagination, and partly because of the rich, colorful life once provided him by the great life-force figure of his father, Eugene now, looking nostalgically back, sees his childhood itself as a Paradise, the loss of which as a result of both his father's death and the disappearance of small-town America in general, he always regards "with an intolerable sense of pain." Paradoxically, therefore, his quests to transcend the limits of mortality, no matter how far and wide they lead him, are always at the deepest level expressive of a desire to recapture what he perceives as the lost pastoral idyll of his childhood by discovering an equivalent Paradise in the present.

II

These quests for transcendence are mainly of four overlapping kinds. One is a quest for *adventure*—for plenitude of experience—which is motivated by a "Faustian" desire to race against death, a voracious passion to conquer time by seeing and doing as much as possible in the brief span of days that life allows: Eugene "was driven by a hunger so literal, cruel and physical that it wanted to devour the earth and all the things and people in it."

A second kind of quest on which he embarks is for *knowledge,* especially that "recorded knowledge" that is to be obtained by " 'reading all the books that were ever printed.' " Through such knowledge Eugene hopes to reach beyond time and death by discovering ultimate meaning—by plumbing "the source, the well, the spring from which all men and words and actions, and every design upon this earth proceeds"; by finding some de-

finitive "answer to the riddle of this vast and swarming earth"; by acquiring
" 'an everlasting and triumphal wisdom.' "

A third quest is for *security*—or, as Wolfe designated it in *The Story of a Novel,* for "a father . . . the image of a strength and wisdom external to . . . [a man's] need and superior to his hunger, to which the belief and power of his own life could be united." In his horror of oblivion, Eugene is yearning for that simple, elemental kind of physical and emotional stability and happiness that the words "father" and "home" connote literally, and that he identifies with the "silence, peace, and certitude" he enjoyed in that lost paradise of his childhood where the foundations of all his other quests were laid as well. The very first episode in the novel—Eugene's journey to Harvard—results not only from his desire for adventure and knowledge, but from his desire to travel to the North, which, because W. O. Gant had been born and raised in Pennsylvania, he envisages as "his heart's hope and his father's country, the lost but unforgotten half of his own soul." After Gant's death, his search intensifies, and reaches a brilliant climax in one of the novel's most moving passages, the eloquent prayer that constitutes the penultimate paragraph of chapter 39:

> Come to us, Father, in the watches of the night, come to us as you always came, bringing to us the invincible sustenance of your strength, the limitless treasure of your bounty, the tremendous structure of your life that will shape all lost and broken things on earth again into a golden pattern of exultancy and joy. . . . For we are ruined, lost, and broken if you do not come, and our lives, like rotten chips, are whirled about us onward in darkness to the sea.

Finally, and most important, there is a fourth way by which Eugene attempts to transcend time and death: this is his quest for *art,* his desire to become a writer. For he not only dreams of art as a means of winning fame and fortune, but, lacking the religious faith he unconsciously craves but cannot attain, ultimately comes to believe that art alone can triumph over flux, and, acting on that belief, begins the process of transforming his life itself into the Earthly Paradise by recapturing the otherwise irretrievable past in memory and rendering it immortal in artistic form. Although he certainly does not think of it in such terms, art becomes, in effect, his surrogate religion.

Before Eugene can appreciate the full significance of art or begin authentically creating it, however, he must first learn that the ideal life he is seeking is unattainable in any other way; he must discover the vanity of all his other quests. The stages of this discovery add up to most of the novel's main action, and are deeply ironic. The basic structural pattern of Eugene's experiences is a series of cycles, each of which (almost like the mood swings of a manic-depressive) consists of some great expectation followed by frustration and disillusionment, some youthful dream shattered by its denial. No matter how often his hopes fail to materialize, they revive, but only inevitably to be dashed again. Nothing ever turns out as he has imagined it would; fantasy and reality always collide; the satisfactions for which he struggles prove unattainable. As in the cycles of futile striving and eternal recurrence described in one of Wolfe's favorite texts, Ecclesiastes, each of the attempts Eugene makes to escape some kind of death only brings him back to death in another form. The pattern of book 1, in which the euphoria that he enjoys while traveling northward on the train gives way to "a feeling of horror" when he stops in Baltimore to see his dying father, thus encapsulates the plot of the novel as a whole: five major cycles are climaxed by his disenchantments with Professor Hatcher's play-writing course at Harvard in book 2; with the Broadway producer who rejects his play in book 3; with New York City, his teaching job, and the Pierce family in book 4; with Starwick in book 5; and with Europe in books 6 and 7. Within these main cycles there are also several smaller ones. In short, although Eugene's hunger is like that of Faustus, his fate is like that of Tantalus, the victim of "a thousand shapes of impossible desire."

Reinforcing the irony produced by this cyclical pattern is Wolfe's use of another device: the alter ego. Eugene's experiences of hope and disillusionment are paralleled throughout the novel by those of various other characters who have also sought and failed. The most important of these characters fall into two groups. One consists of the young, like Eugene's brothers Ben and Luke, his sister Helen, and his friends, Robert Weaver and Frank Starwick—characters of or close to Eugene's own age, whose hopes and disillusionments are more or less contemporaneous with his own (or, in the case of Ben, would have been contemporaneous, if Ben had lived). The other group consists of the old, like Uncle Bascom Pentland, Dr. Hugh McGuire, and, most important of all, W. O. Gant, Eugene's father—characters much farther along in life than Eugene, whose hopes and disillusionments have for the most part taken place a long time in the past or have extended over a great many years, and who now have nothing left to confront but despair and death. Both of these groups of characters function not only to exemplify the kinds of "death-in-life" from which Eugene is confident he can escape, but to comment ironically, as a kind of chorus, on the naivete of that confidence by foreshadowing or playing variations on his inevitable frustrations and defeats. Each is a *memento mori*—a death's head at the feast of life—whose presence in the novel is a constant reminder of that vanity of human wishes that Eugene is trying so hard not to face, but that his own disappointments sooner or later force him to acknowledge. The unromantic reality his alter egos experience and symbolize is very different from his romantic conceptions, but one that he must eventually confront.

Yet the final effect of *Of Time and the River* is far from despairing or cynical. On the contrary, like that of all Wolfe's books, it is profoundly affirmative, for not all of Eugene's quests for an Earthly Paradise that is immune to death end ironically in defeat; his solitary and painful pilgrimage through the darkness leads him ultimately to the light. What distinguishes Eugene from his alter egos and makes possible his transcendence of the trap of morality and futility in which they are caught is his possession of artistic talent. If *Of Time and the River* is a specimen of the bildungsroman, it is also an example of its subgenre, the künstlerroman, because, as I have noted, along with the bitter story of the disillusionments and frustrations resulting from Eugene's quests for adventure, knowledge, and security, and in counterpoint to that story, there has been running throughout the novel another one, less conspicuous, perhaps, but essential to the denouement— namely, that of his successful growth as a writer. This development consists of several clearly marked stages, results in three vital discoveries about the nature of art and the artistic process, and culminates in a feverish act of authentic and redemptive creation.

III

In book 1, which begins where *Look Homeward, Angel* left off, Eugene sets out for graduate study at Harvard, dreaming naively "that he would write a book or play every year or so, which would be a great success, and yield him fifteen or twenty thousand dollars at a crack." He soon discovers, however, that the creation of art is not so easy. For, although in book 2 he enrolls in Professor Hatcher's "celebrated course for dramatists" and there writes a play that we later learn he submits to a Broadway producer, he is plagued by self-doubts that are only too emphatically confirmed in book 3 when his work is rejected. His next effort, a play called *Mannerhouse,* which he writes in book 4 while teaching in New York City, is presumably somewhat better; at any rate, the praise he receives from his friend Joel Pierce and Joel's sister, Rosalind, to whom he reads it does much to restore his confidence. But again self-doubts emerge when he contemplates the great Pierce library, and reflects on the power of wealth to reduce "all the glory, genius, and magic of a poet's life ... [to] six rich bindings, forgotten, purchased and unread." Seeking to regain his inspiration, he travels in book 5 to Europe, where he manages to fill "a great stack of . . . ledgers," and at last begins to recognize that the artist's life consists of "the sweat and anguish of hard labor." Two crises, however, soon develop. The first results from his lack of any coherent artistic purpose: driven by an insane, "Faustian" desire to cram all human experience into "one final, perfect, all-inclusive work," he succeeds only in filling his notebooks with a "mad mélange" of "splintered jottings." The second crisis arises when his old friend from Harvard, Starwick, suddenly appears in Paris with two women from Boston who are in love with him. Eugene becomes infected for a time with Starwick's growing apathy, and consequently falls into a life of idleness and dissipation that brings his writing to a halt and nearly overwhelms him with feelings of shame and guilt. Even after he has broken off with Starwick and the women, he continues in book 6 merely to drift from place to place, accomplishing little or nothing. Nevertheless, he finally recovers and begins writing again, more earnestly than ever before, after his arrival in Tours in the opening two chapters of book 7. Indeed, not only are these chapters among Wolfe's finest lyrical passages, but they carry Eugene's development as an artist as far as the novel will take it, and thus bring *Of Time and the River* as a whole to its true climax and resolution.

To understand what happens in these key chapters and makes them possible we first have to examine three crucial discoveries about art that Eugene has made earlier. One of these concerns the process of creation itself and where it can be performed. Influenced by his desire for an Earthly Paradise in general, Eugene has long hoped to find a place where he can write under the most ideal and romantic conditions. In Orleans, however, he realizes the folly of such a dream; making a giant leap from romanticism to realism, he concludes that, as a condition for the creation of art, an Earthly Paradise of any literal, physical, geographical sort is wholly unnecessary: "he knew now . . . 'the place to write' was Brooklyn, Boston, Hammersmith, or Kansas—anywhere on earth, so long as the heart, the power, the faith, the desperation . . . were there inside him all the time."

A second major discovery, analogous to this, concerns the subject matter of art: just as the artist must look for some never-never land of fantasy and romance in which to create, so he must not try to depict such a place in his work itself, but, drawing heavily upon memory, must faithfully represent the reality of life as he has come to know it. Eugene begins to make this discovery in book 3, after he and some companions are arrested and jailed in Blackstone, South Carolina, for drunken driving. The extreme humiliation he suffers on this occasion leads Eugene to feel "a more earthly, common, and familiar union with the lives of other men than he had ever known," and thus ultimately results in his rejecting Shelley's poetry "of aerial flight and escape into some magic and unvisited domain" in favor of Homer, the poets of the Bible, Chaucer, the Elizabethans, and others, "who wrote not of the air but of . . . the golden glory of the earth, which is the only earth that is . . . the only one that will never die." Another step toward realism and an art based on memory occurs when Eugene writes the play that he reads to Joel and Rosalind Pierce at their estate in Rhinekill. Although this work is uneven in quality, and, as was his earlier one, is still in many respects imitative of stale theatrical conventions, he has begun to use in it "some of the materials of his own life and experience," and to depict "some of the real grandeur, beauty, terror, and unuttered loneliness of America." Finally, to complete his realization that his art is now moving in the right direction there is the town of Rhinekill itself. For this privileged, sheltered world of the Hudson Valley rich is merely the counterpart of the dream worlds created by the Harvard esthetes and Shelley. However painful it is, therefore, to return to the ugliness of New York City, Eugene now knows that upon doing so depends his artistic salvation.

The third and last discovery that leads to the climax of his development as an artist and to the resolution of the novel as a whole occurs during the reading of his play to Joel and Rosalind, when he suddenly realizes, "in one blaze of light," that, of all man's works, art and art alone can achieve timelessness. The passage that describes this epiphany is, in fact, the fullest and most memorable statement of the theme in all Wolfe:

> This is the reason that the artist lives and works and has his being: that . . . he may distill the beauty of an everlasting form . . . cast his spell across the generations, beat death down upon his knees, kill death utterly, and fix eternity with the grappling-hooks of his own art. His life is soul-hydroptic with . . . the intolerable desire to fix eternally in the patterns of an indestructible form a single moment of man's living, a single moment of life's beauty, passion, and unutterable eloquence, that passes, flames, and goes, slipping forever through our fingers with time's sanded drop, flowing forever from our desperate grasp even as a river flows and never can be held.

In these three major discoveries about art, then, lies the key to Eugene's coming-of-age as a writer and hence to the achievement of his quests for transcendence and the resolution of the entire novel. The Earthly Paradise immune to death that he has so futilely sought in his quests for adventure, knowledge, and security, will turn out to be his life as he has already lived it (including, presumably, his quests themselves, with all their cycles of hope and disappointment) when that life has been recaptured by memory and embodied in art. He will be able to confer transcendence upon his own earlier self and experiences by means of the immortalizing and apotheosizing power of the creative process itself. All that remains to complete the design of *Of Time and the River*, therefore, is for such a process to begin, and this is precisely what happens in the two great opening chapters of book 7. The catalyst is an unbearable feeling of homesickness that has been building up in Eugene for months and now becomes profounder and more intense than ever before.

Arriving by chance in the old French town of Tours, and there finding peace and quiet for the first time after months of hectic travel, Eugene falls almost immediately into a rapt, mesmeric, trancelike state that lasts for several weeks, during which he feels himself transported into the very realm of timelessness that he has apprehended so often before. His surroundings virtually disappear from his conscious awareness, and are replaced by pre-ternaturally vivid memories of "home" and teeming impressions of America that from the beginning of the novel have been embedding themselves "in every atom of his flesh and tissue." He knows now that, although he has been "wandering forever," he must return to "the earth [i.e., America] again."

The consequence of all this is not only his literal return a few chapters later, but, far more crucially, his return by means of art. For in Tours all his memories bred of homesickness finally trigger a furious burst of creativity, the object of which is to get every scrap of his remembered experience down on paper, to disgorge all of his life into language:

> He began to write now like a madman . . . all ordered plans, designs, coherent projects for the work he had set out to do went by the board, were burned up in the flame of a quenchless pas-sion, like a handful of dry straw. . . . he wrote ceaselessly from dawn to dark, sometimes from darkness on to dawn again. . . .
>
> And in those words was packed the whole image of his bitter homelessness, his intolerable desire, his maddened longing for return. . . .
>
> They were all there—without coherence, scheme, or reason— flung down upon paper like figures blasted by the spirit's light-ning stroke, and in them was the huge chronicle of the billion

forms, the million names, the huge, single, and incomparable substance of America.

This episode is the point toward which Eugene's development as an artist has been implicitly tending from the beginning, and, as such, it constitutes the novel's climax and resolution. If only in a half-conscious way, Eugene has now begun the process of dealing more compulsively and completely than ever before with what must henceforth be the central subject of his art—America and the life he has already lived there. It is true that his frenzied burst of creativity is very brief; it is both the first and the last of its kind in the novel. But we are not allowed to imagine that such a crucial event will have no long-range consequences, for Eugene's memory, now more powerfully and purposefully activated than ever before, continues to operate srongly even after he leaves Tours, and thus provides a source of inspiration to which his creative impulse will surely return many times in the future. In short, Eugene has embarked upon the task of producing an authentic autobiographical art that will rescue his past from the maw of time, confer upon it "the beauty of an everlasting form," and thereby impart to it a radiant immorality. In doing so, he is at last on the verge of attaining the goal of all his quests—the transcendence of death.

This account of the novel's closure is, of course, incomplete. After chapters 96–97, for instance, Eugene's futile, romantic quests for transcendent adventure, knowledge, and security continue anticlimactically for five more chapters, which culminate in his shipboard meeting with the woman who, in *The Web and the Rock* and *You Can't Go Home Again,* is to be known as Esther Jack, and to become the mistress of Wolfe's next protagonist, George Webber. Distracted, perhaps, by the mere "chronicle" aspect of what he was writing, Wolfe clearly did not know when to stop, and for this, as well as other reasons, *Of Time and the River* is far from being a perfect book. So much I conceded at the outset. Nevertheless, it is also far from being "formless." Considered in its broadest outline, indeed, the form turns out to be nothing less than a late avatar of that age-old, fundamentally religious one so brilliantly described by M. H. Abrams in his distinguished study of romanticism, *Natural Supernaturalism.* This is the design (originating in pagan and Christian Neoplatonism, modified by the nineteenth-century romantics, and passed on to a number of moderns) of the "circuitous journey" or "the great circle," which expresses a vision, in Abrams's words, of "the course of all things" as "a circuit whose end is its beginning, of which the movement is from unity out to the increasingly many and back to unity, and in which this movement into and out of division is identified with the falling away from good to evil and a return to good." In the terms implicitly proposed by *Of Time and the River*, this circle consists of four phases related to the key concepts of "home" or "paradise": paradise itself, paradise lost, paradise sought, and paradise regained. Paradise corresponds to the recollections of preexistence and the romantic dreams that Eugene enjoyed in childhood and even to his childhood itself when in later years he nostalgically recalls it; paradise lost corresponds to the anguished awareness of time and death that comes to him in his youth; paradise sought corresponds to his many (also cyclical) quests for adventure, knowledge, and security; and paradise regained corresponds to the beginning of authentic artistic creation whereby he will finally be able to transcend time and death by making of all the transitory and tormented moments of his life itself a thing of timeless beauty.

Chronology

1900   Thomas Wolfe is born in Asheville, North Carolina, October 3, the last of eight children born to William Oliver Wolfe and Julia Elizabeth Westall Wolfe.

1904   Visits World's Fair in St. Louis with mother and several siblings; Grover Cleveland Wolfe, twin of his favorite brother, Ben, dies.

1905   Attends Orange Street Public School.

1912   Attends North State School, a private school.

1916   Matriculates at the University of North Carolina, Chapel Hill.

1918   Spends summer doing civilian war work. Ben dies, October 19.

1919   Awarded the Worth Prize for essay "The Crisis in Industry." Edits *Tar Heel,* the student newspaper.

1920   Graduates from the University of North Carolina; in September enters the Harvard Graduate School and the 47 Workshop; George Pierce Baker's playwriting course.

1921   His short play *The Mountains* is staged at the Workshop.

1922   Earns M.A. at Harvard. Father dies June 20. In September Wolfe returns to 47 Workshop.

1923   *Welcome to Our City* is staged May 11.

1924   Teaching appointment at Washington Square College of New York University in February. Embarks on trip to England, October 25.

1925   Meets Aline Bernstein, stage designer, at end of voyage back to New York, the beginning of a long and turbulent affair.

1926   On a second European trip, joins Aline Bernstein in the English Lake Country.

1928   *Look Homeward, Angel* completed in March. Wolfe travels to Europe in the summer.

1929   "An Angel on the Porch" published in August issue of *Scribners Magazine*. *Look Homeward, Angel* published by Scribners in October.

1930   Receives Guggenheim Fellowship in March. Departs for Europe May 10. Break with Aline Bernstein, the first of many.

1931   Returns to New York late February and takes up residence in Brooklyn.

1932   "A Portrait of Bascom Hawke," co-winner of a *Scribners Magazine* prize, is published in April issue.

1934   *Of Time and the River* assembled for publication.

1935   Departs for Europe March 2. *Of Time and the River* is released March 8. Returns to New York July 4. Guest lecturer at the Colorado Writers' Conference July 22 to August 9. *From Death to Morning*, a collection of short stories, is published November 14.

1936   *The Story of a Novel*, based on the lectures given at Colorado, is published April 21. Break with Scribners over royalties as well as more personal matters. Wolfe visits Berlin during Olympic Games in August. Libel suit brought against him for "No Door," a story published in *From Death to Morning*.

1937   Suit settled out of court. Wolfe signs contract with Harper.

1938   After a lecture in Portland, Oregon, Wolfe travels through a number of national parks in the West, June 21 to July 2. Falls ill in Seattle. At the Johns Hopkins Hospital in Baltimore, an operation performed September 12 reveals "myriads of tubercles" on the right lobe of his brain. Wolfe dies September 15. He is buried in Riverside Cemetery in Asheville.

1939   *The Web and the Rock* published June 22.

1940   *You Can't Go Home Again* published September 18.

1941   *The Hills Beyond* published October 15.

1948   *Mannerhouse* published.

Contributors

CLYDE C. CLEMENTS, JR. has taught English at Xavier University, New Orleans.

LESLIE A. FIELD is professor of English at Purdue University and the editor of *Thomas Wolfe: Three Decades of Criticism*.

MORRIS BEJA is professor of English at Ohio State University and the author of *Epiphany in the Modern Novel*.

RICHARD S. KENNEDY is professor of English at Temple University. He is author of *The Window of Memory: The Literary Career of Thomas Wolfe* and editor of *Thomas Wolfe: A Harvard Perspective*.

LEO GURKO was professor of English at Hofstra University and author of *The Angry Decade, Heroes, Highbrows and the Popular Mind, Tom Paine, Freedom's Apostle, Joseph Conrad: Giant in Exile, The Two Lives of Joseph Conrad, Ernest Hemingway and the Pursuit of Heroism* as well as *Thomas Wolfe: Beyond the Romantic Ego*.

C. HUGH HOLMAN was Kenan Professor of English at the University of North Carolina and the author of *Three Modes of Modern Southern Fiction* and *The Loneliness at the Core: Studies in Thomas Wolfe*, among other books.

JOHN HAGAN is a member of the Department of English, Literature, and Rhetoric at the State University of New York at Binghamton.

Bibliography

Albrecht, W. P. "The Title of *Look Homeward, Angel*." *Modern Language Quarterly* 11 (1950): 50–57.

Angoff, Charles. "Thomas Wolfe and the Opulent Manner." *Southwest Review* 48 (1963): 81–84.

Aswell, Edward C. "Thomas Wolfe: The Playwright Who Discovered He Wasn't." In Look Homeward, Angel: *A Play Based on the Novel by Thomas Wolfe*, by Ketti Frings, 3–5. New York: Scribner's, 1958.

Baker, Carlos. "Thomas Wolfe's Apprenticeship." *Delphian Quarterly* 23 (1940): 20–25.

Basso, Hamilton. "Thomas Wolfe." In *After the Genteel Tradition: American Writers Since 1910*, edited by Malcolm Cowley, 202–12. New York: Norton, 1937.

Beach, Joseph Warren. *American Fiction, 1920–1940*. New York: Macmillan, 1941.

Bowden, Edwin T. *The Dungeon of the Heart: Human Isolation and the American Novel*. New York: Macmillan, 1961.

Boyer, James. "The Metaphoric Levels in Wolfe's 'The Sun and the Rain.' " *Studies in Short Fiction* 19, no. 4 (1982): 384–87.

Boyle, Thomas E. "Thomas Wolfe: Theme Through Imagery." *Modern Fiction Studies* 11 (1965): 259–68.

———. "Frederick Jackson Turner and Thomas Wolfe: The Frontier as History and Literature." *Western American Literature* 4 (1970): 273–85.

Boynton, Percy H. *America in Contemporary Fiction*. University of Chicago Press, 1940.

Bradbury, John M. *Renaissance in the South: A Critical History of the Literature, 1920–1960*. Chapel Hill: University of North Carolina Press, 1963.

Bredahl, A. Carl, Jr. "*Look Homeward, Angel*: Individuation and Articulation." *Southern Literary Journal* 6, no. 1 (1973): 47–58.

Brodin, Pierre. *Thomas Wolfe*, translated by Imogene Riddick. Asheville, N.C.: The Stephens Press, 1949.

Budd, Louis J. "The Grotesques of Anderson and Wolfe." *Modern Fiction Studies* 5 (1959–60): 304–10.

Burgum, Edwin Berry. *The Novel and the World's Dilemma*. New York: Oxford University Press, 1947.

Chase, Richard. "Introduction" to *The Web and the Rock*. New York: Dell, 1960: 7–19.

Church, Margaret. *Time and Reality; Studies in Contemporary Fiction.* Chapel Hill: University of North Carolina Press, 1963.

Cracroft, Richard H. "A Pebble in the Pool: Organic Theme and Structure in Thomas Wolfe's *You Can't Go Home Again.*" *Modern Fiction Studies* 17 (1971–72): 533–53.

Dessner, Lawrence J. "Thomas Wolfe's Mr. Katamoto." *Modern Fiction Studies* 17 (1971–72): 561–65.

DeVoto, Bernard. *The World of Fiction.* Boston: Houghton Mifflin, 1950.

Domnarski, William. "Thomas Wolfe's Success as Short Novelist: Structure and Theme in *A Portrait of Bascom Hawke.*" *Southern Literary Journal* 13, no. 1 (1980): 32–41.

Evans, Elizabeth. "Music in *Look Homeward, Angel.*" *Southern Literary Journal* 8, no. 2 (1976): 62–73.

———. "Thomas Wolfe: Some Echoes from Mark Twain." *Mark Twain Journal* 18, no. 2 (1976): 5–6.

———. "Thomas Wolfe's Preliminaries to *Of Time and the River.*" *Markham Review* 8 (1978): 5–7.

———. *Thomas Wolfe.* New York: Frederick Ungar, 1984.

Field, Leslie. "Thomas Wolfe on the Couch and in Symposium." *Southern Literary Journal* 5, no. 1 (1972): 163–76.

———. "Thomas Wolfe's Attitude Toward Germans and Jews." *Journal of Modern Literature* 11, no. 1 (1984): 180–85.

Frohock, W. M. "Thomas Wolfe: Time and the National Neurosis." In *The Novel of Violence in America.* 2d ed, 52–68. Dallas: Southern Methodist University Press, 1957.

Geismar, Maxwell. "Thomas Wolfe." In *American Moderns: From Rebellion to Conformity,* 119–44. New York: Hill & Wang, 1958.

Gelfant, Blanche Housman. *The American City Novel.* Norman: University of Oklahoma Press, 1954.

Gossett, Louise Y. *Violence in Recent Southern Fiction.* Durham, N.C.: Duke University Press, 1965.

Gould, Elain W. *Look Behind You, Thomas Wolfe: Ghosts of a Common Tribal Heritage.* Hicksville, N.Y.: Exposition, 1976.

Gray, Richard. "Signs of Kinship: Thomas Wolfe and His Appalachian Background." *Appalachian Journal* 1 (1974): 309–19.

Green, Charmian. "Wolfe's Stonecutter Once Again: An Unpublished Episode." *Mississippi Quarterly* 30 (1977): 611–23.

———. "Wolfe, O'Neill, and the Mask of Illusion." *Papers on English Language and Literature* 14 (1978): 87–90.

Gurko, Leo. *Thomas Wolfe: Beyond the Romantic Ego.* New York: Crowell, 1975.

Halberstadt, John. "The Making of Thomas Wolfe's Posthumous Novels." *Yale Review* 70 (1980): 79–94.

Hampton, Nigel. "Who's Ashamed of Thomas Wolfe?" *CEA Critic* 38, no. 1 (1975): 18–20.

Hartley, Lois. "Theme in Thomas Wolfe's 'The Lost Boy' and 'God's Lonely Man.' " *Georgia Review* 15 (1961): 230–35.

Harvey, Nancy L. "*Look Homeward, Angel:* An Elegaic Novel." *Ball State University Forum* 13, no. 1 (1972): 29–33.

Hawthorne, Mark D. "Thomas Wolfe's Use of the Poetic Fragment." *Modern Fiction Studies* 11 (1965): 234–44.

Hilfer, Anthony Channell. "Wolfe's Altamont: The Mimesis of Being." *Georgia Review* 18 (1964): 451–56.

Hill, John S. "Eugene Gant and the Ghost of Ben." *Modern Fiction Studies* 11 (1965): 245–49.

Holman, C. Hugh. *The Loneliness at the Core: Studies in Thomas Wolfe.* Baton Rouge: Louisiana State University Press, 1975.

———, ed. *The World of Thomas Wolfe.* New York: Scribner's, 1962.

Howell, Elmo. "Thomas Wolfe and the Sense of Place." *South Carolina Review* 11, no. 1 (1978): 96–106.

Idol, John L., Jr. "Thomas Wolfe and Painting." *Re: Arts and Letters* 2, no. 1 (1969): 14–20.

———. "Thomas Wolfe's 'A Note on Experts.' " *Studies in Short Fiction* 11 (1974): 395–98.

———. "Angels and Demons: The Satire of *Look Homeward, Angel.*" *Studies in Contemporary Satire* 1, no. 2 (1975): 39–46.

———. "Thomas Wolfe and Jonathan Swift." *South Carolina Review* 8, no. 1 (1975): 43–45.

———. "Thomas Wolfe and *Moby-Dick.*" *Melville Society Extracts* 57 (1984): 9–10.

Johnson, Pamela. *Thomas Wolfe: A Critical Study.* London: Heinemann, 1947.

Kazin, Alfred. *On Native Grounds: An Interpretation of Modern American Prose Literature.* New York: Harcourt, Brace & World, 1942.

Kennedy, Richard S. *The Window of Memory: The Literary Career of Thomas Wolfe.* Chapel Hill: University of North Carolina Press, 1962.

———. "Wolfe's *Look Homeward, Angel* as a Novel of Development." *South Atlantic Quarterly* 63 (1964): 218–26.

———. "Thomas Wolfe's Last Manuscript." *Harvard Library Bulletin* 23 (1975): 203–11.

———. *Thomas Wolfe: A Harvard Perspective.* Athens, Ohio: Croissant, 1983.

Kennedy, William F. "Economic Ideas in Contemporary Literature: The Novels of Thomas Wolfe." *Southern Economic Journal* 20 (1953): 35–50.

Koch, C. J. "Who Wants the Novel? Fiction in the Era of Film and Television." *Quadrant* 26 (1982): 8–11.

Loggins, Vernon. "Dominant Primordial." In *I Hear America: Literature in the United States Since 1900.* New York: Crowell, 1937.

Maddock, Lawrence. "Thomas Wolfe, A Stone, A Leaf, A Door." *Arizona English Bulletin* 21, no. 1 (1978): 83–86.

McIlvaine, Robert. "Thomas Wolfe's GarGANTuan Family." *Notes on Contemporary Literature* 6, no. 1 (1976): 2–5.

McElderry, Bruce R., Jr. *Thomas Wolfe.* Twayne's United States Authors Series. New York: Twayne, 1964.

Millichap, Joseph R. "Narrative Structure and Symbolic Imagery in *Look Homeward, Angel.*" *Southern Humanities Review* 7 (1973): 295–303.

Morgan, H. Wayne. "Thomas Wolfe: The Web of Memory." In *Writers in Transition: Seven Americans,* 127–51. New York: Hill & Wang, 1963.

Morris, Wright. "The Function of Appetite: Thomas Wolfe." In *The Territory Ahead*. New York: Harcourt, Brace & World, 1958.

Moser, Thomas C. "Thomas Wolfe: *Look Homeward, Angel*." In *The American Novel: From James Fenimore Cooper to William Faulkner*, edited by Wallace Stegner, 206–18. New York: Basic Books, Inc., 1965.

Muller, Herbert J. *Thomas Wolfe*. Makers of Modern Literature Series. Norfolk: New Directions, 1947.

Natanson, M. A. "Privileged Moment: A Study in the Rhetoric of Thomas Wolfe." *Quarterly Journal of Speech* 43 (1957): 143–50.

Norwood, Hayden. *The Marble Man's Wife: Thomas Wolfe's Mother*. New York: Scribner's, 1947.

Nowell, Elizabeth. *Thomas Wolfe: A Biography*. Garden City, N.Y.: Doubleday, 1960.

O'Brien, Michael. "Thomas Wolfe and the Problem of Southern Identity: An English Perspective." *South Atlantic Quarterly* 70 (1971): 102–11.

Phillipson, John S. *Thomas Wolfe: A Reference Guide*. Boston: G. K. Hall, 1977.

Pleasant, John. "Two Train Rides of Thomas Wolfe." *Innisfree* 4 (1977): 3–14.

Pollack, Thomas Clark, and Oscar Cargill, eds. *Thomas Wolfe at Washington Square*. New York: New York University Press, 1954.

Powell, W. Allen. "Thomas Wolfe's Phoenix Nest: The Plays of Thomas Wolfe as Related to His Fiction." *Markham Review* 2 (1971): 104–10.

Priestly, J. B. "Introduction" to *The Web and the Rock*. London: Heinemann, 1947: ix–xii.

Reaver, J. Russell and Robert I. Strozier. "Thomas Wolfe and Death." *Georgia Review* 16 (1962): 330–50.

Reeves, Paschal. "Thomas Wolfe: Notes on Three Characters." *Modern Fiction Studies* 11 (1965): 275–85.

———, ed. *Studies in* Look Homeward, Angel. Columbus, Ohio: Merrill, 1970.

Rothman, Nathan L. "Thomas Wolfe and James Joyce: A Study in Literary Influence." In *A Southern Vanguard*, edited by Allen Tate, 52–77. New York: Prentice-Hall, 1947.

Rubin, Louis D., Jr. *Thomas Wolfe: The Weather of His Youth*. Baton Rouge: Louisiana State University Press, 1955.

———. *Thomas Wolfe: A Collection of Critical Essays*. Englewood Cliffs, N.J.: Prentice-Hall, 1973.

———. "Thomas Wolfe and the Place He Came From." *Virginia Quarterly Review* 51 (1975): 183–202.

Ruppersburg, Hugh M. "The Narrator in *Look Homeward, Angel*." *Southern Humanities Review* 18 (1984): 1–9.

Ryssel, Fritz Heinrich. *Thomas Wolfe*. Translated by Helen Sebba. New York: Frederick Ungar, 1972.

Schneider, Duane. "The Re-emergence of Thomas Wolfe." *Mississippi Quarterly* 37 (1984): 195–200.

Scribner, Charles, III. "Crying Wolfe." *Princeton University Library Chronicle* 45, no. 3 (1984): 225–229.

Sloyan, Gerald S. "Thomas Wolfe: A Legend of a Man's Youth in His Hunger." In *Fifty Years of the American Novel: A Christian Appraisal,* edited by Harold C. Gardiner, 197–215. New York: Scribner's, 1952.

Snell, George. "The Education of Thomas Wolfe." In *Shapers of American Fiction: 1798–1947,* 173–87. New York: Dutton, 1947.

Snyder, William. *Thomas Wolfe: Ulysses and Narcissus.* Athens: Ohio University Press, 1971.

Spiller, Robert E. *The Cycle of American Literature: An Essay in Historical Criticism.* New York: Macmillan, 1955.

Steele, Richard. *Thomas Wolfe: A Study in Psychoanalytic Literary Criticism.* Philadelphia: Dorrance, 1976.

Trilling, Lionel. "Contemporary American Literature in Its Relation to Ideas." In *The American Writer and the European Tradition,* edited by Margaret Denny and William H. Gilman, 144–49. Minneapolis: University of Minnesota Press, 1950.

Untermeyer, Louis. "Thomas Wolfe." In *Makers of the Modern World,* 726–35. New York: Simon & Schuster, 1955.

Walser, Richard. *Thomas Wolfe: An Introduction and Interpretation.* American Authors and Critics Series. New York: Barnes & Noble, 1960.

———. "On Faulkner's Putting Wolfe First." *South Atlantic Quarterly* 78 (1979): 172–81.

———, ed. *The Enigma of Thomas Wolfe: Biographical and Critical Selections.* Cambridge: Harvard University Press, 1953.

Walser, Richard. "The Angel and the Ghost." In *Thomas Wolfe and the Glass of Time,* edited by Paschal Reeves, 63–65. Athens: University of Georgia Press, 1971.

Wank, Martin. "Thomas Wolfe: Two More Decades of Criticism." *South Atlantic Quarterly* 69 (1970): 244–56.

Warren, Robert Penn. "A Note on the Hamlet of Thomas Wolfe." In *Selected Essays,* 170–83. New York: Random House, 1958.

Watkins, Floyd C. *Thomas Wolfe's Characters: Portraits from Life.* Norman: University of Oklahoma Press, 1957.

———. "Rhetoric in Southern Writing: Wolfe." *Georgia Review* 12 (1958): 79–82.

———. "Thomas Wolfe and Asheville Again and Again and Again . . ." *Southern Literary Journal* 10, no. 1 (1977): 31–55.

Wheaton, Mabel Wolfe and LeGette Blythe. *Thomas Wolfe and His Family.* Garden City, N.Y.: Doubleday, 1961.

Acknowledgments

"Symbolic Patterns in *You Can't Go Home Again*" by Clyde C. Clements, Jr. from *Modern Fiction Studies* 11, no. 3 (Autumn 1965), © 1965 by Purdue Research Foundation, West Lafayette, Indiana. Reprinted by permission.

"*The Hills Beyond*: A Folk Novel of America" by Leslie A. Field from *Thomas Wolfe: Three Decades of Criticism,* edited by Leslie A. Field, © 1968 by New York University. Reprinted by permission of New York University Press.

"The Escapes of Time and Memory" (originally entitled "Thomas Wolfe: The Escapes of Time and Memory") by Morris Beja from *Epiphany in the Modern Novel* by Morris Beja, © 1971 by Morris Beja. Reprinted by permission of the author, Peter Owen Ltd., and the University of Washington Press.

"Wolfe's Fiction: The Question of Genre" by Richard S. Kennedy from *Thomas Wolfe and the Glass of Time,* edited by Paschal Reeves, © 1971 by the University of Georgia Press. Reprinted by permission of the University of Georgia Press. The excerpts are reprinted by permission of Paul Gitlin.

"*The Web and the Rock*" by Leo Gurko from *Thomas Wolfe: Beyond the Romantic Ego* by Leo Gurko, © 1975 by Leo Gurko. Reprinted by permisson of Harper & Row Publishers.

"The Web of the South" by C. Hugh Holman from *The Loneliness at the Core: Studies in Thomas Wolfe* by C. Hugh Holman, © 1975 by Louisiana State University Press. Reprinted by permission.

"Structure, Theme and Metaphor in *Look Homeward, Angel*" by John Hagan from *American Literature* 53, no. 2 (May 1981), © 1981 by Duke University Press. Reprinted by permission.

"*Of Time and the River*: The Quest for Transcendence" by John Hagan from *Thomas Wolfe: A Harvard Perspective,* edited by Richard S. Kennedy, © 1983 by Croissant and Company. Reprinted by permission.

165

Index

What's Happened To Our High Schools?

JOHN FRANCIS LATIMER

*Assistant Dean of Faculties
and Professor of Classics,
The George Washington University*

Public Affairs Press, Washington, D. C.

44001

ABOUT THE AUTHOR

By 1929, when he received the Ph.D. in Classics from Yale at the age of 26, John Francis Latimer had been a public high school teacher of Latin and coach for one year, principal-superintendent for one year and an Instructor at Vanderbilt University for another. After his graduate studies at Yale he taught successively at the Taft School, Knox College, and Drury College. He is now Professor of Classics, Executive Officer of the Classics Department, and Assistant Dean of Faculties at The George Washington University.

Dr. Latimer is a member of the Managing Committee of the American School of Classical Studies in Athens, of the American Philological Association, the Archaelological Institute of America, the American Classical League, and of the Executive Committee of the Classical Association of the Atlantic States. He was president of this latter association from 1955 to 1957.

A naval officer during World War II, he served in the Atlantic and Pacific areas for two years and received four battle stars. At the present time he holds the rank of Captain in the U.S. Naval Reserve.

Copyright, 1958, by Public Affairs Press
419 New Jersey Avenue, S.E., Washington 3, D. C.

Printed in the United States of America
Library of Congress Catalog Card No. 58-6843

INTRODUCTION

Historians will undoubtedly characterize the period between October 4 and November 4, 1957, as the prelude to a real educational awakening on the part of the American people. On the first of these two dates, as everybody knows, the Russians launched Sputnik I. On the second, they sent Laika on her epochal oneway flight in Sputnik II.

While these dramatic events were still on the front page, the United States Office of Education, by a rather fortuitous and ironical coincidence, published its controversial study, *Education in the USSR.* Aroused and alarmed by what seemed to be the obvious relationship between Russia's scientific achievements and her system of education, we immediately intensified the probe of our own system. This probe had been in progress intermittently in the twelve years following the end of World War II, but it lacked that sense of urgency that the Sputniks provided.

Overnight we began to ask ourselves and our leaders what had happened to our self-acknowledged superiority in science and technology. Didn't a larger proportion of our boys and girls attend high school, finish, and go on to college than anywhere else in the world? Weren't our graduate schools the best in the world? Didn't we lead the entire world in production of Ph.D.s? Why then hadn't we been the first to put an orbiting satellite into space? Had our system of public and private education somehow failed?

The last question summed up all the rest. It cut deepest and hurt the most because all of a sudden we knew the answer: *We, the American people, have failed in our educational responsibilities. We have failed ourselves, but worse than that, we have failed our children.*

How have we failed ourselves and our children?

Not simply by our failure to provide enough competent teachers. Not simply by our failure to provide better facilities and more space. Not simply by our failure to educate properly the most gifted.

These failures are tragic enough. But *we have compounded the tragedy by our failure to realize the importance of the curriculum in secondary education, and by our failure to sense the vital connection between education and national security.*

As these words are being written there is little doubt that the American people are grimly conscious of some hard educational facts:

iii

we have fallen not simply far short of the Russians but far short of our own capabilities and potentialities in the production of scientists and engineers.

Predictions and warnings of this have been appearing almost daily in the public press since 1950. As a people, however, we are prone to postpone action until a crisis of some sort jars us from our lethargy.

A crisis of that sort has indeed come upon us—as is plainly evident in the Seven-point Program recently presented to President Eisenhower by the Department of Health, Education, and Welfare. Whether Congress will accept this program in whole or in part is not yet known, but of one thing we may be sure: Whether by neglect or design, we have made our public schools what they are. *If we now think they are not what they should be, we should not blindly plan to change them until we know what they have been doing and how they came to be doing it.*

We do not naively suppose that scientists are born and not made. If the Russians feed their elementary and high school students a diet heavy with mathematics and science and foreign languages, should we therefore do the same? What part should the humanities play in the education of a scientist? What part should science play in the education of nonscientists? If the Russians gear their educational methods and studies to the pace of the most gifted, is that the proper path for us? If they permit no electives, place the less gifted in less difficult studies, and send only the elite to college, are those the solutions to our probelms? Is a democracy capable of coping with the dilemma of providing for the proper education of the many *and* the few ?

These are not easy questions to answer and most of them cannot be answered merely by the expenditure of more money. But answer them we must.

This study, begun now some four years ago, attempts to present some fundamental facts about our educational system that will, it is hoped, help us to understand our educational problems more clearly. It centers mainly but not exclusively on the high school curriculum. It traces the changes that have taken place in high school studies, primarily since 1890, and relates to those changes student enrollments in the various subjects. It covers the entire curriculum from 1889-90 through 1948-49 in six different years selected as nearly as possible at ten-year intervals. Data for foreign languages are continued through the fall of 1954; for the other cumulative subjects—mathematics and science—through the fall of 1956.

Does the choice of subjects in high school determine the choice of an undergraduate major in college? Do student enrollments in mathematics, science, and foreign languages have any relationship to each other? Do they vary widely among geographical regions? Have these variations themselves changed over the years? Have boys always outnumbered girls in the cumulative subjects? What geographical regions send the largest proportions of public high school graduates to college? Were the public high schools more nearly preparatory schools for college in the two decades before and after 1900 than they are today?

These are some of the questions this study attempts to answer.

The answers may or may not be pleasing; in many cases they are most certainly not final. For education, particularly secondary education, is inherently dynamic in a democratic society. As it changes, its quality always depends primarily on the quality of public concern. Our high school education was not *good before* and *bad after* the two Sputniks were put into orbit. Its quality did not magically change overnight. What *did* change was our *attitude* toward it. Our national security was not endangered by the two small spheres circling the earth or by the fact that the Russians put them there first. But it was and is endangered by our unwillingness to pay the mental and financial price necessary to develop and maintain a sound educational program at all levels of our educational house. The essential ingredients of that program must be science *and* the humanities, *not* science *or* the humanities.

We must face these facts realistically; to that end this study is dedicated. As it takes its place among the many that have been made of our schools, a word to the reader may be in order: Although there are many cross references, a deliberate effort was made to write each chapter as a separate and independent unit. A variety of statistical information, not covered in the text, or broken down in a different way, is contained in the Appendices. These data make it possible for the reader to draw his own conclusions, in agreement or disagreement with those suggested by the writer.

One final note: The use of facts and figures is not meant to imply that the *quality* of education can be measured by statistics. But by means of these facts and figures, cold and lifeless though they may seem, we may be able to take the educational pulse of America and to prescribe with confidence for her educational health in the years to come.

JOHN F. LATIMER

Washington, D. C.

ACKNOWLEDGEMENTS

Over the several years this study has been in preparation my debt to friends and associates has piled high. It is a pleasant sort of debt because it can never really be paid. But it can be acknowledged and this I gladly do.

Some of the creditors are mentioned in appropriate notes close, as it were, to the scenes of their contributions. *Gratias eis quam maximas ago.*

Of the others I would make special mention of several. Miss Rose Marie Smith, Specialist in Educational Statistics in the U.S. Office of Education, helped me find my weary way through the morass of numbers and kept me up to date with information and publications issued by the Office of Education. Dr. Kenneth E. Brown, Specialist for Mathematics, furnished some pre-publication data from his most recent pamphlet (No. 120) on science and mathematics, at a time when such help was most needed. Dr. Ray C. Maul, Assistant Director of the Research Division of the National Education Association, explained a few of the intricate problems connected with teacher supply and demand. None of these of course should be charged with what may seem, in the opinion of some, errors of fact or of interpretation.

I would mention also Dr. Mitchell Dreese, who was Dean of the College of General Studies of The George Washington University when work on this volume began, and Dr. Oswald S. Colclough, Dean of Faculties, under whom it was completed. The encouragement they gave by permitting flexibility in my administrative schedule was an important complement to the time thus gained.

Only three people in addition to the publisher read the complete type-script. Each of the other two read it *in cursu* and somehow managed to survive. As chief critic of style and content I owe much to Dr. Craig R. Thompson, professor of English at Lawrence College. He could not entirely recast the writing habits of a lifetime but what he saved the readers from they will never know.

My wife knows because she played an even larger part in their salvation. With her it has been a thrice-read tale—and more. No one knows better than she the long hours and hard work that writing entails. No one knows better than I the blessings of a sympathetic patience and an understanding ear.

J.F.L.

CONTENTS

CHAPTER I

THE RISE OF PUBLIC EDUCATION

Nothing in the history of education can compare with the rise and development of the American system of free public education. Nothing in that system reflects more clearly the influence of democracy than the gradual evolution of the public high school and the unique role it has come to play in our educational and national life.

In colonial times the principle of elementary education for all was early established. The Protestant church required of its members a reading knowledge of the English Bible; the colonial government required of all inhabitants a reading knowledge of its laws.[1] Personal salvation depended upon the one, civil obedience on the other. Thus each householder had a religious and civil duty, in the absence of a public system of education, to provide the members of his family with the training necessary for reading the commandments of God and the laws of man. The affairs of daily life also made it practical to include some instruction in writing and arithmetic.

Different communities varied so widely in their methods of providing elementary instruction in these three subjects that in New England some states passed regulatory laws and set up machinery for their enforcement. But the laws were neither widely obeyed nor strictly enforced. Public sentiment in time proved more effective. In the middle and southern colonies, where distances were greater and settlements less numerous, such matters were of local concern and initiative. In all the colonies teachers were difficult to obtain, and schools, whether taught by a local "dame" or by some "itinerant" pedagogue, were limited in number and poor in quality for many years. The wonder is that they existed at all, and that the arrangements, whatever they were, always included provisions for children and orphans of the poorer class.

On the secondary level education was much more restricted in purpose and scope. The primary purpose was to prepare youth for college and thus to maintain an educated class from which would come ministers, and teachers, and citizens fitted for leadership in legislative and judicial bodies. Outside of New England such education was also considered necessary to prepare members of the landed aristocracy for their roles as country gentlemen or squires. Particu-

1

larly in the South it had long been the custom to send young men to colleges in England, and often to the grammar schools there, in preparation for such a life. George Washington's older brother was among those so educated, and he himself had all but started when destiny intervened.

Although grammar schools began with what we call the fourth or fifth grade, for many years there was little connection between them and the elementary schools. Many seven-year-olds had to be given special home instruction by parents or tutors before they could enter the grammar school. The expense of such instruction and the cost of tuition served to restrict such education to a relatively small minority.

Another and even greater barrier to larger enrollments was the curriculum. Since the curriculum of the early colleges was primarily Latin and Greek, the grammar schools' had no choice but to get their pupils ready for such studies, and the students had no choice but to accept such academic fare. Many of them could not see it through. Latin received the greater emphasis, and the extent to which it was studied can scarcely be realized today. The usual procedure in grammar school called for seven years of Latin and three or four years of Greek. The pupil spent the first two years in memorizing Latin forms, vocabulary, and grammar. Graded readers were then introduced and these were followed by standard Latin authors—Caesar, Cicero, and Vergil—and several usually read now in college, if they are read at all. Greek was studied less intensively and extensively. Since Latin was studied first, a certain knowledge of its grammar was assumed, and the early Greek grammars were often written in Latin. The Greek authors most read were Xenophon and Homer, but The New Testament in Greek with a Latin translation probably received the greatest attention.

Since the few colleges in existence required a speaking knowledge of Latin for entrance until about 1700, the grammar school also emphasized its oral use. So great was the emphasis on writing and speaking Latin that some parents complained that their children had difficulty in speaking and writing English. There was no formal study of English grammar. It was learned through the study of Latin and Greek. Latin writers served as models of elegant style for original compositions in Latin prose and poetry. Some knowledge of ancient history and life was gleaned from the Latin and Greek authors studied in class and perhaps from some outside reading assigned to students in advanced classes.

This was the type of secondary education that prevailed throughout

the colonies down to the Revolutionary War, and there is no doubt
that it did not appeal to many students whose parents were well able
to pay tuition charges. By modern standards they were almost ridicu-
lously low and not excessive even for the colonial period. Information is lacking about the number of schools and their total enrollments. It is fairly certain that each town or community of any size
had at least one grammar school of sorts and that the heaviest concentration was in New England.[3] Some of them became famous in
their own day, and several in New England have maintained their
reputation to the present time.

Although many of the early grammar schoolmasters were ministers,
those with the greatest reputation were laymen and might even be
called professionals. The most famous of these was Ezekiel Cheever.
He began teaching in Quinnipiac, now New Haven, in 1638. Seventy
years later he retired as headmaster of the renowned Boston Latin
School, only a few months before his death. Not only did he set a
record for teaching that has never yet been equalled, but most of the
prominent New Englanders of his day were his pupils, and a little
Latin text he wrote was the first of its kind written and published in
America. In a funeral sermon delivered September 8, 1708, two weeks
after Cheever's death, one of his former pupils, Cotton Mather, said
of him that he was a teacher "than whom New England had known
no better." Many of his students joined in paying similar tributes.

Most of the teachers, however, were not comparable to Cheever;
the scarcity of good teachers was a perennial problem then as now.[4]
One of the difficulties was inadequate salaries. In the course of his
sermon Mather had a few things to say on the subject that have a
strangely modern tone, even in his pompous rhetoric:

"These our School-Masters, deserve a great Encouragement. We
are not wise for our Children if we do not greatly encourage them.
The PARTICULAR PERSONS, who have their children, in the Tutelage of
Skillful and Careful School-Masters, ought to make them suitable
recompenses. Their Stipends are generally far short of their Deserts.
They deserve Additional Compensations . . .

"To feed our Children, to Cloath our Children, To do anything for
the Bodies of our Children; . . . we count no Expense too much; At
the same time to have the minds of our Children Enriched with the
most valuable Knowledge, . . . To What Purpose? is the cry: a little
Expense, how heavily it goes off! My Brethren, such things ought
not so to be."[5]

But they were; and the way of the schoolmaster, like that of the transgressor, has always been hard.

Teacher shortages, teacher salaries, and the curriculum—these three, but the curriculum was the greatest factor in the grammar school's decline. As population and wealth increased and social distinctions became less important, dissatisfaction with this type of education and its narrow curriculum became stronger and stronger. Not all students wanted to prepare for college. In place of so much Latin and Greek they hoped to substitute a few other courses that would be of more direct and immediate help in the shop and office or on the farm. But the curriculum had been fixed and theirs was not to reason why.

By 1700, however, another type of school beyond the elementary level had been set up in many of the larger towns and cities. They were privately conducted, and classes were generally held in the evening during the winter or summer months, and sometimes both, for the convenience of those who had daytime work. This arrangement also made it possible to use teachers who were employed full time during the day.[6]

The schools were open to any who wished to attend, and many of the students were sent by masters to whom, under varying legal requirements, they had been apprenticed. It was the duty of the master to look after the spiritual welfare of his charges and to have them trained in some useful work. The apprentices, both boys and girls, with the proper training, could become largely self-supporting and thus no longer dependent on public or private bounty. The evening schools, accordingly, were primarily vocational or practical in nature, and taught such courses as advanced mathematics, geography, map-making, navigation, surveying, astronomy, English, and even foreign languages. For the girls there were additional courses in needlework, china painting, and quilt making.

Such schools undoubtedly added to the dissatisfaction with the grammar schools and their narrow curriculum. Many families had capable sons who had no desire to go to college or to concentrate on Latin and Greek for six or seven years. These parents wanted schools for their sons that were a little more "respectable" than the evening schools but which would offer some of the subjects taught in them. They tried to get the curriculum of the grammar school changed or expanded, but to no avail.

Such resistance to change led eventually to the downfall of the grammar schools. It was Benjamin Franklin, that father of so many

different things, who finally succeeded in breaking their monopoly. With other interested and wealthy Philadelphians he founded a private academy in 1751. It had separate masters for each of three different schools—mathematical, English, and Latin. The last had been included somewhat against Franklin's wish, but he yielded to those who wished preparation for college to be one of the functions of the academy. In 1754 a philosophical school was added in which such subjects as logic, rhetoric, natural and moral philosophy were taught to advanced students. In 1755 the academy was reorganized. The Latin and philosophical schools were designated as the college, the English and mathematical schools as the academy. The college was named the College of Philadelphia and became in time the University of Pennsylvania.

Although Franklin's academy did not meet all of his expectations and hopes, it did set in motion a pattern that changed the direction of secondary education in this country. The timing could not have been more propitious. By the Revolutionary War the idea had been widely accepted. The war checked but did not stop the movement, and two academies that later became nationally famous, Phillips Andover and Phillips Exeter, were actually founded while the war was in progress. The close of the war gave the movement renewed impetus. America had finally won educational as well as political and economic independence, and the time was ripe for the idea of education as a public responsibility.

The first definite formulation of the idea came from the fertile brain of Thomas Jefferson. In 1779 he proposed to the Virginia House of Delegates a plan to establish a system of free public education in that commonwealth. The plan was too advanced for the times—and too expensive; it was never put into operation. But undoubtedly it fired the imagination of national and educational leaders, and probably played a part in influencing national legislation that soon followed.

In 1787 the Continental Congress passed a law known as the Northwest Ordinance, which provided the administrative machinery for the government of that vast region and set forth the arrangements under which the new states to be formed from it would be admitted to the union. One provision set aside the sixteenth section in each township for the maintenance and support of schools. This laid the foundations for the creation of permanent school funds which eventually formed a part of each state budget. Two years later Massachusetts made its district school independent of town authorities, and other states passed similar laws which gave each district local control over

its own schools. In 1791 the adoption of the Tenth Amendment gave the states all powers not reserved to the federal government. This was interpreted as authorization for the states to establish state-controlled systems of education, and at varying intervals each state proceeded to put that principle into effect.

By 1800 the movement for state systems of education was underway, and primarily on the two levels of elementary and higher education. By 1850 the concept of state taxation to support such undertakings had been generally accepted. Although not all states had both types of education until after 1870, the need for public high schools to fill the gap between the elementary school and college became more and more apparent. Some public provision had to be made for those who wished to prepare for college, and for the larger number who wished to prepare for more practical pursuits. The private academies, however, were performing both functions so well that their very existence was at once a hindrance and a help in the movement to establish free education on the secondary level. The very excellence of their performance for a long time made it seem unwise to replace them. But they were not under public control, and as private institutions they charged tuition. In time these two facts worked against them and helped to pave the way for the public high schools, which were patterned after them.

The rapidity with which the academies had spread after the Revolutionary War was ample evidence of the educational needs they were meeting. Some adopted the idea of broad curricula advocated by Franklin. Some were strictly college preparatory; others were strictly vocational. Some admitted boys only, some girls only, some both. They provided many denominations with the answers to their educational problems and religious needs. Most of them were under private control and governed by self-perpetuating boards; all received charters, and in some cases, authority to grant degrees, from various state legislatures. With the exception of a few that were set up to provide educational facilities for the poor, all charged tuition. Many of them provided training for teachers in the public elementary schools. Since none had to be bound by tradition or college entrance requirements, they suited their courses of study to the wishes of local communities, and became in effect the community colleges of their day.

The influence of the private academies in our educational history was enormous. The educational opportunities they offered gave great impetus to the concept of free public high schools. They served as models in some respects for manual-labor schools, which were imported

from Europe and flourished briefly between 1800 and 1840, and for military schools which became very popular after the founding of the U. S. Military Academy in 1802. They fostered education for women and stimulated interest in teacher training and education. Many of them developed into normal schools or expanded into colleges to which some remained attached as special preparatory schools or departments.

Most important of all perhaps was their role in shaping and developing the public high school system. Despite the wide variety and flexibility of their curricula, after 1800 the academies became the principal gateway for entrance into college. For this reason, and because of their unique contributions to education, many states supported them with public funds. In a few states a movement was started to have a system of academies, one in each county. Both of these developments were in line with the theory of state-founded and state-supported institutions of higher learning, which was making considerable headway in practice. There was one difference. Except in a relatively few cases the academies remained under private control and continued to charge tuition. Private control in the case of early colleges was one of the very reasons for the eventual establishment of state universities. The same logic had to apply to the academies.

The movement to establish public high schools was slow in starting and slow in making headway. It had many obstacles to overcome. The very existence of private academies was an obstacle in itself and in many communities pride in local academies was deep-rooted and strong. These factors created in those communities a reluctance to supply by taxation, facilities for all which many had been willing to provide for their own children as means and opportunity allowed. But there was an increasingly large number of citizens who could not afford such education for their children or who believed that the concept of free public education, to be consistent, should include education on the secondary level.

This feeling was strongest in the towns and cities where the concentration of industrial workers and tradesmen was building up a large middle class who felt that their needs and rights should be considered. It is not strange, therefore, that the first two public high schools that were opened in 1821, were located in two rapidly growing industrial centers, Boston and Portland. A few other cities and towns in Massachusetts and in neighboring states soon followed suit. In 1827 Massachusetts passed a law requiring a public high school in every town with 500 or more families. Several New England states passed

similar laws, and the actions of these New England states marked the real beginning of the public high school movement. By 1880 there were fewer than a thousand high schools throughout the country, but their growth since then has been one of the phenomena of our educational history. In 1900 the number of high schools reached 6,000, the number of private academies in 1850. The high schools had double the enrollment of the 1850 academies and almost double the number of teachers. Beginning in 1890 the high school enrollments approximately doubled each decade through 1930. Since that time the increases have been proportionately less rapid, but the numbers have been truly staggering. After a peak enrollment of six and one-half million in 1940-41, the depression-caused decrease set in and continued through 1948-49. Since that year enrollments have gradually increased, and in 1954-55 they passed the 1941 mark. By 1959-60 they are expected to exceed eight million.

As the number of high schools increased, the academies began to lose ground. By a pedagogical fate, just as the academies had replaced the old grammar schools, the high schools gradually replaced their academic parents. By 1890 the situation was no longer in doubt. For the academies the result was somewhat ironic. They contracted their broad curricula and became in effect the new grammar schools of the late nineteenth century. As college preparatory schools they developed special techniques and found ready public acceptance. In that capacity they are best known today, and in them many discriminating parents find the kind of education and instruction they want their children to have.

Strongly influenced by the academies, the early high schools adopted their slogan: Preparation of youth for practical life. It is interesting to note that the curriculum of the "English Classical School," as the first high school was named in Boston, did not include any foreign languages, ancient or modern. As the name implied, the curriculum centered around English—grammar, literature, composition, and declamation. The next heaviest concentration was in mathematics which included arithmetic, algebra, plane geometry, navigation, surveying, and at least one additional course not named. Other subjects were ancient, modern, and American history; natural philosophy—natural science was the later name—including astronomy; logic, moral and political philosophy. Great emphasis was put on public speaking during the first two years. Science came only in the last year. The course lasted for three years and was open only to boys twelve or

more years of age.   Separate high schools for girls were established
also, but most high schools were for both sexes.

In time the curricula of the high schools varied as much as those
of the academies after which they were patterned, and the new subjects introduced by both types caused some changes in college entrance requirements.   By 1850 most colleges had added to their list
algebra, geometry, geography, and ancient history.   By 1880 physics
and chemistry, several of the natural sciences, solid geometry and
trigonometry, English literature and rhetoric were either required
or acceptable.   By that same date many of the colleges also accepted
modern foreign languages, but in most instances still insisted on four
years of Latin.   Advanced mathematics was allowed by many colleges
as a substitute for Greek.

Since the number of college-bound high school students was increasing, most high schools had to add Latin to their curricula.   Many
added Greek and modern foreign languages because of local demands.
For the great majority of students, however, high school ended their
formal education.   To satisfy their needs and demands had been the
primary function of the early high schools.   To meet the needs and demands of both groups put a double burden on the high schools that
grew increasingly heavy.   This dual function caused instructional, administrative, and financial problems that have not yet been satisfactorily solved.

An additional complicating factor was introduced by the passage
of state compulsory education laws.   Massachusetts led the way in
1852.   Many states vigorously opposed laws of this kind, and only
twenty-six had enacted such legislation by 1890 and thirty-two by
1900.   It was 1918 before the other twelve had come into the fold.
Even without compulsory attendance, high school enrollments would
have increased enormously in the natural course of nature and events.
But the presence of a great body of students who had to stay in high
school against their inclination created a situation for which there
were no real educational or administrative precedents.

Throughout the years the widely differing interests and abilities of
willing and eager students have presented enough problems in themselves.   Those presented by unwilling or indifferent students have
added enormously to the complex and difficult tasks of administrators
and teachers and taxed the ingenuity and patience of all.   The combined weight of all these diverse problems has had a great influence
in the development of teaching methods and in the expansion of the

curriculum.   Each of these would require separate treatment, but only the curriculum fits into the pattern of this study.

[1] The first embodiment of this principle is found in the *Massachusetts Law of 1642*. See *Cubberley*, pp. 12-26.   For references and bibliography see Appendix A.

[2] The full name was Latin Grammar School.   Since English grammar was not studied in England or America until well after 1700, the name was usually shortened to Latin School or Grammar School.

[3] Although the title is somewhat misleading, a very convenient and interesting account of our elementary and secondary school systems down to 1787 is found in "Public Schools During the Colonial and Revolutionary Period in the United States," by The Rev. A. D. Mayo. CR 1893-94, I, pp. 639-738.

[4] The number and caliber of the early teachers have perhaps been underestimated. For an excellent account of the teacher and his contributions to American education and life, see *The American Teacher*, by Willard S. Elsbree, American Book Co., 1939.

[5] Mather's funeral sermon bears the title, *Corderius Americanus*.   It was adapted from the Latinized surname of Mathurim Cordier, a famous French teacher who died in the year Shakespeare was born, 1564.   With a Latin title, but written in English, the sermon is one of the most amazing documents in American literature.   See "Ezekiel Cheever and His Accidence," by John F. Latimer, *The Classical Weekly*, Vol. 43, No. 12 (March 6, 1950), pp. 179-183.

[6] *Knight* (1), pp. 122-23. *Cubberley*, pp. 428, 587-88, puts the date after 1800.

CHAPTER II

EDUCATION TAKES COUNT

The year 1867 marked a turning point in the history of public education in this country. In March of that year President Andrew Johnson appointed Henry Barnard the first United States Commissioner in the newly-created Department of Education. In July 1869 the Department lost its independent status and was made part of the Department of the Interior under the title Office of Education. The title was changed to Bureau of Education in 1870 but back to Office of Education in 1929. In July 1939 the Office was moved from the Department of the Interior to the newly-established Federal Security Agency, and in April 1953 it became a part of the Department of Health, Education, and Welfare.

The purpose of the original Department of Education, as stated in the enacting law, was to collect "such information and facts as shall show the condition and progress of education in the several States and Territories, and of diffusing such information respecting the organization and management of school systems and methods of teaching as shall aid the people of the United States in the establishment and maintenance of efficient school systems, and otherwise promote the cause of education throughout the country."[1]

Barnard interpreted the provisions of the law literally and liberally. The annual reports which he initiated surveyed the whole realm of public and private education from the primary school through college. They were contemporary documents that enabled educators and laymen in one section to compare their educational problems and progress with those in all other sections of the country, and with those in many foreign countries. They presented detailed summaries of educational congresses and exhibitions at home and abroad. They became the best single source in America of information about the theories of prominent educators, past and present, throughout the world.

This broad treatment of education had begun in several educational journals that flourished intermittently in a few of the states before 1850. It was particularly noticeable in the thirty-two volumes of the *American Journal of Education*, which Barnard himself founded, edited, and published from 1855 to 1882. It was the first publication

of its kind in this country that was national—and international—in
status and scope. It brought Barnard into national prominence, and
became his model for the reports he wrote as U. S. Commissioner of
Education.

Barnard's reports and those of his successors naturally gave the
greatest amount of attention to American education. Some of the
then current topics have a familiar ring. In 1870, for example, there
were discussions of kindergarten culture; medical education; illiteracy;
school supervision; society, crime, and criminals; and school finances.
In 1886-87 (in 1882-83, the annual reports had been changed to coincide with the school year) there were special articles on the perennial
problem of shortening and enriching school programs; in 1889-90,
on methods to be employed in the reformation of juvenile offenders;
in 1899-1900, on vaccination requirements in city schools; in 1909-10,
on the physical welfare of school children, college and high school
standards; and in 1914-15, on increasing facilities for practice teaching, national aid for vocational education, the kindergarten and educational experimentation, and the education of backward children.

Not so familiar are such items as: the relations of education to
labor (1870); the English language in Indian schools (1886-87);
educational training for railway service (1898-99); introduction of
domestic reindeer into Alaska (1899-1900); movable schools of domestic science (1909-10); influence of state inspectors of high schools
(1914-15).

One of the most important functions of the Bureau of Education
was to act as a central clearing house for curriculum matters at all
levels. In addition to specific articles dealing with curriculum problems
and developments, each annual report contained various kinds of
statistical tables. Although Barnard published many valuable data
during his three years as Commissioner, the first systematic efforts to
obtain curriculum information on the high school level did not begin
until 1871. Between 1871 and 1949 the reports varied considerably,
not only in completeness and accuracy, but also in the type and
arrangement of statistical data presented.

During the first period, 1871-1875, the tables prepared by the Bureau gave state and national enrollments in three general curricula—
English, classical, and modern languages. The figures were from
private secondary schools only. The number of schools reporting
increased from 638 to 1,143, and their enrollments from 80,000 to
108,000 during the period.

In the second period, 1876 to 1885-86, an effort was made to include

statistics from public high schools. Although the number of public high schools reporting increased from 192 to 471, and their enrollments from 23,000 to 70,000, most if not all of them were in city systems. During the same period the number of private secondary schools reporting increased from 1,229 to 1,440, and their enrollments from 106,- 600 to 151,000. Some general curriculum information, with state and national enrollments, was given for the private schools, but not for the public high schools.

Although there were variations from year to year, during both of these periods the national figures for private schools showed in general that enrollments in the classical and modern languages curricula were approximately the same. Together they totaled about half of the enrollments in the English curriculum. The number of students preparing for the classical course in college, on the other hand, was usually about twice as large as the number preparing for the scientific course both in college and in special scientific schools.

As the number of public high schools reporting to the Bureau increased, their enrollments became sufficiently large to merit separate tabulation of statistics. This was done for the first time in 1886-87. The figures were presented in two separate tables, one for schools supported wholly by public funds, the other for those only partly supported by such funds. There were 419 schools in the first category, 96 in the second. Their combined enrollments equalled 80,000. The total enrollment of the simon pure public schools outnumbered that of the others six to one.[2]

The curriculum data provided set a pattern that was to continue for many years. Instead of enrollments in each of three curricula—classical, modern languages, and English—those for five different subjects were tabulated. These were Latin, Greek, French, German, and English.[3]

Subject percentages were given for each state, for each of five geographical regions into which the states were divided, and for the country as a whole. Thus, for the first time in the history of American education, it was possible to get some idea of what the public high school students were studying, and how the subject enrollments varied, in the different sections. That the list of subjects was far from complete was indicated by the tabulation for 1887-88. In that year figures and percentages for mathematics, physics, chemistry, and other sciences not named, were added. Since all of these figures came primarily from city school systems,[4] two years more were to

elapse before a fairly comprehensive picture of the high school curriculum appeared.

This was made possible by a startling development. In 1888-89
the number of public high schools reporting had increased to 713.
Their total enrollment was 125,500. In that same year 1,324 private
secondary schools reported, with a total enrollment of 146,500. One
year later the situation was abruptly reversed: 2,526 public high
schools reported, with a total enrollment of 203,000. This was in sharp
contrast to a total enrollment of 95,000 reported in 1,652 private
schools. The number of public high schools had not more than tripled
within the space of one year; the Bureau had simply succeeded in
reaching more of them outside of cities. The public high school had
clearly become the dominant feature on the secondary education
landscape.

Before describing some of the statistical changes that took place
in 1889-90, which continued for varying periods, it is necessary to add
a few words about the annual reports. They continued to appear each
year through 1914-15. But the tremendous increase in the number of
high schools and in high school enrollments made the task of gathering and tabulating statistics more and more complex and expensive.
Beginning in 1916 the reports were issued biennially. The last complete report covered the biennium 1952-54.[5]

The tremendous increases in high school enrollments also affected
the gathering and publication of curriculum statistics. From 1886-87
through 1905-06 individual subject enrollments and percentages were
published each year, but thereafter at varying intervals: 1909-10,
1914-15, 1921-22, 1927-28, 1933-34, and 1948-49.[6] Statistics of enrollments and percentages according to curricula also varied. Through
1909-10 enrollments and percentages were given in two curricula,
classical and scientific. Between 1910-11 and 1913-14 figures were
given for eight different curricula: classical, scientific, commercial,
manual training, teacher training, agricultural, domestic economy,
and academic. In 1914-15 enrollment figures in the scientific, and
classical curricula were omitted; they were possibly included under
the academic. After 1914-15 no curriculum statistics of any kind appeared except for the four years indicated above. In those years
enrollments according to curricula were not given, and regional tabulations were discontinued.

Several other features of the annual reports deserve mention. Each
of the 18 reports between 1890 and 1910 inclusive that contained complete curriculum surveys also gave information about the college plans

of the students. One set of data gave the number and percentage of the total high school population that were preparing for college. Another set broke this down according to sex, and according to the college curriculum, classical or scientific, for which the students were preparing. Still another, the total number and percentage of the graduates who were *prepared* for college, the percentage of boys who were prepared, and the percentage of girls. These last data did not indicate the particular curriculum for which they were prepared.

Most of this information, except that dealing with the two curricula, was also given in the four curriculum surveys made between 1915 and 1934, or could be obtained from data contained in them. A special table in the survey of 1933-34 summarized these statistics for graduates of the classes of 1921, 1925, 1929, and 1933.[7]

Another special feature of considerable importance for this study remains. Because of its bearing on the curriculum problem, discussion of it is reserved for the next chapter.[8]

[1] CR 1870, p. 5. For an explanation of the abbreviations used in this study see Appendix B.

[2] CR 1886-87, Table 31, pp. 496-99; Table 33, pp. 512-13. Tables 32 and 34 gave statistics for private schools. For a useful statistical review of the number of all secondary schools and students reported to the Bureau of Education between 1871 and 1894, see CR 1893-94, I, pp. 36-37.

[3] In the tabulation of subjects in private schools for girls, Greek and English were omitted. In the private schools for boys and in those for both sexes, another category, "not distributed," was added. These differences made it impossible to compare subject enrollments in the public high schools with those in the private schools, interesting as such a comparison might have been.

[4] Despite their incompleteness, the figures and percentages for these two years are used in Chapter IV, where the developments of the different subject matter fields are traced.

[5] Chapters of report were published in 1956 and 1957.

[6] From 1890 through 1910 the statistics included the number and percentage of boys and of girls studying the various subjects. From 1915 through 1934 only figures were given, but these made it possible to calculate the respective percentages. For this type of information in certain subjects see Appendix C.

[7] See Appendix D for several historical tables dealing with high school students and college.

[8] This statement is not intended to imply that such discussion will exhaust the various types of information given in the reports issued by the Office of Education. Only those have been mentioned which fit into the purpose of this study.

CHAPTER III

AN INNOCENT PARADOX

In our system of public education the high school has long played a dual role. As pointed out in Chapter I, its original function was to prepare students for practical life. But under the pressure of diverse needs of a democratic society this function was gradually enlarged to include preparation for college. In its attempts to carry out this twofold mission, the high school was caught on the horns of a perplexing curriculum dilemma.

The story of this dilemma has been strangely neglected in the current controversy about the high school and its place in our educational life. It is to be found in the reports published by the United States Office of Education. But valuable as those reports are, they have become, with one exception, the all but forgotten documents of American education. And paradoxically enough, that one exception contains the innocent cause of some of the confusion that exists today about the development of the high school curriculum. An explanation of the paradox is in order.

A brief account of the curriculum surveys made by the Office of Education was given in the preceding chapter. Although the surveys varied in the amount and kind of statistical information presented, two features remained constant in all the surveys made between 1889-90 and 1948-49. Among the various tables there was always one that gave state and national subject enrollments, and another that gave corresponding percentages for certain subjects.

In 1889-90 another table was added that gave national subject enrollments and percentages only. It provided a convenient national summary of curriculum developments and showed at a glance the proportion of high school students enrolled in various subjects. As the summary table appeared year after year, it became historical in nature. In the Annual Report for 1894-95, for instance, the summary table showed the proportion of high school students enrolled in various subjects each year between 1889-90 and 1894-95 inclusive. In the Annual Report for 1899-1900 the historical summary table gave similar percentages for the years 1889-90 to 1899-1900 inclusive. In

the Report for 1904-05, it covered the years 1894-95 to 1904-05, but in the period 1909-1910, the years 1889-90 to 1909-10 were covered.[1]

In 1914-15 three changes were made in the historical summary table: actual subject enrollments as well as percentages were given; instead of using each annual summary table since 1889-90, those at five-year intervals were chosen, and the total high school enrollment for each of those years was included. This format and type of selectivity occurred in each of the other four historical summary tables published.[2]

Through 1914-15 the subjects listed in the historical summary tables corresponded very closely to those in the longer and more detailed statistical tables. The differences between the two first became noticeable in 1899-1900, but they did not become pronounced until 1921-22, as the following table shows:

TABLE A[1]

CONTRAST BETWEEN NUMBER OF HIGH SCHOOL SUBJECTS TABULATED IN DETAILED STATISTICAL TABLES AND IN HISTORICAL SUMMARY TABLES IN CERTAIN YEARS BETWEEN 1889-90 AND 1948-49

	1889-90	1899-1900	1909-10	1921-22[3]	1933-34[3]	1948-49[3]
Detailed Tables	13	29	35	68	111	141
Historical Tables	13[2]	18	23	44	47	52

[1] The Annual Reports for these years were used as the primary basis for this study. For the number of subjects in the "detailed tables," see Chapter V, Table 14.

[2] Since the table for this year contains statistics for that year only, it is not strictly historical.

[3] During these years some related subjects were grouped under a single heading in the historical summary tables. The figure 44, 47, and 52, therefore, are not quite accurate.

In this table the number of subjects was listed in the second line as they were given in the historical summary tables of the year indicated. In 1933-34 and again in 1948-49, however, the historical summary tables omitted some of the subjects previously listed in those of a given year. These numerical differences are shown in the table on the next page.

TABLE B [1]

CONTRAST BETWEEN THE NUMBER OF HIGH SCHOOL SUBJECTS TABU-
LATED IN DETAILED STATISTICAL TABLES IN CERTAIN YEARS BE-
TWEEN 1889-90 AND 1948-49 AND THE NUMBER TABULATED FOR THOSE
YEARS IN THE HISTORICAL SUMMARY TABLES OF 1933-34[2] AND 1948-49[3]

	1889-90	1899-1900	1909-10	1921-22	1933-34	1948-49
Detailed Tables	13	29	35	68	111	141
Historical Table 1933-34	12	16	21	43	47	
Historical Table 1948-49	12	14	20	40	46	52

[1] See footnotes 1, 2, and 3 of Table A above.
[2] *Bul. 1938, No. 6*, Table 1.
[3] BS 1948-50, Ch. 5, Table 7.

Although the differences between the figures in the historical summary tables of 1933-34 and 1948-49 are slight, the contrast between
them and the figures in the detailed tables is progressively greater
from 1889-90 on. This has led to the paradox mentioned in the second
paragraph of this chapter.

Chapter 5 of the Biennial Survey for 1948-50 contains the last curriculum survey on a national basis made by the U. S. Office of Education. It is naturally more widely available and readily accessible
than any of the others. Various critical and defensive comments made
in recent years indicate that Table 7 of this chapter has been used
as the basis of comparison between the curriculum of today and that
of fifty and sixty years ago. Tables A and B show at a glance how un-
safe and misleading a comparison based on such a source would be.
A few small examples will partially illustrate the point.

Table 7, referred to above, lists Earth Science as having been taught
from 1900 on. Reference to the original documents shows that the
subject was first listed in 1948-49. In that year astronomy, geology,
physical geography, and possibly a subject called earth science were
all grouped together in Table 7 under the heading *earth science*.[3] The
first three subjects were listed separately through 1933-34.

Reference to the original documents also shows that astronomy was
taught in the high schools of the country from 1895 through 1933-34,
and Greek from 1890 through 1927-28. The omission of these two
subjects from Table 7 might lead to the erroneous conclusion that they
had never been offered in the high schools at all.

But the most startling omission of all is English, which is not listed until 1900. What would this mean to the casual reader of Table 7? That some time between 1890 and 1900 English was finally introduced into the high school curriculum? And what would the same reader judge about the percentage of students enrolled in English? Table 7 shows a steady increase between 1900 and 1949. Subject enrollments, as the table correctly shows, did increase during that period. What the table does not correctly show is that proportionately subject enrollments were greater in 1910 and 1915 than before or since. English was in the curriculum in 1890 and long before—in two forms: Rhetoric and English Literature. The Office of Education did not collect reliable data on the former until 1894-95 or on the latter until 1897-98. From 1900 through 1915 even the figures and percentages given tell only half the English story!

These examples show some of the limitations of Table 7 and with what caution it must be used even for the subjects actually listed. It does provide a convenient overview of curriculum developments in "certain" subjects between 1890 and 1949. That is all. To use it as a complete and sufficient summary of the curriculum story is to mistake its purpose; to draw conclusions on the basis of partial evidence can only result in confusion and misunderstanding.

One additional fact will emphasize the importance and necessity of presenting all the evidence before the developments that have taken place in the high school curriculum can be made plain to the American people. The fact is very simple, but it has been largely overlooked in recent years: Before 1909-10 not a single historical summary table listed a single non-academic subject. In 1909-10 only two were listed, agriculture and domestic economy. Since the subjects listed in each historical summary table were repeated, with some variations and omissions, in later tables, to the casual observer or commentator one conclusion might seem reasonably obvious, to wit: before 1909-10 the high schools offered only academic subjects. As the original documents of the curriculum surveys receded more and more into the limbo of the past, such a conclusion might be considered even more reasonable in recent years than ever before.[4] But reasonable or unreasonable, the conclusion is wrong, as the next chapter will show.

---

[1] The 1909-10 summary table was based on the summary tables of 18 years. As pointed out in Chapter II, statistics on individual subject enrollments and percentages

were published each year between 1889-90 and 1905-06, and thereafter in 1909-10, 1914-15, 1921-22, 1927-28, 1933-34, and 1948-49.

[2] For the years in which they appeared in the Annual Reports see Note 1 above.

[3] BS 1948-50, Ch. 5, Table 7. See also pp. 13-14, and the writer's Chapter IV, Table 3.

[4] Chapter 5 of BS 1948-50, which contains Table 7, referred to so often, was published in the fall of 1951.

A BAKER'S DOZEN

The three-thousandfold growth in high school enrollments since 1890 has brought in its wake many problems. Public discussion has produced great awareness of many of them, such as teacher shortages and salaries, inadequate school buildings and equipment, and has put these and related problems into sharp fiscal and educational focus.

But in our concern for such tangible matters we have tended to overlook the real foundation of our educational house—the course of study or curriculum. It too has had a phenomenal growth. At the rate of six courses each academic year it would take a student almost 46 years to complete all of the 274 courses offered by the high schools in 15 or more states in 1948-49![1] At the same rate a student could have finished all the courses offered in 1889-90 in a maximum of six years.

Such quantitative changes between 1890 and 1949 did not take place all at once, but they did occur more rapidly than is commonly known. The rate at which new subjects came into the curriculum, the nature of the additions, and the shifts in educational emphasis that resulted, make a story that is known primarily to school administrators and historians. Some account of that story, as part of our educational history, may have interest in itself. Some acquaintance with it may give us a better background for understanding the educational problems that confront us today.

It was pointed out in Chapter II that the curriculum pattern in public high schools first began to emerge in 1889-90. Between that year and 1948-49 the U. S. Office of Education published 26 Annual Reports and 17 Biennial Surveys. These 43 reports contained 23 complete curriculum surveys. Six of these, selected as closely as possible at ten-year intervals, were used as the primary basis for this study. They appeared in 1889-90, 1899-1900, 1909-10, 1921-22, 1933-34, 1948-49.[2]

Tables listing all subjects offered during each of these six years would be extremely interesting and useful. They would show the progressive additions to the curriculum in all subject matter fields, as the high school expanded its efforts to satisfy the diverse educational needs and abilities of a constantly increasing high school population.

21

Such comprehensive tables for the years after 1909-10, however, would be impractical because of their length. Comments about so many different subjects in the last three survey years would become confusing. The trees would be lost in the forest. To overcome these difficulties, at least in part, it seems feasible and logical to present the additions as they occurred in each of the thirteen broad subject matter fields into which the high school curriculum was eventually divided—a baker's dozen.

In the tables that follow statistics for each separate subject are given as percentages. Each percentage shows the proportion of high school students studying a given subject in each of the six selected years. To give some approximate clue to the actual numbers, the total high school enrollment in thousands, grades 9-12, is given, in two separate figures for three of the years, immediately under each year listed.[3] These figures are repeated in each of the thirteen tables.

Each table also contains total percentages, and the total number of subjects offered during a given year. The "total percentages" provide a convenient way of comparing all enrollments in one subject matter field with those in another. Since many students often study more than one subject in a given field, the subject enrollments in that field often represent, *not different* students but *all* students taking different subjects in the field at the same time. English is a good example (see Table 5). Total percentages, therefore, show the relative strength or popularity of each subject matter field in the same year, and indicate the proportionate changes that took place in each field year after year.[4]

The Bureau of Education published fairly complete statistics on only four of the thirteen subject-matter fields for 1890. Data on three others were published for 1900, and on three more for 1910. Information on all thirteen was published for the first time for the year 1914-15.

These facts determined the order of presentation, with one exception, for the tables that follow. That exception, Teacher Training, is placed at the end of the chapter for two reasons: separate statistics on specialized courses, which were undoubtedly offered, were not available. Although it played a negligible role in the history of the high school curriculum, it is included as a separate subject-matter field.

After the statistical data are presented in each table, a brief historical sketch traces the developments within the subject-matter field, with comments on some of the more significant changes. As will be noted in various instances, many of the subjects were actually in the

high school curriculum some years before the Office of Education began to collect statistics on them. When the year in which the data were first published does not coincide with the first entry in a table, the date is given in parenthesis under or after the subject.

TABLE 1[1]

MATHEMATICS: PERCENTAGE OF PUBLIC HIGH SCHOOL STUDENTS GRADES 9-12 ENROLLED IN MATHEMATICS BY TYPE OF COURSE IN CERTAIN YEARS BETWEEN 1889-90 AND 1948-49

	1890	1900	1910	1922	1934	1949
Enrollment in 1000's	203	519	739	2,155	4,497	5,399
			915	2,230	5,621	
Algebra	45.4	56.3	56.9	40.2	30.4	26.8
Geometry[2]	21.3	27.4	30.9	22.7	17.1	12.8
Trigonometry (1891-92)		1.9	1.9	1.5	1.3	2.0
General Mathematics					3.0	13.1
Arithmetic[3]				10.5	4.4	
Mathematics Review[4]						0.3
Total Percentages	66.7	85.6	89.7	74.9	56.2	55.0
Total Subjects	3	4	4	6	6	7

[1] Primary statistical sources for each year in this and subsequent tables are given in Appendix B. Specific reference to them and to other sources will be made as necessary. For the two enrollment figures between 1910 and 1934, see the reference in Note 3 of text. For subject percentages in the fall of 1952, 1954, and 1956, see Note 11 below.

[2] Figures for plane and solid geometry were not separated until after 1921-22. They show that plane geometry was largely studied for a year, solid, for a half-year. In this table they count as two subjects.

[3] In BS 1948-50, Ch. 5, Table 7, the figures and percentages for 1922 and 1924 are given under the entry for general mathematics. Arithmetic is not listed.

[4] Although several subjects or courses are included, the figures are negligible. All are counted as one subject.

Mathematics played a relatively small part in the curriculum of the colonial grammar schools. Although students learned some of the elements of arithmetic before entering the grammar school, for many years little effort was made to add to the instruction already given. The early colonial colleges included arithmetic in their curricula, and did not require it for entrance until after 1802.

The practical need for mathematics, as preparation for trade and business, was first met by the evening schools that began to spring up toward the end of the seventeenth century. Students in these schools did not usually go to college. After 1750 the private academies, following the lead of the evening schools, taught such subjects as commercial arithmetic, algebra, geometry, surveying, and navigation.

Their mathematics curricula were more extensive than those in most colleges and were instrumental in causing the colleges to add algebra (about 1820) and geometry (about 1844) to their entrance requirements. After 1821 the early public high schools, for many years primarily in cities, adopted the mathematics pattern of the academies. By 1887-88, and probably some years before that date, mathematics in all of its branches was the most popular high school subject.[5]

Among the individual subjects in mathematics, algebra has been consistently the strongest. Through 1933-34 there were generally two courses, elementary and advanced. By 1948-49 an intermediate course had been added. The table shows that algebra's percentage increased up to 1910. According to the records it increased only through 1905-06, when it reached 58 percent. Although it had dropped only slightly by 1910, its decrease after that was rather rapid. This percentage decrease was probably caused primarily by the decline of enrollments in elementary algebra. It is fairly certain that this was the case between 1933-34 and 1948-49. In both of these years enrollments in second-year algebra equalled about one-third of those in elementary algebra. But the percentage of ninth grade students enrolled in elementary algebra dropped from 70 in 1933-34 to 63.5 in 1948-49.[6]

One factor in the percentage decline of elementary algebra enrollments has been the competition of arithmetic and general mathematics. Even if it is true that only advanced arithmetic was offered in 1921-22,[7] in 1927-28 an elementary course, under the term *general mathematics*, was added.[8] In 1933-34 elementary and advanced arithmetic and general mathematics were listed separately, and in 1948-49, general mathematics and advanced general mathematics. Although arithmetic was not listed at all in the latter year, it was assumed, when it was reported as a subject in the ninth grade, that it was general mathematics.[9] It is probably pure coincidence that the percentage in algebra and general mathematics (both courses) in 1948-49 totaled approximately the percentage of algebra alone in 1921-22.

Since plane geometry would not ordinarily be studied by a student who had not had at least a year of algebra, decline of elementary algebra percentages meant an almost inevitable decline of those in plane, but not necessarily in solid geometry or in trigonometry. In 1933-34 enrollments in plane geometry were almost nine times as large as those in solid; in 1948-49, almost seven times as large. During this period actual enrollments in plane geometry decreased, those in solid geometry and in trigonometry, increased. The explanation would seem fairly obvious. General mathematics, which increased consid-

erably during this same period, attracted the weaker students away from first-year algebra. The beginning algebra students were better on the whole, and a larger number of them continued beyond plane geometry into solid geometry and an even larger number into trigonometry. This was probably the first time in high school history that trigonometry enrollments were larger than those in solid geometry. The percentage of students enrolled in trigonometry was higher between 1891-92 and 1897-98 than in any year since, through 1948-49. The lowest was 2.3% in 1897-98; the highest was 2.9%, in 1893-94.[10]

As the table shows, the turning point in mathematics was reached in 1910. Between 1890 and 1910 the percentages in algebra and geometry increased; proportionately, geometry's gain was slightly greater. During the twenty-year span geometry climbed slowly to its percentage peak; algebra reached its peak in 1906, but maintained a higher level in 1910 than in 1900. After 1910 a proportionate decline for both subjects set in. Between that year and 1922 algebra's loss was proportionately greater; between 1922 and 1934 the proportionate losses of the two subjects were about equal, but between 1934 and 1949 those of geometry were significantly larger.

Trigonometry, listed first in 1891-92, reached its percentage peak quickly—in 1893-94. After a period of proportionate decline through 1904-05, it began a gradual recovery, and in 1910 regained its 1900 level. Between 1910 and 1934 it reached an all-time low-water mark, but by 1949 it was slightly above its 1900 level.

Arithmetic, listed first at its percentage peak in 1922, hit a deep depression in 1934, but with the help of general mathematics reached a new peak in 1949. Despite the assistance of these two subjects, however, the total percentage in mathematics was less in 1949 than the percentage of algebra alone between 1897 and 1910.[11]

From colonial times down to about 1850 Latin and Greek constituted the educational twin suns around which the rest of the curriculum revolved. They were the be-all and know-all and almost end-all of the schoolboy's existence.

During this whole period, Latin was the major planet. To read Latin like English was a commonplace; to write Latin in a barbarous and anglicized imitation of Cicero was the mark of superiority; to speak Latin—as many did in some fashion—was a pre-ordination, first for Harvard or William and Mary or Yale, and then for the ministry or law or pedagogy.

TABLE 2

FOREIGN LANGUAGES: PERCENTAGE OF PUBLIC HIGH SCHOOL
STUDENTS GRADES 9-12 ENROLLED IN FOREIGN LANGUAGES BY TYPE
OF COURSE IN CERTAIN YEARS BETWEEN 1889-90 AND 1948-49

	1890	1900	1910	1922	1934	1949
Enrollment in 1000's	203	519	739	2,155	4,497	5,399
			915	2,230	5,621	
Latin	34.7	50.6	49.0	27.5	16.0	7.8
German	10.5	14.3	23.7	0.6	2.4	0.8
French	5.8	7.8	9.9	15.5	10.9	4.7
Greek	3.1	2.9	0.8	0.09		
Spanish			0.7	11.3	6.2	8.2
Italian				0.02	0.2	0.3
General Language					0.01	0.2
Total Percentages	54.1	75.6	84.1	55.0	35.7	22.0
Total Subjects	4	4	5	6	6	6

Between 1850 and 1890, Latin and Greek apparently went into an eclipse from which Greek never recovered. The earliest statistics available, although incomplete and perhaps inaccurate, show that the percentage of Latin enrollments declined from 37.0, in 1886-87,[12] to 34.7, in 1889-90. That was a low point for Latin until 1917-18 or 1918-19. During this period it reached a high point of 50.8% in 1903-04. In the same period, between 1898-99 and 1905-06, a little over 50% of the high school students studied Latin each year. In the six years immediately preceding 1898-99 the percentage varied from 43.1 to 49.7; from 1909-10 to 1913-14, it varied from 49.0 to 40.0.

The study of Latin has been declining since 1903-04. Its greatest loss was between 1909-10 and 1914-15, when it declined from 49.0% to 37.3. This was almost equalled by the loss between 1921-22 and 1933-34, as shown on the table.

Greek, never as strong as Latin even in colonial times, began to decline still further after 1886-87, when it reached a high point of 4.0%. It fell below 3.0 for the first time in 1899-1900. Its greatest loss came between that year and 1909-10, a period during which it was finally abolished as a college entrance requirement. Although it was listed among the regular high school subjects through 1927-28, after that year it was offered in only a few high schools of several states. It is now almost a lost continent on the high school map.

One factor in the decline of Greek was undoubtedly the growing

popularity of German and, to a less extent, of French. Some years before 1800 the academies had introduced French and German, and occasionally Italian, into their curricula. The early high schools, also emphasizing "practical" subjects, enlarged their language offerings for a time. But the opposition of the classicists was strong and qualified modern language teachers were scarce. In the 1870's, however, French and German won the final skirmish with Greek and Latin and became acceptable for entrance into most colleges.[13]

Although German declined between 1886-87 and 1889-90, after the latter year it increased gradually to its percentage peak of 24.4 in 1914-15. If it had not been for World War I, it almost surely would have overtaken Latin by 1921-22. But the war put a stop to all that. The Germans lost on land, on sea, and in the American classroom, where their language has been all but lost ever since. Its slow gains through 1933-34, and for a few years after, were again interrupted, and it became a war casualty for the second time.

Of the three modern languages, German was almost twice as strong as French until 1899-1900, about two and one-half times as strong between 1900 and 1909-10, almost three times as strong in 1914-15. French did not reach its percentage peak until 1921-22, but until recently it has declined consistently since then. Spanish began struggling for a foothold around 1900, and finally gained a place on the linguistic altas in 1909-10. It also reached its percentage peak in 1921-22. After a period of decline through 1933-34, it began to climb and in 1948-49 nosed out Latin for the first time as the leading high school foreign language.

Between 1890 and 1915 Latin was considerably stronger than all the other foreign languages combined. In 1927-28 the others pulled slightly ahead and increased their lead by a small margin in 1933-34. In 1948-49, with the weak help of Italian and general language, they outnumbered Latin students almost two to one.[14]

The battle of science for a place in the high school galaxy took place between 1850 and 1890. Natural philosophy, as physics was first called, and chemistry were considered practical subjects, in contrast to languages, literature, and history, and their values for mental discipline were long doubted. By 1887-88, however, the battle had been won. In that year over 72% of the high school students were enrolled in science courses. Physics was in the lead with 25.2%. Chemistry came next with 12.9%. Other science courses, not identified, totaled 34.5%.[15]

TABLE 3

SCIENCE: PERCENTAGE OF PUBLIC HIGH SCHOOL STUDENTS GRADES 9-12 ENROLLED IN SCIENCE BY TYPE OF COURSE IN CERTAIN YEARS BETWEEN 1889-90 AND 1948-49

	1890	1900	1910	1922	1934	1949
Total Enrollment in 1000's	203	519	739	2,155	4,497	5,399
			915	2,230	5,621	
Physics	22.8	19.0	14.6	8.9	6.3	5.4[1]
Chemistry	10.1	7.7	6.9	7.4	7.6	7.6[2]
Physical Geo. (1894-95)		23.4	19.3	4.3	1.6	
Geology (1894-95)		3.6	1.2	0.2	0.1	
Astronomy (1894-95)		2.8	0.5	0.1	0.1	
Earth Science						0.4[3]
Zoology			7.0	1.5	0.6	0.1
Physiology (1894-95)		27.4	15.3	5.1	1.8	1.0
Botany			15.8	3.8	0.9	0.1
Biology			1.1	8.8	14.6	18.4
General Science				18.3	17.7	20.8
Aeronautics						0.3
Total Percentage	32.9	83.9	81.7	58.4	51.3	54.1
Total Subjects	2	6	9	10	10	11

[1] Includes advanced and applied physics, fundamentals of electricity, radio and electronics, and fundamentals of machines. Enrollments in each of these were so small that the percentages were negligible. Not counted as separate subjects.

[2] Includes applied chemistry, which had a minute percentage.

[3] See Ch. III, Note 3. Counted as three subjects.

Although these figures were not complete or wholly accurate, there is little doubt that physics and chemistry were only two of several science subjects being offered in the high schools of the day. In 1889-90 statistics were confined to physics and chemistry, but five years later four other sciences were reported, two of which, physical geography and physiology, had enrollments larger than physics and considerably larger than chemistry. Physical geography increased during the next year. Although it decreased slowly until 1914-15, it maintained a sizeable lead over physics until 1909-10, but was only slightly ahead in 1914-15. Physiology followed almost exactly the same pattern. It ran, slightly but consistently, ahead of physical geography until 1904-05, fell slightly behind in 1909-10, and considerably behind in 1914-15. In 1921-22 physics, which had been declining slowly since 1893-94, was almost as strong as physical geography and physiology combined. Physics continued to lose through 1948-49, and the other two by that year had almost disappeared from the curriculum. Physical geogra-

phy was grouped with geology and astronomy, which were listed for
the first time in 1894-95, under the general term of earth science. If
physiology had been less human, it might have suffered the same
anonymity.

Through 1909-10, as indicated above, physical geography and
physiology were the chief rivals of physics for high school science
honors. Chemistry, which fluctuated less than the other three, was
the fourth member of the quartet until 1909-10, when it was replaced by a newcomer, botany, which ranked second to physical geography that year. Botany entered in full flower, but it faded rapidly,
and by 1948-49 was hanging on by only a stamen. Zoology entered
the lists with botany, but at a lower level, and by 1948-49 it was being
kept alive by the artificial heartbeats of a frog.

The greatest drop in the science field took place between 1909-10
and 1921-22. In this period the five leading subjects, physics, physical
geography, physiology, botany, and zoology suffered their most drastic
losses, and two new subjects entered the field. The two newcomers,
biology and general science, were destined to attract over half of the
total high school enrollments in science, and this they proceeded to do
as early as 1927-28, possibly a year or two before. In 1933-34 these
two subjects alone had 62% of the enrollments in science; in 1948-
49, 72%.

A law of diminishing returns seems to have been at work in the
sciences. Statistics on four new subjects were collected in 1894-95.
A year later enrollments in science reached their high point and lacked
only a little of tripling enrollments of 1889-90. The addition of three
other subjects in 1909-10 did not check the general decline, however,
which had begun after 1895-96. Between 1909-10 and 1921-22 chemistry and biology alone increased, but their gains, augmented greatly
by general science, were not enough to offset the decreases in all other
science subjects. The general decrease continued through 1933-34,
despite a slight gain in chemistry and a considerable gain in biology.
Between 1933-34 and 1948-49 chemistry held its own; the increases in
biology and general science were sufficient to offset the losses in all
other subjects and to show a slight gain in the whole field.[16]

The changes that took place in the number and variety of social
studies constitute one of the most striking phenomena in the development of American secondary education. During the colonial period
history did not appear as a separate subject. Some ancient history
was learned in connection with the study of Latin and Greek authors.

TABLE 4

SOCIAL STUDIES: PERCENTAGE OF PUBLIC HIGH SCHOOL STUDENTS
GRADES 9-12 ENROLLED IN SOCIAL STUDIES BY TYPE OF COURSE IN
CERTAIN YEARS BETWEEN 1889-90 AND 1948-49

	1890	1900	1910	1922	1934	1949
Enrollment in 1000's	203	519	739	2,155	4,497	5,399
			915	2,230	5,621	
General History[1]	27.3	38.2	55.0			
English History					2.9	0.5
Ancient History				17.2	6.8	1.5[2]
Medieval History				15.4[3]	6.2[3]	
Modern History						2.1
American History				15.3	17.4	32.3[4]
World History (1927-28)					11.9	16.2
State History					0.4	2.7
Latin American History						0.5
Industrial History					0.2	
Civil Gov't. (1897-98)		21.7[5]	15.6[5]	19.3[5]	6.0	8.0[6]
Com. Gov't. (1914-15)					10.4	9.5[7]
Psychology (1894-95)		2.4	1.0	0.9	0.3	0.9
Geography					2.1	
American Geography						0.6
World Geography						5.0
Prob. of Dem. (1927-28)					3.5	5.2
International Relations					0.2	0.2
Economics				4.8	4.9	4.7
Sociology				2.4	2.5	3.4
Consumer Education						0.6
Occupations					3.0	3.9
Orientation						2.1
Social Studies					2.5	
Total Percentages	27.3	62.3	71.6	78.2	78.8	99.4
Total Subjects	4	7	7	10	18	20

[1] This was the term used in 1889-90. In the next two surveys given in the table the entry read: "History (other than United States)." In BS 1921-22, Ch. 6, Tables 33 and 34, enrollments and percentages for four separate history subjects were given for the first time: American, English, ancient, medieval and modern. The historical summary table (Table 32) for that year lists these four as being in the curriculum since 1889-90, but the figures and percentages were not separated until 1921-22, as just indicated.

[2] Includes medieval history.

[3] Includes modern history (European).

[4] Approximately 9.5% of the total high school enrollment studied U. S. history in the ninth grade (Note 17 below), and 22.8%, in grades 10-12 or 31.6% of the total enrollment in those grades.

[5] Includes community government or civics. Enrollment figures for the two subjects were separated in 1914-15, combined in 1921-22, and separated thereafter.

[6] This was 11.1% of the enrollment in grades 10-12.

[7] See note 17.

The *Epitome* of Roman history, written by Florus in the second century, and the *Breviarium* of Eutropius, a survey of Roman history written in the fourth century, were common grammar school texts. Bilingual editions of these and of other classical historians and biographers, such as Herodotus, Thucydides, Livy, Suetonius, Tacitus, and Nepos, were in vogue, but they were read more for their grammatical or literary values than for their historical content.

Ancient history was first introduced into the curricula of the private academies, which began to spring up after 1750, and the early public high schools followed their example. By 1844 it was listed among college entrance requirements, and by that time courses in general history were being taught in many of the high schools and academies. It included ancient, English, medieval and modern European history.

Up until 1870 the teaching of American history was largely confined to the elementary schools. Although it was introduced in many high schools after that date, it did not make much headway until after the first world war. The first separate statistics on it appeared in the curriculum survey of 1921-22. Ancient history was still in the lead, with medieval and modern history next, American history a close third, and English history a weak fourth. Of these four only American history showed a gain in 1933-34, and again in 1948-49. By the end of this period the other three had almost disappeared from the curriculum, possibly because of the introduction of world history, first listed in 1927-28. The sevenfold increase in state history between 1933-34 and 1948-49 is an interesting local phenomenon, but it probably had little influence on the study of other subjects in history. It is also interesting to note that the Good Neighbor Policy had little effect on the high school history curriculum.

The social studies curriculum expanded slowly until 1921-22. After history, psychology was the first to enter. Never strong, it reached its percentage peak in 1894-95. By 1933-34 it had almost faded away, and its hold on life in 1948-49 was still precarious. Civil or American government entered the listings at its peak. Although community government or civics came in around 1909-10 or earlier, statistics for civil and community government were not separated until 1914-15. The former was slightly in the lead. By 1927-28 civics, which was primarily a ninth grade subject, had gained a two-to-one lead, but that lead was slightly reduced in 1933-34. During the period between that year and 1948-49 civil government made a small gain, despite competition with problems of democracy, a newcomer in 1933-34. The introduction of problems of democracy, which combines the funda-

mentals of civil government, sociology, and economics, may account for the slight decrease in economics and for only slight increases in civil government and sociology. Since all of these subjects are offered usually in grades 10-12, they probably had little influence on enrollments in civics in 1948-49, estimated for that year as 9.5% of the total high school enrollment.[17]

Geography as a separate high school subject was first listed in 1933-34. By 1948-49 it had been separated into world and American geography, with the former leading a little over eight to one. Study of occupations and social science studies were first listed in 1933-34. The latter, which were general in nature, did not last long and apparently succumbed to the depression. Other social studies, such as international relations, consumer education, orientation, and industrial history, have played a very minor—and inconsequential—role in the curriculum.

Although many social studies were added from 1921-22 on, the study of history always received major emphasis. Enrollments in history doubled between 1889-90 and 1909-10. Although it has declined proportionately since 1910, its gains in the period between 1933-34, when it reached its low point, and 1948-49 were greater than its losses between 1921-22 and 1933-34. Increase in the study of American history accounted for most of the gains. In 1948-49 enrollments in American history were 62% of all history enrollments. World history came next with 31%, far in advance of ancient history, the leading subject in history through 1921-22.

The next most popular field was civil and community government. Although 1899-1900 saw the greatest proportion of student enrollment, its greatest loss was between that year and 1909-10. It made a strong recovery by 1921-22, dropped back slightly in 1933-34, but regained some of its loss by 1948-49.

Social studies as a whole have been increasing since 1889-90. Their greatest percentage gain came between 1890 and 1900, but this was almost matched between 1933-34 and 1948-49. Through 1921-22 history and government attracted 90% or more of enrollments in the field. Although this proportion dropped to 75% in 1933-34 and to 70% in 1948-49, by the latter date the total enrollments in social studies for the first time almost equalled the total high school enrollment of the entire country. Between 1890 and 1949 the number of social studies had increased fivefold, the total percentage almost fourfold. Only physical education and English could boast comparable records.

TABLE 5

ENGLISH: PERCENTAGE OF PUBLIC HIGH SCHOOL STUDENTS GRADES 9-12 ENROLLED IN ENGLISH BY TYPE OF COURSE IN CERTAIN YEARS BETWEEN 1889-90 AND 1948-49

	1900	1910	1922	1934	1949
Enrollment in 1000's	519	739	2,155	4,497	5,399
		915	2,230	5,621	
Rhetoric (1894-95)	38.5	57.1			
			78.6[1]	90.5[2]	92.9[2]
English Literature (1897-98)	42.1	57.1			
Journalism			0.1	0.7	1.9
Dramatics			0.1	0.8	1.5
Public Speaking			1.7	2.3	4.4
Penmanship			1.7	0.3	0.4
Spelling			0.7	0.4	
Literature				0.4	
World Literature					0.1
Reading				0.01	
Creative Writing and Composition				0.2	0.1
Short Story				0.01	
Novel				0.02	
Bible				0.08	0.2
Library Training				0.3	
Debate					0.3
Radio Speaking and Broadcasting					0.1
Remedial English					0.7
All other English					0.5[3]
Total Percentages	80.6	114.2	82.9	96.0	103.1
Total Subjects	2	2	7	14	15

[1] Figures and percentages for rhetoric and English literature were combined in 1921-22, but they were counted as two subjects. The percentage 78.6 was corrected to 76.7% in BS 1948-50, Ch. 5, Table 7. Since Table 7 did not contain four of the 1921-22 subjects in English, some of which might also have needed slight correction, the original percentage of 78.6 for 1921-22 was retained for the sake of consistency.

[2] Enrollments in English given separately in each of the four grades 9-12. The four courses are counted as one subject.

[3] Several subjects, not listed separately, are counted as three.

The formal study of English entered the secondary curriculum relatively late. During most of the colonial period intense and prolonged concentration on the classics provided all the knowledge of English grammar that seemed necessary. Although the development of a fine writing style and the cultivation of literary appreciation were two of the aims of grammar school education, these objectives were sought through the translation of Latin authors into English and the translation of English prose and poetry into Latin. English

grammar as a separate subject was introduced into the curricula of
the evening schools that sprang up toward the latter part of the seventeenth century. The private academies of Franklin's day, and later,
added courses in literature and declamation, and by 1800 courses in
English grammar and literature, composition, and declamation were
standard features in the secondary schools. After 1819 the colleges began to require English grammar for entrance, but it was fifty years
more before English composition and literature began to receive
similar recognition.[18] By that time the public high schools were
spreading rapidly, and courses in English had been in their curricula
from the beginning, in 1821.

Although the first reliable statistics on English enrollments were not
published until 1894-95, there were earlier indications of the importance of English in the public high schools. In 1879-80 students enrolled in the English curriculum outnumbered those in the classical
and modern languages curriculum more than two to one. Out of a
total high school population of 110,000, 67,000 were enrolled in
the English curriculum.[19] In 1886-87, the first year in which separate
subject enrollments were given, 37% of the high school students were
enrolled in English. A year later the percentage had jumped to 61.8,
the largest for any of the eight subjects listed separately.[20] Most
likely the percentage was based on enrollments in rhetoric and in
English literature. Rhetoric was first listed, however, in 1894-95,
and English literature in 1897-98. In the three curriculum surveys
of 1905-06, 1909-10, and 1914-15 students in these two subjects, which
were the only ones listed in English, were the equivalent of a little
more than the total high school enrollment. Through 1905-06 registrations in English literature were slightly larger than those in rhetoric.
In that year rhetoric overtook Latin for the first time and from 1909-
10 through 1914-15 passed English literature by a small margin.
After 1905-06 rhetoric replaced algebra as the leading high school subject, with English literature a close second.

The year 1921-22 marked a decided change in the English curriculum. The statistics for rhetoric and English literature were
merged under the generic term of English. Rhetoric and English
literature seemingly disappeared from the scene—some think forever.
In that same year five new subjects were listed for the first time, all
weak, but with public speaking and penmanship leading the five.
The percentage in English, pure and undefiled, dropped slightly below
its 1900 level and considerably below the level maintained between

1901-02 and 1914-15. It rose in 1927-28, dropped back slightly in 1933-34, and by 1948-49 was almost back to its 1927-28 level.

In the meantime proliferation of courses had proceeded apace. Although the number from 1933-34 on was double or nearly double the number in 1921-22, most of the newcomers were apparently offered in comparatively few of the schools. Among them, public speaking was almost as strong as the others combined. It, along with journalism and dramatics, showed some gains between 1933-34 and 1948-49. Several others made less gains during that period, were merged in statistics for others, or disappeared altogether. One noteworthy newcomer in 1948-49 was remedial English—in the opinion of many, none too soon.

Business and commercial subjects have been taught in the secondary schools of the United States ever since the latter part of the seventeenth century. The evening schools, mentioned in Chapter II, apparently started the practice, and many of the private academies included such courses in their curricula. After the Revolutionary War, industry and business expanded so rapidly that the evening schools and academies could not meet the increased demands for such training, even with the help of public high schools. In many of the larger cities, therefore, privately-owned-and-operated commercial schools and colleges sprang up. Although earlier statistics are lacking, in 1871 the Bureau of Education received reports from sixty such institutions with a total enrollment of nearly 6,500 students. By 1890 the number had increased to 250; the total enrollment was nearly 82,000. In addition, there were 25,000 other students in the private academies and colleges and in the public high schools.[21] By way of parenthesis, it is interesting to note that the number of males decreased from 96% in 1871 to 72% in 1890.[22]

The widespread demand for business education was not confined to the high schools. Many of the elementary schools offered bookkeeping in the eighth grade. The practice had become so prevalent that President Eliot of Harvard was moved to protest against it. He based his opposition on the purely practical ground that the system taught was never "used in any actual business." More than that, he argued that it would be better academically and businesswise for the young students to spend more time on arithmetic.[23]

It is not known what influence President Eliot's suggestion had on the elementary schools. More than likely it was a coincidence that the first definite information about commercial education and en-

TABLE 6

BUSINESS EDUCATION: PERCENTAGE OF PUBLIC HIGH SCHOOL
STUDENTS GRADES 9-12 ENROLLED IN BUSINESS EDUCATION
BY TYPE OF COURSE IN CERTAIN YEARS
BETWEEN 1889-90 AND 1948-49

	1900	1910	1922	1934	1949
Enrollment in 1000's	519	739	2,155	4,497	5,399
		915	2,230	5,621	
General Business Course	4.2	11.0			
Bookkeeping	13.2		12.6	9.9	8.7
Commercial or Business Law	1.8		0.9	3.2	2.4
Commercial or Economic Geography	2.5		1.7	4.0	1.7
Business Arithmetic			1.5	4.9	4.6
Typewriting			13.1	16.7	22.5
Shorthand			8.9	9.0	7.8
Office Practice			0.4	1.6	2.0
Salesmanship and Advertising			0.3	0.7	1.0
Business English (1927-28)				0.9	1.0
Elementary or General Business Training (1927-28)				6.1	5.2
Machine Operation				0.2	
Business Organization				0.4	
Accounting				0.1	
Cooperative Office Training					0.4
Retailing					0.5
Cooperative Store Training					0.3
Consumer Economics					0.7
Commercial History			0.4		
Other subjects			2.3		
Total Percentages	21.7	11.0	42.1	57.7	58.8
Total Subjects	4	1	10	13	14

rollments in the public high schools appeared two years later in the
Commissioner's Report for 1893-94. In that year 5.2% of the students
were reported in the commercial course. There was no indication of
separate subjects or sexes.[24] By 1900, however, as Table 6 shows,
nearly 22% of high school students were enrolled in business subjects. Of the four courses listed, bookkeeping was considerably
stronger than the other three combined.[25] Out of 4,393 schools and
colleges, public and private, that reported such courses in 1900, over
half, or 2,893, were public high schools. The modern trend, mentioned above, was plainly evident: nearly 52% of the students were
girls.[26]

During the next ten years a rather surprising development took place. By 1905 the number of public schools reporting commercial and business courses had increased to nearly 3,500. A little over 26% of the students were enrolled in four different courses.[27] In 1910 the number of reporting schools had dropped to 1,440, with only 11% of the students enrolled. Enrollments by subjects were not reported.[28]

It could not be determined whether there was an actual decrease in the number of high schools offering business education courses, or simply a decrease in the number reporting them. Since 1910 the spiral has gone steadily up. In 1922 over 5,000 schools reported bookkeeping; in 1934, over 7,000. Schools reporting the other subjects varied considerably. In 1922 they ranged from over 4,000 (typewriting) to less than 200 (office practice); in 1934, from over 8,500 (typewriting) to less than 100 (accounting). The number of schools was not reported in 1948-49. Since 1915 typewriting has consistently led the field. Bookkeeping and shorthand have kept a respectful distance in a near-tie for second place. While the other commercial and business subjects individually have not attracted large enrollments, all the different subjects together have made the whole field one of the strongest in the high school curriculum.

Manual or industrial training was not a feature of colonial education. The grammar schools concentrated on academic subjects as preparation for study of the liberal arts in college. A system of apprenticeship, of learning by doing, provided practical instruction for entrance into trades and vocations. The prevalent economy of a rural and farming population made household chores under parental tutelage a necessity for girls and boys in most homes. This type of practical training continued to be widespread well into the nineteenth century and has not yet disappeared in many sections of the country.

After 1800, however, America began to make rapid progress in industry and technology. The concentration of industries in cities created a growing demand for skilled labor, and private trade schools were gradually set up to meet the needs. The early high schools, following the lead of the academies, introduced commercial courses to satisfy the business side of industrialization, but had to look elsewhere for models of trade and vocational training.

These models came initially from the land-grant colleges set up under the provisions of the Morrill Act of 1862. The first institution to offer trade and industrial courses was apparently the Illinois Industrial University, now the University of Illinois, in 1871.[29] Other

TABLE 7

VOCATIONAL AND NONVOCATIONAL SUBJECTS: PERCENTAGE OF
PUBLIC HIGH SCHOOL STUDENTS GRADES 9-12 ENROLLED IN
VOCATIONAL AND NONVOCATIONAL SUBJECTS BY TYPE OF
COURSE IN CERTAIN YEARS BETWEEN 1889-90 AND 1948-49

	1910	1922	1934	1949	Non-Vocational 1949
Enrollment in 1000's	739	2,155	4,497	5,399	5,399
	915	2,230	5,621		
Industrial Arts or Manual Training	8.6	10.5	6.3		0.2*
Vocational Related Subjects			0.08	0.4	
Shop Mathematics or Industrial Arts Mathematics				0.7	0.1
Trade Science				0.4	
Diversified Occupations				0.2	
General Industrial Shop				0.07	
General Shop			1.2		8.0*
Machine Shop			0.8	0.8	
Automobile Mechanics			0.8	0.7	0.4
Mechanical Drafting				1.2	
Mechanical Drawing		2.6	6.6		5.6*
Carpentry				0.3	
Cabinet Making				0.3	
Radio				0.2	
Electrical Work			0.7	0.4	1.2
Printing		0.2	1.1	0.3	1.6
Metal Work		0.4	0.5		3.6
Sheet Metal				0.2	
Aviation				0.1	
Welding, Forge and Foundry			0.2		
Welding				0.07	
Cosmetology				0.1	
Woodworking			2.1		6.3*
Ceramics			0.03		0.1
Architectural Drafting			0.2		
Pattern Making			0.1		
Farm Shop			0.3		
Handicrafts					0.5*
Home Mechanics					0.2
Photography					0.1
Other subjects uncommonly offered				0.4	
Total Percentages	8.6	13.7	21.0	6.8	27.9
Total Subjects	2	4	15	18	13

* See Appendix E.

colleges followed suit. Land-grant colleges included such courses in
their curricula, and "agricultural and mechanical colleges," as they
were originally named, were eventually founded in most of the states.

These had separate departments devoted to mechanical and industrial arts.

In the meantime some of the colleges found it expedient or necessary to organize such courses on the high school level. The first school of this type, the St. Louis Manual Training School, opened in 1880 under the auspices of Washington University. Although a few other colleges established similar schools, a movement to incorporate such training as part of the public school system was making rapid headway. One of the chief factors in this progress had been the manual training exhibits of European countries at the Philadelphia Centennial Exhibition in 1876. These exhibits had shown what could be done on elementary and secondary levels and had aroused considerable public and educational interest. In a nationwide debate which followed, there were educators on both sides and some in the middle. Proponents enumerated the mental, moral, spiritual, and economic values of such training, one by one. Their arguments could be summed up in an epigram coined by one ardent advocate: "Put the Whole Boy to School."[30]

Arguments on the opposing side could be summed up in three unepigrammatic phrases: beyond the proper functions of the public school, debasement of education, too expensive.

Even in the early stages of the debate, however, it had become obvious that the hand would join the head throughout the public school system. As early as 1880 Jamestown, N. Y., had made manual training courses obligatory, except for girls in high school.[31] In 1890, thirty-five cities reported such courses in their public school systems. 69,748 students were enrolled in them, in both elementary and high school grades.[32] Of these, 6,763 were on the high school level. Since the individual reports in many instances combined figures for all grades, the total number of students taking such courses in grades 9-12 could not be estimated with any assurance. On the basis of the figure given above, at least 3.3% of the high school students were enrolled in manual training courses in ordinary high schools. Four years later, when the data were more complete, the percentage was 6.2.[33]

The figures and percentages just given do not take into account students enrolled in public manual and industrial training high schools. They were first set up in Chicago and Baltimore, in 1884. By 1900 they had been established in at least 16 cities. The 8,696 students who received manual training instruction in them that year constituted 1.6% of the total high school enrollment. Although man-

ual training courses were also being offered that year in the ordinary high schools of 169 cities, enrollment figures were not available.[34]

A fairly complete and accurate statistical picture for the whole country first became clear in 1909-10. The total percentage for that year, given in Table 7 above, was based on figures for students in the two types of schools just mentioned. About 3.6% were in ordinary high schools and 5.0% in separate manual training high schools.[35]

Although the Commissioner's Reports for 1889-90 and 1899-1900, as indicated above, listed individual manual training subjects, no attempt was made to calculate separate percentages. Of the fifteen subjects listed in Table 7 for 1934, all were offered in 1890 except those dealing with automobile mechanics, electricity, and vocational related subjects. Two subjects offered in the earlier years had dropped out, at least in terminology, long before 1934: chipping and filing, and sloyd—a term for wood carving, borrowed from the Swedes. In this country it was apparently deemed very suitable for girls.

From 1909-10 through 1914-15 the separate subjects were grouped primarily under the heading: manual or industrial training. Mechanical drawing, which had been the most popular single course in the field from the beginning, was given a special listing in 1914-15 and thereafter. After 1909-10 the statistics for ordinary and manual training high schools were combined, but in 1921-22 separate listings began to re-appear and to multiply. Although the nonvocational aspects and values of manual training courses were stressed in the debate that took place between 1880 and 1900, it was 1949 before any real distinction was made in the subject matter grouping. In that year the equivalent of one-third of the high school population received training in all phases of the subject-matter field, but students in nonvocational subjects outnumbered the others four to one. Perhaps that had been something of the situation all along, particularly after 1922.

To summarize—manual training courses appeared in the high school curriculum much sooner than has been generally realized. Although subject and combined percentages through 1909-10 seem small in comparison with leading academic subject-matter fields, they were actually much larger than indicated. The lack of sufficient data made it impossible to put the picture in proper focus before 1909-10. After 1922 the subjects grouped under manual arts began to appear separately. Except for a change in terminology and the addition of a few new subjects made possible by technological progress, the subjects listed in 1934 were strikingly similar to those

offered in 1890. Subject changes that took place between 1934 and 1949 were greater than those that occurred between 1890 and 1934.

TABLE 8[1]

HOME ECONOMICS: PERCENTAGE OF PUBLIC HIGH SCHOOL STUDENTS GRADES 9-12 ENROLLED IN HOME ECONOMICS BY TYPE OF COURSE IN CERTAIN YEARS BETWEEN 1889-90 AND 1948-49

	1910	1922	1934	1949
Enrollment in 1000's	739	2,155	4,497	5,399
	915	2,230	5,621	
Home Economics	3.8	14.3	7.9	
Sewing			1.9	
Cooking			1.3	
Child Care			0.1	0.2
Home Nursing			0.2	0.8
Foods (nutrition and dietetics)			2.3	2.9
Clothing			2.7	3.8
Family relations			0.1	0.5
Interior Decorating and House Planning			0.1	0.1
Costume Design or related arts			0.1	0.1
Homemaking				14.3
Homemaking General				0.8
Home Management				0.8
Consumer Buying[2]				
Total Percentages	3.8	14.3	16.7	24.3
Total Subjects	2	4	10	10

[1] Between 1934 and 1949 several changes in course names were made. Those not indicated in the table or text were as follows: *Home Nursing* in 1934 added *health* in 1949; *interior decorating and house planning* became *the house* in 1949.

[2] Listed under Social Studies, Table 4.

Household work or domestic economy entered the high school curriculum in the early 1880's along with other manual training subjects. This was only natural since cooking and sewing, the forms in which it first appeared, were considered manual arts.[36] Of the 35 cities that offered manual training in their public school systems in 1889-90, 16 gave courses in sewing and 12 in cooking. (See note 32 on p. 55). In 1893-94, of 95 such cities, 43 gave courses in sewing, 26 in cooking.[37] By 1900 the number of such cities had increased to 169, but information about work in sewing and cooking, or any other separate subjects, was not made available. In that year, however, of the 16 separate public manual training high schools listed, 11 offered courses in sewing and 10 in cooking. (See Note 34).

As was true of manual training subjects, the situation in domestic

economy remained very much confused until 1909-10. In that year the number of ordinary high schools reporting domestic economy had increased to 491; only 257 reported manual training courses. The students in domestic economy constituted 3.8% of the total high school enrollment, as against 3.6% for those in manual training.[38] In addition, however, there were 10,189 girls enrolled in 59 public manual training high schools throughout the country.[39] Although many of these were undoubtedly taking courses in domestic economy, in addition to the other subjects just mentioned above, the exact number could not be determined.

In 1922 the real situation in domestic economy, now changed to home economics, came to light. With the figures in both types of schools combined, home economics pulled slightly ahead of manual training. It fell behind in 1934, but was catching up by 1949.

In 1934 it was possible to see in some detail for the first time the range of efforts being made to promote the domestic felicities of modern living. Home economics, that reassuring catchall, remained in the lead as befitted a basic course. Sewing and cooking, as some might have feared, yielded to the more tangible objects of their affections, clothing and foods. These two increased in 1949, with three year-courses in each. Cooking and sewing lost their separate identities by being subsumed under homemaking. This was not a newcomer to the field but another name for the basic course. It was divided into four year-courses and commanded nearly 60% of all registrations in home economics.[40]

Throughout our history farming has been the backbone of our economic life. Yet instruction in the elements of agriculture has played a very minor role in secondary education. This is all the more strange when it is realized that agricultural societies to promote such studies at all levels were formed a few years before 1800. Although they did not succeed in establishing courses of instruction in the high schools, they did stimulate publication of books and periodicals dealing with agriculture, and the organization of agricultural fairs. Both of these activities had some educational influence.

In the early part of the nineteenth century a few private agricultural schools were organized and some of the universities introduced courses in agriculture and horticulture. Three states founded agricultural colleges between 1857 and 1859, but colleges of this kind did not begin to increase until the Morrill Act of 1862 gave federal aid and impetus to the movement. In that same year the Department of

TABLE 9

AGRICULTURE: PERCENTAGE OF PUBLIC HIGH SCHOOL STUDENTS
GRADES 9-12 ENROLLED IN AGRICULTURE BY TYPE OF COURSE IN
CERTAIN YEARS BETWEEN 1889-90 AND 1948-49

	1910	1922	1934	1949
Enrollment in 1000's	739	2,155	4,497	5,399
	915	2,230	5,621	
Agriculture	4.7	5.1	2.9	6.7
Animal Husbandry			0.3	
Horticulture			0.1	
Soils and crops			0.3	
Poultry			0.02	
Total Percentages	4.7	5.1	3.6	6.7
Total Subjects	1	2	5	4

Agriculture, which had existed in embryo as a minor division of the
Patent Office, was given independent and national status.[41]

The activities of the colleges and of the new Department in giving
extension courses and in holding institutes for farmers possibly helped
to delay the introduction of agricultural courses in the public high
schools.   Some of the agricultural colleges had such courses on the
high school level, and interest in them began to grow.   By 1905 a few
private and public schools were teaching elementary courses in the subject and three normal schools in at least one state were beginning to
train teachers of such subjects for the public schools in that state.[42]

But not until 1910 did the high school study of agriculture
cut any sort of national furrow.   By 1915 the furrow had become a bit
longer and deeper; the number of schools reporting agriculture had
increased from nearly 1,800 to 4,390, and the percentage of students
had almost doubled.   In 1917 the national government stepped in
with the Smith-Hughes Bill to assist the states in establishing vocational high schools.   In 1922, however, although the number of schools
reporting had increased to 5,200, the national percentage, like an
ornery mule, took two steps backward from its position of 1915.   The
future farmers of America suffered a slight setback and the cattle on
a thousand hills moaned low.[43]

In 1934 agricultural courses were listed under separate subjects
for the first time.   The previous pattern, however, was reinstated in
1949, except that enrollments were given in each of the four years into
which the courses had been organized.   Most likely the courses
covered essentially the different subjects listed in 1934.

Since agricultural courses have only sectional appeal and are offered more widely in some regions of the country than in others, the national percentages may be misleading. In 1910, for example, when such information was given, the percentage of students studying agriculture in the North Atlantic and in the Western Divisions was 1.15 and 1.16 respectively. The greatest concentrations were in the South Atlantic and South Central Divisions, with 11.6% and 16.22 respectively. The North Central Division trailed along with 5.03%. In 1915 the sectional percentages had changed very little, and there is no reason to believe they have changed materially since.

TABLE 10

PHYSICAL EDUCATION: PERCENTAGE OF PUBLIC HIGH SCHOOL STUDENTS GRADES 9-12 ENROLLED IN PHYSICAL EDUCATION BY TYPE OF COURSE IN CERTAIN YEARS BETWEEN 1889-90 AND 1948-49

	1900	1910	1922	1934	1949
Enrollment in 1000's	519	739	2,155	4,497	5,399
		915	2,230	5,621	
Physical Education			5.7	50.7	69.4
Health					26.7*
Hygiene and Sanitation			6.1	6.5	4.5*
Safety					3.4*
Driver Education					3.8
Military Drill	2.0		2.7	1.2	1.3
Total Percentage	2.0		14.5	58.4	109.1
Total Subjects	1		3	3	6

*See Appendix E.

Our colonial ancestors paid more attention to the mind than to the body. Despite their devotion to the literature and thought of Greece and Rome as food for the mind, they gave no heed to ancient ideas about the values of physical training as a part of education. This was perhaps natural in a country where distances were great and means of travel limited. The daily life of children, whether those of a farmer, tradesman, or clergyman, involved considerable exercise and play in many forms outside of school hours. This was considered sufficient for growing bodies, if indeed any thought was given to the matter at all.

But growing urbanization and higher standards of living began to have some effect. Around 1850 unhealthy conditions in schools finally caused severe criticism and during the next 50 years the neces-

sity for physical culture, as it was then called, and for instruction in health and hygiene was gradually recognized. But progress was slow. In 1886-87, out of 419 high schools supported wholly by public funds, 90 reported equipment for physical culture.[44] In 1889-90 only 91 out of 2,526 high schools reporting had gymasiums.[45]

In that year Boston appointed a director of physical training for its public schools. This was possibly the first position of its kind in the country.[46] In January 1891, about 1,100 teachers "were engaged in an honest attempt to teach the Ling free standing movements" in Boston's grammar and primary schools. 190 or more of these teachers had attended the Boston Normal School of Gymnastics, which had been founded in 1888.[47]

The major emphasis in Boston, and elsewhere during this period, was on physical training in the elementary grades. But the movement was growing and spreading upward into high school. In 1899-1900 military drill was given in 132 high schools, including three in Indian Territory, in 33 states and the District of Columbia. A total of 10,259 boys took part in the drills, or 4.7% of the male high school enrollment.[48] Nearly half of these were in Massachusetts; over half were in four New England states, where nearly one-third of the high schools reporting military drill were located.

Encouraging signs of progress could be seen by 1910. In that year 5% of the high schools had departments of physical education; 8% gave instruction in gymnastics, 10% in athletics, and 16% in hygiene. 20% of the schools had athletic fields, 7% gymnasiums, 1% military drill.[49]

Experience during the first world war brought out the great need for a better and more widespread system of physical education in the public schools. In 1915 the U. S. Army rejected 80% of those who volunteered; the Navy, 75%, and the Marine Corps, 83%. The rejections were based on physical disabilities of various kinds. It was estimated that 50% of the disabilities recorded by the Navy, and 40% of those recorded by the Marine Corps could have been prevented or corrected by proper remedial measures in childhood.[50]

Although the responsibility of the high schools for such a large percentage of rejectees could not be determined, it was estimated that not more than 50% of public high school graduates could have met the physical standards set by the Army and Navy. The shock of these revelations was immediate but shortlived. The shortcomings of one proposal, compulsory military training for high school students, which was adopted in a few states, soon became obvious. A more

comprehensive system of physical training, combined with instruction in health and hygiene, was needed, but it was slow in coming. In 1921-22 only 356 high schools out of about 14,000 reported physical training; 319 reported military drill; 1,652, courses in health and sanitation. The number of students involved was the equivalent of only 14.5% of the total high school enrollment. Boys outnumbered girls by not more than the width of a pair of bloomers.[51]

The greatest progress came between 1927-28 and 1933-34. The percentage of students in physical education jumped from 15 to almost 51. In the latter year, however, nearly half of the public high schools reported no such training. In hygiene and sanitation the situation was much worse. Only a little over one-sixth of the high schools had these subjects in their curricula. Military drill, as might have been expected, diminished to the size of a button on a platoon captain's coat.[52]

World War II revealed continued deficiencies in the high school program of physical training and education. As a result, many states made physical training compulsory and instituted new courses in health. Although many students in 1948-49 were not receiving instruction in the basic elements of physical education, health, and safety, the total number involved in all courses was for the first time equivalent to a little more than the total high school population. Physical education had become the second leading subject matter field in the high school curriculum.

Those twin handmaidens, music and art, had no part in the academic pattern of colonial times. The religious clime forbade the making of a "joyful noise unto the Lord" in church, and academic discipline had no thought for its possible need or use in school. The concept, *vita brevis,* was a theme for constant admonition and frequent practice. *Ars Longa* was only another Latin phrase to be memorized without regard for any practical application.

The notion of music and art as educational instruments entered our public school system via Boston. The introduction of art, in the form of drawing, came in 1821. The attempt was not very successful there nor in the few other cities where it had been tried by 1850. Real impetus was given to the movement by the realization, gained by American visitors to the London Exhibition in 1851, of the industrial purposes which art might serve. In 1860, drawing was made optional in the schools of Massachusetts, and a required subject in the high schools, in 1864. In 1868 the requirement was extended to several

grades below the high school level. Two years later the teaching of drawing was made compulsory for all public schools, and all towns of 10,000 or more inhabitants were required to give free instruction in industrial or mechanical drawing to persons over fifteen years of age. During that same year, 1870, the position of state supervisor of drawing and art was set up, probably the first of its kind in the country. In 1874 the Massachusetts Normal Art School opened, the first state supported school of its kind in the country. Its specific purpose was to train public school teachers of drawing and art.[53]

TABLE 11

MUSIC: PERCENTAGE OF PUBLIC HIGH SCHOOL STUDENTS GRADES 9-12
ENROLLED IN MUSIC BY TYPE OF COURSE IN CERTAIN YEARS
BETWEEN 1889-90 AND 1949-49

	1922	1934		1949*
	2,155	4,497		5,399
	2,230	5,621		
Vocal Music (1914-15)	21.9	17.9		
Instrumental Music (1914-15)	3.2	3.2	0.2	0.3
Music Appreciation or Studies (1914-15)	0.2	1.2	4.1	6.3
Orchestra		1.2	1.6	2.4
Band		1.3	6.2	9.4
Chorus			8.4	12.9
Glee Club			6.1	9.3
General or Public School Music			2.9	4.5
Theory and Practice			0.1	0.2
Harmony			0.5	0.7
Total Percentage	25.3	24.8	30.1	46.0
Total Subjects	3	5	9	9

*The first column under 1949 gives corrected percentages. See Appendix E.

At the Centennial Exhibition held at Philadelphia in 1876 the special exhibits of art work done in schools attracted favorable attention and created a new wave of enthusiasm among laymen and educators alike. By 1886-87 a shade over one-fourth of the students in city public high schools were enrolled in free-hand drawing. The students represented 375 schools, out of a total of 419 that reported, located in 25 states and the District of Columbia.[54] Although detailed statistics for 1889-90 were not given, approximately half of the 2,500 public high schools that reported had made drawing compulsory.[55] The type of drawing, whether free-hand or mechanical, was not specified. In another table for manual training in city public schools, how-

TABLE 12

ART: PERCENTAGE OF PUBLIC HIGH SCHOOL STUDENTS GRADES 9-12
ENROLLED IN ART BY TYPE OF COURSE IN CERTAIN
YEARS BETWEEN 1889-90 AND 1948-49

	1922	1934	1949*	
Enrollment in 1000's	2,155	4,497	5,399	
	2,230	5,621		
Freehand Drawing (1914-15)	14.7	5.5	2.6	7.1
Art-Craft-Design		2.7	0.4	1.0
Art Appreciation		0.2	2.5	6.9
Applied Art		0.1	0.8	2.1
Commercial Art		0.1	0.3	0.7
General Art			1.8	4.7
School Service Art			0.6	1.7
Total Percentage	14.7	8.6	9.0	24.2
Total Subjects	1	5	7	7

*The first column under 1949 gives corrected percentages; the second, original percentages.
See Appendix E.

ever, there were entries for drawing, free-hand drawing, and mechanical drawing.[56] But despite the confusion in terminology and the lack of definite and accurate information about it, art instruction in all public schools was a matter of increasing concern. Almost every Commissioner's Report between 1870 and 1900 had many references to and comments about the general problem.

The same was true of music. Its development paralleled very closely that of art. It too started in Boston. After an auspicious beginning about 1836, there was an almost immediate diminuendo. The idea spread slowly throughout New England and the rest of the country. On the elementary school level there is some evidence that singing, the form in which instruction was first given, was connected with physical training. It was considered most useful for strengthening the lungs and for developing the speaking voice.[57]

There is little doubt that the teaching of music spread more rapidly than the teaching of art. A special survey made by the Bureau of Education in 1885 showed that seven-eighths of all public school pupils were receiving instruction in music that year. The following year it was reported that it was "systematically taught in nearly every city school in the country."[58]

The encouraging information contained in the survey may partially explain why no attempt was made to collect similar data for many

years.   The Bureau's statistical staff was small, and music, together
with art, was in a rather special category.   Neither music nor art
was required for college entrance; strictly speaking, neither was vocational in nature.   The cultivation of both had apparently been widely
accepted as legitimate public school functions.

How well were the schools doing the job?   Not well at all in music,
was the verdict of a special commission that had come over from England to study American education.   It found a great "neglect of musical talent among the school children."[59]   It also felt that drawing
should not be considered a manual training subject, and that its teaching methods were undeveloped.[60]

What effects this report had on the teaching of music and art in
the public schools is not known.   It can scarcely be disputed, however,
that instruction in these two fields did not keep pace with the expanding high school population.   In 1904-05, out of 188 cities with a population of more than 25,000 that reported to the Bureau of Education,
142 had supervisors of music in their public school systems, and 156,
supervisors of art.[61]   The number of students could not be estimated.

The first definite information about high school enrollments in music and art was reported for the session of 1914-15.   In that year 31.5%
of the total high school enrollment received instruction in vocal music
in 3,520 high schools; 22.9% received instruction in drawing, in 3,090
high schools.[62]   These were the largest percentages reported for any
year in these two subject matter fields.   Because of its possibilities
for various kinds of group activities, music had naturally crescendoed
more than art by 1914-15.   Since then the gap between the two has
widened considerably.   It reached a three-to-one scale in 1933-34 and
has grown slightly larger since.

The greatest changes in music came between 1934 and 1949.   By
the former year bands and orchestras had made a formal entry, with
the brass only slightly in the lead.   By 1949 the strings had stepped
up their volume slightly, but the wind and percussion instruments
even more.   Music appreciation, which was struggling for recognition
in 1922, merged with music studies in 1934 but had regained independence of movement by 1949.   Among the new alignments in 1949,
chorus took a commanding lead in vocal music, with strong support
from glee club activities.   Public school music, aided by harmony,
theory and practice, sounded a timid, professional note, but the whole
high school ensemble was decidedly on the up beat.

Art has shown the opposite trend.   In the simple, unsophisticated
days of 1915 and 1922, students could give vent to their artistic feel-

ings only in drawing. By 1934 this was not considered a sufficient outlet, and several courses were added to afford fuller expression. The result, numerically if not artistically, was a decided drop in total percentage.[63] Drawing still maintained a two-to-one popularity but barely managed to hold first place over art appreciation in 1949. Third place went to general art, one of the two new courses that year. The other was school service art, so called because students who wished to do so might work at school-wide projects, in which service was possibly more important than art. Despite the two added courses, the total percentage for 1949 was greater than that for 1934 only by the thickness of a painter's pallette.

TABLE 13

TEACHER TRAINING: PERCENTAGE OF PUBLIC HIGH SCHOOL STUDENTS GRADES 9-12 ENROLLED IN TEACHER TRAINING BY TYPE OF COURSE IN CERTAIN YEARS BETWEEN 1889-90 AND 1948-49

	1900[1]	1910[2]	1922	1934	1949
Enrollment in 1000's	519	739	2,155	4,497	5,899
		915	2,230	5,621	
Teacher Training *or* Principles of Teaching	2.6	1.9	0.9	0.1	0.002
Normal Review			0.1		
Total Percentage	2.6	1.9	1.0	0.1	0.002
Total Subjects	1	1	2	1	1

[1] CR 1899-1900, II, p. 2087.
[2] CR 1909-10, II, p. 1096. References for the other years are found in Appendix B.

Teacher training in the United States first started in the private academies, which began to spring up after 1750. They apparently did not introduce special courses for that purpose, however, until well after 1800. A pioneer step in that direction was taken by the Lancastrian Schools, many of which were founded in this country between 1815 and 1830. The use of older students as monitors, under the general supervision of the headmaster or teacher, involved practical application of rote teaching methods. Although the system was neither very successful nor lasting, it did show the necessity for developing methods of group instruction, and stimulated interest in free public schools.[64]

The influence of the academies on the development of teacher train-

ing was twofold: their lead in introducing teacher-training courses was followed by the early public high schools, and they became the model for the first teacher-training school in America, established in 1823, in Concord, Vermont, by the Reverend Samuel R. Hall.[65] Although the new school's curriculum was largely academic, the three-year course also included a review of elementary school subjects, and provided opportunity for observation of teaching and for practice teaching. Toward the end of the three-year course, students were given a special series of lectures on "The Art of Teaching." After six years of experience the founder of the school set forth his principles in a volume, *Lectures On Schoolkeeping*, published in 1829. This was the first professional work of its kind written and published by a native American.[66] It was widely sold and read, and influenced writing on educational matters for many years.

The success of Hall's school strengthened the hands of those who advocated state establishment and support of teacher training schools. Massachusetts again led the way, and in 1839 the first state normal school in the country opened in Lexington.[67] The idea of public normal schools spread slowly until about 1870. By that date many states had one or more of such schools, and some of the larger cities had incorporated them in their public school systems. In 1900 the Bureau of Education received reports from 172 public normal schools and teachers colleges, and 134 under private control. In addition, 243 universities and colleges reported departments of education or professional courses in that subject matter field.[68] Only one state reported no public normal school or no state university offering such training.

By 1900 most normal schools had begun to raise their entrance requirements from elementary to high school graduation. The leading subjects in the typical normal school of this period included the "history of education, the theory of education, school oragnization and supervision, school management and discipline, school hygiene, psychology and child study, ethics, school laws, and practical pedagogy."[69]

In 1870 the typical normal school included four years of high school work in its offerings. Its purpose was the same as that in 1900, namely, to prepare teachers for the elementary schools. At a meeting of the American Normal School Association in 1870, a special committee recommended for elementary teachers the course of study and training listed on the next page. The course was to take two years, and each year was divided into two terms of 20 weeks each.[70]

Subject	Number of weeks	Order
English (grammar, reading, elocution)	60	Omitted 4th term
Arithmetic (through ratio and proportion, roots, mental processes)	40	1st yr.
Algebra (to quadratic equations)	10	2nd yr., 1st term
Geometry (4 books)	40	1st yr., 2nd term 2nd yr., 2nd term
Writing and drawing (free)	20	1st yr., 1st term
Drawing (Perspective. Drawing of simple objects)	20	1st yr., 2nd term
Geography (U. S., Europe, Asia, world map construction, methods of rapid delineation, phenomena of ocean and atmosphere, terrestrial astronomy)	60	Omitted 4th term
Botany (Morphology of leaves; stem; roots, analysis and classification of plants)	16-18	1st year
Physiology	32	1st yr., 1st term 2nd yr., 2nd term
Natural philosophy (Physics)	20	2nd yr., 1st term
Geology (General principles, field work, classification of specimens)	20	2nd yr., 2nd term
Chemistry (Nomenclature, study of elements and compounds, lectures and laboratory)	30	2nd year
Vocal and physical training (Free calisthenic exercises; musical notation and reading through key of *C*; chorus)	20	1st yr., 1st term
Vocal and physical culture (Reading and singing in all scales and keys; transposition; chorus; rhythmic exercises)	20	1st yr., 2nd term
History (American)	20	2nd yr., 1st term
Science of government	20	2nd yr., 1st term
Bookkeeping (Theory and practice in double entry and in business forms)	20	1st yr., 2nd term
Theory and practice of teaching (Observation and criticism of teaching primary reading and number classes)	20	1st yr., 1st term
Theory and practice of teaching (Lessons and criticism of methods in language, form ,and place)	20	1st yr., 2nd term
Theory and practice of teaching (Practice and criticism of object lessons; management and methods with advanced classes)	20	2nd yr., 1st term
Theory and practice of teaching (School organization, discipline, and management; school laws; history of education)	20	2nd yr., 2nd term
Ethical instruction (Manners and morals; foundation of right habits)	20	1st yr., 1st term
Philosophy of education, including mental philosophy (Nervous mechanism; the senses; sensation, perception, observation, memory, reason, imagination; principles and methods of training inferred from the above)	20	2nd yr., 2nd term

With its report the committee gave some statistics on the teacher training situation throughout the U. S. at the time. Out of 200,-000 public school teachers, it was estimated that 40% were without previous experience. If all the students in all the schools for training teachers, both public and private, became teachers, seven out of eight of the inexperienced teachers would still be without special training for their work. The committee also expressed the opinion that "one of the best methods of teaching how to teach any subject is actually to teach that subject upon the most approved plan." But that method should not be "exclusively relied upon. Special drill in the art of teaching should be constant accompaniment of the course."

To what extent the proposed curriculum was adopted by the normal schools or adapted by the public high schools could not be determined. In 1886-87 there were 50,000 students training to become teachers in the four different types of institutions that reported to the Bureau of Education. About 90% of these were in public and private normal schools. Of the remainder, students in the normal course in public and semi-public high schools outnumbered teachers-in-training in 58 reporting colleges a shade under two-to-one.[1] The public school students taking the normal course constituted 3.7% of the total high school enrollment reported that year. Most of the schools were in city systems.

The rapid growth of the public high schools after 1870 enabled the normal schools to raise their entrance requirements gradually and in time to drop their high school departments altogether. By 1900, as pointed out above, they were concentrating on professional courses in education. The high schools, on the other hand, in response to the increasing demand for teacher training, had introduced normal courses into their curricula. Although no information was given in 1870, and none could be found later about the names and contents of such courses, one thing does seem fairly certain: The increase in the number and standards of the normal schools was instrumental in raising the requirements for the granting of teachers' certificates. This, in turn, decreased the need and the practicality of teacher-training courses in the public high schools.

[1] BS 1948-50, Ch. 5, p. 6. A course is one year's study of a subject. A subject such as English, for example, is usually divided into four courses of a year each.

[2] No curriculum survey was made between 1933-34 and 1948-49. The next one is scheduled for 1958-59.

[3] The explanation for two different figures in 1910, 1922, and 1934 is given in Appendix G, Table 36, Notes 2-4.

[4] The total number of subjects will be discussed as necessary in connection with each table.

[5] CR 1887-88, Table 38, p. 490. The equivalent of 86 percent of the students in high schools supported wholly by public funds, that reported to the U.S. Bureau of Education, were enrolled in mathematics courses. Other sources for the colonial period and later include: *Kandel*, pp. 122, 169-77, 397-462; *Knight* (1): 122-3, 375-76, 427-31; *Johnson*, 133, 147, 301-17; *Brown*, 131-35, 231-32, 237-47, 300-03, 371, 417, 425; *Meriwether*, 158-81; *Cubberley*, 26-81, 288-339.

[6] *Bul. 1938, No. 6*, p. 12; BS 1948-50, Ch. 5, p. 15. A break-down of this type was not possible before 1927-28. In that year 27% of the total high school enrollment was in elementary algebra (*BS 1926-28*, p.966), which constituted a little more than 72% of grade 9.

[7] BS 1926-28, p. 966.

[8] *Ibid.*, p. 1064.

[9] BS 1948-50, Ch 5, p. 16, Note 10. See Note 3 of Table 1 above. The contents of the elementary course apparently represent "a final attempt to pound home the basic operations of arithmetic." See *Dyer et al*, p. 22.

[10] CR 1909-10, II, Table A., p. 1139. The figures and percentages for plane and solid geometry, as usual, were combined. These percentages show that trigonometry was not "at an all-time high" in 1948-49, as stated in BS 1948-50, Ch. 5, p. 16.

[11] This comparison was made between the data in this table and those in CR 1909-10, Table A, p. 1139. For the relationship of mathematics to all other subject-matter fields throughout this entire period, see CH. V, Table 14. By the fall of 1952 the percentage of students in algebra had dropped to 24.6; in geometry, to 11.6; in trigonometry, to 1.7; but in general mathematics it had risen to 15.0 The total percentage was 52.9 See *Bulletin 1953, No. 5*, Table 49. In the fall of 1954 algebra had a slight increase to 24.8% and trigonometry a striking increase, to 2.6. The reference for these percentages, *Pamphlet No. 118, 1956*, Table 11, shows a slight decrease for geometry, to 11.4. The writer, however, using the data in *School Life* (May 1955), p. 126, and (June 1956), p. 6, calculated the percentage for geometry as 11.7. He also calculated 12.2 for general mathematics, which was not covered in the pamphlet. Another special study by the Office of Education for the fall of 1956 showed 28.7% for algebra; 13.6 for geometry, and 2.9 for trigonometry. These figures were given to the writer in advance of publication by Dr. Kenneth E. Brown, who conducted the study. They are to be found in *Pamphlet No. 120, 1957*, Table 16.

[12] CR 1886-87, Tables 31 and 33, pp. 496, 512. The statistics were based primarily on reports from public high schools in city systems. See Ch. II, notes 2 and 4.

[13] *Brown*, p. 248; *Cubberley*, p. 315.

[14] In 1954-55 the percentage for Latin was 6.9; for French, 5.6; for Spanish, 7.3; for German, 0.8. See *PMLA*, LXX, No. 4, Pt. 2 (September 1955), pp. 52-56.

[15] CR 1887-88, p. 490.

[16] In the fall of 1954 enrollments in physics and chemistry constituted 4.6% and 7.3%, respectively, of the total high school enrollment; biology, 19.6%. See *Pamphlet No. 118, 1956*, Table 2. No statistics were reported on general science. If it increased proportionately as much as biology its percentage would have been 22.2 This estimate, as it happens, was probably somewhat high. In the fall of 1956 its percentage was 21.8; biology, 20.5; chemistry, 7.5. Physics alone had a slight decrease to 4.4. These figures are to be found in *Pamphlet No. 120 1957*, Table 3.

[17] In BS 1948-50, Ch. 5, Table 3, enrollments in civics are given for grades 7, 8, or 9. It was estimated, however, that one-third of the ninth grade students were enrolled in the subject. (*Ibid*. p. 9). On the basis of enrollments in ninth grade English, 9.5% is approximately correct. The same percentage also studied American history in the ninth grade.

[18] *Kandel*, pp. 363-64; *Knight* (1), p. 375; *Brown*, pp. 231-32, 371; *Cubberley*, p. 315.

[19] CR 1880, Table VI, pp. cvi-cvii.   [20] See Notes 12 and 5 above.

[21] CR 1889-90, II, p. 1610. Statistics for all types of schools were combined. For the period before 1889-90, see CR 1892-93, II, p. 2020.

[22] CR 1892-93, II, p. 2020.

[23] CR 1889-90 (published in 1893) II, pp. 1126-27. The remarks were made in an address to the National Education Association on February 16, 1892.

[24] CR 1893-94, I, p. 65; II, p. 2171. The first reference gives the total high school enrollment, the second, subject registrations.

[25] CR 1899-1900, II, pp. 2478-79.

[26] *Ibid*. pp. 2469, 2474.

[27] CR 1904-05, II, pp. 815 (enrollment), 1226-27 (subject registrations).

[28] CR 1909-10, II, pp. 1249, 1258.

[29] *Dexter*, p. 408. Between 1775 and 1835 a "manual labor movement" made considerable headway in the country. Many colleges, academies, and theological schools combined such a feature with their academic work, but the movement collapsed from practical difficulties of finance and administration. Undoubtedly its influence, however, helped to prepare the way for the Morrill Act. See *Knight* (1) pp. 380-84.

[30] It was made in an address by C. M. Woodward, Director of the Manual Training School of Washington University, in Boston, on December 16, 1885. The address was published in the *Boston Herald* of December 17, 1885, and in pamphlet form by the Social Science Association of Philadelphia, in 1886. This information was given in a special article by Woodward, "The Rise and Progress of Manual Training," (CR 1893-93, I, pp. 895-96). The whole chapter, pp. 877-949, surveyed the development of the manual training movement in this country and in Europe, including Russia, down to 1893-94. Unless otherwise indicated, it is the primary source for the statements made in this section.

[31] CR 1893-94, II, Table 20, p. 2095. This was the earliest instance found of such courses, obligatory or otherwise, in the public school system of any American city.

[32] CR 1889-90, II, pp. 1351-56. The table gives 36 as the number of cities, but Washington, D. C. was listed twice. In CR 1899-1900, II, p. 2438, and in CR 1904-05, II, p. 1168, the number of cities for 1890 is given as 37.

[33] CR 1893-94, II, Table 20, pp. 2097-2113. The percentage is minimal. As in 1889-90, in many cases figures for all grades were combined.

[34] CR 1899-1900, II, Ch. 40, Tables 1 and 4. The writer made the additions and calculated the percentage given. The figure 169 did not include cities in which instruction in mechanical drawing was given.

[35] CR 1909-10, II, Ch. 26, Tables 161 and 168. Both percentages are minimal. The figures in Table 161 were from 257 high schools in nearly all of the 48 states. No school was included that did not report at least 20 students in manual training courses. The writer made the additions from the list of schools given in Table 168, and calculated both percentages.

[36] The introductory remarks about manual training in the preceding section are generally applicable to domestic economy.

[37] CR 1893-94, II, pp. 2097-2113.

[38] CR 1909-10, II, Table 137 (domestic economy), Table 161 (Manual training). The percentage of 3.8 in Table 8 above represents 27,933 students. Of these 1,546 were boys. The percentage of 3.6 in Table 7 above represents 26,637 students. Of these 9,803 were girls, most of whom were probably taking mechanical drawing, clay modeling, and wood carving. See Note 35 above.

[39] Ibid. Table 168, Pt. 1.

[40] BS 1948-50, Ch. 5, p. 23, and Table 3. This was the first year such a division appeared for home economics. In Bul. 1938, No. 6, Table 3, the division into years was made for English, foreign languages, and mathematics, but a large number of students had to be placed in an "undesignated" category for lack of more specific information or designation by the reporting schools.

[41] CR 1904-05, I, pp. 244-48.

[42] CR 1904-05, I, pp. 251-53.

[43] Time, (August 8, 1955) carried the welcome news that the "national F.F.A. program" had made tremendous strides since the disheartening days of 1922. That organization was not in existence then, but one hopes that some agronomic license may be allowed in such terrestrial matters.

[44] CR 1886-87, pp. 534-43. Most of these schools were in city systems. The writer made the count.

[45] CR 1889-90, II, pp. 1394-1485. The writer made the count.

[46] Ibid., pp. 1106-08. This could not be verified. In the winter and spring of 1890 a Boston School Committee made an extensive tour to observe systems of physical training in the public schools of the West and South. Their administrative organization for physical training was not covered in the reference cited.

[47] Ibid. The Ling system was built on a series of rhythmic movements, all starting from one basic position. There were ten types of exercises. See Ibid., pp. 1103-06 for an account of Ling and his system.

[48] CR 1899-1900, II, pp. 2174-2350. The writer made the count and calculated the percentage.

[49] CR 1909-10, I, pp. 138-47. No estimate could be made of enrollments.

[50] CR 1915-16, I, pp. 317-19.

[51] BS 1920-22, II, pp. 590, 573, 590. In 1914-15 military drill was reported in only 119 schools. A little over 50% of the boys in those schools engaged in the drills— 1.2% of the total high school enrollment. CR 1915-16, II, p. 477.

[52] BS 1926-28, pp. 1085, 1069; Bulletin 1938, No. 6, Tables 2 and 3.

[53] CR 1870, p. 167; Cubberley, pp. 355, 428-29, 467-69.

[54] CR 1886-87, pp. 496-97. Mechanical drawing enrolled 8.8%.

[55] CR 1889-90, II, pp. 1394-1485. The writer made the count.

[56] See Note 34 above.

[57] CR 1870, p. 167; CR 1886-87, pp. 237-38. For a brief account of its beginning in Boston, and its development elsewhere in the country, see CR 1899-1900, I, pp. 349-55. See also Cubberley, pp. 355-56, 428.

[58] CR 1886-87, p. 237; Circulars of Information of the U. S. Bureau of Education, No. 1, 1886, pp. 41-78. See Dexter, p. 406. According to Dexter (p. 407) the proportion was even greater in 1901. The number of high school students in music could not be estimated for 1885-86 or for 1886-87. Most likely the great majority were in the lower grades.

[59] From "Extracts From the Report of the Mosely Educational Commission to the United States of America, October-December 1903," in CR 1904-05, I, p. 15. In a short, introductory article, W. T. Harris (*Ibid*. pp. 1-10), stated that the purpose of the Commission was "to find out the educational causes and conditions which have contributed to the rapid industrial development of the United States," and recommended it to the careful attention of American readers. The survey covered the whole range of education, public and private, academic and technical, at all levels, and was published in a 400-page book by the Cooperative Printing Society (Limited): London, 1904.

[60] *Ibd.*, p. 23.

[61] *Ibid.*, pp. 217-23.

[62] CR 1915-16, II, pp. 499 and 503. In 1909 the Music Teachers' National Association held its 31st annual meeting (no previous mention of this organization was found), and in 1910 the American Federation of Arts held its first annual convention. CR 1909-10, I, pp. 121 and 54 respectively.

[63] The percentage for drawing in 1922 may have been based on some enrollments in mechanical drawing. The statistics in *Bul. 1938, No. 6*, Tables 1 and 2, did include mechanical drawing under the entry, "Drawing and art." Since separate data for the subject were given, however, in Table 3, it was listed with the vocational and nonvocational subjects in Table 7 of this study.

[64] For brief accounts of Joseph Lancaster, the English schoolmaster, see *Cubberley*, pp. 128-37; *Knight* (1), pp. 66, 163-67. See also *Brown*, pp. 250-51.

[65] *Cubberley*, pp. 375-76; *Knight* (1), pp. 309-29.

[66] Three other books had actually preceded it, all published in Philadelphia. The first, *Schulordnung*, was written in German by Christopher Dock, in 1750, but not published until 1770. In 1808, Joseph Neef, a former associate of Pestalozzi in Switzerland, published a *Sketch of a Plan and Method of Education, founded on the Analysis of the Human Faculties and Natural Reason*. In 1813, Neef published his *Method of Instructing Children Rationally in the Arts of Writing and Reading*. Although none of these three had much more than local circulation, Neef made his books known in Louisville, Kentucky and in New Harmony, Indiana, where he taught. See *Cubberley*, p. 325, Note 1.

[67] *Cubberley*, pp. 378-84.

[68] CR 1899-1900, II, Ch. 38, pp. 2067-2117. New York University was probably the first to offer such courses, in 1832. See *Knight* (1), p. 334.

[69] *Knight* (1), p. 329.

[70] CR 1870, pp. 404-05. The meeting was held in Cleveland, August 15, 1870. The committee's whole report was published in pp. 399-405.

[71] CR 1886-87, p. 455. The public high schools outnumbered the semi-public over six to one.

SPLIT-LEVEL EDUCATION

The public high school is the product of our American democracy. Its growth reflects the social, political, and economic changes that have taken place in our national life. Its development reveals the evolving concept of secondary education from colonial times to the present. The history of its curriculum shows the changing pattern of our educational ideals and practices.

Earlier chapters traced in summary fashion the genealogy of the high school from its remote ancestor, the grammar school, to the private academy, the direct progenitor of the early high school and the connecting link between the two. Each stage showed advances over the one preceding in two different ways: extension of educational opportunities, and expansion of the curriculum. These two developments went hand in hand and with them came for the first time the idea that secondary education should be provided for two different groups, those who were preparing for college, and those who were not.

This has been one of the most influential concepts in the history of American education. It was primarily responsible for the founding of academies and later on of public high schools. It broke the academic stranglehold of the colleges, planted the seed of the elective system on both levels, and altered the entire pattern of secondary and collegiate education.

The original intent of the academies was to serve the educational needs of the non-college group. But they could not break entirely with academic tradition. To the more "practical" subjects, which they had planned to offer exclusively, public opinion compelled them to add those required for college preparation. The expanded curricula of the academies, in turn, compelled the colleges to examine their entrance requirements. Between 1800 and 1820 they began to require arithmetic, geography, English grammar, and algebra, in addition to Latin and Greek.

The early public high schools, beginning in 1821, were also unsuccessful in their attempts to establish complete academic independence. Their influence, however, together with that of the academies, brought about further changes in the colleges. Between 1820 and 1875 they began to recognize and to accept such "non-academic"

subjects as geometry, history, physical geography, English composition, physical sciences, and modern foreign languages.[1]

The transition period between 1821 and 1890 marked the high point of the academies, ended their dominance in the field, and brought secondary education largely under public control. It was a period of great and prolonged educational confusion. Scientific and industrial developments were changing the pattern of American life. Population shifts into large and growing urban centers created a new type of citizen and intensified demands for an enlargement of the high school curriculum to meet the needs of a new industrial and commercial age.

When the Department of Education was set up in 1867, it soon discovered that the high school curriculum was a coat of many colors. Local communities, with a characteristic spirit of independence, had organized their high schools to meet local demands. The system of state control was in its infancy or was not yet born in some states, tottering to its feet in some, rapidly maturing in others. Courses multiplied and then faded away. Students moving with their families from one section of the country to another found it difficult to adjust to a new program of studies. Each college had its own standards and method for admitting students. Parents with college-bound children complained because the schools devoted too much time to subjects not acceptable to the colleges of their choice. Other parents complained because the schools were too much concerned with subjects of no immediate practical value in business and industry. The American high school had growing pains.

One of the first tasks of the Bureau of Education was to find out what the schools were doing. Although the number of public high schools was increasing rapidly during this period, the first information about curricula came only from private schools. Enrollments were generally reported for three curricula: English, classical, and modern foreign languages. Separate reports were made on other schools, also private, primarily devoted to business and commercial subjects, manual and industrial training, music, and art. Many of these had courses on both high school and college levels, but enrollment figures were usually combined.[2]

The first survey of high schools supported wholly by public funds covered the year 1886-87. That year for the first time, enrollments were also recorded for separate subjects—Latin, Greek, French, German, English, free-hand drawing, and mechanical drawing. All of the information was given in addition to the customary report on

enrollments by the two curricula, classical and scientific.[3] No information was given about any courses in mathematics, science, or history.

In the following year the omissions in mathematics and science were partially filled in,[4] but it was 1889-90 before history was added. During the intervening year, enrollments were given in four curricula for public high schools located in cities with populations of 4,000 and above.[5] Another table gave a list of manual training courses and enrollments in all grades in public schools of 28 cities.[6]

Some additional details of the history of the curriculum, covering thirteen broad areas of human knowledge and endeavor, were presented in the last chapter. These details included a short historical sketch of various subjects in each subject-matter field before 1890. Thirteen separate tables listed the subjects, old and new, as they were tabulated by the United States Office of Education between 1890 and 1949. Each table, in terms of individual and total percentages based on total high school enrollments, showed the changes in a single broad field of study for each of six different years.

That type of presentation, made necessary by the accelerated addition of subjects after 1890, could not show the changing pattern of the high school curriculum as a whole. It did show piece-meal the changes that took place in each of the subject-matter fields. To evaluate those changes, we must see them on a broad canvas. To determine their educational significance, we must examine them in their relationship to each other. For this purpose the table below combines the thirteen separate tables into one.

This table possibly presents the most complete statistical summary of curricular developments in our public high schools between 1890 and 1949 that has ever been published. It shows at a glance their scope and depth. It makes plain the twofold function of the high school that has made it the pivotal point in our educational system. It provides the factual evidence for an evolving theory of split-level education that has come to dominate the high school scene.

Although the curriculum survey of 1889-90 was far more extensive than any made up to that time, lack of adequate data limited the tabulation to subjects in only four of the thirteen broad fields. With the possible exception of agriculture, however, it is quite certain that all of the subjects listed in 1910 and even 1922 were in the curriculum before 1890.[7] Their very omission, and the rather startling changes that took place between 1890 and 1900 require an explanation that is important for understanding Table 14.

After 1870 many of the private academies became preparatory

TABLE 14

SUMMARY OF PERCENTAGE CHANGES IN SUBJECT MATTER FIELDS
AND OF SUBJECTS ADDED IN PUBLIC HIGH SCHOOLS GRADES 9-12
IN CERTAIN YEARS BETWEEN 1889-90 AND 1948-49 [1]

		1890	1900	1910	1922	1934	1949
	Enrollment in 1000's	203	519	715 915	1,255 2,230	4,967 5,621	5,399
1	Mathematics	66.7 (3)	85.6 (4)	89.7 (4)	74.9 (6)	56.2 (6)	55.0 (7)
2	Foreign Languages	54.1 (4)	75.6 (4)	84.1 (5)	55.0 (6)	35.7 (6)	22.0 (6)
3	Science	32.9 (2)	83.9 (6)	81.7 (9)	58.4 (10)	51.3 (10)	54.1 (11)
4	Social Studies	27.3 (4)	62.3 (7)	71.6 (7)	78.2 (10)	78.8 (18)	99.4 (20)
5	English		80.6 (2)	114.2 (2)	82.9 (7)	96.0 (14)	103.1 (15)
6	Business Education		21.7 (4)	11.0 (1)	42.1 (10)	57.7 (13)	58.8 (14)
7	Vocational and Nonvocational Subjects			8.6 (2)	13.7 (4)	21.0 (15)	34.7 (31)
8	Home Economics			3.8 (2)	14.3 (4)	16.7 (10)	24.2 (10)
9	Agriculture			4.7 (1)	5.1 (2)	3.6 (5)	6.7 (4)
10	Physical Education		2.0 (1)	(1)	14.5 (3)	58.4 (3)	109.1 (6)
11	Music				25.3 (3)	24.8 (5)	30.1 (9)
12	Art				14.7 (1)	8.6 (5)	9.0 (7)
13	Teacher Training		2.6 (1)	1.9 (1)	1.0 (2)	0.1 (1)	0.002 (1)
	Total Subjects	13	29	35	68	111	141

[1] The numbers under the dates represent the total high school enrollment in the nearest whole number of thousands. The numbers in parenthesis under each percentage show the number of different subjects in a broad subject matter field. Percentages are underscored to indicate the year in which they reached a maximum. To the left side of the table references are given to the appropriate tables of Chapter IV.

The percentages were obtained by dividing the total number of students studying all subjects in a given subject matter field by the total high school enrollment for that year. Since duplicates (the same student enrolled in two or more subjects in a single broad field, such as English, or social studies) could not be excluded, the percentages show the comparative student concentrations in different subject matter fields. They do *not* show the exact proportion of separate students in a given field.

The figures and percentages (all additions and many subject percentages calculated by the writer) were taken from or based on statistics published by the U.S. Office of Education for the years indicated. See Appendix B.

schools for college. Since the colleges still stressed Latin, Greek, and mathematics, the academies gradually tended to neglect most subjects except those. The public high schools, on the other hand, had been compelled to add the principal college subjects. They had also broadened their curricula to satisfy increasing demands for additional subjects. Among these were modern foreign languages, modern history, natural science, and sociology. Many high schools also offered vocal music, shorthand writing, cooking, bookkeeping, calisthenics, and woodworking. (See Note 9). In the meantime more states were passing compulsory education laws.[8] These laws and a rising birth rate were bringing ever larger numbers into the high schools. As the curriculum expanded to meet their greatly diversified backgrounds, capacities, and educational interests, the dual function of the high school became increasingly apparent and difficult. Many of the new subjects were not acceptable for admission to college. Some of the older subjects failed to meet rising college standards. Many short courses, particularly in science, were offered, and some subjects were taught one way for college entrance, another way for more immediate and practical use. Both groups of students suffered educationally, and the number of students going to college from the public high schools was proportionately less in the early 1890's than before 1870.[9]

These and related problems demanded intelligent action and planning. In 1892 the National Education Association appointed a Committee of Ten, with Harvard's president Charles W. Eliot as chairman, to study the entire situation and to make recommendations dealing with it. This committee divided the high school curriculum into nine groups of related subjects and appointed nine sub-committees of ten members each to study them and to make recommendations about their place in the high school pattern.[10] These subjects were: (1) Latin; (2) Greek; (3) English; (4) Other Modern Languages (German and French); (5) Mathematics (arithmetic, algebra, plane and solid geometry); (6) Physical Sciences (physics, chemistry, astronomy); (7) Natural History (biology, botany, zoology, physiology); (8) History, Civil Government, Political Economy; (9) Geography (physical geography, geology, meteorology).

In each of their meetings the sub-committees found it necessary to consider the subjects in relation to elementary and higher education, to teacher training and teaching methods. The comprehensive nature and thoroughness of the final Report make it one of the important documents in the history of American education.[11].

Of the many interesting recommendations three or four had special

significance. One of these had to do with the correlation of elementary and high school studies. The pattern should be set in the lower grades and carried through high school. The study of Latin and modern languages should begin at least by the fifth grade. (The strides made in that direction since 1951 have been slow in coming, but they would receive the Committee's full endorsement.) Less time should be spent on arithmetic than the elementary schools were then giving, to make room for a graduated approach to algebra, plane and solid geometry. Algebra should be taught in connection with arithmetic; the two geometries in connection with drawing, but related to arithmetic and elementary physics. After elementary instruction of this sort in mathematics, the student, at age 14, should go into the formal sudy of algebra, then into plane and solid geometry and trigonometry. The physical sciences should be introduced in the lower grades also, while the students' powers of observation and natural curiosity were very strong and capable of rapid development. Experiments which involved use of simple measuring instruments would bring the child into direct contact with objects and be a valuable preparation for laboratory experiments later on.

The study of natural history or science should begin in the primary grades and continue on through at least one year in high school. No texts were necessary, but the work should be coordinated with the study of literature, language, and drawing. By the use of notebooks and drawing, students would be trained in the art of expression as well as observation.

A coordinated program of history study should be worked out, four years in the grades, and four in high school. The first two years should deal with mythology and biography preparatory to the study of general and American history and the history of various countries, including Greece and Rome. To be properly studied and taught, history should be associated with English, ancient and modern languages, physical and commercial geography. U.S. history should be coordinated with civil government. Students should be required to keep notebooks, and to make abstracts and maps, the last in connection with drawing. English themes should be written on historical subjects. Civil government should be introduced orally in the lower grades, but a text with collateral readings should be used in high school where the emphasis should be on comparative government.

The recommendations on geography were the most revolutionary of all. It was defined as a study of the "physical environment of man." It should include not only a description of the earth, physical geog-

raphy, but the elements of botany, zoology, astronomy, meteorology, commercial geography, government, and ethnology—man's racial divisions and characteristics. Since it involved so many different elements the study should begin in the lower grades and proceed in logically arranged courses step by step through the high school. It, too, would be associated with English and drawing, in addition to the other subjects mentioned.

It was conceded by all the subcommittees that natural science, foreign languages, and mathematics should be substantial parts of education. The committee on English felt that it should be given at least equal status with foreign languages and should, because of its comprehensive nature, be basic to the study of all other subjects. The essentials of grammar should be taught in the lower grades, and good English, both oral and written, should be required by teachers of all subjects. This requirement should extend to the high schools where the study of all subjects should contribute to the pupil's training in English. All students should study English for four years in high school. The courses should include literature, training in oral and written expression, historical and systematic grammar. The history of the development of the English language should be part of every student's knowledge. Grammar and word study should go hand in hand, and particularly useful for that purpose would be the study of Latin, French, and German. The study of words could be used to illustrate the political, social, intellectual, and religious development of the English race. The history and geography of English-speaking peoples would also fit into such a pattern of English studies. And finally, the committee recommended that admission of a student to college should depend primarily on his ability to write English, as shown in his examinations in subjects other than English.

There were naturally some objections to the Committee's rather ambitious and idealistic program. Chief among these was the mental strain it might impose, particularly on the younger pupils in the elementary grades. It was argued that the present course of study had already proved difficult for many of them; the proposed curriculum would be even more strenuous.

This opinion had been anticipated and the full report included the answering argument. It was true that some of the children had experienced some difficulty in their studies. In the opinion of the Committee this had stemmed not so much from lack of ability as lack of interest. The current courses concentrated too much on the study of grammar, arithmetic, and geography in which learning by rote mem-

ory played the major role. Memory was not learning and too great dependence on it stifled the child's imagination and left unused and undeveloped many latent capabilities. The new program would not be easy, but presented in the right way it would arouse the child's interest, appeal to his imagination and develop his powers of reason and observation, which were greater than commonly supposed. To say that a child of only average ability could not learn the elements of algebra and science, for example, was to assume as true something that had not even been tried. Motivation based on interest was a powerful factor in all learning. When the program had been used for a while and proved too difficult for some, teaching methods rather than pupil's ability might be the cause. Much would be demanded of the children, perhaps even more of the teachers. Later on, when new and better methods of teaching had been developed and better textbooks written, if the program still proved too difficult for some, proper adjustments and changes would have to be made for them.[12]

There is little doubt that the Committee's philosophy had been influenced by two ideas that had long held sway in educational circles: that it was the business of the schools to impart knowledge as a basis for good citizenship, and to develop mental training by disciplinary drill. By tradition, the subjects best suited for accomplishing both of these purposes were Latin, Greek, and mathematics. To these the Committee, in keeping with modern needs and developments, added English grammar, composition, and literature; history, modern foreign languages, civil government, geography, physics, chemistry, physical geography, and several other science subjects. But they gave chief emphasis to the values of mental discipline, for which they had the support of a new psychological theory.

Under this theory, which was developed between 1860 and 1890, the mind was thought to be divided into several separate compartments, each of which controlled different faculties, such as judgment, will, memory, reason, imagination, and feelings. It was assumed that mastery of certain subjects trained the separate faculties and that the mental discipline thus acquired was "transferred" for mastery of other subjects.[13] Since this involved an educational process that was the same for all students, essentially the same type of curriculum was necessary for all.

With this in mind, and in view of the different interests and abilities of students, the Committee drew up four suggested curricula: Classical (three foreign languages, one modern), Latin-Scientific (two foreign languages, one modern), Modern Languages (two foreign

languages, both modern), and English (one foreign language, ancient or modern). Common to all four curricula were English (4 years), mathematics (3 years), history (3 years), a foreign language (4 years), and science (3 years: physics, chemistry, and physical geography.)

The Committee felt that these subjects were essential for a well-rounded high school education. It realized that many students, from choice or necessity, left high school after the first or second year, and that the high schools as a whole did not "exist for the purpose of preparing boys and girls for colleges." It was even more important for them than for the others to have at least the rudiments of a good education. What could be better for them than an introduction to the fundamentals of linguistic, literary, historical, mathematical, and scientific knowledge? Latin, German, or French, and English represented the first two fields; history, the second; algebra and geometry, the third; physical geography, and physics or chemistry, the fourth.

Because of the student's continuation in school and because sound educational planning suggested it, the Committee believed that choice of a particular curriculum should not be made until after the first, or better still, after the second year in high school. Accordingly, most of the subjects for the first two years were the same in all four curricula. The chief differences were in the selection of a foreign language and the substitution of botany or zoology for history in the second year of the Latin-Scientific, and Modern Languages curricula.

Of the four programs open to students the Committee expressly stated that the two emphasizing Modern Languages and English, because of the conditions of teacher training in the United States, "must in practice be distinctly inferior to the other two." A student who successfully completed any of the four, however, should be acceptable for college work. If the Committee's recommendations were "*well carried out*" (italics added), they "might fairly be held to make *all* of the *main* subjects taught in the secondary schools of equal rank for the purposes of admission to college or scientific school. They would all be taught consecutively and thoroughly, and would all be carried on in the same spirit; they would all be used for training the powers of observation, memory, expression, and reasoning; and they would all be good to that end, although differing among themselves in quality and substance."

Programs of that sort were badly needed "because the pupil may now go through a secondary school course of a very feeble and scrappy nature—studying a little of many subjects and not much of

any one, getting, perhaps, a little information in a variety of fields, but nothing which can be called a thorough training."

Some of the subjects commonly taught in many schools of the day, as the Committee noted, did not appear among their specific curricular recommendations. The omission of such subjects as drawing, music, and elocution did not imply that they should not be offered. But *how* they should be introduced as *supplementary* to other courses was a matter for local school authorities, rather than for the Committee, to decide. Drawing, in particular, was "to be used in the study of history, botany, zoology, astronomy, meteorology, physics, geography, and physiography." This kind of drawing was, in the opinion of many, the most useful type—"namely, that which is applied to recording, describing, and discussing observations." Its use might not "prevent the need of some special instruction . . . but it ought to diminish the number of periods devoted exclusively to drawing." Also, in the "large number of periods devoted to English and history there would be some time for incidental instruction in the elements" of ethics, economics, metaphysics, and aesthetics. "It is through the reading and writing required of pupils, or recommended to them, that the fundamental ideas on these important topics are to be inculcated." And finally, if a need should be felt for more subjects "thought to have practical importance in trade or the useful arts," they could be offered as options for some of the science courses in the third and fourth years of the English Curriculum." [14]

The influence of the Committee of Ten's Report was felt in several ways. It caused widespread discussion of the principles and purposes of education among laymen and professional educators alike. It focused attention on the public high school and its dual role in our educational system: the connecting link between the elementary school and college; and the end of formal education for the great majority of students. It "soon led to considerable uniformity in secondary school courses throughout the United States." [15]

Two other reports made during this period were also influential in bringing about uniformity in high school subjects and in college entrance requirements: The Committee of Fifteen on Elementary Education,[16] and The Committee on College Entrance Requirements.[17]

Among the recommendations of the last named committee there were several which pertained particularly to the high school curriculum:

Although the elective system was recognized, it should not be unlimited. A certain number of subjects should be required for admis-

sion to college: foreign languages (four units, no language in less than two units); mathematics (two units); English (two units); history (one); science (one). Two years of the same science was better than a year each of two different sciences. In addition to a year (one unit) in American history and civil government, colleges should also accept one-half year of intensive study of some period of history, particularly of the United States. The colleges should also accept one unit of economics, which should include a course in elementary political economy and instruction in commercial geography and industrial history. The colleges should accept, in general, high school subjects taught four periods a week for one year under competent instruction.

This last recommendation involved a principle that came to be known as the "equivalence" of subjects. The Committee of Ten had made a similar recommendation, but both committees plainly had in mind subjects that were academic in nature. Although the Committee on College Entrance Requirements expressly stated its belief that all subjects were not of equal disciplinary or cultural value, its recommendation undoubtedly paved the way for later acceptance of such a principle and for many additions to the list of subjects acceptable for college entrance.[18]

There is little doubt that the nation-wide discussion of the reports made by these committees was primarily responsible for the changes that took place in the high school curriculum between 1890-1910.[19] In the curriculum survey of 1894-95, within nine months of the Committee of Ten's Report, rhetoric and three additional subjects in science were listed for the first time. By 1897-98 all but three of the subjects it had recommended had been included.[20]

The outstanding curriculum development in the period from 1890 through 1910, as Table 14 shows, was the increasing proportion of students enrolled in the five subject-matter fields stressed by the two committees. During the same period more non-academic subjects were tabulated. The increasing proportion of enrollments they attracted showed up significantly between 1910 and 1922, when the distribution and concentration of high school studies gave unmistakable evidence of decided changes. These changes became even more evident in the period between 1922 and 1940.

To put this evidence into clearer focus for the entire period between 1890 and 1949, it would be helpful to group the data of Table 14 by related fields. The analysis below provides the basis for the grouping.

Different as they are in content, foreign languages, mathematics, and science have one common characteristic: they are all cumulative

in nature. One does not begin the study of algebra with quadratic equations, or the study of French with one of Racine's comedies, or of physics with Einstein's theory of relativity. In each subject it is necessary to begin with basic forms or concepts and proceed by gradual, logical steps from the elementary to the complex. Each successive step depends on the ones preceding and all form parts of a related whole. Learning such subjects calls for consistent mental effort that cannot be relaxed without the risk of failure or added difficulties. These three subject-matter fields by common consent have long been considered the most difficult in the high school curriculum. They form Group A.

English and social studies form Groups B and C respectively. Although they have many things in common, the general content of subjects in the two fields is widely different. In each field the emphasis is on extensive reading, analysis, and interpretation. Research papers are often assigned in which attention is paid to orderly presentation, clear expression and thought, accurate information and, in English at least, to grammar and spelling. While English composition also permits creative effort, in social studies that element is largely confined to method of presentation. Recitations in both fields are conducted by lecture or by lecture-discussion techniques, if class size allows.

Group D includes business education, vocational and nonvocational subjects, home economics and agriculture. Their subject matter varies greatly, but the content of each combines some theory with practical application. Emphasis is given to the cultivation of some ability, skill, or hobby that will be useful or enjoyable in the home, on the farm, or in the business world. Learning in these fields has been called training, to distinguish it from the more purely bookish type.

Physical education, music, and art, for the sake of convenience, are put in Group E.[21] These three fields, each so different from the others, have one common purpose: to provide opportunity for the discovery and cultivation of special talents. They afford outlets for creative and recreational activities that promote physical or artistic health and enjoyment. Art, in contrast to the other two, encourages and stimulates individual effort. Music and physical education add to that, teamwork and group play. All three tend to develop habits of coordination, determination, and patience. Music and art stress esthetic appreciation and values.[22]

Comparison of Tables 14 and 15 shows that the pattern is essen-

TABLE 15

PERCENTAGE TOTALS OF SUBJECT-MATTER FIELDS IN THE
HIGH SCHOOL CURRICULUM, GRADES 9-12, ARRANGED IN GROUPS
BY TYPE OF COURSE IN CERTAIN YEARS BETWEEN 1889-90 AND 1948-49

GROUP	1890	1900	1910	1922	1934	1949
Total enrollments in 1000's	203	519	739 915	2,155 2,230	4,497 5,621	5,399
A. Cumulative Subjects	153.7	245.1	255.5	188.3	143.2	131.1
Number of fields	3	3	3	3	3	3
Number of subjects	9	14	18	22	22	24
B. English		80.6	114.2	82.9	96.0	103.1
Number of fields		1	1	1	1	1
Number of subjects		2	2	7	14	15
C. Social Studies	27.3	62.3	71.6	78.2	78.8	99.4
Number of fields	1	1	1	1	1	1
Number of subjects	4	7	7	10	18	20
D. Practical Subjects		21.7	28.1	75.2	99.0	124.4
Number of fields		1	4	4	4	4
Number of subjects		4	6	20	43	59
E. Health, Music, Art		2.0		54.5	91.8	148.2
Number of fields		1	1	3	3	3
Number of subjects		1	1	7	13	22

tially the same for both. By 1910 the cumulative subjects and English, Groups A and B, had reached their greatest proportion of student enrollments.[23] Between that year and 1922 both groups had their sharpest drops.[24] Group A continued to lose, and reached its lowest point in 1949. After 1922 English arrested its descent, but by 1949 it was still some distance below its 1910 peak.[25] All the other groups continued the increases which had begun with additional subject tabulations, and came to their peaks in 1949.[26]

On the basis of statistical evidence, then, it is possible to analyze the broad changes that took place in the high school curriculum and to see how they fit in with educational developments in each of the three periods between 1890 and 1949.

In the first period, 1890 through 1910, the cumulative subjects and English dominated the scene. Student concentration in the cumula-

tive subjects alone was greater than that in all other subjects combined. Social studies made impressive gains and practical subjects showed signs of growing strength. Music, art, and physical education played insignificant roles.

This was the period during which the philosophy of the Committee of Ten and of the Committee on Entrance Requirements had the strongest influence. That philosophy stressed the values of intellectual and cultural discipline. It held that the purpose of high school education was the same for all students: to sharpen one's mental powers, to broaden one's intellectual and cultural horizons, to develop maturity of thought and judgment, to instill a sense of responsibility for intelligent participation in public affairs, and to strengthen character. All students, to the extent of their ability, no matter what their ultimate goals might be, should be introduced to the five great realms of human thought and experience: English language and literature; foreign languages and literatures, particularly Latin; mathematics, algebra and geometry; science, particularly physics, chemistry, and physical geography; history, including civil government. A course of study based on such subjects, for four years, or even for two years, would be the best possible preparation for individual development and civic usefulness. The longer course would also serve as the best avenue to college.

During this same period the work and philosophy of John Dewey began to exercise an influence that was to have a profound effect on the high school curriculum. His thesis that education is life and not preparation for life, and the psychological investigations of G. Stanley Hall and others paved the way for a new approach to study of the curriculum through observation and experimentation. The contrast between the old and the new educational theories was pointed up in a criticism of the Committee of Ten and the other two committees.

Their work was "dominated by subject-matter specialists, possessed of a profound faith in the value of mental discipline. No study of pupil abilities, social needs, interest, capacities, or differential training found a place in their deliberations. The basis of their recommendations throughout was that of individual judgment. It was twenty years afterward before any use was made of investigations as to curriculum content, or any experimental work was made as to grade placement and the organization of the materials of the curriculum. As the committees supported one another, their views became accepted and the reconstructed curriculum which followed soon became crystalized and difficult to change. There was much vigorous dissent from

teachers, but for a long time it was not influential. A change came
only as we turned from college presidents and professors, subject-
matter specialists, and private school executives, whose interests were
in mind training, scholarship as such, and knowledge for knowledge's
sake, and who compiled their reports by armchair philosophic methods, to students of educational practices who applied the experimental
and quantitative method to the solution of educational problems and
built their report on the results of experimental research." [27]

The change mentioned above came with the investigations of another committee appointed by the National Education Association in
1911: Committee on the Economy of Time. Its four reports, published between 1915 and 1919, were "believed to have marked a turning point in the study of the curriculum in the United States." [28] The
purposes of the Committee were "to bring about economy of time in
the work of schools by the use of scientific methods, to determine the
'socially worth-while instructional materials', their proper placement
in the grades, and their organization to fit what was called the 'life-
needs' of the pupils, and to eliminate those materials that were no
longer considered to be of real worth." [29]

The effects of this "life-adjustment" concept, as it was later called,
were plainly evident in the transition period between 1910 and 1922.
Proportionately the cumulative subjects and English lost considerable
ground, but still remained the leading fields of study. The cumulative
subjects constituted the strongest single group, social studies made
only minor gains, but practical subjects accelerated rapidly. Health,
music, and art secured a strong foothold.[30] The focal point of secondary education was definitely shifting from emphasis on subject-
matter to emphasis on the pupils and their life-adjustment needs. The
old idea that pupils should conform to the curriculum was giving way
to the new concept of adapting the curriculum to fit the wide diver-
gence of student interests and capacities.

During the next period, 1922 through 1949, this movement gained
considerable momentum and the positions of the five groups changed
radically (Table 15). Through 1934 the cumulative subjects (Group
A) remained in the lead; practical subjects (Group D) passed English (Group B) for second place. Health, music and art (Group E)
came next to Group B, and social studies (Group C) came last.

By 1949 further shifts had occurred. Group E replaced Group A
in the lead. Group D came third, Group B, fourth, and Group C,
last. For the second time—the first time was in 1934—the subjects in
Groups C and D totaled more than half of the subjects in the entire

high school curriculum. Student concentration in those two groups for the first time was almost as great as the concentration in Groups A and B. Although Group A remained the strongest academic subject-matter field, its loss in proportion of enrollments between 1910 and 1949—124.4—was exactly the same as student concentration in Group D in 1949. Coincidence or not, the decline in the proportion of student enrollments in the cumulative subjects between 1910 and 1949, and the simultaneous increase of enrollments in practical subjects constitute one of the most striking developments in the history of the high school curriculum.

This development did not come all at once or in isolation from other changes. Between 1910 and 1922 the number of subjects listed in the cumulative subjects increased from 18 to 22; those in English, from 2 to 7; in social studies, from 7 to 10, and those in health, music, and art, from 3 to 7. The most phenomenal increase, however, was in practical subjects—from 6 to 20.[31] The number in this group doubled, with a little to spare, between 1922 and 1934. In 1934 and in 1949 student concentration in business education alone was greater than that in foreign languages, science, or mathematics. In 1949 vocational and nonvocational subjects, and home economics had also passed foreign languages.[32] The subjects in Group D as a whole made up 41.8% of the entire curriculum and equalled the number listed in Groups A, B, and C combined (Table 15).

The decided changes that took place in the high school curriculum after 1910, and increasingly between 1922 and 1949, reflected the influence of the new educational philosophy—primarily that of John Dewey. The aim of education was no longer almost exclusively intellectual, but social. Since there was little or no transfer of training, all subjects were of equal educational value if they appealed to the interests of the student. The main function of the school was to foster individual growth in keeping with each child's innate capacities, and to make each child a useful member of society by making school life a replica of the larger life outside.[33] The objectives of secondary education might be summed up in the "seven cardinal principles" that should govern the organization of high school curricula: health, command of fundamental processes, worthy home-membership, vocation, civic education, worthy use of leisure, ethical character.[34]

Although the statement and discussion of these objectives attracted considerable attention, they were too vague and comprehensive to have much immediate and direct influence on the high school

curriculum.[35] They did serve, however, to reemphasize the social purposes of education during the period of adjustment that followed World War I. This happened to be the period also when the last few states adopted compulsory education laws and most states revised and strengthened previous enactments (see Note 8 on p. 78). The entry and retention of more and more students in high school, with their greatly diversified interests, backgrounds, and capacities, increased the demands for additional subjects. The extension of educational opportunities to increased numbers, the goal of "at least a high school education for all," and the social adjustment philosophy—all these helped to bring about the changes in the high school curriculum so noticeable between 1922 and 1949.

But there were two other factors, somewhat contradictory in nature. One of these was a two-pronged assumption that an increase in numbers meant a decrease in average ability, and that in the past only the best students finished high school and continued on to college. Evidence has been cited and recent tests have been made that indicate that both of these assumptions are unfounded.[36] Between 1900 and 1920 a student's chance of finishing high school increased from 16 to 45 out of 100. If those trends continued, for students born in 1940 the chance increased to 62. If they still continue, the chance has increased to 70, for those born in 1950. The chances of entering college increased, for those same years, from 10 to 16 to 22 to 25; of finishing college, from 3 to 9 to 15 to 18.[37]

Do these statistics mean that the average intelligence of students has been decreasing, while the number of students has been increasing enormously? Do they mean that only the best students have finished high school and continued on to college? There is no doubt that more and more students *have* finished high school and that more and more *have* entered college. If only the best students have finished high school and entered college, then the *number* of *best* students has certainly increased. It does not necessarily follow, however, that only the best students finish high school. In recent years 38% of the most capable students who finished high school did not enter college.[38] Is it illogical to assume that some of the *best* students drop out of high school before they finish?

This was a problem of concern to educators in the period around 1890 and before. It has been of no less concern since. But only in comparatively recent years have detailed studies been made to determine the reasons for the failure of many students to complete their high school education. The reasons are naturally varied and num-

erous. Among them are: lack of interest in the work or of ability to
do it; the feeling of being "lost in the shuffle" of a large mass of students; indifference of teachers; economic conditions; the difficulty of
transferring from one course of study to another; desire for greater
independence and freedom from conformity; community environment; poor health.

These were some of the more common causes. Although they were
based on conditions in school systems of cities with more than 200,-
000 population, as reported in 1950, there is little basis for believing
that adolescent motives vary to any great extent because of school
size or lapse of time.

It is not surprising that the greatest number of drop-outs occurs
at age 16, when compulsory education usually ends, and most students are in or between the ninth and tenth grades.[39] What is surprising perhaps is the fact that the percentage of drop-outs is apparently greater for students in vocational than for those in academic
courses.[40]

This may simply indicate that academic courses are better taught
than those of a vocational nature and attract better students. On
the other hand, since academic subjects are admittedly more difficult,
some students undoubtedly yield to the lure of the easier path. The
boredom that often results is probably difficult to distinguish from
the frustration of too great mental strain—and probably more frequent.[41]

Since the high school curriculum was much more varied between
1922 and 1949 than between 1891 and 1922, it would be interesting
to compare the drop-out rates of the two periods. Incomplete and
uncertain data for the earlier period make this unfeasible. It is possible, however, to get some clues about the influence of the two types
of curricula on the percentage of students prepared for, or actually
attending college after high school graduation.[42]

In 1891 almost 29% of the high school graduates were prepared
for college. In 1900 the percentage had increased slightly to a little
over 30. By 1910, when the number preparing for other institutions
was included for the first time, the total percentage reached 49. In
1915, it was 52%; in 1922, 46.4. In 1928, at the height of prosperity,
it was 42.8.[43] In 1934, during the depression, the percentage dropped
to 25. In 1952, it had risen almost to the 1922 level—44.8.[44]

Although the percentages before and after 1915, as pointed out
(Note 42) above, are not exactly comparable, those within each period may be compared with each other. Between 1891 and 1915,

while the percentage of graduates prepared for higher institutions increased from 28.6 to 52.1, the number of graduates increased from 23,000 to 176,000 — an increase of 665%. During this same period the total high school enrollment increased 505%. Between 1922 and and 1952, a slightly longer period, the number of graduates increased from 243,000 to 1,196,000—an increase of 293%, while the percentage of graduates entering higher institutions had a slight decrease from 46.4 to 44.8. During this period the total high school enrollment increased 164%.

In each period, as these figures show, the number of graduates increased more rapidly than the number of high school students as a whole. In both cases the rate for the earlier period was considerably faster—1.7 times as fast for the increase of graduates and 3 times as fast for the increase in total enrollment—at a time when high school enrollments were largely concentrated in mathematics, science, foreign languages, chiefly Latin, English, and history. Although the figures give no clue to the quality of the work, the great increase in the number of graduates *prepared* for college does *not* suggest a decrease in the average level of intelligence or ability. Neither does it prove or disprove that only the best students graduated.

At the beginning of the second period, although they were still fairly strong, mathematics, foreign languages and science had gone noticeably down the scale of student attention. Even English had suffered a temporary relapse. By 1934 and increasingly by 1949 it was apparent that a new type of secondary education was in vogue, and that a new concept of split-level education had been evolved.

The new concept was based on the assumption mentioned above, that large increases in numbers meant a decrease in the average level of intelligence. It therefore followed that a curriculum primarily academic or bookish in nature, was not suitable for the growing masses of high school students. Their minds were not too susceptible of mental discipline. In place of physics or chemistry they needed general science; in place of algebra, general mathematics. Since they needed subjects of practical and immediate value, foreign languages were a waste of time for most. Although English should remain a required subject for three or four years, grammar had to be diluted, and the study of literature, almost perforce, had to be turned into an obstacle race in reading.

Among the social studies, with better citizenship and civic betterment as worthy objectives, history of the past was unimportant. Contemporary problems were best solved in the light of contemporary

knowledge of national and international affairs. American history should become—and did after 1928—the leading subject, even if the neglect of ancient and European history isolated it from the logical stream of historical development. To give students a better grasp of the current scene, American history should be supported by such courses as problems of democracy, orientation, occupations, sociology, economics, world geography, and world history.

But there are other sides of a well-developed, socially adjusted personality. Man does not live by mind alone. Certain practical or domestic arts should supplement mental training for both sexes. Dexterity of hand, familiarity with machines and tools, acquaintance with business methods and procedures—all these would serve many practical needs of daily life. They would lead to self-sufficiency and in many cases to self-support.

Nor should health and cultural pursuits be neglected. The proper care of the body, cultivation of sports that could be followed in later life, development of artistic and musical talent—all these would yield rich dividends in physical well being, in esthetic enjoyment, and in rewarding use of leisure time.

There is little doubt that the relatively modern practice of adapting courses of study to the individual student's interest and ability is more intelligent than a system of rigid requirements with *no* flexibility. There is also little doubt that an almost unlimited number of widely different electives presupposes a greater maturity of judgment than most students possess, or a more effective counseling service than scientific tests and measurements have yet produced. It cannot be denied that the proportion of students who finish high school has been gradually increasing since 1890. Neither can it be denied, on the other hand, that the more flexible curriculum during the period 1922 through 1949 failed to increase the proportion of graduates attending higher institutions.

The primary function of the high school has never been and is not now the preparation of students for college. The number of students who drop out has always been greater than the number who finish, and the number who finish has always been greater than the number who go to college. The kind of education both groups receive can constitute one of our nation's greatest assets or become one of its greatest liabilities.

The new form of split-level education may be the salvation of many students. The less difficult and more practical subjects may be the only ones they can master under ordinary teachers and in crowded

classrooms. That some students are not capable of strenuous mental effort is unfortunately true. But split-level education often results, not from lack of ability, but from *under-estimation* of a student's capacity, by himself, his parents, or his adviser, or from the very human tendency, to which even students are prone, to follow the path of least resistance. Those who make the wrong choice in high school, whatever the reason, often realize it too late to make the necessary substitutions or to change their objectives. The effect on a student can be disastrous, in lowered morale and self-confidence, in loss of interest, and in lack of adequate preparation for college or for the larger world outside. Here is the educational fallow ground we must cultivate. Here is the educational wasteland we can and must reclaim.

[1] *Cubberley*, p. 315, lists the separate subjects and the dates they were first accepted by leading colleges. See *Brown*, pp. 231-32, 371-72, for a similar list.

[2] It is interesting to note that business and commercial schools, mostly under private control, were offering Spanish, along with French and German, as early as 1873 (CR 1873, p. 581). Separate professional courses were not listed that year, and were first noted in CR 1877, pp. 372-75. By 1889-90 the list of professional courses had been considerably enlarged, and Latin and Greek had been added to the languages taught (CR 1889-90, II, pp. 1621-28).

[3] See Chapter II, Notes 2 and 4.

[4] CR 1887-88, p. 490.

[5] CR 1888-89, II, pp. 831-52. The four were: classical, English or scientific, commercial, teacher training, and "other courses and unclassified." No data were given for separate subjects.

[6] *Ibid.*, pp. 1363-66. It was impossible to separate statistics for the high schools from those of the lower grades.

[7] In addition to the comments above, see comments under various tables in Chapter IV.

[8] By 1890, 26 states; by 1900, 32; the remaining 12 by 1918. By 1916 most of the states had amended the laws previously passed. See CR 1915-16, II, p. 22, for separate state provisions and dates.

[9] CR 1892-93, II, pp. 1402-64; *Brown*, pp. 416-17.

[10] On President Eliot's committee were five college presidents, three headmasters of private academies and high schools, one college professor, and the Commissioner of Education, W. T. Harris. Of the ninety members of the nine sub-committees, forty-seven were from colleges or universities, forty-two from secondary schools, and one was a government official, formerly a college professor. Among the members were some of the best known educators of the day: Woodrow Wilson, William C. Collar, Benjamin I. Wheeler, George L. Kittredge, Charles H. Grandgent, James Harvey Robinson, Ira Remsen, and Francis W. Parker, to name only a few.

[11] The Report is summarized in CR 1892-93 (published in 1895), II, pp. 1415-1446. Various comments are given, pp. 1440-91. The complete report was published as

Report of the Committee of Ten on Secondary School Subjects, by the American Book Company, 1894. The Bureau of Education distributed 30,000 copies of the volume and it went through many editions. (CR 1893-94, I, p. 469).

[12] The importance of the relationship between elementary and high school work had been recognized. In 1893 the NEA had appointed another committee to make a study of the elementary schools, under the chairmanship of W. H. Maxwell, Superintendent of Schools, Brooklyn, N.Y. Known as the Committee of Fifteen, its report was printed in CR 1893-94 (published in 1896), I, pp. 469-556. The report was also published under the title, "Report of the Committee of Fifteen on Elementary Education—With the Reports of the Sub-Committees: On the Training of Teachers; On the Correlation of Studies in Elementary Education; On the Organization of City School Systems." The American Book Company, 1895. The separate volume also contained opinions of various educators on the three main topics, in three appendices. These appendices did not appear in the Commissioner of Education's Report. Instead, a supplementary chapter (14) in his report contained "Verbatim Reports of Recitations in Arithmetic and Languages in the Schools of Kansas City, Missouri," by Superintendent J. M. Greenwood, a member of the Committee.

[13] *Cubberley,* pp. 513-14.

[14] These would presumably be in addition to bookkeeping and commercial arithmetic, permissible options for algebra in the second and third years, but with no specific curriculum indicated. See the general subject-matter Tables II and III of the Report, pp. 37 and 41. If the algebra option were elected, geometry would be the mathematics subject in the second and third years.

[15] *Cubberley,* pp. 542-43.

[16] See Note 12 above. It was composed of public school superintendents of twelve city systems, one state superintendent, one university president, and the U. S. Commissioner of Education.

[17] The preliminary report was published in *School Review* (June, 1896), and the complete report in *Journal of Proceedings and Addresses,* of the National Education Association (Chicago, 1899). The chairman was A. F. Nightingale, superintendent of Chicago high schools. In addition to a secretary, who was principal of the high school in Denver, there were twelve other members, three each from the four regional associations of secondary schools and colleges. The final report was based on the views "of many specialists in secondary and higher education." See *Knight* (2) pp. 99-102.

[18] See *Brown,* p. 388 and pp. 381-89; *Kandel,* pp. 472-85; *Knight* (2), pp. 99-102. The Committee made three other recommendations of great importance; teachers in secondary schools should have a college education, or its equivalent; gifted students should be encouraged to finish high school in a shorter length of time than that required by most students; the high school course of study should be organized on a unified six-year plan, beginning with the seventh grade. This was the beginning of the junior high school movement, as it was later called. Of several grade combinations, the 6-3-3 plan was most widely adopted. See *Knight* (2), pp. 51-54. *Cubberley,* pp. 554-56, 631-32.

[19] Since the complete report of the Committee on Entrance Requirements was not published until 1899, the Committee of Ten's Report exercised the major influence down to 1900. The Committee of Fifteen, it will be remembered, dealt with the curriculum in grades one through eight. Although it was concerned also with the correlation of studies on both levels, its influence on high school curriculum was general.

[20] These three, botany, biology, and zoology were first tabulated in CR 1909-10, II, pp. 1178, 1181, 1183-84. In Table A, p. 1139, figures for biology were combined both with those for botany and with those for zoology. Meteorology was never tabulated. Apparently it was considered a part of physical geography. See Chapter IV, Table 3 above.

[21] With the exception of courses in health, hygiene and sanitation, individual subjects in this group generally come under extracurricular activities. Driver education may be used, however, to round out a course of study for sub-average students.

[22] Although teacher training is listed as a subject-matter field (Table 14), it does not logically fit into any of the five groups. It played an extremely minor role in the curriculum.

[23] Although Table 14 shows science at its peak in 1900, its actual peak came in 1895-96 (Chapter IV, Table 3 and comments). Since the peaks for mathematics and foreign languages came in 1910, the percentage of the group as a whole increased through that year.

[24] Mathematics dropped considerably between 1910 and 1915, but the addition of arithmetic and general mathematics in 1922 checked its decline for a few years. Science declined considerably between 1900 and 1905. The addition of three new subjects in 1910 (see Note 20 above) kept its percentage that year only slightly below its 1900 level. But the addition of general science, and an increase in biology in 1922 could not keep the whole science field from its severest loss, between 1910 and 1922.

[25] The peak was maintained through 1915. A new method of tabulation accounted for part of the decrease between that year and 1922. The various schools reported enrollments in English in so many different ways that separate statistics for rhetoric and English literature could not be continued after 1915. BS 1920-22, II, p. 533.

[26] Some of the individual subject-matter fields, as indicated in comments on the appropriate tables of Chapter IV, reached their peaks in 1915: music, art, and agriculture. By 1949, however, only art was considerably below its 1915 peak. Since 1915 was not one of the years listed, Table 14 shows art at its peak in 1922, music and agriculture, in 1949.

[27] *Cubberley*, pp. 543-44.

[28] *Knight* (2), p. 103. See Cubberley, pp. 544-45.

[29] *Knight* (2), p. 103.

[30] Between 1910 and 1922 enrollments in Groups C, D, and E increased 455%, or four times as rapidly as those in Groups A and B, which increased 114% in the same period. High school enrollments, on which the subject percentages were based, increased 191%.

[31] See Table 15 for the number of subjects listed in the other years. The number listed in 1915 was the same as in 1910 for each group except health, music, and art (Group E). Since the Office of Education did not collect complete statistics on the subjects in Groups D and E until after 1915, the contrast between their status in 1910 and 1922 seems greater than it actually was. The total percentage for each of the five groups in 1915 was as follows: A, 215.6; B, 114.2; C, 67.4; D, 49.5; E, 55.6. In 1922 an increase in physical education was more than offset by a decrease in music and art. For the 1914-15 statistics, see CR 1915-16, II, pp. 477, 500-503, 535.

[32] Music was also ahead of foreign languages, but it is doubtful if there was any "competition" between those two fields. For all of these comparisons, see Ch. IV, Tables 6, 2, 1, 7, and 8 respectively.

[33] See *Kandel,* pp. 486-87; *Cubberley,* pp. 506-07; *Russell-Judd,* pp. 456-57; *Knight* (1), pp. 521-24.

[34] *Kandel,* pp. 489-90. The principles were set forth in *Cardinal Principles of Secondary Education,* U.S. Bureau of Education, *Bulletin* 1918, No. 35. It was the work of the Commission on the Reorganization of Secondary Education, which was appointed in 1913 by the National Education Association. Ten different subject-matter committees reported on English, social studies, natural sciences, modern languages, ancient languages, household arts, manual arts, music, business, and agriculture. There was another committee on the relationship of high school and college, and a reviewing committee. In addition to these reports, a special committee of the Mathematical Association published a *Report on the Reorganization of Mathematics in Secondary Education* (1923). A committee of the American Classical League issued its *Classical Investigation* (1925), and two American and Canadian Committees on Modern Languages published *Reports on Modern Language Teaching* (1929 and 1930). See *Kandel,* pp. 488-89. *Knight* (2), pp. 102-05.

[35] *Kandel,* p. 490.

[36] Students in two high schools were given the same psychological tests at an interval of 15 years. Although the number of students had increased markedly during the period, the average scores and variability of scores of the two sets of students had no significant differences. Between 1931 and 1942 the high school graduates entering the University of Minnesota maintained a highly constant average percentile rank. See *Wolfle,* p. 173.

[37] *Wolfle,* p. 172.

[38] *Wolfle,* p. 175.

[39] These and other statements in this section were based on information contained in U.S. Office of Education *Circular* No. 269 Reprint, 1953. See pertinent comments on Tables 36 and 37 of Appendix G.

[40] For a discussion of this problem and others, and of suggested remedies, see the first reference cited in the preceding note.

[41] In some high schools (see Note 39) that offered all types of courses the drop-out rate was higher than in those whose offerings were more strictly academic.

[42] This distinction is necessary. Between 1891 and 1915 the percentages indicate the proportion of graduates *prepared* for college and other higher institutions. Between 1922 and 1952 the percentages indicate the proportion that presumably entered college after graduation in the preceding year. The comparison between the percentages before and after, therefore, is merely suggestive. See Appendix D for additional details.

[43] Calculated from the figures given in CR 1926-28, Ch. 24, Table 50. See Note 42 above. For the years 1910 through 1934 the separate percentages for college alone were 34.0, 35.9, 32.1, and 21.3 respectively. No separate breakdown was made for 1952. "Other higher institutions" included Agricultural and Mechanical (Land Grant) Colleges, Scientific Schools, Normal Schools, and Teachers Colleges, as distinguished from Liberal Arts Colleges.

[44] In 1940 the percentage was 35.2; in 1944, 30.8, and in 1950, 40.6. These percentages were calculated from BS 1950-52, Ch. 1, Table 6. The percentages in this note, it should be pointed out, were based on data that included figures for private schools. Those for public high schools alone could not be determined. Presumably they would be slightly lower.

CHAPTER VI

SUBJECT, GRADE, AND COLLEGE

By etymology the word *school* means *leisure*. Among the Greeks it was the time an adult had free from his daily routine. Since he often spent such spare time in listening to a lecture or in taking part in an intellectual discussion, the word came to designate pursuits of that kind, and finally, the place for such pursuits. To a Greek the term *schoolwork* would have been completely foreign and strange or—to use his word for it—hopelessly barbaric.

We have examined this barbaric activity — American high school style — in the last two chapters. In them we traced the development of the high school curriculum as it expanded to meet the diverse needs and interests of a progressively dynamic and democratic society. We listed different subjects as they were tabulated by the United States Office of Education and entered the combat zone of the high school mind. Each table was a statistical barometer of the changing academic weather, and from their composite reading we charted its amazing course from the stern scholastic calm of the Gay Nineties to the elective confusion of the Nuclear Age.

In all of the tables, whether for separate subjects, subject-matter fields, or related fields within a group, percentages based on total high school enrollments showed the changing proportion of students in each of those three categories. By applying the percentages to the total enrollment, always given to the nearest thousand, it was possible to calculate actual enrollments by subject, subject-matter field, or group, in a given year. In 1890, for example, the total high school enrollment was 203,000. Of these, 45.4% or 92,000, studied algebra. In 1949, out of an enrollment of 5,399,000, students in algebra numbered 1,449,000—26.8%. Between the two dates total enrollments had increased 2560%; students in algebra, 1475%. Stated in another way, 45 out of every 100 students studied algebra in 1890; in 1949 the number was 27 out of every 100. If the 1890 percentage had been maintained in 1949, in that year algebra would have gained 980,000 students.[1]

Similar statistics could be derived for all subjects, subject-matter

fields, or groups, from the various tables in Chapters IV and V. Separately or in combination, the percentages and the figures on which they were based show the emphasis each subject or field or group received in the high school curriculum between 1890 and 1949. They show the *breadth* and scope of the main educational developments that took place in that period.

But there are several closely related and important parts of these developments that such subject-matter statistics did not touch upon. They did not show the grades in which many separate subjects by custom or design had been offered. In what grades, for instance, were chemistry and physics usually studied? In the last 20 years chemistry generally has been offered in the 11th grade, physics in the 12th. Were those their positions in 1890? If not, in what grades were they taught? When were they shifted to grades 11 and 12? Was first-year algebra in grade 9 followed by second-year in grade 10, and then by plane geometry, solid geometry, and finally trigonometry?

These questions must be answered, if possible, so that other significant data may be collected and analyzed. The statistics on algebra, given above, showed that the number of algebra students increased tremendously between 1890 and 1949, but that the proportion of such students decreased progressively after 1910. Did similar decreases take place in the various courses in algebra and mathematics in relation to the grades in which they were taught? Did the grades in which they were taught have any influence on enrollments? Did the introduction of new courses in certain grades affect enrollments in other courses or subjects offered in the same grades, or in the next grade of a sequence? Did the sequence of courses in one subject affect the sequence in another?

Many of these questions probably cannot be answered with absolute finality. Even tentative answers, however, may provide additional details of interest to educational history and may suggest possible solutions for some of the educational problems that confront us today.

During the last sixty years the increase in high school enrollments has been caused by rising birth rates, extension of educational opportunities, and longer continuance in high school. Although college enrollments have also increased tremendously in this period, most students still end their formal education with high school while many others drop out before they graduate. The type of education they receive is of the utmost importance to them as individuals and as citizens. The type of education is equally important for those who continue to college, and determines in a large measure their choice of

specialization, particularly in fields that are unavoidably connected with the country's vital role and leadership in world affairs.

Some years before 1890, expansion of the high school curriculum, which had been in progress for many years, had created a considerable lack of uniformity in high school offerings and in college entrance requirements. The Committee of Ten set up by the National Education Association to study the situation and to make recommendations, published its report in 1894.[2] The gist of its recommendations was contained in four tables. Table I coordinated the recommendations of nine Subcommittees or Conferences, as they were called, assigned the task of studying the nine subject-matter fields into which the high school curriculum had been divided. Each Conference included in its list not only high school and elementary subjects, but also the sequence, grade by grade, in which they should be offered. Table II, confined to high school subjects, followed this sequence and showed the amount of time, the number of years within a four-year program, and the number of periods per week that would be required if all subjects were offered.

The Committee of Ten itself in Table III changed the grade sequence of several courses, and reallocated the amount of time and the number of periods for many subjects—changes that would permit a single program of studies in which all subjects could be included. In Table IV the Committee took into account the diverse interests and abilities of high school students and divided the subjects into four different curricula, with some subjects common to all. This arrangement necessitated a few new changes in sequence and in the number of periods for certain courses and subjects.

The four "model" curricula (Table IV) apparently received more attention than the single program of studies. A "time table" summary of the four curricula appeared in at least three of the Annual Reports of the Commissioner of Education.[3]

It is not known to what extent subject assignments by grade differed from the practice current in the Committee's day. In some respects there could have been no difference. All four-year sequences, such as those in foreign languages, English, or history, would naturally begin in the ninth grade. The principal question would be what languages and what histories should be studied. Other main problems would doubtless center around the proper sequence in mathematics and on the relationship of that sequence to the sequence of certain sciences, particularly the order in which physics should best be placed.

TABLE 16[1]

TIME-TABLE FOR FOUR COURSES OF STUDY
SUGGESTED BY THE COMMITTEE OF TEN

	Classical				Latin-Scientific				Modern Languages				English			
	1	2	3	4	1	2	3	4	1	2	3	4	1	2	3	4
Latin	1	1	1	1	1	1	1	1					1	1	1	1
Greek			1	1												
French		a	a	a		a	a	a	1	1	1	1	b	b	b	b
German		1	1	1		1	1	1	a	1	1	1	b	b	b	b
Algebra	1		½	½	1		½	½	1		½		1		½	½
Geometry		1	½			1	½			1	½			1	½	
Trigonometry				½				½				½				½
Astronomy							½				½					½
Physics	1				1				1				1			
Chemistry			1				1				1					1
Physical Geography	1				1				1				1			
Physiography[2]								c				c				c
Geology								½				½				½
Meteorology							½				½					½
Botany		—				1				1				1		
Zoology		d				d				d						
Physiology								½				½				½
History	1	1		e	1		1	e	1		1	e	1	1	1	1
English	1	1	1	1	1	1	1	1	1	1	1	1	1	1	1	1

a German or French.   b Latin, German, or French.   c Geology or physiography.
d Botany or zoology.   e Trigonometry and higher algebra, or history.

[1] References were given in Note 3 of the text. The figures 1 and ½ indicate the amount of time in terms of an academic year. The number of periods per week is not shown. They varied for different subjects and occasionally for the same subjects in different curricula. The general pattern was as follows: in the first year of a foreign language, classes met five times a week, thereafter, 4 times. Mathematics and history classes in grade 9 met 4 times each; in grades 10 and 12, 3 times; in grade 11, 2 times (in the English curriculum, 4 times). All science courses met 3 times. English in grade 9 met 4 times; in grade 10, 3 or 4 times in the English curriculum, 3 times in the others; in grade 12, 2 times in the classical curriculum, 4 times in the others. Each of the four curricula had a total of 20 periods a week for each of the 4 high school years.

[2] "A more advanced treatment of our physical environment in which the agencies and processes involved, the origins, development, and decadence of the forms presented, and the significance of the earth's face are the leading themes . . ." *Committee of Ten*, p. 209.

The changes made in the grade assignments of physics and chemistry are revealing.

The Conference on Science recommended that chemistry be taught before physics and that physics be taught in the twelfth grade. It recognized that this was "plainly not the logical" order but one required by the necessity of more mathematics, considered essential for the study of physics but not of chemistry. In its Table III the Committee of Ten reversed this order to insure at least a half year of physics before meteorology was taken up in the second half of grade 11, and a whole year before physiography was studied in grade 12. With this arrangement students would have first-year algebra in grade 9 (4 periods), plane geometry and second-year algebra in grade 10 (2 periods each) in preparation for physics in grade 11. With physics they could finish second-year algebra and solid geometry (2 periods each).

In its model curricula, however, the Committee placed physics in grade 10. Its reasoning was twofold: the first two years should be the period in which students could explore their interests and capabilities. It was important for them to discover their several aptitudes before they chose which curriculum they would follow. Physics best represented the "inorganic sciences of precision" in which all students should have some experience. Since many students, from necessity or choice, left school after grade 10, that grade was the best place for physics.

How widely the model curricula were adopted by the schools could not be determined. By 1910 the Committee's *Report* had become "famous" and "for seventeen years" its recommendations had "been the inspiration of many thousands of high school principals and teachers whose aim has been to live up to the model courses of study arranged by that committee." [4]

Table 17 below tests the possibility that many schools did follow the model curricula, in whole or in part. To make this test it was assumed that the subject enrollments, as given in the selected curriculum surveys, represented the students in the grade to which the subject had been assigned by the Committee of Ten. Total enrollments in physics, for example, presumably came from grade 10. The percentage for physics, therefore, shows what proportion of students in that grade studied physics in a given year.

In examining this table there is one principle that must be kept in mind. All percentages should form a theoretically possible pattern. Any percentage greater than 100, for example, shows immediately that the grade allocation of that subject is wrong. It is obviously impossible for a subject to have more registrations from a grade than

TABLE 17

ENROLLMENTS IN CERTAIN COURSES IN PUBLIC HIGH SCHOOLS
EXPRESSED AS THE PERCENTAGE OF STUDENTS IN THE GRADE OR
GRADES SUGGESTED FOR THE COURSES BY THE COMMITTEE OF TEN:
1889-90 TO 1954-55 [1]

	1890 [2]	1900 [3]	1910 [4]	1922 [5]	1934 [6]	1949 [7]	1955 [8]
High School enrollment	203	519	915	2230	5621	5399	6584
Grade 9 enrollment	87	223	393	869	1827	1641	1998
Grade 10 enrollment	53	135	248	608	1540	1491	1782
Grade 11 enrollment	37	93	163	427	1231	1242	1500
Grade 12 enrollment	26	68	111	326	1023	1026	1304
Grades 9,11,12 enrollments	150	384	667	1602	4081	3909	4802
Grades 10 and 11 enrollments	90	228	411	1035	2771	2733	3282

Grade(s)	Course or Subject	1890	1900	1910	1922	1934	1949	1955
9,11,12	Algebra 1,2,3 [9]	61.4	76.1	77.9	55.2	40.7	37.1	34.9
10 & 11	Geometry	48.1	62.4	68.8	48.9	34.4	25.8	22.8
12	Trigonometry	--	14.6	15.3	10.5	7.4	10.6	13.0
11	Astronomy	--	15.5	3.0	0.3	0.2	--	--
10	Physics	87.1	73.2	54.0	32.6	22.9	19.5	17.0
12	Chemistry	78.9	58.9	56.6	50.3	41.6	40.9	37.0
9	Physical Geography	--	54.4	45.1	10.9	4.9	--	--
12	Geology	--	27.6	9.5	1.1	0.6	--	--
10	Botany	--	--	58.2	14.0	3.3	0.5	--
10	Zoology	--	--	25.6	5.6	2.2	0.4	--
12	Physiology [10]	--	209.4	125.8	34.8	10.0	5.2	--

[1] Figures immediately under the dates give the total high school enrollment to the nearest thousand. For a discussion of grade enrollments in 1890 and 1900, and of the particular situation from 1910 through 1934, see Appendix G. Although the recommendations of the Committee were not known in 1890, the grade locations of Table 16 were assumed for that year. Percentages underscored mark the year in which they reached the highest point. To facilitate comparison all percentages were carried through 1955. For percentages based on total high school enrollments, see Chapter IV, Table 1 (Mathematics) and Table 3 (Science).

[2] CR 1889-90, II, pp. 1388-91.
[5] BS 1920-22, II, pp. 580-94.
[3] CR 1899-1900, II, pp. 2129-36.
[6] *Bulletin 1938, No. 6*, Table 3.
[4] CR 1909-10, II, pp. 1169-81.
[7] BS 1948-50, Ch. 5, Table 3.
[8] *Pamphlet No. 118*, Table 3 (Science) and Table 12 (Mathematics); *School Life* (June 1956), pp. 6-7.

[9] For the sake of uniformity and convenience the three courses in algebra, elementary (first-year), intermediate (second-year), and advanced (college algebra), are called algebra 1, 2, and 3 respectively.

[10] Anatomy and hygiene, with physiology, formed a half-year course, 3 periods a week.

the number of students in that grade. Since physiology in grade 12 or in grade 11, does not conform to this principle in 1900 and 1910, it could not have been offered exclusively in either of those grades in those years.

Although no other subject percentage runs contrary to this principle, that fact does not "prove" that the grades assigned to each subject are necessarily correct. There are other factors to be considered. One of these involves a comparison with subject percentages based on total high school enrollments. Subject percentages worked out on this basis show that physics and chemistry were at their highest percentage points in 1890; that astronomy, physical geography, geology, and physiology were at their highest points in 1900, and algebra and geometry, in 1910. Except for trigonometry, all the percentages in this table follow that pattern exactly, subject for subject.

This is not surprising. Registrations in each subject are the same in the corresponding years of the three tables. They form the appropriate common base into which total high school or grade enrollments are divided to obtain the necessary percentage in a given year. Despite the great differences in size between the two kinds of enrollments and the resulting percentages, the comparable subject percentages not only reach their peaks in the same years, they all begin to decline in the period immediately following their peaks. In this respect trigonometry also conforms to the expected pattern.[5]

If the comparison between total enrollment and grade enrollment percentages is carried a step further, it throws some doubt on the grade assignment of at least one course. In Chapter IV, Table 3, chemistry shows a percentage increase between 1910 and 1922. Table 17 shows a decrease. Although it is unlikely that a grade enrollment would show the same proportionate increase or decrease in a given period as the total enrollment, the percentage decrease for chemistry in this table deviates a little too much. Another grade 12 subject, trigonometry, shows a percentage decrease in both tables. Both of these instances mean, not that enrollments in grade 12 are incorrect, but that chemistry is probably in the wrong grade in 1910 and 1922.

Support for this tentative conclusion was found. In 1934 chemistry and physics had become the "predominating sciences of the third and fourth years."[6] Even as early as 1928 physics had become "generally a fourth-year subject."[7] Since chemistry had passed physics in enrollments for the first time in 1928,[8] it is unlikely that physics would have been shifted to compete with it in the same grade. It is more likely that chemistry had shifted from grade 12 to grade 11 *before*

1928, if indeed it had ever been exclusively in grade 12 at all. On the other hand, if chemistry *had been* in grade 12 and physics in grade 10 during most of the time between 1890 and 1922, when grade 10 was consistently twice the size of grade 12, this would easily account for the two-to-one proportion of registrations in physics over those in chemistry between 1890 and 1915. In 1922 chemistry narrowed the gap remarkably.[9] This lends further support to the doubt about chemistry expressed above. Perhaps between 1915 and 1922 chemistry was shifted to grade 11 and physics to grade 12 or—and this seems more logical—neither had been exclusively in the grades recommended by the Committee.

There was no conflict in the order preferred by the Conference on Science—physics before chemistry—and the order preferred by the Committee—physics before meteorology and physiography. There was a conflict of opinion about the amount of mathematics needed for physics. The Committee's final shift of physics to grade 10, with only a year of algebra as preparation, seemed to imply that the Conference was wrong about the need for more mathematics. At any rate, the Committee's views won out—on paper.

On the practical side, however, there was an unexpected development. Although the Conference on Geography had doubts about the availability of suitable textbooks and adequately prepared teachers in meteorology and physiography, the Committee expressed hopes that both might be supplied. Apparently these hopes were not met. Neither subject was ever listed in any of the curriculum surveys. This left a gap in all of the curricula except the classical, and may partly explain the meteoric rise in popularity of physiology and, to a much less degree, of geology, both assigned to grade 12 (Table 16). But the former, as pointed out above, was obviously not exclusively in grade 12 in 1900 and in 1910. Its percentage for grade 11 in 1900 would also have been well above 100. Only grades 11 and 12, or 10 and 11, would yield a plausible percentage for 1900 and 1910. Since it had never been assigned to any grade except 12, the former seems more logical. Geology, without doubt, was always in grade 12.

If physics had been shifted to grade 12 by 1922, as seems likely, it would not be logical to assume that it was shifted from grade 10. There must have been a period in which it was first in grades 10 and 11 and then in 11 and 12. A shift from grade 10 to grades 10 and 11 by 1900 would be a natural step, and from that position, to grades 11 and 12, by 1910. Although these shifts would have made physics and chemistry partial competitors with each other and with physiology

in 1900 and complete competitors in 1910, registration figures for each would not have made this impossible. In 1900 those for physiology were greater than those for chemistry and physics combined. But in 1910 the latter two combined pulled ahead of the former. This was the year in which botany and zoology were first listed in grade 10. It is unlikely that the two of them would have attracted nearly 84% of that grade if they had been competing with physics. Their rather drastic decreases by 1922 were caused by the marked rise of biology.

The final shifts of chemistry and physics to grades 11 and 12 would also explain another development. Each of them, in contrast to physiology and geology, was a year's course. This undoubtedly helped them to become the leading sciences in their respective grades. As early as 1915 physics had overtaken physiology and geology combined. By 1922 chemistry too had moved ahead. In its grade neither subject has had a rival in the field of science since those years.

Of the other subjects listed in Table 17 the locations of plane and solid geometry and algebra 2 are the only ones open to question. By 1928 plane geometry, which is primarily a year-course, had "shifted from a second or a third year subject to an almost exclusively second-year subject." [10] Before that year solid geometry, which is usually a half-year course, must have been in grade 11 or 12. The location of the two geometries probably meant that algebra 2, before 1928, was in grade 10, primarily as a half-year course, and was shifted to grade 11 when plane geometry was shifted to grade 10. [11] Since 1934, without question, plane geometry in grade 10 has usually come between algebra 1 in grade 9 and algebra 2 in grade 11. This might very well explain the decrease in algebra 2 students between 1934 and 1949. It might also be a contributing factor in the decrease of students in physics during the same period.

"Arguments" such as these do not of course "prove" that all the various shifts mentioned in the last few pages took place exactly at the times or in the ways indicated. The next table takes these possibilities into account and shows what the percentages would have been if they had been carried out.

This table lists all of the principal subjects and courses in mathematics and science offered in the public high schools between 1890 and 1955. It shows the most likely possibilities for their respective grade locations before 1934, with the resulting percentages, and underscores those that seem most probable. Before that date complete certainty is impossible without additional information; after 1922 no subject

TABLE 18

ENROLLMENTS IN MATHEMATICS AND SCIENCE IN PUBLIC HIGH SCHOOLS EXPRESSED AS THE PERCENTAGE OF STUDENTS IN THE GRADE OR GRADES IN WHICH THE COURSES WERE REASONABLY CERTAIN OR KNOWN TO HAVE BEEN OFFERED: 1889-90 TO 1954-55 [1]

Course or Subject	Grade(s)	1890	1900	1910	1922	1934	1949	1955
Algebra 1,2,3	9, 11, 12	64.1	76.1	77.9	55.2			
Algebra 1,2,3	9, 10, 11	52.1	64.8	64.7	47.0			
Algebra 1	9					70.1	63.5	60.3
Algebra 2[2]	11					34.9	29.9	28.5
General Math[3]	9				31.7	22.8	42.9	40.1
P. & S. Geometry	10, 11	48.1	62.4	68.8	48.9			
P. & S. Geometry[4]	10, 11, 12	37.3	48.1	54.1	37.2			
P. & S. Geometry	10, 12	54.8	70.1	78.6	54.1			
Plane Geometry	10					55.1	40.2	37.3
Solid Geometry[5]	12					10.8	9.2	11.4
Trigonometry[5]	12		14.6	15.3	10.5	7.4	10.6	13.0
Physics	10	87.1	73.2	54.0	32.6			
Physics	10, 11	51.3	43.3	32.5	19.2			
Physics	11, 12	73.3	61.4	48.7	26.5			
Physics	12				61.1	34.5	28.5	23.2
Chemistry	12	78.2	58.9	56.6				
Chemistry	11, 12	32.5	24.9	22.9	21.9			
Chemistry	11				38.6	34.6	33.2	32.2
Geology	12		27.6	9.5	1.1	0.6		
Physiology	11, 12		88.4	51.0	15.1	4.5	2.3	
Astronomy	11		15.5	3.0	0.3	0.2		
Biology	10			3.9	32.2	53.3	66.8	72.6
Botany	10		58.2	14.0	3.3	0.5		
Zoology	10		25.6	5.6	2.2	0.4		
Physical Geography	9		54.4	45.1	10.9	4.9		
General Science[6]	9				46.9	54.6	68.4	73.0

[1] See Table 17 for grade enrollments. Unless otherwise indicated, references for subject enrollments are the same as those given in the appropriate notes to Table 17. Percentages underscored indicate the writer's choice of grade shifts for different courses down to 1934. For a few possible changes in 1955, see Appendix G, Note 11.

[2] Algebra enrollments were first broken down in 1928. It is assumed that the figures for 1934 do not include algebra 3. Separate enrollments in algebra 3 were specificaly given in 1949 for the first time. In that year registrations in it were 3.3% of grade 12. BS 1948-50, Ch. 5, p. 57.

[3] In 1922 the term *arithmetic* was used. The term *general mathematics* was first used in 1928. In 1934 both terms were used, but in the other two years, only *general mathematics*.

According to BS 1926-28, p. 966 only advanced arithmetic was taught in 1922. In 1934 elementary and advanced arithmetic and general mathematics were listed separately. For lack of other information, all were assigned to grade 9. In 1949 general mathematics, advanced general mathematics, and mathematics review were listed separately. All were assigned to grade 9. The percentage for general mathematics definitely in grade 9 alone was 42.2.

[4] The figures for plane and solid geometry were first broken down in 1928.

[5] See Note 4, Table 19 below.

[6] The percentage for 1955 was estimated by the writer on the basis of the trend in general science as compared with biology.

assignment to grade is really in doubt. Percentages not underscored (before 1934) are kept to make them readily accessible for other judgments. Shifts in grade location prevent the underscored percentages from forming an observable pattern, but those for the same grade(s), underscored or not, show the patterns or trends unaffected by shifts.

A comparison of this table with Table 16 shows that after 1922 there was only one change in the grade location of any course in mathematics—solid geometry was shifted from grade 11 to grade 12. Algebra 3, omitted from Table 18, since it was identifiable by registrations only in 1949, was in grade 12 in both tables. The main difference between the two was the addition of general mathematics, or arithmetic, first listed in 1922.

It is interesting to note that in 1922 and afterwards physics and chemistry were in the order and in the grades originally suggested by the Conference on Science and not in the grades or the sequence shown in Table 16. Of the six other sciences listed in Table 16, all except physiology had disappeared by 1949. Since 1922, two newcomers, general science (grade 9) and biology (grade 10), together with chemistry and physics have formed the main rungs in the tapering ladder of high school science studies.

Among these four subjects, although the study of one in grade 9 or 10 may encourage or discourage study of one in the next higher grade, there is no fixed or necessary sequence. General science is usually, but not necessarily, studied before biology, biology before chemistry, chemistry before physics. But physics may be the first science to be attempted.[12]

In contrast to this, the study of mathematics, by tradition if not by inherent necessity, has long followed a grade sequence. The introduction of a new course, general mathematics, has served to lengthen the ordinary sequence and to postpone the study of elementary algebra, after its usual starting point, if not to divert some students from it altogether. The appearance of a new course, advanced general

mathematics, first listed in 1949, suggests that some diversion has resulted.

Although such courses may provide mathematical training for students who would or could not otherwise receive it in high school, they probably also represent an attempt to overcome inadequate preparation in the lower grades. In that respect such courses may mark the beginning of another vicious cycle, for the colleges in their turn have found it necessary to add high school algebra to their freshman curriculum.[13] Since the majority of high school students who study general mathematics *may* not *enter* college, there may be no connection between increasing enrollments in that subject and the mathematical shortcomings of college freshmen. On the other hand, those who are compelled to study it in high school or do study it before they begin elementary algebra must thereby postpone the normal sequence at the beginning, and most likely are forced to shorten it at the end. The latter result may only be surmised; the results of initial postponement may be illustrated by a few statistics.

In 1922 registration in arithmetic, listed that year for the first time, made up 31.7% of grade 9 (Table 18), or approximately 275,500 students (all enrollments from Table 17). If it is assumed that registrations in algebra 1 were 75% of all algebra students,[14] they constituted 77% of grade 9, or approximately 669,000. Registrations in both subjects totaled 944,500 students, 75,500 more than enrollments in grade 9. It cannot be proved that all or most of these students were in algebra 1; it is certain they were not in grade 9.

In 1928 the situation apparently changed; registrations in the two subjects equalled only 98% of enrollments in grade 9. In 1934, as Table 18 shows, they equalled only 92.9%. But in 1949 they were 106.4%, and in 1955, 100.4%.

During all of these years, however, including 1922, it is not possible to say how many students in grade 9 were actually studying algebra 1 or general mathematics. It can simply be stated that the number was a certain percentage of enrollments in that grade, with a strong and natural assumption that the great majority came from grade 9. If some of these came from grade 10—another likely assumption—the potential registrations in plane geometry, generally a grade 10 subject, would be reduced. Similarly, potential registrations in algebra 2, a grade 11 subject primarily, would also be reduced. In both cases, actual grade enrollments and percentages in both subjects would very likely decrease. This did not happen between 1922 and 1934, but it did happen between 1934 and 1949. Between 1949 and 1955,

TABLE 19
CONTRAST BETWEEN THE RATE OF INCREASE OR DECREASE IN
SUBJECT ENROLLMENTS WITH THAT OF CORRESPONDING GRADE
ENROLLMENTS IN PUBLIC HIGH SCHOOLS BETWEEN 1922 AND 1955 [1]

	1922	1934		1949		1955	
Total high school enrollments in 1000's	2230	5621	+152.1	5399	-3.9	6584	+21.9
Enrollments							
Grade 9	869	1827	+110.2	1641	-9.9	1998	+21.7
Algebra 1	669	1281	+91.5	1042	-18.6	1205	+15.6
General Mathematics	276	417	+51.1	704	+68.1	801	+13.8
General Science [2]	408	998	+144.6	1122	+12.4	1458	+29.9
Grade 10	608	1540	+153.3	1491	-3.2	1782	+19.5
Plane Geometry	430	849	+97.4	599	-29.5	665	+11.0
Biology	196	821	+318.8	995	+21.3	1294	+30.0
Grade 11	427	1231	+188.3	1242	+0.3	1500	+20.8
Algebra 2 [3]	224	430	+91.9	404	-6.0	432	+6.9
Chemistry	165	426	+158.2	412	-3.3	483	+17.2
Grade 12	326	1023	+213.8	1026	+0.9	1304	+27.2
Trigonometry [4]	34	76	+123.6	109	+43.4	170	+55.9
Solid Geometry [4]	76	110	+44.7	94	-14.5	149	+58.5
Physics	199	353	+77.4	292	-17.2	303	+3.7

[1] Figures for total high school and grade enrollments are taken from Table 17. In all cases, except the two algebras and the two geometries in 1922, the subject registrations were calculated from data in Table 18. In 1922 algebra 2 registrations were about 25% of all algebra students (see page 93). In 1928 and 1934 plane geometry was 88% of all geometry registrations (BS 1926-28, pp. 1065-66, and *Bulletin 1938 No. 6*, pp. 46-48.) The same percentage was assumed for 1922. In 1949 and 1955 comparable percentages were 86 and 88 respectively. But see Note 4 below. For possible different enrollments in 1955 and resulting percentage changes, see Appendix G, Note 11.

[2] The figures for 1955 were based on the percentage estimated by the writer in Table 18. See Note 6, Table 18.

[3] In 1949 and 1955 algebra 3 figures were not included. It could not be determined whether they were included in the other two years or not.

[4] Trigonometry and solid geometry are primarily one-semester courses and are usually offered twice each academic year. If the situation in 1954-55 is typical, enrollments in the second semester are smaller than those in the first. In the fall of 1954, 7.4% of the students in grade 12 studied trigonometry. After adjustments were made for drop-outs, registrations in the second semester brought the total up to 170,000, which was 13.0% of grade 12. (*Pamphlet No. 118*, p. 17). Registrations in solid geometry, however, were not adjusted for second-semester additions, according to the writer of *Pamphlet No. 118*. In the fall of 1954 the registrations amounted to 6.5% of grade 12. If they had been adjusted for second-semester additions, it is estimated by this writer that registrations for the year would have totaled 149,000. In making the estimate it was assumed that the adjustments would have been comparable to those in trigonometry. The following proportion, therefore, was set up: 7.4: 13 as 6.5: X. This gave 11.4% for X. This percentage was applied to the enrollment in

grade 12 and yielded 148,656. This figure, rounded off to 149,000, is used in this table instead of the figure 85,000 given in *School Life* (June 1956), p. 6. The writer does not
maintain that it is absolutely accurate, but simply that it is much closer to the actual registrations in solid geometry than 85,000. The official estimate was 147,000 (Pamphlet No. 120).

although subject registrations by grade increased, among these four
subjects in 1955 the numbers in algebra 1 and plane geometry were
considerably smaller than they had been in 1934. Algebra 2 had made
a slight gain, but general mathematics had almost doubled.

The total high school and grade enrollments increased between
1922 and 1934, decreased between 1934 and 1949, and increased between 1949 and 1955. The last table shows how these enrollment
fluctuations compared with registrations in all courses in mathematics,
and in science.

This table reveals several instances of a development that is very
rare, if not unique, in high school history. Between 1922 and 1934
enrollments in two subjects, biology and chemistry, increased at a
more rapid rate than high school enrollments. Biology and general
science increased at a more rapid rate than enrollments in their respective grades.

In the next period, 1934 to 1949, enrollments in five subjects—
algebra 1, plane geometry, algebra 2, solid geometry, and physics—
decreased more rapidly than high school enrollments. Of these algebra
1 and plane geometry decreased more rapidly than their respective
grades; the other three, and chemistry, decreased, even though their
grades showed slight increases. General mathematics, general science,
and biology showed increases while their grades decreased; trigonometry had a much larger proportionate increase than grade 12.[15]

Between 1949 and 1955 enrollments again increased. Only four
subjects, however, increased more rapidly than enrollments in high
school and in their respective grades—general science, biology, solid
geometry, and trigonometry.

Throughout the entire period, 1922 to 1955, four subjects showed
continuous increases. Two of these, general mathematics and general
science, were in grade 9. One was in grade 10—biology; and one,
trigonometry, was in grade 12. Three other subjects, in addition to
these four, had larger registrations in 1955 than in 1934—solid geometry, chemistry, and algebra 2, but the gains in algebra were fractional.

It is interesting to note that between 1922 and 1949 grade enrollment gains were consecutively and progressively greater from grade 9
through grade 12. This was true also in the period between 1934 and
1949 when the loss in grade 9 was proportionately greater than the
loss in grade 10, and the gain in grade 12 was proportionately greater

than the gain in grade 11. The breaking of this pattern between 1949 and 1955, when the gain in grade 9 was proportionately greater than that of grade 10 and of grade 11, suggests that the estimates in 1955 were slightly wrong, either for grade 9 or for grade 11, or possibly for both. The gains for 9 were probably a little too great, and for 11, a little too small.

A comparison of this table with Table 18 shows that the decreases in subject percentages by grade between 1934 and 1949 *were accompanied by decreases in actual subject enrollments for the first time in the history of the high school curriculum.* This fact gains added educational significance because the increases in enrollments by grade were proportionately greater for grade 10 than grade 9, for grade 11 than grade 10, and for grade 12 than grade 11. As students remained longer and longer in high school, proportionately fewer and fewer of them studied the advanced subjects taught in the upper grades. This tendency was apparently checked in 1955 as compared with 1949. If enrollments in the upper grades, however, continue to increase more rapidly than those in grades 9 and 10, more students must enroll in algebra 1 before sizeable increases can be expected in plane geometry and algebra 2. These two courses, beyond question, are the feeding ground for solid geometry and trigonometry, and most likely for physics. Adequate preparation in these three subjects, in turn, determines to a large extent the number of college majors in these and related fields. And from the college majors must come the trained personnel who go into business and industry, private and governmental, and into graduate schools for the additional training necessary to meet the needs and requirements for teaching and for leadership in scientific activities.

This interlocking relationship between lower-and-upper-level courses and between high school and college is plainly evident in many other fields. Although the rise of general mathematics undoubtedly contributed to the declining enrollments in algebra 1 and therefore, in plane geometry and algebra 2, there were other influences at work. The period after 1910, and particularly after 1922, as the tables in Chapter IV show, was marked by rapid proliferation of a wide variety of courses. Many of these did not attain great student strength, but their very numbers helped to spread their appeal. In general, only required courses managed to survive such divisive onslaughts with any success, and even these showed signs of diminishing compulsion in the upper grades. English is the best example. As a "required" subject, it offers a forceful contrast to foreign languages.

TABLE 20

ENROLLMENTS IN ENGLISH AND IN FOREIGN LANGUAGES IN PUBLIC HIGH SCHOOLS EXPRESSED AS THE PERCENTAGE OF ENROLLMENTS IN THE GRADE IN WHICH THEY ARE USUALLY OFFERED: 1933-34 TO 1954-55[1]

		1934[2]			1949[3]			1955[4]		
		5621			5399			6584		
Total English in 1000's		5089	90.5		5016	92.8		6169	93.7	
Course	Grade									
I	9	1696	92.8	33.3	1564	95.3	31.2	1900	95.1	30.8
II	10	1430	92.8	28.1	1397	93.7	27.8	1684	94.5	27.3
III	11	1165	94.6	22.9	1198	96.4	23.9	1493	97.5	24.2
IV	12	798	78.0	15.7	856	83.4	17.1	1095	84.0	17.7
Total Foreign Languages in 1000's		1997	35.5		1165	21.0		1357	20.6	
All Foreign Languages										
I	9	1058	57.9	52.9	647	39.4	55.5	758	37.9	55.8
II	10	727	47.2	36.4	419	28.1	35.9	484	27.2	35.7
III	11	160	13.0	8.2	80	6.4	6.9	98	6.5	7.2
IV	12	48	4.7	2.4	19	1.9	1.7	16	1.2	1.2
Total Latin in 1000's		902	16.0		422	7.8		454	6.9	
I	9	460	25.2	51.0	236	14.4	55.9	257	12.8	56.5
II	10	338	21.9	37.5	156	10.4	36.9	172	9.6	37.8
III	11	71	5.8	7.9	23	1.9	5.4	21	1.4	4.6
IV	12	33	3.2	3.6	7	0.7	1.7	5	0.4	1.1
Total French in 1000's		611	10.9		255	4.7		369	5.6	
I	9	315	17.2	51.6	134	8.2	52.6	201	10.1	54.4
II	10	224	14.5	36.7	91	6.1	35.5	128	7.2	34.7
III	11	61	4.9	10.0	25	2.0	9.9	35	2.3	9.4
IV	12	11	1.1	1.7	5	0.5	2.0	6	0.5	1.5
Total Spanish in 1000's		350	6.2		444	8.2		481	7.3	
Course	Grade									
I	9	205	11.2	58.4	254	15.5	57.1	272	13.6	56.6
II	10	119	7.7	34.1	156	10.5	35.2	165	9.3	34.4
III	11	22	1.8	6.2	29	2.3	6.4	38	2.5	7.9
IV	12	5	0.5	1.3	6	0.6	1.3	5	0.5	1.1
Total German in 1000's		133	2.4		43	0.8		53	0.8	
I	9	78	4.3	58.5	23	1.4	52.5	29	1.4	54.3
II	10	45	2.9	34.1	16	1.1	38.1	19	1.1	35.9
III	11	6	0.5	6.7	4	0.3	8.5	5	0.3	8.9
IV	12	-1	---	0.7	-1	---	0.9	-1	---	0.9

[1] The figures under the dates give the total high school enrollment to the nearest thousand. The figures underscored, as indicated, give the total enrollment in English, in all foreign languages, and in each language separately, in the same manner. The corresponding percentages, based on the total enrollment, are underscored. The other figures give the field or subject enrollments in each grade according to the year of the course. The corresponding percentages are in the column next to the figures, and show the proportion of grade enrollments in each year of each subject. Percentages in the adjoining column show the proportion of language enrollments in each year of the four-year language sequence. For enrollments by grade in each year listed, see Table 17 above, or Appendix G. The rounding off of decimals occasionally causes the sum in the second percentage column to fall 0.1 below 100.0%.

[2] In this year enrollments in each of the four regular classes in English and in foreign languages were broken down for the first time. By dividing the total English or foreign language enrollments into each of the course enrollments (I through IV), the proportion of the total enrollments in each course enrollment was determined. In each of the five subjects, as it happened, many students could not be classified in one of the four courses. In English, for example, 3,775,051 students were enrolled in English I through IV. Of these, enrollments in English I constituted 33.3%, in English II, 28.1%, etc., as shown in the table. There were 282,691 "undesignated" students, however, and 13,352 in half-year courses, that had not been included in the English enrollments just given. All regular English enrollments, therefore, totaled 4,071,094. Without any possibility of verification it was assumed that the unclassified students were divided in the same way as those in classes I through IV. But the English enrollments were from schools that represented only 80% of the total high school enrollment in the country. The correction of 4,071,094 for 80% gave 5,088,867 for the total English enrollment. The English I, English II, etc., percentages were then applied to this total. The appropriate products were then divided by enrollments in the corresponding grade — the total high school enrollment and enrollments in each grade were also corrected for 80%—and yielded the percentages shown. The same procedures were used for each of the four languages. For the 80% "correction," see *Bulletin 1938, No. 6*, p. 9 (repeated in BS 1948-50, Ch. 5, pp. 5, 16, 27). For grade distribution, see Appendix G, Table 36; for subject enrollments, *Bulletin 1938, No. 6*, Tables 1, 2, and 3. For subject percentages in other English subjects, see Chapter IV, Table 5.

[3] BS 1948-50, Ch. 5, Tables 3 and 7.

[4] Data for foreign languages were taken from PMLA, pp. 52-56. On the basis of figures given, the percentage of total enrollments in all languages, and in each language separately, was determined for courses I through IV, as shown in the table. The language enrollments and percentages in the survey were based on a total enrollment of 4,520,505 in the schools covered. Of these, 6.9% were enrolled in Latin, 5.6% in French, etc., as indicated in the table. The writer applied these percentages to the total high school enrollment for 1954-55, estimated by Foster and Hobson (*School Life*, May 1955), and to the results, the percentages for Latin I, French I, etc., referred to above. These results were then divided by the enrollments in grade 9, grade 10, etc., as estimated by Foster and Hobson, for the percentage of grade enrollments in each language course, as shown in the table.

Although no data were available on English for this year the writer estimated enrollments in the subject as 93.7% of the total high school enrollment as forecast by Foster and Hobson (*School Life*, May 1955). He then estimated the percentage of total English enrollments in English I, English II, etc. These percentages gave the figures for those enrollments which, in turn, yielded the appropriate grade percentage in each course. For possible different enrollments and resulting changes in grade percentages of foreign languages, see Appendix G, Note 11.

This table should be compared with Table 18 for percentage trends, and with Table 19 for enrollment trends. It shows the same general characteristics of both. Actual subject registrations decreased between 1934 and 1949, but increased between 1949 and 1955. In English, however, the percentage of total registrations and of those by grade also increased, except in English I between 1949 and 1955.[16] If this is substantially correct, it would indicate that English is be-

coming more and more a required subject for all four of the high school years.

Nothing better illustrates the influence of the elective system on enrollments than the changes that have taken place in the position of foreign languages in the high school curriculum. More than any subjects, they show the effects of decreasing enrollments in a four-year sequence in which each higher course is dependent upon the one immediately preceding it. Like most of the other cumulative subjects, increasing enrollments and decreasing percentages went hand in hand through 1934. When the two statistical elements both went in the same direction between 1934 and 1949, the drop in foreign languages was more drastic than that of any other subject-matter field.

This drop was approximately 42% in all foreign languages. By courses it was progressively larger for each consecutive course. In those of the first year it was 38%; of the second year, 42%; of the third year, 52%; of the fourth year, 60%.

Three of the languages followed this pattern in varying degrees. The overall decrease in Latin was 53%. Latin I decreased 49%; Latin II, 54%; Latin III, 68%; Latin IV, 79%. For French the overall decrease was 58%; for French I, 57%; French II, 59%; French III, 59%; French IV, 54%. In German the overall decrease was 68%; in German I, 70%; German II, 64%; German III, 33%. In German IV there was a negligible increase. In contrast to losses in each of these Spanish increased 27% between 1934 and 1949. Spanish I increased 24%; Spanish II, 31%; Spanish III, 32%; Spanish IV, 20%.[17]

It is interesting to note that in all languages combined and in Latin the loss in the second year was the same or close to the overall loss. In French the same thing was true in French I and in French II. In German, German I was closer than German II. In Spanish the increase in Spanish II was closer to the overall increase than Spanish I. In each of the languages and in all languages combined, it is also noteworthy that the proportion of enrollments in the second-year course to total enrollments was more uniform and changed less than the proportion in any other year. These facts, together with the tremendous drop after the second-year course, emphasize the strategic importance of second-year language study.

The developments between 1949 and 1955 bear out this conclusion. In this period registrations in all languages combined increased 14%. The increase in Language I was 15%; in Language II, 13%; in Language III, 24%. But in Language IV there was a 14% decrease.

Among the separate languages there was considerable variation.

The overall increase in Latin was 8%. Latin I increased 9%; Latin II, 10%. Latin III, however, decreased 9%; and Latin IV, 29%. In French the overall increase was 45%. French I increased 50%; French II, 41%; French III, 40%; French IV, 20%. In Spanish the overall increase was 8%. Spanish I increased 7%; Spanish II, 6%; Spanish III, 31%. Spanish IV, however, decreased 16%. In German the overall increase was 23%. German I increased 26%; German II, 16%; German III, 25%. German IV remained about the same.

In this period, although there was not the same relationship between increases in second-year courses and total increases as in the preceding period, the proportion of second-year to total enrollments remained remarkably consistent. The tremendous drop after the second year of study decreased slightly in Spanish and German, but increased slightly in Latin and French.

Between 1934 and 1955 developments in English and in foreign languages were in striking contrast. In 1934 enrollments in English I and II constituted 61% of all enrollments in the four regular English courses. In 1955 that proportion had dropped to 58%. In 1934 enrollments in Language I and II constituted 89% of all foreign language enrollments. In 1955 that proportion had reached approximately 92%, with step-ladder variations among the four languages—89% for French, 90 for German, 91 for Spanish, and 94 for Latin. In effect each language had become a two-year instead of a four-year sequence.

This change, which began before 1934, points once more to the second-year course as the vital spot in all foreign language study. This is made clear by another contrast with English.

Enrollments in English I, as Table 20 shows, outnumber those in Language I more than two to one. Almost nine out of ten students in English I will go into English II, if the 1955 situation has continued, and nine out of ten of those, into English III. Almost two out of three students in Language I will continue into Language II, but only one out of five in Language II will continue into Language III. Comparable figures for the separate languages show, in order, two out of three, and one out of eight in Latin; in French, almost two out of three, and three out of eleven; in Spanish, three out of five, and a little more than one out of four; in German, two out of three, and a little more than one out of five. Fifty-seven out of a hundred students in English I will continue into English IV. Two out of a hundred in Language I will continue into Language IV. In Latin, Spanish, and German comparable figures for each are not quite two; in French, three.

Although the numbers are considerably smaller, the *proportion* of students in the first year of a foreign language who continue into the second year compares favorably with continuation from English I into English II. The great differences come after the second year, when the proportion of those continuing foreign language study takes such a decided drop.

In mathematics, although the decided drop seems to come after algebra I, this is by no means certain. The reason for the uncertainty is the flexibility of the mathematical sequence, which permits algebra I to be followed by plane geometry or algebra II. The findings of a special study on mathematics may throw some light on this complicated problem.

In 1952-53 it was estimated that 1,135,800 students were enrolled in algebra I throughout the United States. Of these 76% were in grade 9, 20% in grade 10, 3% in grade 11, and 1% in grade 12.[18] In that same year, it is estimated, 559,000 students were enrolled in plane geometry, of whom 64% were in grade 10, 26% in grade 11, 8% in grade 8, and 2% in grade 9. Estimates for algebra II gave 334,000, of whom 30% were in grade 10, 51% in grade 11, 17% in grade 12, and 1% in grade 9.[19] On the basis of these figures there is only one valid comparison that can be made: the number of students in grade 9 enrolled in algebra I as compared with the number of students in grade 10 enrolled in plane geometry and algebra II.[20] In grade 9 the number of students in algebra I was 863,208. In grade 10 the number enrolled in plane geometry was 357,880 and in algebra II, 90,000. The total of these two—448,000—constituted 52% of grade 9 enrollments in algebra I.

Since these figures were for the same year, they do not indicate what percentage of students who studied algebra I in grade 9 continued with plane geometry and algebra II the following year in grade 10. Neither do they make allowance for drop-outs between grades 9 and 10, or failures in algebra I. Nevertheless they probably make it reasonably safe to say that about one out of two students who study algebra I in grade 9 will continue with plane geometry or algebra II in grade 10.

The next sequence involves students in grade 11 who study one of these two subjects, or possibly both. Again, no allowance can be made for drop-outs or failures. It is merely assumed, without any possibility of proof, that a student in either subject in grade 10 would not be in that same subject in grade 11. From the percentages given above, in 1952-53, grade 11 students of plane geometry totaled 145,300;

of algebra II, 170,300. The combined figures—316,000—constituted 70% of plane geometry and algebra II enrollments in grade 10. On this basis, it seems reasonably safe to say that seven out of ten students who studied plane geometry or algebra II in grade 10 will continue with the other subject in the sequence in grade 11. This compares very favorably with the nine out of ten students who will go from English II to English III, and contrasts sharply with the two out of ten who will go from Language II to Language III.

The final sequence, trigonometry and solid geometry in grade 12, presents complications similar to those already mentioned. In 1952-53, it is estimated, approximately 100,000 students were enrolled in each of these subjects, which are predominantly one-semester courses. Of the trigonometry enrollments about 83%—or 83,000—were in grade 12, and of those in solid geometry, about 78%—78,000.[21] The total—161,000—constitutes 51% of registrations in plane geometry and algebra II in grade 11. On this basis, about one out of two students in plane geometry or algebra II in grade 11 will continue into trigonometry and solid geometry in grade 12.

These figures, uncertain though many factors are, probably give a more realistic picture of the situation in mathematics than do those in Tables 18 and 19. Although they were based on the study of conditions in a relatively small number of schools for only one year, the schools were carefully selected by type, size, and location. Even if conditions have changed in the period between 1952-53 and 1954-55, the figures serve to emphasize this fact: enrollments in a given course, expressed as the percentage of pupils in the grade where the course is usually taught, do just that and no more. They cannot show how many students from that grade were actually in the course. For that reason they cannot be used to predict how many students in a given course in a given grade will study the next course of the sequence in the next grade. Only a special study of the kind illustrated above can give that kind of valuable information.

Table 20 above is a good example of the difference between the two kinds of data just mentioned. Since English is becoming more and more a required subject in each of the four high school years, the sequence of English I, English II, etc., requires that a student follow it in that order. Although failures occur, the continuation rates from one course to the next have a more realistic relationship to corresponding grade enrollments than have any other subject-matter sequences.

In foreign languages a completely different situation has developed.

They, too, must be studied in proper sequence, but most students end their language work after the first two courses. If they take up a second language they ordinarily do so while they are in grades 11 and 12. Although their number is undoubtedly small, their presence in courses I and II, usually offered in grades 9 and 10, makes the relationship between grade enrollments and corresponding course registrations somewhat unrealistic. In this respect, cross-grade registrations in language courses are similar, though less extensive, to those in mathematics. Since the second year for second-language students would coincide with their senior high school year, their graduation tends to increase the big drop in registrations between the second- and third-year of all language courses.

Tables 18 and 20 could not of course take any of these factors into account. They simply show course registrations as a percentage of enrollments in the grade in which the course is usually taught. Since all percentages are derived in the same way, they have some value for marking the successive changes that have taken place at various levels in the subjects listed. For the years 1934 through 1955 Table 20 goes one step beyond Table 18 and adds actual enrollments. Table 19 supplements Table 18 in this respect and goes one step beyond Table 20 by adding percentages to show increase or decrease in course or subject registrations during the twenty-one-year period. Similar data for the courses in Table 20 are given in the text.

The actual enrollment figures, together with the percentages to indicate the extent of increase or decrease, are of some interest in themselves. But they also suggest an important question: Do they have any value for predicting an increase or decrease in the number of high school students who may specialize in certain subject-matter fields in college? [22]

A student's program of high school studies is the result of many different factors: subjects available, college entrance or school requirements, personal inclination, parental and community influence, and the like. But what about the students whose programs, whatever the reasons, include four years of a foreign language, or chemistry and physics, or trigonometry and solid geometry? Does the increase or decrease in the number of registrations in these subjects have any bearing on the number of college students who major in these and related fields?

As a companion to Tables 19 and 20 and as an aid to predictive analysis, the table below lists the number of undergraduate majors in certain subjects between 1947-48 and 1954-55.

TABLE 21

COLLEGE MAJORS IN CERTAIN SUBJECTS AND SUBJECT-MATTER FIELDS BETWEEN 1947-48 AND 1954-55 [1]

	1948	1950	1952	1953	1954	1955
Total number first degrees in 1000's	272	434	332	305	293	287
Physics	2126	3414	2247	2005	1952	1996
	0.78	0.78	0.68	0.66	0.67	0.69
Chemistry	7429	10619	6819	5959	5791	5920
	2.7	2.4	2.1	1.9	2.0	2.1
Other physical sciences [2]	5169	10372	3089	2466	2137	2600
	1.9	2.4	0.93	0.84	0.73	0.91
Biology	6739	10428	6960	5959	5847	5493
	2.5	2.3	2.1	1.9	2.0	1.9
Other biological sciences [3]	5952	6994	4236	3748	3519	3557
	2.2	1.6	1.3	1.3	1.2	1.2
Total sciences	27,415	41,827	23,351	20,136	19,246	19,566
	10.1	9.7	7.0	6.6	6.3	6.8
Mathematics	4266	6392	4721	4396	4090	4034
	1.6	1.5	1.4	1.4	1.4	1.4
Engineering [4]	31096	52246	30549	24189	22329	22589
	11.4	12.0	9.2	7.9	7.6	7.9
Business and commerce [5]	38371	72137	46683	40706	40944	41655*
	14.9	16.8	14.1	13.3	14.0	14.5
Other applied social sciences [5]	3705	9014	13068	6091	7647	8057*
	1.3	2.1	3.9	2.0	2.6	2.8
Basic social sciences [6]	29560	43678	31199	28918	27774	27666
	10.8	10.1	9.4	9.5	9.5	9.6
Education [7]	29694	46635	62951	61520	56817	53254*
	10.8	10.7	18.9	20.2	19.4	18.5
Foreign Languages (all)	4241	5160	4418	4068	3793	3548
	1.5	1.2	1.3	1.3	1.3	1.2
Classical (Latin and Greek)	498	671	683	562	571	512*
	0.18	0.15	0.21	0.18	0.19	0.18
French	1281	1473	1385	1202	1268	1279
	0.47	0.34	0.42	0.39	0.43	0.45
German	334	540	415	381	327	315
	0.12	0.12	0.13	0.12	0.11	0.11
Spanish	1827	2132	1605	1438	1210	1206
	0.67	0.78	0.48	0.47	0.41	0.42
Russian	7	36	43	54	68	60*
Others	294	308	287	431	349	·176
History [8]	9245	13567	10216	9576	9385	9540*
	3.3	3.1	3.1	3.1	3.2	3.3
Economics [8]	9002	14573	8595	7313	6728	6364
	3.3	3.4	2.6	2.4	2.3	2.2
Public Administration		273	297	309	383	386
English [8]	12614	17246	14087	12667	12566	13099*
	4.6	4.6	4.3	4.1	4.3	4.6

¹ All figures were taken from *Earned Degrees* (See Appendix A) for the year indicated. The figures under the dates represent to the nearest thousand the total number who received their first undergraduate degree in a given year, i.e., B.A., B.S., C.E., etc. Those receiving graduate degrees—M.A., Ph.D., Ed.D., and the like, were not included. The other figures *show the actual number* and percentage of those who received their first degree with a major or specialization in the subjects or subject-matter fields indicated. The figures underscored show the largest number recorded during the seven-year period. Those marked with an asterisk had an increase in 1955 over 1948. For the sake of interest and comparison many subjects and fields were added for which high school figures and subjects would have no predictive value. Comments will be made about some of them below, and in a few cases additional high school information given.

In 1955-56 the total number of first degrees was 311,298. Because of a change in the method of tabulation, statistics in some of the fields are not comparable to those of preceding years. Thus, in Table 6 (old method) the biological sciences show a decrease in 1955-56 over 1954-55, but in Table 4 (new method), a sizeable increase. Physical sciences are the same in both. Physics increased to 2,335 in number and to 0.75 in percentage; chemistry increased to 6,178, but its percentage decreased to 1.99. Mathematics, the same in both tables, increased to 4,660 and 1.48%.

² Astronomy, geology, metallurgy, meteorology, and a number of physical sciences not identified. All of these had slight increases in 1955-56.

³ Anatomy, bacteriology, biochemistry, botany, entomology, physiology, zoology, and a number of biological sciences not identified. Of these only bacteriology and zoology increased in number in 1955-56; all decreased in percentage.

⁴ All engineering fields were grouped together. In 1955-56 the number increased to 26,312 and the percentage to 8.45.

⁵ In addition to business and commerce (accounting, and "other"), the applied social sciences include public administration (given separately), social work, and social sciences unclassified. All except social work had numerical and percentage increases in 1955-56.

⁶ Economics, history (both given separately), sociology, political science. All increased numerically in 1955-56; political science and sociology decreased slightly in percentage.

⁷ It is interesting to note that Education was the only separate major field that did not reach its peak in 1949-50 when college enrollments and graduates reached their all-time high. Its number in 1954-55 as compared with 1947-48 was proportionately much greater than that for any other subject or field. In 1955-56 the various entries in this field were considerably changed. There was an overall increase in number but a slight decrease in percentage.

⁸ Undergraduate majors in history, regardless of college enrollments or the number of graduates, make up slightly more than 3% of the graduates; those in economics, slightly more than 2%; and those in English, about 4.5%. In 1955-56 the number of majors in each of these subjects increased slightly, the percentages remained practically the same. It seems clear that high school enrollments in these subjects have little influence in college.

This table gives a very good cross-section of under-graduate studies and majors in recent years. Between 1947-48, the first year such statistics were made available in such detail, and 1949-50, returning veterans brought college enrollments and graduating classes to an all-time high. Although there was a steady decrease between 1950 and 1955, each class in this period was larger than any during the pre-war years. Many high school graduates entered college also, directly after graduation, during all these years. While the presence of the veterans, whose college education has been delayed, may weaken the predictive value of high school enrollments in mathematics, science, and foreign languages, nevertheless certain comparisons may be made and some tentative conclusions drawn from them.

Between 1934 and 1949, as Tables 17 and 18 show, high school

enrollments decreased, and many subject registrations by grade decreased in actual numbers and in percentages. Neither table could show the fluctuations of enrollments in grades 11 and 12. Enrollments in those grades increased to their peak between 1934 and 1941. Between 1941 and 1947 there were variations down and then up to a second peak. In 1947-48 grades 11 and 12 were slightly larger than those grades in 1948-49.[23] This fact is important because certain subject registrations by grade were smaller in actual numbers and in percentages in 1949 than in 1934.

In 1947-48, it is estimated 28.4% of 1,030,000 high school seniors, or approximately 292,500 students, studied physics.[24] One year later approximately 292,000 students were enrolled in physics (Table 19). Since the members of these two classes who entered college immediately would theoretically have graduated in 1952 and 1953 respectively, the college class of 1952 might be expected to have a few more majors in physics than the class of 1953. As Table 21 shows, it had 242 more.

In 1947-48, to take another example, there were 491,000 high school students of chemistry.[25] Subject registrations a year later, in 1948-49, totaled 412,000 students (Table 19). The members of these two classes who entered college after their senior year would theoretically have graduated in 1953 and in 1954 respectively. In line with predictive expectations, chemistry majors in the class of 1953 outnumbered those in the class of 1954. Although the difference was smaller than might have been anticipated—168 (Table 21)—the likelihood that most students were in high school a year after they had studied chemistry was a possible factor.

Other physical science majors in college, fields for which high school registrations in chemistry and physics might be predictive, showed the same developments as majors in chemistry and physics. The number of such majors was larger in 1952 than in 1953 and in 1953 than in 1954. This was also true in biology and in the other biological sciences (Table 21).

It cannot of course be proved that the high school figures for 1947-48, on which these comparisons and predictions rest, were absolutely accurate. The differences between the number of college majors in physics and particularly in chemistry were somewhat less than might have been expected. If it was justifiable, however, to add majors in the other fields cited, the potential predictive value of registrations in high school chemistry and physics together might be considered fairly strong.[26]

A similar analysis for mathematics and foreign languages is made more difficult by the lack of any special studies to fill the gap between the high school curriculum surveys of 1933-34 and 1948-49. Nevertheless, as Tables 19 and 20 make plain, registrations in all mathematics courses, except in general mathematics and in trigonometry, decreased between 1934 and 1949, and in all language courses except Spanish. It may not be illogical, therefore, to assume that enrollments in these courses—exclusive of the exceptions just noted—followed the pattern of chemistry and physics in 1947-48 as compared with 1948-49. If the assumption is justified, there should be more college majors in mathematics, Latin, French, German, and possibly in engineering, in 1952 than in 1953, and possibly more in 1953 than in 1954. This was true for mathematics, engineering, and German. Latin and French had more in 1952 than in 1953 or 1954, despite a slight increase in 1954 over 1953 (Table 21).[37] Spanish, contrary to expectations, followed the pattern of German.

Two contradictory elements for predictive purposes in mathematics and engineering—the decrease in plane and solid geometry and algebra II registrations as against an increase of those in trigonometry—illustrate the complex nature of the predictive process. The decreases in solid geometry and algebra II offset the increases in trigonometry by approximately 7,000 students. On this basis, perhaps decreases in the number of college majors in mathematics and engineering should have been expected. On the other hand, at least in engineering, it is quite likely that peak enrollments in that broad field in 1949, 1950, and 1951, caused some concern about future job opportunities and intensified competition. It is noticeable that the engineering field between 1952 and 1954 decreased not only in numbers but in percentages as well. The number in mathematics also decreased, but the proportion to all majors remained approximately the same in each of those three years.

Among the foreign languages the tremendous enrollment drop in Latin, French, and German between 1934 and 1949 undoubtedly had reduced college majors in those subjects long before 1947-48. The continued high school decrease assumed for 1947-48 and 1948-49 would have been reflected, if at all in college, only in the classes of 1952 and 1953, when the numbers involved had become even more relatively insignificant.

The high school developments in Spanish, which ran contrary to expectations in college, illustrate an important factor in all language study. Although it is possible for a student to begin a language in

college and major in it, the amount of work this would require in the last two years adds considerably to the difficulty. Most language majors come into college with at least two years of a language, and more often with four. Sometime before 1948-49 Spanish became the most popular foreign language in high school. Although increases took place in third- and fourth-year courses, the greatest increases were in the courses of the first two years. More students were entering college with some knowledge of Spanish than ever before, but that knowledge was rusty from two years' lack of use. This would make it necessary in most cases to shift to another foreign language, even to satisfy a two-year requirement for the bachelor of arts. As Table 21 shows, Spanish majors were about 50% larger than those in French between 1948 and 1950. That gap had narrowed considerably by 1952, and by 1954 French had passed Spanish for the first time. An additional contributing factor in this development may be read in Table 20.

Between 1934 and 1949 all enrollments in French decreased markedly, including those in French III and IV. During the same period all enrollments in Spanish had increased markedly, including courses of the last two years. In 1934, however, French III enrollments were nearly three times as large as Spanish III, and French IV enrollments were a little over twice as large as Spanish IV. Although Spanish had gone ahead in the last two categories by 1949, during most of the period French was probably in the lead or at least equal to Spanish. In 1949 Spanish III was considerably ahead of French III, but Spanish IV was only slightly ahead of French IV. By 1955, with general increases in both languages, Spanish III's lead over French III had been reduced, but French IV was ahead of Spanish IV. This development, which had started in high school after 1948-49, showed predictable results in college. In 1955, and even in 1954, French majors outnumbered those in Spanish, and French majors in 1955 had increased over those in 1954.

The same predictable results also worked out for Latin. Between 1949 and 1955 enrollments in Latin III and IV decreased (Table 20). There was a smaller number of classics majors in 1955 than in 1954 (Table 21).[28]

The proportion of second-year enrollments to total enrollments, as pointed out earlier in this chapter, remained remarkably uniform in all languages.[29] But the increase in the proportion of the first-year course to all courses, between 1934 and 1955, was greater for Latin than for any other language. By 1955, as a result of the de-

creases in the proportion of Spanish I, it was about the same for Latin and Spanish. It is extremely doubtful if this means, as was suggested above for Spanish, that more students are taking up Latin as a second language. The numbers involved do not support such an inference. What it does mean, however, is that, fewer though they may be in the aggregate as compared with the numbers immediately before and after 1934, more students are going into college ill prepared to continue in Latin. Because of the lapse of two years' time their knowledge of Latin has become dim with disuse. Far from being qualified to major in Latin, most of them are compelled to shift to another language to satisfy requirements for the bachelor's degree. This is an important contributing factor in the decline of Latin majors, just as it is for Spanish.

In proportion to the number of high school students enrolled in it, and particularly in courses III and IV, German has far more college majors than any other foreign language. Although the numbers involved are small, both in high school and in college, the decrease in German IV between 1949 and 1955 produced the expected results in college. German majors were fewer in 1955 than in 1954 (Table 21).

As Table 19 shows, enrollments in every mathematics and science course in high school increased between 1949 and 1955. College majors in every related subject and field increased in 1955 over 1954, except in biology and in mathematics.

Although the greatest high school increases were in solid geometry and trigonometry, their predictive value may be greater for engineering than for mathematics proper.[30] The increases in algebra II and plane geometry were comparatively slight, and their principal grade locations, 11 and 10 respectively, probably reduced their predictive value. Nevertheless recent studies have portrayed a situation in mathematics more serious than the college figures indicate.

A study published in 1954 revealed that 62% of the colleges in the country had to teach high school algebra to their entering freshmen. A year later another study gave the report of an engineering school that 72 per cent of its entering students were not qualified for the regular freshman course in mathematics.[31]

Whether the experience of the one school is typical for all engineering schools or not, the two reports supplement each other. Since all of the students had been duly admitted, presumably because they had taken the proper courses, including mathematics, with the proper grades and had been recommended by their principals, it must be

assumed that they were average or above average in ability, character, and temperament.

Why then do so many colleges find it necessary to teach sub-freshman algebra? Why are so many students unprepared for college algebra or trigonometry as freshmen, after they have successfully completed the prerequisite courses in high school?

The answers to these questions are too variable and complex to be conclusive. And yet two of the answers lie ready at hand.

The student who plans to enter a college that requires two years of mathematics for entrance, and one year after entrance, is in something of a dilemma, whether he knows it or not. If he studies algebra I in grade 9, while arithmetic is presumably fresh in his mind, he then may have the choice of plane geometry or algebra II in grade 10. If he is in one of the smaller schools, he may have to wait a year to get his choice. If he has good teachers, he may take both courses as they are offered. But he has met the requirements by the end of grade 10, or he may have an extra year at the end of grade 11. In grade 12 he takes physics or chemistry but not mathematics. Is he ready for college algebra or trigonometry when he reaches college, after being away from algebra for one and possibly two years?

Could the student solve this problem by studying general mathematics in grade 9, algebra I in grade 10, and algebra II and plane geometry in grades 11 and 12, as they might be available? If he studied algebra II in grade 12, there would be a year's gap after algebra I. If he studied it in grade 11, there would be a year's gap before college. Which would be better—or worse—for a student not overly fond of mathematics anyway? Is the sequence any better for the student who does like the subject and wants to include trigonometry or solid geometry for entrance into an engineering school?

The report from one engineering school cited above would seem to indicate that it is not. Common sense would agree. Traditional though it may be, what sense does it make to separate algebra into two levels, interpose a year of geometry between, separate it from its companion piece by the second level of algebra, and top them all with trigonometry for half a year? Are there no principles common to plane and solid geometry and trigonometry? Are there no common bonds of logic between algebra and geometry?

Experiments are now being carried on, not to discover common principles, but to use those that have long been known, in a new approach to the teaching of mathematics. From the experience gained in these experimental classes in a selected number of high schools it is

expected that a four-year integrated course of study will be developed, together with suitable textbooks and teaching methods.[32] These changes in high school will most likely cause similar changes in the lower grades and possibly in college. Undoubtedly they will bring about an increased emphasis and interest in the study of mathematics at all levels and make such study a more effective educational instrument for an ever larger number of students in our public schools.

In the field of foreign languages another approach has been made to solve the problem of declining enrollments. Within the last few years informal oral instruction, primarily in French and Spanish, has been introduced in the elementary grades. The movement has spread throughout most of the states, and preparation has begun of a series of teaching manuals appropriate to the different grade levels.[33]

How this program, if it continues to grow, will affect foreign language study in high school and college cannot yet be judged. The vast majority of language students will continue to begin such study in high school, particularly in Latin, for some years to come. As more students enter high school with previous language training, however, changes will undoubtedly occur in methods and texts for all languages, including Latin. Out of these changes will come eventually a coordinated course of language study, extending from the grades through high school into college, that will more nearly suit our educational needs as leader in the community of free nations.

Those needs will not be met by mathematics and foreign languages alone. They must be supplemented with a carefully coordinated program of science studies, on which our national security so unavoidably rests.

The subject-matter of these three fields may change and methods of instruction may vary, but within the foreseeable future we shall neglect them at our peril.

[1] All figures were calculated from data given in Ch. IV, Table 1, and rounded off to the nearest thousand.

[2] See Chapter V, for a general discussion of the *Report*, and Note 11 for references.

[3] CR 1904-05, II, p. 822; CR 1905-06, II, p. 695; CR 1909-10, II, p. 1134.

[4] CR 1909-10, II, p. 1133 (published in 1911).

[5] In Chapter IV, Table 1, its percentage was 1.9 in 1900, and 1.86, rounded off to 1.9, in 1910. In Table 17 above the slight increase in 1910 over 1900 is due to the size of grade 12, which did not increase proportionately quite as much as the total high school enrollment. For the percentages and pattern in science, based on total high school enrollments, see Chapter IV, Table 3.

[6] *Bulletin 1938, No. 6*, p. 14.

[7] BS 1926-28, p. 966.

[8] *Ibid.*, pp. 1066-67.

[9] A convenient reference for these facts is BS 1948-50, Ch. 5, Table 7.

[10] In BS 1926-28, p. 966, from which this quotation was taken, the word *geometry*, rather than *plane geometry*, was used. Since the statement came on the heels of "what portion of geometry is plane geometry," and with no mention of solid geometry in the paragraph, the reference to plane geometry seemed unmistakable. Otherwise, the statement would mean that plane and solid geometry, before 1928, were studied together as a year's course. In 1934, the first time such information was made available, registrations in plane geometry as a year-course constituted 98% of all registrations in the subject; registrations in solid geometry as a half-year course, 84% of all registrations in the subject. See *Bulletin 1938, No. 6*, pp. 47-48.

[11] In 1934 registrations in advanced algebra as a year-course constituted 68% of all registrations in the subject; in 1949, in intermediate algebra, 81%. See *Bulletin 1938, No. 6*, p. 46, and *BS* 1948-50, Ch. 5, p. 55. In 1934 advanced algebra may have included algebra 3. Since the only separate figures for algebra 3 (in the second reference, p. 57) show that it was a half-year course for 65% of the students, the presence of algebra 3 figures in 1934 would probably have increased the number of half-year students.

[12] The numbers who have studied all four sciences in the various years could not be determined. This would make an interesting and useful study—if it has not been done.

[13] According to one recent study 62% of the colleges were caught in the cycle. W. L. Williams, "What the colleges are doing about the poorly prepared student," in *American Mathematical Monthly*, 61 (February 1954) 86-88, quoted by *Dyer et al*, p. 23. In 1955 an engineering school reported that 72% of its entering freshmen had to take refresher courses in mathematics before they could do normal first-year work. *Engineering and Scientific Manpower Newsletter* No. 89 (February 14, 1956), quoted by *Dyer et al*, p. 23.

[14] In 1928 they were 76.8%, and in 1934, 74.6%. Percentages were calculated from BS 1926-28, p. 1065, and *Bulletin 1938, No. 6*, p. 46.

[15] See, however, Note 4, Table 19.

[16] The division of registrations in English I through IV in 1934, as explained in Note 1, Table 20 above, could not be made with absolute certainty. If the division for that year was approximately correct, the proportion of English I registrations decreased between 1934 and 1949, and this assumed decrease was carried through 1955 (see second percentage column in Table 20). The proportion of English II also showed a slight decrease in the whole period. Both of these developments were in contrast to increases in the proportions of English III and IV, with 1934 again as the starting point.

[17] All calculations were based on figures in Table 20. Percentages were rounded off to the nearest decimal.

[18] *Bulletin 1953, No. 5*, Tables 15 and 17.

[19] *Ibid.*, pp. 16 and 21; Tables 24 and 28.

[20] It is obviously impossible to tell from the data given how many students in grade 11 enrolled in plane geometry or algebra II might have studied the other subject while they were in grade 10, or might be studying the two concurrently in grade 11.

[21] *Ibid.*, pp. 23-26; Tables 31 and 35. The latter table shows that about 15% of trigonometry registrations were in grade 11, and about 22% of solid geometry. The remaining 2% in trigonometry were postgraduate students.

[22] See p. 106.

[23] These statements are based on statistics in BS 1950-52, Ch. 1, Table 12, reported by state systems. Enrollments based on state reports are usually larger than those based on reports from individual secondary day schools, from which subject registrations and percentages are derived. In 1948-49, for example, enrollments in grade 12 from the latter source wer 1,026,000 (Table 17 or 19), or only 91.1% of the number reported in the former source, 1,126,000 (Table 12 in this note). Grade 11, to take a second example, was 98% as large. The figures were 1,242,000 (Table 17 or 19) and 1,267,000 (Table 12 in this note) respectively.

[24] The percentage was obtained from Table 4 of a special study *Bulletin 1950, No. 9*. Apparently, it was based exclusively on enrollments in grade 12 of the selected schools. This writer then applied it to the total enrollment in that grade throughout the United States as given in BS 1950-52, Ch. 1, Table 12, after it had been corrected in the way indicated in the preceding note. It was assumed that the correction necessary in 1948-49 would have been the same in 1947-48.

[25] The percentage, 39.4, was based on enrollments in grade 11 of the selected schools (*Bulletin 1950, No. 9*, Table 4.) This percentage was applied to the total enrollment in grade 11 throughout the country, after it had been corrected in the way indicated in Note 23 above.

[26] As Table 19 shows, biology was the only high school science, except general science, that had increasingly larger registrations between 1934 and 1955. Even though its high school enrollments have been consistently and considerably larger than those in physics and chemistry combined, in college, majors in the physical sciences have been consistently larger than majors in the biological sciences. High school enrollments in biology therefore would seem to have no predictive value. Since it is primarily a grade 10 subject many biology students undoubtedly study chemistry or physics before they finish high school.

[27] Majors in the classical languages (Table 21) include those in Greek and possibly those in classical archaeology. High school studies, except Latin of course, and possibly history, have very little bearing on the latter two subjects.

[28] See Note 27.

[29] See the second percentage column in Table 20.

[30] See Note 26 above for a discussion of a similar situation in biology.

[31] See Note 13 above.

[32] The experiments are being conducted under the direction of a Committee on Secondary School Mathematics at the University of Illinois (*Dyer et al*, pp. 23-24). A special grant to aid in this work was made by the Carnegie Corporation. See its *Annual Report* for 1956, pp. 39-40, 66.

[33] *Status of Foreign Language Study in American Elementary Schools*, by Kenneth W. Mildenberger, published by the U.S. Department of Health, Education, and Welfare (Washington, February 1956).

CHAPTER VII

THE JANUS LOOK

No American can study the history of our public high school without a feeling of awe at its growth and a sense of pride in its accomplishments. Its development into a national institution without sacrifice of state and local control is an example of educational leadership that has no parallel in any other country. The simultaneous evolution of this institution's dual function as an instrument of education and an agent of social change is unprecedented even in the annals of our own democracy.

This evolution may be divided into five broad periods. Each period maintained some continuity with the past and at the same time was naturally subject to the modifying force of contemporary and often conflicting opinions. Each period, that is, in succession bore the peculiar imprint of its own times in which, consciously or unconsciously, the seeds of change were constantly being sown.

During the colonial peroid, when secondary education was considered the prerogative of a favored minority, the curriculum used was one inherited from a tradition based upon aristocratic ideas of culture and class. Granted that it was inevitable for the Pilgrims and Cavaliers to transplant the only system of education they knew, the result was in many ways grotesque. In no other phase of our history has there been a greater incongruity between the practical needs of daily life and the curriculum of secondary and higher education. What stronger contrast could there be than the multitudinous activities of a struggle with primitive nature and man and the study of Greek and Roman literature? And yet, far from being an unrelieved exercise in futility, those selfsame studies pursued from grammar school into college by successive generations helped to produce a leadership that carved national independence out of almost unyielding odds.

No man can prove that an education of this kind, limited in number of students and in subject matter, prolonged — or shortened — the struggle one agonizing whit. It is clear, nevertheless, that the restriction of educational opportunities and consequent dissatisfaction with

a curriculum geared so exclusively to the past ushered in the next phase—the founding of private academies and the introduction of subjects conceivably of more immediate and practical use.

But the private academies, despite their original aims, could not make a complete break with tradition. The classical impulse was too ingrained and the college influence too dominant in a society that continued to show at least token obeisance to the ideals of culture and discipline. Large segments of that society, however, were becoming increasingly conscious of the possible connection between education and day-to-day living. Many of the academies, founded in all parts of the country, catered to the demands for such practical subjects as English grammar, surveying, business arithmetic, bookkeeping, history, and modern foreign languages; many combined such courses with the usual Latin and Greek, and still others were merely grammar schools under the new name.

Soon after the close of the Revolutionary War the academies largely replaced the grammar schools, in name if not altogether in spirit and purpose. The birth of the Republic and the growth of school-age population called for more and more schools at the secondary level. The academies provided the first answer and with their more extensive and flexible curricula they became the community colleges of their day.

But a private enterprise, however dedicated to the public good, meant private control of a public enterprise that was supported primarily by tuition fees. Both of these—private control and tuition fees—eventually ran counter to the spreading idea of free elementary education, and led to the third period of development—the creation in 1821 of a new instrument of democratic education, the public high school.

In keeping with its initial purpose, to prepare youth for the practical affairs of contemporary life, the curricula of the early high school were broadly vocational in content and scope. As the movement spread from industrial centers throughout the country, however, the original intent was gradually enlarged. Public sentiment compelled high schools, as it had compelled the academies before them, to add college preparatory subjects to their curricula. Under the mounting pressure of the dual function this imposed, made more complicated by compulsory education and a rising birth rate, the high schools enlarged their curricula beyond the bounds of effective educational control and plain common sense.

This expansion was in full bloom when the Federal Department of

Education was set up in 1867. Through systematized and informative publications it gradually made the American people and its leaders aware of the need for greater uniformity in subject matter and higher standards in secondary education. For the first time in our history we faced the necessity of applying to education the principle we had already learned in winning our political freedom: *uncontrolled excess leads to chaos and subsequent reform.* This realization paved the way for the fourth stage of the high school's development, which began with the Report of the Committee of Ten in 1894.

This Report was more than a blueprint of curriculum reform; it was also the *embodiment of the most profound, practical, and democratic philosophy of education ever enunciated in America.*

It was the most profound because it cut through the shams and shibboleths of the immediate and the practical to the basic needs of the individual and of our democratic society in the dawning world of the twentieth century. It was the most practical because it set an educational pattern that could be tailored to any high school regardless of size. It was the most democratic because it made no distinction between the educational welfare of those who were going to college and those who were not.

The essence of the Committee's philosophy may be summarized in four guiding principles: (1) The high school should specialize in broad, general education in the liberal arts and sciences which helped to form Western Civilization and on which man's destiny largely depends. (2) Out of the many broad fields of human knowledge, those must be selected which lay the foundation for civic and cultural development, mental and moral growth. (3) The subjects must be ones in which instruction can be given in classes graded in sequence from the elementary grades through high school, by teachers skilled in the use of methods appropriate to each level. (4) They must be subjects for which, by continuous and cooperative effort, improved texts and teaching methods can be developed and progressively kept up to date.

These precepts are as valid today as they were in 1894. It is good educational sense for our high schools to teach what they and they alone are best able to teach. It is practical and economical not to add to the burden of the schools—and of the taxpayers—an almost unlimited number of subjects many of which could be learned as well, perhaps even better, outside of school. It is democratic to make the same kind of basic education available to all, within the limits of individual capacity.

To translate their philosophy into action, the Committee set up a

four-track curriculum. Each track in this curriculum had graduated courses of study in five subject-matter fields: English, mathematics, foreign languages, history and government, and science. The four courses of study differed from each other mainly in two ways: in the foreign language designated (ancient or modern), and in the number of periods per week devoted to various subjects. It was contemplated that most students would graduate with four years of English and a single foreign language, and with at least three years of mathematics, science, and history and government.

For nearly thirty years the philosophy of the Committee of Ten was the predominating influence in secondary education. That influence was greatest from 1894, the year its Report was published, to 1910, but it remained strong through 1922. This is the period, it is significant to recall, when the number of high school students increased almost 1000% and the number of graduates, approximately 1200%.[1] Contrary to popular and to much educated opinion, this was *not* the period in which the majority of public high school graduates went to college.[2] Nevertheless during this period student concentration in science, mathematics, and foreign languages reached a maximum, both in percentages based on total high school enrollments and, for science, in those based on enrollments in grades in which these subjects are usually offered.[3]

At no time before or since have the high schools of this country worked with such unanimity and singleness of purpose. At no time did it seem more certain that secondary education had at last found a solid foundation of permanent value. Actual subject-matter content might change—and surely it would with new discoveries and with old interpretations revised in the light of added knowledge. New methods of teaching would surely be inevitable with advances in the field of psychology and in the embryonic science of education. To incorporate and correlate all of the myriad facets of learning and teaching into a related whole would demand new texts, but the five subject-matter fields would continue to be the *pentateuch* of the high school curriculum.

But during the very period in which the cumulative subjects in the Committee's four-track curriculum were attracting the largest proportions of students in high school history, a different philosophy of education was gaining wide support. In this philosophy education was considered not so much a training and disciplining of the mind as a process of developing social and civic awareness and responsibility. The life-adjustment theory shifted emphasis from formalized

drill to cooperative problem-solving, from subject matter to the student and his individualized needs.

Added impetus was given to these concepts by the tremendous and rapid growth of high school enrollments. More students meant more personalized differences and interests and consequently a greater number and variety of subjects to meet the greater diversity of life-adjustment demands. The attempt to meet these needs ushered in the fifth stage of high school development: over-expansion of the curriculum—for the second time.[4]

The Committee of Ten had recognized that diversity of individual interests and capacities would require different subject matter and treatment. It had provided some choice among the sciences and a few options for those whose bent or intent did not extend to algebra or ancient languages. It had not seen fit to prescribe the number of such practical subjects as business education, home economics, industrial arts, physical education and the like. The need and facilities for such activities and studies would vary wisely and decisions about them were proper matters for community judgment and local boards. The same could be said of music and art.

Nor was expansion confined to nonacademic subjects. Many new social studies were added to inculcate civic and social responsibilities. Courses in English were reorganized and special courses created, in an attempt to relate "literature and life."

Once such a movement was started it was difficult to stop. A few figures will illustrate. In 1910 there were 35 subjects in the curriculum, of which 27 were in the five academic fields stressed by the Committee of Ten. By 1922 the 27 had increased to 39, and the 8 to 29, for a total of 68. In 1934 additions were in full swing. The 39 had become 54—15 new subjects, all in English and social studies—and the 29 had become 57, for a total of 111. In 1949 the pendulum reached perhaps its widest arc. The 54 academic subjects had become 59, the nonacademic had become 82, for a total of 141, divided into some 274 different courses![5]

The effects of this expansion may be easily traced in the shifts of educational emphasis that resulted. In 1910 there were proportionately more students studying foreign languages, or mathematics, or science, or English, or social studies, than were studying all of the nonacademic subjects combined. English led the field with registrations equivalent to 114% of the total high school enrollment, mathematics came next with the equivalent of 90%; then foreign languages, with

84%, and social studies with 72. The seven nonacademic fields had the equivalent of 28%.

By 1922 the five academic fields still led, but there was a noticeable shift in the educational wind. English remained at the top with the equivalent of 83% of the total enrollment, followed by social studies with 78%. Among the three cumulative subject-matter fields, which had been significantly close together in 1910, mathematics was far in the lead with 75%, then science with 58%, and foreign languages with 55%. These three fields had suffered drastic losses on a proportionate basis, in sharp contrast with the other academic fields,[6] and in decided contrast with proportionate gains in the nonacademic fields. Chief among these was business education, which had a phenomenal increase between 1910 and 1922 from 11% to 42%. All of the subjects in the seven fields have the equivalent of 130% of the total high school enrollment.[7]

Although total losses or gains were less striking in the next period, ending in 1934, the general trend of the preceding period was maintained. Social studies made a slight gain to 79%; English, with 96%, had made a strong recovery from statistical confusion. The three cumulative subjects continued to decline: mathematics to 56%, science to 51, and foreign languages to 36. These were in sharp contrast with business education, which now enrolled 58% of the total high school. For the first time in high school history there were more students in business education subjects than in mathematics or science or foreign languages. Enrollments in the two fields of vocational and nonvocational subjects and home economics were greater than those in all foreign languages. All enrollments in nonacademic subjects, which attracted 28% in 1910, were now equivalent to 211% of the high school enrollments and considerably larger than those in mathematics, science, and foreign languages combined.

But the climax was still to come. In 1949 for the first time in high school history enrollments in home economics (24%)[8] or in vocational and nonvocational subjects (35%) were greater than those in all foreign languages with 22%; combined, they were greater than those in mathematics, with 55%, or in science, with 54%. Business education, with 59%, held its lead over mathematics and science, although the latter had made a slight gain since 1934. English, the leading high school subject since 1902,[9] climbed once more beyond the total high school, with 103%, but had to yield the palm at last to physical education, which attained that distinction for the first time with 109%. Social studies came next with 99%. Enrollments in the four practical

subject-matter fields were almost as large as those in mathematics, science, and foreign languages combined.

Because of the tremendous increases in high school enrollments these shifts in educational emphasis attracted relatively little attention. Although the declining percentages of students studying mathematics, science, and foreign languages after 1910 caused a vague feeling of concern among conservative educators, continuous increases in the actual number of students in those fields seemed reassuring enough to prevent extensive alarm. After all, in 1909-10, when the equivalent of 90% of high school students studied mathematics in some form, only about 13% of the high-school age population—those 14 to 17 years old—were in high school. In 1948-49, when 55% were studying mathematics, approximately 63% of the high-school age bracket were in high school.[10]

But aside from the great increase in educational opportunities and in the holding power of the schools, there were other and perhaps more significant implications. In 1909-10 only the intellectually "elite" were in high school. It is not strange that 90% of them studied mathematics, particularly in view of the restricted curriculum. But times have changed since 1910. Our high schools have become more "democratic." It could not be expected that nine out of ten students should study mathematics, for which many of them would have slight ability and even less use. Other subjects in the curriculum would more nearly satisfy their needs—and interests.

The contrast in actual numbers of course is rather staggering. The equivalent of about 800,000 studied mathematics in 1909-10; about 2,960,000, in 1948-49. In the latter year there were more students in alegbra 1 alone than in the entire high school in the former year, and almost as many in general mathematics.[11]

What is overlooked in all such overwhelming statistics is one very simple but crucial fact: if the equivalent of 90% of the students in 1948-49 had studied mathematics, in that year alone the equivalent of 1,900,000 more students would have been added.

After 1910, at any rate, *increasing enrollments but decreasing percentages* became the expected pattern in the three cumulative subject matter fields. When foreign languages broke the pattern, with fewer students in 1948-49 than in 1933-34, there were cries of educational anguish—among language teachers and a few world-minded and culture-conscious citizens. Although mathematics also broke the pattern in the same year, this fact largely escaped attention because, except for geometry, the record seemed to show larger subject—and total—

enrollments in 1948-49 than in 1933-34.[12] The actual facts were somewhat different.

Between 1933-34 and 1948-49 the total high school enrollment decreased about 4%. Among the four high school grades, however, decreases took place only in grades 9 and 10; grades 11 and 12 each had slight increases. Enrollment decreases might have been expected, therefore, in the subjects taught in grades 9 and 10 but not in those taught in grades 11 and 12. Yet they occurred in all four grades. *For the first time since 1910, and probably earlier, there were decreases of enrollments in algebra 2 (grade 11), in solid geometry (grade 12) despite enrollment increases in these two grades. In the same period, decrease in algebra 1 was proportionately almost twice as great as the decrease in grade 9; decrease in plane geometry proportionately almost ten times that of grade 10.*[13]

These developments were not confined to foreign languages and mathematics; they occurred in science also. Here the contrast was equally striking. General science and biology had increased enrollments in grades 9 and 10 despite the decreases in those two grades. Chemistry and physics, on the other hand, both had decreases despite the increases in grades 11 and 12, small though they were. *For the first time since 1893-94 physics and chemistry had simultaneous decreases in enrollments and percentages.*[14] *For the first time since 1910 there were simultaneous decreases in enrollments and percentages of most of the cumulative subjects.*[15]

The reason was not simply the competition and attraction of subjects that were less strenuous in their mental demands. That had its effect. Nor was it the correlary idea that increasing enrollment meant a corresponding decrease in the average level of intelligence. That too played its part. Added to these were several other rather complex but inter-related reasons. Chief among them were the failure to develop better teaching methods and texts, the shortage of good teachers, and the gradual dissipation of a once almost evangelistic belief in the disciplinary value of education.

No other subjects in the curriculum require more thorough knowledge and teaching skill than mathematics, science, and foreign languages. But knowledge alone is not enough; teaching skill alone is not enough. The two must be combined to a high degree of excellence. Such a combination can do much to overcome the handicaps of a poor textbook, but effective teaching demands all three—expert knowledge, teaching skill, and a textbook that enhances both.

These are attributes and assets that do not come by simple chance

or divine intervention. To obtain and foster and improve them requires constant vigilance and determined, cooperative effort on the part of professional and academic experts alike, at all levels of our educational system.

Unbelievable at it may now seem, cooperation of this kind has never existed between teachers of arts and sciences in college and those who teach teacher-training courses. On the contrary, such a feeling of antipathy and distrust has grown up that the educators of this country are virtually divided into two opposing camps, each with its own till-death-us-do-part brand of camp followers.

From the small beginning of a few courses offered in some of the academies, the training of teachers has long been one of our most important educational activities. Early in the nineteenth century, however, when the movement for such training began to gather force, the liberal arts colleges could not see beyond their stuffy academic fronts. In due and immediate course separate normal or training schools were established. The first in 1823 was the institutional progenitor of a lusty breed.

The breach, thus begun, has been hard to bridge. The liberal arts colleges have admitted Departments of Education to their cloistered circle and Schools of Education have been set up in most universities. For all that, two vitally related educational functions for the training of teachers have been kept essentially separate. Professors of academic subjects have tended to stress mastery of content and to deride study of methods. In their seasoned judgment, unwarped by excessive acquaintance with teaching techniques, knowledge of subject matter is the one requisite for good teaching. If the teacher really knows the subject, plain common sense, plus the teacher's intuitive experience, will take care of teaching methods. Good teachers are born, not made.

Professors of Education, on the other hand, have tended to glorify methodology and to minimize content. Once a teacher has learned tested teaching methods in a particular subject for a particular age-group, the application of those methods along the lines dictated by psychological research will result in good teaching. The task of the teacher is to guide the student in a learning situation which varies greatly for individuals. Since each person must learn for himself, the student is helped most, not by the teacher's knowledge of the subject, but by his knowledge of how to teach that subject.

This intramural debate has waned considerably of late and there are signs that a new era, one of cooperation, has now begun. The

teacher shortage has made it necessary to bring back or to accept for the first time many who do not meet usual professional requirements. This has happened most frequently perhaps in mathematics and science. Knowledge and enthusiasm for a subject have often proved effective substitutes for attested teaching-methods courses, and the educational heavens of the profession have not fallen! Although a millenium is not yet to be expected, there has been a slight apocalypse.

Proponents of the liberal arts and science have also begun to learn the salutary lesson that methods *are* important. Although there are other factors involved in the long continued decline in the proportion of students in mathematics, science, and foreign languages, the failure to use proper teaching methods is one of the most significant. This is not the fault of professional educators. There is little doubt that more effective teaching methods have been developed. There is little doubt also that many teachers have been unable—or unwilling—to learn them. But the leaven will spread, for new methods mean new textbooks, and new textbooks will spread the gospel among the hardened and unregenerate righteous who, perhaps more often than any others, stand in the need of prayer and repentance.

But reforms in teaching methods and texts do not stop there. Almost inevitably both point to a more fundamental change—a reorganization of the curriculum, in whole or in part. Such a change in mathematics is already under way to a limited degree in high school, and at least in prospect for the junior high school. Only within the last year or so have we learned the apparently amazing fact that principles of abstract thought and of symbolic logic, presented by competent teachers, are not beyond the interest and grasp of the average student. In time a coordinated course of study will undoubtedly result. It will extend from the lower grades through high school into college, and a special series of texts will be developed for each of the three public school levels.[16] Improved texts and teaching methods will revolutionize the study and teaching of mathematics in this country and make it an educational instrument second to none in the curriculum.

Although these results in themselves would make such steps desirable, they will be enhanced by their effect on science. Recent and recurring developments have dramatized as rarely before in intellectual history the vital connection between these two distinct but related fields. Even if the study of mathematics had no educational value as a separate discipline, its possible influence on and applica-

tion to scientific thought would make it indispensable in the modern world.

Improvements of this sort in mathematics, accomplished or planned, make parallel reforms in science all the more imperative. Indeed the rapidity with which scientific knowledge has expanded in the last decade and most likely will continue to expand complicates the task to a degree not found in other subject matter fields, even in mathematics. If a textbook, for example, is not to be outdated by the time it is published, how can the author and publisher decide with any degree of assurance when a "safety period" has been reached or how long it will last? The tremendous cost of publishing such texts and the risk of new discoveries, particularly in physics and chemistry, do much to explain the outmoded courses most high schools offer in those two subjects. Although general science and biology always have larger potential registrations in grades 9 and 10 than chemistry and physics in grades 11 and 12, this does not explain the actual decline of enrollments in physics and chemistry between 1934 and 1949 as against increase of enrollments in general science and biology.[17] The explanation, in part, is very simple: lack of modernized texts and teaching methods. Although enrollments in chemistry increased in 1954-55 and again in 1956-57, only in the latter year was the increase in number matched by an increase in percentage—for the first time since 1909-10! Enrollments in physics increased in both of those years, but national percentages continued to decrease. Its percentage based on grade 12 showed a slight increase in 1956-57.[18]

In our concern for mathematics and science, important as they are for our national security, we must not overlook the importance of foreign languages. They too play a vital role in national defense. All nations try to keep abreast of current developments throughout the world as they are reflected in the social, political, economic, military, and scientific activities within and without each country. The compilation, organization, translation, interpretation, and correlation of masses of highly complex and technical material cannot be entrusted to amateurs. These various tasks must be performed by and under the direction of linguistic experts upon whom our national leaders depend for a continuous flow of digested and annotated information. Failure to understand and consequently to translate vital material correctly could imperil the safety of the free world.

The knowledge such responsibilities require cannot be obtained except by a rigorous study. The road to mastery in this field is also long and difficult, but the need has never been greater. Even on the diplo-

matic front, where facility in languages would seem indispensable, we often offend our friends and weaken our influence by the self-protective assumption that ours is the only language worth knowing.

The State Department has an intensive language training program in its Foreign Service Institute and the Armed Services give excellent training to many officers and enlisted men. All of these activities have some elements of a "crash" program, as it is sometimes called. Despite the great need for language experts and for diffusion of linguistic knowledge, we have somehow failed to capitalize on one of our greatest opportunities. Among the thousands of armed service personnel stationed in numerous countries all over the world, what incentives and opportunities are offered in language training and instruction? With native instructors readily available, why do we leave such matters on a purely voluntary basis and not incorporate language study as part of the serviceman's training abroad? We send a handful to language schools in this country, and then fail to organize language classes in situations and places where they would be most effective.

This disregard for foreign languages is painfully evident throughout our educational system. Although encouraging progress has been made in the past few years with language instruction in elementary schools, the effect on high school foreign language study has just begun to be noticeable. In 1933-34 the equivalent of about 36% of the high school students studied one or more foreign languages. By 1954-55 *the figure had dropped to a little below 21%*. In both of those years and in the intervening period approximately 90% of all students enrolled in a foreign language studied it usually for only two years.

By way of contrast, in 1955-56 it is reported that 100% of students in classes VIII, IX, and X of Russian-speaking schools studied a foreign language: about 40%, German; 40%, English, and "remaining 20% either French, or in a few schools, Spanish or Latin." The students begin the language in class V and apparently study the same language for six years. It is interesting to note that in classes V and VI the language is studied four hours a week, and in the remaining three years three hours a week.

Mathematics, which begins with class I and continues through class X, is studied six hours a week each year. Arithmetic is the subject through class V, algebra and geometry, in classes VI through X, to which trigonometry is added in class IX and an introduction to calculus in class X.[19]

In American high schools in 1956-57 the equivalent of 110% of

grade 9 studied general mathematics (43%) and elementary algebra (67%). About 42% of grade 10 studied plane geometry, 32% of grade 11, intermediate algebra, 15.8% of grade 12, trigonometry, and nearly 12.7% of grade 12, solid geometry.[20]

There is also a strong contrast in the two systems with the amount of science studied. The Russian student studies biology for two periods a week in classes IV through VI, three periods in class VII, two in class VIII, and one in class IX. He begins physics with two periods a week in class VI, increases it to three in VII and VIII, to four in IX, and to 5/4 in X.[21] He starts chemistry in class VII with two periods a week, increases it to three in IX and the first semester of X, and to four in the second semester of X.

In this country in 1956-57 slightly over 67% of students in grade 9 studied general science; 74% of grade 10, biology; 34% of grade 11, chemistry; and 24.5% of grade 12, physics.[22]

The work load of a Russian student in each of the last three years of secondary school is given as 33 hours a week. During those three years, by way of summary, he spends an estimated 3,267 class hours on all subjects studied. Of these, 445.5 hours or almost 14%, are devoted to Russian language and literature; 594 hours or 18%, to mathematics; 396 or 12%, to history; 379.5 or 11.6%, to physics; 297 or 9%, to foreign languages; 280.5 or 8.6%, to chemistry; 99 hours, or 3%, to biology; 33 hours or 1%, to astronomy. The remaining hours are taken up with physical education (198 hours), technical drawing (99 hours), practical study of agriculture, machine construction, and electrotechnology (198 hours), constitution of the USSR (33 hours), and psychology (33 hours). Apparently there are no electives.

A program of this sort is obviously not geared to the average student. At the same time the attempt has been made to provide adequate teachers and to avoid oversize classes. The student-teacher ratio was 33.1 to 1 in primary-secondary schools in 1927-28; in 1955-56, it was 17 to 1. The corresponding ratio in the United States in the latter year is given as 26.9 to 1.[23]

Student-teacher ratios, derived by dividing the number of students by the number of teachers, obviously give an average. Although information of this sort may be useful, it may also be deceptively comforting, because it may conceal situations in which the average is far from representative. Much more significant would be data about the number of students in language, in mathematics, and in science classes, or in any class where size affects, not the quality of teaching, but its effectiveness. The organization and presentation of material reveal

quality or the lack of it in varying degrees. But teaching, though good in quality, may be frustratingly ineffective when class size prevents individual attention and response. Age and maturity are factors to be considered also, but the type of subject matter is usually a better guide in determining proper class size.

During a period of general teacher shortage, however, the problem of class size is usually pushed to the background by one more insistent and immediate—the mad scramble for teachers. Unless conditions change radically, the scramble now going on will continue, and the teaching fields most seriously affected in high school—and in college—will continue to be the very subjects which are irreplaceable in the education of scientists and engineers. To make the vicious circle complete, the mad scramble for engineers, scientists, and technologists, in government, in business and industry, and in the armed services has enticed many prospective and actual teachers away from the very positions in high school and college that are indispensable for training the very experts industry and government so badly need.[24]

There is little doubt that poor salaries in teaching are one of the basic reasons for teacher migration in the United States and a strong factor in keeping many away for whom teaching would otherwise have a powerful appeal. Under such conditions two things are absolutely imperative: increasing of salaries and making the best possible use of those actually engaged in teaching.

What is the "best possible use"? The answer is so obvious that it seems absurd to state it. In a period of increasing shortage of teachers, a shortage which is not uniform in all states or in all subjects, many teachers tend to be compelled to teach subjects for which they are not fully qualified. Although this cannot always be avoided, its prevalence is undoubtedly a factor in causing some teachers to seek other kinds of employment. For there is one thing certain: having him teach the subject he is best prepared to teach, is the best possible use of a teacher. It makes for the kind of morale that enables a teacher to do his best and makes him want to keep on teaching. Besides that, it is just plain common sense.

True, the human and practical elements involved make this a complicated problem. Fortunately two reports are available that will reveal more clearly its nature and possibly suggest some solutions. A special table in each of these makes it possible to compare the number of new teachers employed in each of the two years in the public high schools of the states listed, and the teaching assignments by major and minor subject-matter fields.[25]

Since there are 19 different fields listed by name, the possible major and minor combinations are somewhat numerous. Only a comparatively few can be mentioned.

In English, for example, in 1954-55 there were 3,668 new teachers. Of these only 2,091 taught English and nothing else. The remaining 1,577, or 43%, taught an additional subject in one of the other 18 named fields. Most of them were in social science, foreign languages, speech, library science, physical education (girls), mathematics, journalism, general science, and commerce. In the order named these teachers ranged in number from 551 to 49. Only one was assigned to physics, two to chemistry, and four to biology. Not counting the 12 in agriculture, the 23 in art, and the 25 in home economics, English teachers are a versatile lot!

But there is another side to the story. In the same year, 1954-55, there were 927 other new teachers to whom English was assigned as a second subject. The largest number, as might be expected, came from those qualified in social science as a major subject—254, or 27%. The next largest, as might also be expected, came from foreign languages— 11%, and then commerce and music, with 10% each.

If all those teaching English are considered (3,668 plus 927), approximately 45% taught it exclusively and 20% as a second subject. In 1955-56 these percentages were about 49 and 16 respectively.

It might be supposed that in subjects considered somewhat more highly specialized than English—mathematics, foreign languages, and science—a different situation might hold. The difference is mainly in degree.

In 1954-55 there were 191 new teachers of physics. Of these 122 taught physics exclusively. The remaining 69 taught in 11 other fields, but 45 out of the 69 taught related subjects, chemistry (17), general science and mathematics (14 each). Of all those teaching physics, however, only 35% taught it exclusively and 44% taught it as a second subject. In 1955-56 comparable figures were 28% and 54%.

Chemistry fared somewhat better. Of all teaching the subject in 1954-55, 33% taught it exclusively and 33% as a second subject. In 1955-56 comparable figures were 30% and 38%. Biology changed from 31% and 44% to 23% and 45%; general science, from 35% and 39% to 35% and 37%; mathematics, from 44% and 25% to 45% and 26%; foreign languages, from 31% and 41% to 36% and 40%; social studies, from 43% and 35% to 41% and 37%.

During the two-year period there were some developments which

the figures cited above perhaps do not entirely make clear. The total number teaching each of these eight subjects increased, in varying degrees, but the number teaching exclusively physics or chemistry or biology or mathematics decreased. This was not the case in the other four subjects. The number teaching physics or chemistry *and* a second subject also decreased. The total increase in those two fields was caused by an increase in those teaching each of them *as* a second subject. Those teaching biology or mathematics *and* a second subject and those teaching each of them *as* a second subject also increased. Teachers of the other four subjects increased in all three respects— those teaching the subject exclusively, those teaching it *and* a second subject, and those teaching it *as* a second subject. It is interesting— and disturbing—to note that in 1954-55 the number teaching physics or biology or general science or foreign languages as a second subject was larger than the number teaching any of them exclusively. This was also true for each of these subjects *and* for chemistry, in 1955-56, and in each case the number teaching each of them as a second subject increased. The number teaching each of the other subjects— English, mathematics, and social studies — as a second subject increased, but in neither year was that number as large as the number teaching each subject exclusively, which also increased.

These statistics, limited though they are in the period and geographical area covered and restricted to new teachers, indicate the type if not the extent of one of the most serious educational problems we face: the recruitment and effective use of teachers. There can be little doubt that the kind of teaching assignment a teacher gets is an important factor in keeping that teacher in the profession. It is also important for getting the best kind of teaching.

The usual high school teacher has one major subject and one or two minor subjects in which teaching competence is assumed. Often the subjects are in the same general field, such as physics and chemistry, biology and general science, or they are in combinations of kindred subjects, such as mathematics and a science, English and a foreign language, or history and English.

Although there are many factors involved, it is logical to assume that a teacher's major assignment would and should be in the field of his major preparation and competence. All teachers are not outstanding, even in their specialties, but they are likely to be at their best in those subjects. There is little doubt that teaching assignments often violate good academic practice and sound educational principles. Expediency is not exclusively a political rationalization. Who has not

seen pitiful instances of a history teacher grappling with algebra? a Latin teacher straining at chemistry? an English teacher puzzling over physics? These are not uncommon cases; others with smaller and varying degrees of absurdity are perhaps more common. And how often could they have been avoided?

It is not maintained that combinations of this sort are deliberately planned or even permitted except on some ostensibly plausible basis. It *is* maintained that they occur too frequently, either because of an administrative machinery that makes judicious interchange of teachers within a given system unnecessarily difficult—if not impossible altogether—or because of sheer inertia.

What kind of sense does it make for an excellent teacher of French to have her schedule filled out with two classes in general science when a competent teacher of general science in another high school half a mile away has his schedule filled out with two classes in French? Or what if the two schools are even farther apart? What if there is no money in the budget for transportation of these two teachers on that kind of a local exchange program? What if the adoption of such a program would call for advance estimates of course and subject needs, registrations, and teachers?

These are not insoluble problems, but they would require meticulous planning and a high degree of cooperation and good will among teachers, administrators, students, and parents alike. To use the specialized abilities of all of our high school teachers to the fullest possible extent is sound economy and good educational sense. To use to the maximum our teachers of foreign languages, science, and mathematics is absolutely essential if we are to develop an educational program best suited to the needs and to the times in which we live.

Within the past six or seven years a custom, once standard practice in this country, has been taken out of mothballs and revived with modern improvements. In a few communities and schools it had never been entirely discarded. These, together with others strategically scattered, reinstituted the old colonial custom of teaching foreign languages in the elementary grades. In those benighted days the language was usually Latin, but in these latter days it is more likely to be French and Spanish. As the distinguished scholar, writer, and teacher of English, Miss Mary Ellen Chase, said to a group of Smith College alumnae and their husbands recently, "Of course children love foreign languages, and the less they understand one the better they like it." Nearly half a million American youngsters last year proved Miss Chase is right, as many enthusiastic parents will proudly testify.

And that number will grow as soon as more teachers are trained to use the texts and methods that have been developed for this linguistic awakening.[26]

But how does this relate to the high schools? In a very practical yet perhaps not so simple way.

It is a well known fact that, great as the teacher shortage is in certain fields in high school, it is even greater for elementary schools as a whole. There are many language teachers in high school—though many more are desperately needed—who are teaching other subjects besides their specialty. By wise and careful planning many of these could fill out their schedules by setting up courses of language study in the lower grades and by training teachers in those grades to give the actual language instruction. Some of the high school teachers might even teach a language class or two in the grades. Or is there some law that says they can't?

Although World War II exploded the carefully nurtured myth of our language ineptitude, we Americans have not yet overcome a deep-rooted prejudice against the study of foreign languages. At a time when our need has been greatest, it is scarcely a proof of our foresight or our so-called practicality that in recent years nearly half of our high schools have offered no foreign languages at all.[27] This has naturally been reflected in college, and it was only in 1955-56 that a slight increase of graduates with a major in foreign languages began to check the downward trend in numbers and percentage that began after 1947-48. The language program in the elementary schools has already made itself felt in high school, if reports from individual schools and teachers here and there are at all representative. The slight increase in modern language majors in college in 1955-56 may indeed be the first faint fruits of a revival of foreign languages.[28]

As indicated earlier in this chapter, such a revival in science and mathematics has definitely started. The movement began in time to be reflected in enrollments in 1956-57 and would undoubtedly have gathered momentum from the coordinated efforts of the most concentrated and sustained educational drive this country has ever experienced. At a fortuitous moment two things happened, neither connected with the other, and yet they served to illustrate effect and cause in that order: the Russians launched Sputnik I and Sputnik II, and the Department of Health, Education, and Welfare launched *Education in the USSR*. From seeing evidence of Russian pioneering achievements in science with the naked eye, the public had a chance to read and hear about the educational system that produced them.

After both initial shocks had passed into retrospect some of the sober second thoughts would seem to indicate that a complete revamping of our educational system was perhaps not yet in store. That system had its weaknesses, and the chief among them was the flexibility of the curriculum. And yet, perhaps it was not so much that as the kind of intellectual atmosphere produced as the result of that flexibility under an elective system.

There is no doubt about it, the atmosphere is not one conducive to the study of mathematics, science, and foreign languages. Is it, on the other hand, conducive to study of English and social studies, particularly history? The answer here would also seem to be No.

What kind of atmosphere, then, do we find in our high schools?

Until very recently it has been the atmosphere that hard work not only doesn't pay, it's not necessary. Why study the hard subjects? You can get into college without them; if you're not going to college you don't need them anyway.

It is ironical, is it not, that we, self-congratulated leader of the free world, creators of what is technologically the richest civilization in man's short history, originators of the idea of free public education and developers of the most extensive system of public education ever known—it is ironical, is it not, that we should take our cue in education from those who are the very antithesis of everything we believe and stand for?

It it doubly ironical because the Committee of Ten gave us in 1894 the pattern we need today. We followed it for some twenty brave years, but only in part, for we failed to work out the recommended sequences in mathematics, science, and foreign languages to extend from the lower grades through high school.[20] We altered the pattern on both levels by the introduction of courses emphasizing social adjustment and civic betterment, and somehow in the main failed to accomplish either. Then, to cap the climax of irony, the cold war taught us what we did not have the wit to see for ourselves, that the Committee of Ten was right: *education that stresses and combines mental discipline and cultural values is not only the best but in the long run the most practical.*

Could it be that the Russians studied the Committee's Report and followed its recommendations? Their reported stress on science, mathematics, foreign languages, social studies, and their own language and literature, throughout grades or classes I to X, corresponds almost exactly with the recommendations of the Committee of Ten. But let us give them due credit. It would scarcely have been necessary for

them to follow any pattern but that of plain common sense. That must be our pattern too.

Within the last few years the number of high school students has passed the pre-war peak, and the number to graduate and enter college is getting larger each year. At the present rate, however, only between six and seven out of ten students who enter the ninth grade finish high school, and only about 50% of those who finish enter college. Since the mortality rate in college is high, *from 25 to 30% of our high school graduates must come the great majority of leaders in all the activities, public and private, that make up the complex diversity of American life.* From this comparatively small group must come the majority of our elementary school teachers. The potential source for high school and college teachers, for doctors, engineers, scientists, is even smaller, because preparation for these and many other professions requires from one to four years of graduate training beyond college. The kind of education a relatively small group of students is now receiving and will receive is a matter therefore of the utmost importance and concern.

But what about the large percentage (35-40) of our students who do not finish high school? What about the 50% of high school graduates who do not enter college, many of whom are far above average in ability? What about the 50% who enter college but fail to graduate? Is the kind of education *they* receive unimportant? Is the kind of education they receive in high school a telling factor in their undeveloped potentialities? Whatever the reasons, many and varied as they are, the accumulated waste is a tragic loss for the individual and for the society in which he could be a vital part.

The prevention or reclamation of such waste has long given concern, and the efforts to that end are receiving increased public attention. These efforts, it is now more than ever realized, must include ways and means of developing to the full the capacities of all students and of speeding up the educational process for those who can combine speed with thoroughness.

In "the great talent hunt" now in progress,[30] it is significant to note the great stress given to "general education" in contrast with "narrow specialization." Business and industry and government are increasingly looking for highly trained specialists, but they are realizing more and more, as many universities have, that the future will "demand specialists who are capable of functioning as generalists."[31]

The need for specialists with "educated talents" will increase and the quality of the education they receive will depend in large measure

on the *fusion of liberal arts and sciences*. Education of this kind cannot be postponed until college; it must begin in high school, or better still, in the lower grades.

All over the country, in awareness of the need, high schools are reinstating the out-of-favor curriculum proposed by the Committee of Ten, in which mathematics, science, foreign languages, history and English are the principal subjects. Students are admitted to this course of study on the basis of their ability and their college plans. In some schools a program of this kind, with smaller and more selected groups, is solving the problem of the "gifted child" by making it possible for him to proceed at his own pace. In recognition of the superior quality of work and greater amount of material covered, some colleges are admitting graduates of such programs into appropriate courses beyond the usual freshman level.

There is little doubt that the number of high schools offering programs of this kind will increase, and that the very emphasis given to the required subjects will cause more students to seek and prepare for admission to them.

This is not only reasonable; it is almost inevitable. And if this is true, it will bring thousands of additional students into mathematics, science, foreign languages, history, and probably English.

There have been and are many students in high school for whom the cumulative subjects have been considered too difficult. Under our system of massive education many students *have* avoided them because they *are* difficult. These are two entirely distinct but related matters. The substitution of one subject for another is not always done on the basis of ability or even of comparative interest; it is often done through expediency and the climate fostered by companionship and environment, both at home and at school. Willing self-deception and self-indulgence are not traits confined exclusively to adults. Many students pass through school without ever really testing their ability or doing what they really want to do. In most cases they find it out— often too late.

In the past we have attempted to solve the problem of the slow learner and the lower-average learner by subjects non-academic or more practical and vocational in nature. But with great advances in knowledge of psychology and improvement of educational techniques and teaching methods, it is time for us to readjust our philosophy and to rethink our educational goals.

It is true that there will always be some students unable to learn as rapidly as others. Does it necessarily follow that the educational

pattern for them should be markedly different from that of others? Metabolism rates are not the same for all, yet all must use oxygen. Should not education follow the same principle? If mathematics and science and foreign languages are increasingly important today, should knowledge of them be confined to the intellectually *elite*?

Creative leadership in these three fields is imperative. But widespread diffusion of such knowledge among all members of our democracy is also imperative. Why should we say to some of our students: "You need this kind of knowledge because you can learn it," but to others, "You do not need this kind of knowledge because with our present texts and teaching methods and large numbers of students, you cannot learn it"? What sort of education is it that does not give a student some acquaintance with the three branches of human endeavor which now more than ever before enter into every phase of human life?

The proper solution for the slow-learner is not the notion of "easier" subject-matter. Tremendous as the task will be, it lies rather in the development and use of special texts and teaching methods and in grouping according to ability, that will give the less gifted an education that will differ in *quantity, not in kind*, from that of his more gifted fellows. This is the essence of democratic education today, the opportunity to learn, at one's own pace and ability, the basic principles of those subjects without which life in the modern world is inconceivable.

It is no accident that the main core of those subjects is the same in all civilized countries: mathematics, science, foreign languages, history' and one's own native tongue. The logic and principles of mathematics, the laws of science, the lessons of history are the same, no matter in what language they are studied and learned. Native tongues differ, but each is the gateway to its own procreation of culture, thought, and communication. Foreign languages differ, but they constitute the media for the transmission of ideas and for the cross-fertilization of cultures.

These are the subjects around which coordinated courses of study for all students, regardless of ability, should be built, from the grades through high school. The opportunity to learn them is each student's new educational bill of rights. To give each student that opportunity is to acknowledge his rightful heritage, to enlarge his usefulness as a citizen, and to perpetuate the purposes and processes of democracy itself.

[1] Calculations are based on figures in Tables 36 and 38 in Appendix G for the period 1890 to 1922.

[2] It is not actually known *what* percentages of its graduates went to college between 1890 and 1915. It *is* known that about 30% were prepared *for* college in 1893 and in 1900, and 49% in 1910, 34% for liberal arts colleges, and 14.9% for other higher institutions. This is the first time such a distinction was made. In 1915 comparable percentages were 35.9 and 16.2 (CR 1915-16, II, pp. 454-55). In the fall of 1921 a little more than 31% of the June graduates entered college, and 14% entered other higher institutions—the first specific information of this kind published. See Tables 24, 27, 29 and comments, in Appendix D.

[3] See Table 14 in Ch. V and Table 18 in Ch. VI. Enrollments by separate courses were first given for mathematics in 1927-28 (CR 1926-28, pp. 1064-66), and for English and foreign languages in 1933-34. See Table 20 in Ch. VI.

[4] See Table 14 and comments in Ch. V.

[5] See Table 14, Ch. V, and BS 1948-50, Ch. 5, p. 6.

[6] A new method of tabulating enrollments in English made it appear that English had also decreased proportionately. For comments on this, see Ch. IV, Table 5. All the figures and percentages in this section, unless otherwise indicated, are based on Tables 1-13 in Ch. IV, which are summarized in Tables 14 and 15 of Ch. V.

[7] Undoubtedly many of the subjects were in the curriculum in 1910 but adequate statistics had not been reported. The situation in business education in 1910 is a case in point. See Ch. IV, Table 6 and comments.

[8] Since over 99% of the students were girls, the percentage means that there were more girls in home economics in 1948-49 than there were girls *and* boys in Latin during that year. See Ch. IV, Table 8.

[9] See CR 1909-10, II, Table A (p. 1139) and Table 14 in Ch. V.

[10] BS 1950-52, Ch. 5, Table A traces these percentages between 1890 and 1952. Although 1948-49 was not included, the writer estimated its percentage on the basis of those given for 1946 and 1952.

[11] For the figures in 1948-49, see Table 10 in Ch. VI; for those in 1909-10, calculations were based on the larger enrollment figures in Table 1, Ch. IV. Although it is not likely that many students enroll in two different mathematics courses at the same time, the term *equivalent* is used in recognition of that possibility. In other words, the percentages and numbers do not necessarily mean different students. It is naturally impossible to determine the number of duplicate enrollments in any subject-matter field. This consideration, whether mentioned specifically or not, applies to all figures given in this study.

[12] Enrollment figures in the 1933-34 curriculum survey were based on reports from schools enrolling 80% of all high school students (*Bulletin 1938, No. 6*, pp. 9 and 20; BS 1948-50, Ch. 5, pp. 5 and 27). In the historical summary table in the latter reference (Table 7), the smaller enrollment figures were used without an explicit monitory footnote about the matter. There was no such footnote, for that matter, in the corresponding table (Table 2) in the former reference.

[13] See Ch. VI, Table 19 for mathematics and science, Table 20 for foreign languages and English.

[14] See CR 1909-10, II, Table A (p. 1139).

[15] See Ch. IV, Tables 1-3, and Ch. V, Table 14.

[16] See Ch. VI, Note 32 and related comments in text. For a short but interesting account of the new developments, written for laymen, see "The Wonderful World of

Why," in *Saturday Review* (Nov. 2, 1957), pp. 42-45, by Helen Rowan.* In the same issue (p. 45) John Lear writes of the Commission on Mathematics set up in 1955 by the College Entrance Examination Board with a grant from the Carnegie Foundation. Its function is to explore ways and means of speeding up changes in the mathematics curriculum in high school. Mentioned also is the Carnegie grant to Dr. John Mayor of the University of Maryland to "modernize the arithmetic now taught in junior high school." The *Committee of Ten* (Table I and pertinent comments) suggested a course of study in grades 1 through 8 in which, in addition to arithmetic, "Algebraic expressions and symbols and simple equations" were to be introduced. From the fifth through the eighth grades one period a week was to be given to "concrete geometry." In the *Report* of the Committee of Fifteen (pp. 93-95) algebra was assigned five periods a week in grades 7 and 8 in place of arithmetic. Geometry was not included.

* Miss Rowan's account was apparently adapted from a longer article in the Carnegie Corporation of New York *Quarterly* (October 1957) of which she is editor.

[17] See Ch. VI, Table 19, and comments earlier in this chapter. For need of new texts and teaching methods, see "Starving Our Potential Scientists" by Kenneth E. Brown, reprinted from the 1955 November-December issue *Armed Forces Chemical Journal*; *Quarterly Report* of the Carnegie Corporation of New York, January, 1955, and various reports of the National Science Foundation. For a short account of a research program conducted at Teachers College, Columbia University, to improve "current high school and chemistry courses," see *New York Times* (Nov. 17, 1957), p. 49. See also the excellent summary: "U.S. Science, Where It Stands Today," in *Time* (Nov. 18, 1957), and Dr. Benjamin Fine's alarming report about science teachers in *The New York Times* (Nov. 24, 1957).

[18] See previous Note and Table 18. See also Tables 2, 3, and 5 of Pamphlet No. 118, and Tables 3, 4, and 7 of Pamphlet No. 120.

[19] *Education in the USSR*, p. 74 and Tables 6, 7, 8 for foreign languages. These tables also contain data on all other subjects mentioned in this section. The curriculum is discussed in pp. 67 to 83. Unless otherwise indicated all information was taken from these sources. *Korol* (see Appendix A) presents material on Russian education in a different way, but it corroborates the figures and percentages given in this chapter. Tables 9, 11 and 13 of his chapter 2 correspond to above Tables, 6, 7, 8.

[20] *Pamphlet No. 120, 1957*, Table 17. *Pamphlet No. 118*, 1956, Tables 3 and 12, was apparently the source for the statement in *Education in the USSR*, p. 67, that in June 1955 "less than a third of the American high school graduates had taken a year of chemistry, about a fourth had a year of physics, and less than a seventh had taken advanced mathematics." The statement about mathematics is probably inaccurate. See Table 19, Note 4.

[21] The use of "5/4" indicates five periods in the first semester, four in the second.

[22] *Pamphlet No. 120*, 1957, Table 7. Apparently the Russians have nothing that corresponds to general science. Apparently too they have decided that physics should be studied before chemistry. This was probably the order in our high schools until about 1910. See Ch. VI, Table 18, and pertinent comments.

[23] *Education in the USSR*, p. 86 and Footnote 16. It is assumed that these ratios are based on statistics that include *shifts*. If the data given are now applicable, grades I-IV are in school from 8 a.m. to 12 or 1 p.m.; grades VII and X, for an hour longer, 1 or 2 p.m.; and grades V, VI, VIII, and IX, generally to 7 or 8 p.m. In 1929-30 the student-teacher ratio in secondary day schools in this country was 24.4; in 1951-52 it was 23.2 (BS 1950-52, Ch. 5, Table A).

[24] The report entitled *Teacher Supply and Demand in Colleges and Universities* (November 1957) makes this very plain on the college level. It also has many facts and figures about the situation in high school.

[25] The data for 1954-55 are found in Table 4 of "A Brief Summary of the 1955 Teacher Supply and Demand Report," and those for 1955-56, from Table 8 of "The Postwar Struggle to Provide Competent Teachers." There were 29 states common to both tables, two in the first year that did not appear in the second, and five in the second that did not appear in the first. Of the 29 common to both, 15 were located in the Middlewest and Far West; 6 in the Middle Atlantic States and New England; the remaining 8 in the South and Southwest. In both tables the word "new" refers to teachers who were not teaching in the year immediately preceding the fall of 1954 and of 1955 respectively.

[26] See Note 33 and pertinent comments in Ch. VI.

[27] PMLA, pp. 52-56. This special study (see Appendix A) indicated that 56% of the high schools offered foreign languages, and 43.6%, modern foreign languages. In 1933-34, the last time such data were given, 63% offered Latin, 35% offered French, and 17%, Spanish. The percentages were calculated by the writer from data in *Bulletin 1938, No. 6*, Table 3. It could not be determined what percentage offered modern languages alone or in combination with Latin. For additional information, see "Latin in the Public Secondary Schools," by S. D. Atkins, J. L. Heller, and P. L. MacKendrick, in *The Classical Journal* 51 No. 6-8 (March, April, May 1956), 269-73; 309-12; 365-7.

[28] See pertinent comments and Table 21 of Ch. VI, for situation between 1947-48 and 1954-55. For changes in 1955-56, see *Earned Degrees*, Tables 4, 6 and 7. The last table (No. 7) shows that majors in all languages constituted 1.27% of all first-degree graduates. French was in the lead with 0.45%, Spanish next, with 0.43%, classical languages, 0.16%, and German, 0.12%. As Table 21 shows, the gains over 1953-54 were slight; Latin actually had a slight decrease. For a short but challenging article on the educational and national importance of language study for this country, see "Foreign Languages in American Education," by Ernest M. Wolf, in *Journal of Higher Education* 27, No. 9 (December 1956), 485-88, 513.

[29] Foreign languages were discussed briefly in the text above. For mathematics, see second half of Note 16. As a science sequence in the lower grades the Committee recommended that natural phenomena be studied five periods a week and botany and zoology for at least two periods a week in grades 1-8. Study of the latter in particular should be associated with literature, language, and drawing. The Committee realized that elementary teachers would be unprepared to guide their pupils in observation of natural phenomena and recommended that special science teachers or superintendents be appointed to instruct the teachers. See Committee's *Report*, pp. 25-28, 34-35. The Committee of Fifteen (pp. 75-95 of its *Report*) agreed in principle with the Committee of Ten, but recommended that the amount of time be reduced to two hours a week.

[30] This telling phrase is used as the title of the introduction to the *Annual Report* of the Carnegie Corporation for 1956, by its president, John W. Gardner, and commented on editorially by the *New York Times* (January 27, 1957).

[31] Gardner, *op. cit.*, pp. 22-23.

BIBLIOGRAPHY

Publications of the United States Office of Education are the primary sources of information for this study. To avoid space-filling repetitions in the list of these publications, the various titles and governmental affiliations of the Office of Education, with dates, are given below:

1867   Department of Education, an independent agency.

1869   Office of Education, under the Department of the Interior.

1870   Bureau of Education, under the Department of the Interior.

1929   Office of Education, under the Department of the Interior.

1939   Office of Education, under the Federal Security Agency.

1953   Office of Education, under the Department of Health, Education, and Welfare.

PRIMARY SOURCES

Footnote references to the primary sources occur so frequently in the text that a simple form of abbreviation, as shown below, was adopted. Each abbreviation is followed by a date indicating the period or year covered by the report. In most cases the period is that of an academic rather than a calendar year. Most dates, accordingly, are in the form 1889-90, etc.

I. BOUND VOLUMES

CR: Report of the Commissioner of Education. (These reports appeared annually between 1867 and 1916. Volume I or II is given, as appropriate.)

BS: Biennial Survey of Education. (The first of these appeared for the biennium 1916-18. Ordinarily these were issued as separate chapters, with different dates of publication. References to the surveys covering each biennium between 1916-18 through 1932-34 are to the bound volumes I or II, as appropriate, with the single exception noted below.)

II.   SEPARATE CHAPTERS, REPORTS, OR STUDIES

Bulletin 1938, No. 6: "Offerings and Enrollments in High-School Subjects 1933-34." (A part of the survey of 1932-34, but not printed in the bound volume.)

Bulletin 1940, No. 2, Ch. 1: "Statistical Summary of Education, 1937-38."

BS 1948-50, Ch. 5: "Offerings and Enrollments in High-School Subjects 1948-49." (Published in 1951.)

BS 1948-50, Ch. 1: "Statistical Summary of Education, 1949-50. (Published in 1953.)

Bulletin 1950, No. 9: "The Teaching of Science in Public High Schools, 1947-48." By Philip G. Johnson.

BS 1950-52, Ch. 5: "Statistics of Public Secondary Day Schools 1951-52." (Published in 1954.)

BS 1950-52, Ch. 1: "Statistical Summary of Education, 1951-52." (Published in 1955.)

Bulletin 1953, No. 5: "Mathematics in Public High Schools." By Kenneth E. Brown. This study covers the year 1951-52 and the first semester of 1952-53.

Circular No. 269: "Why Do Boys and Girls Drop Out of School, and What Can We Do About It?" Report of a Work Conference on Life Adjustment Education, held in Chicago, January 24-27, 1950. (Reprint 1953.)

Earned Degrees: "Earned Degrees Conferred by Higher Educational Institutions." The first of these reports covered the year 1947-48, the last, 1955-56. The title of each includes the specific year.

Pamphlet No. 118, 1956: "Offerings and Enrollments in Science and Mathematics in Public High Schools." By Kenneth E. Brown. Brown.

Pamphlet No. 120, 1957: "Offerings and Enrollments in Science and Mathematics in Public High Schools, 1956." By Kenneth E. Brown.

School Life (Feb. 1953): "High School Retention: How Does Your State Rate?" By Walter H. Gaumnitz. *School Life,* 35, No. 5, pp. 69-71 (Feb. 1953).

School Life (May 1955): "Elementary and Secondary School Enrollment in the Public School System of the United States, By Grade, 1949-50 Through 1959-60." By Emory M. Foster and Carol Joy Hobson. *School Life,* 37, No. 8 (May 1955).

School Life (May 1956): "Public School Enrollment By Grade—1953-54." *School Life,* 38, No. 8 (May 1956).

School Life (June 1956): "High School Enrollments in Science and Mathematics . . . some facts and figures." *School Life,* 38, No. 9 (June 1956).

BS 1952-54, Ch. 4, Sec. 1: "Statistics of Higher Education: Faculty, Students, and Degrees, 1953-54." (1956.)

BS 1952-54, Ch. 1: "Statistical Summary of Education, 1953-54." (1957)

BS 1952-54, Ch. 2: "Statistics of State School Systems, 1953-54." (1956).

SECONDARY SOURCES

Brown, Elmer E.: *The Making of our Middle Schools.* Longmans, Green, and Co., 2nd ed. (New York, 1905).

Committee of Ten: Report of the Committee of Ten on Secondary School Studies. With the Reports of the Conferences arranged by the Committee. Published for the National Education Association by the American Book Company (New York, 1894).

Committee of Fifteen: Report of the Committee of Fifteen on Elementary Education. With the Reports of the Sub-Committees: On the Training of Teachers; On the Correlation of Studies in Elementary Education; On the Organization of City School Systems. Published for the National Educational Association by the American Book Company (New York, 1895).

Classical Investigation: The Classical Investigation conducted by The Advisory Committee of The American Classical League. Part One, General Report. Princeton University Press (Princeton, 1924).

Cubberley, Elwood P.: *Public Education in the United States.* Revised and enlarged edition. Houghton Mifflin Co. (Boston, 1947).

Dexter, Edwin Grant: *A History of Education in the United States.* The Macmillan Co. (New York, 1906).

Dyer et al.: Problems in Mathematical Education, by Henry S. Dyer, Robert Kalin, and Frederic M. Lord. Educational Testing Service (Princeton, 1956).

Johnson, Clifton: *Old Time Schools and School Books.* The Macmillan Co. (New York, 1925).

Kandel, I. L.: *History of Secondary Education.* Houghton Mifflin Co. (Boston, 1930).

Knight (1): *Education in the United States.* 3rd revised edition. By Edgar W. Knight. Ginn and Co. (New York, 1951).

Knight (2) : *Fifty Years of American Education,* 1900-1950. The Ronald Press Co. (New York, 1952).

Korol, Alexander G.: *Soviet Education for Science and Technology*. Published jointly by The Technology Press of Massachusetts Institute of Technology and John Wiley and Sons, Inc. (New York 1957).

Latimer, John F.: A Mimeographed Report of enrollments in twelve subjects in the fields of mathematics, science, and foreign languages in certain high school systems throughout the United States for the years 1951-52, 1952-53, and 1953-54. A survey made from March-September 1954. The George Washington University, Washington, D. C.

Maul, Ray C.: "A Brief Summary of the 1955 Teacher Supply and Demand Report." Reprinted from *The Journal of Teacher Education* (March 1955). Prepared by the NEA Research Division under the supervision of Ray C. Maul.

Meriwether, Colyer: *Our Colonial Curriculum 1607-1776*. Capital Publishing Co. (Washington, 1907).

PMLA "Foreign Language Offerings and Enrollments in Public High Schools 1954-55." Publications of *The Modern Language Association*, 70 (No. 4, Pt. 2, September 1955), 52-56.

Russell-Judd: The American Educational System. By John Dale Russell and Charles H. Judd. Houghton Mifflin Co. (Boston, 1940).

Teachers for Tomorrow: Published by The Fund for The Advancement of Education as Bulletin No. 2 (November 1955).

White House: A Report to The President. By the Committee for The White House Conference on Education. U.S. Government Printing Office, Washington, D. C. (April 1956).

Wolfle: America's Resources of Specialized Talent. The Report of the Commission on Human Resources and Advanced Training. Prepared by Dael Wolfle, Director. Harper & Brothers (New York, 1954).

Education in the USSR: U.S. Department of Health, Education, and Welfare, Office of Education (November 1957).

Knapp & Goodrich: Origins of American Scientists, by R. H. Knapp and B. H. Goodrich, University of Chicago Press (1952).

NEA Research Bulletin: "The Postwar Struggle To Provide Competent Teachers," National Education Association *Research Bulletin*, Vol. XXXV, No. 3 (Oct. 1957).

A CHRONOLOGICAL LIST OF REFERENCES
MOST FREQUENTLY USED

To save time and space a list of the most frequently used references is given below, with appropriate entries as to year, volume, chapter, tables, and pages.

- B: Bulletin
- BS: Biennial Survey of Education
- CH: Chapter
- CR: Commissioner's Report
- G: Graduates
- GE: Grade enrollment
- HT: Historical Table
- SE: Subject enrollments
- TE: Total high school enrollment
- T: Table

Roman numerals always refer to *volumes*. Entries unnecessary are omitted.

Year	CR or BS	T E	G E	S E	G	H T
1889-90	Same	II,1388		II,1388-92	II,1389	II,1392
1899-1900	Same	II,2129		II,2129-39	II,2130	II,2123
1909-10[1]	Same	II,1130	II,1130	II,1174-84	II,1143	II,1139
1914-15	1915-16	II,448	II,448	II,490-503	II,454	II,487
1921-22[1]	1920-22	II,534	II,535	II,580-601	II,559	II,578-79
1926-27	1926-28	p. 976	p.976	pp.1058-87	p.1042	pp.1057-58
1933-34[1]	1932-34	Ch.5,T.1	B.1938,No.6, p.9,Note 1	B.1938, No.6,Ts2-4	Ch.5,p.57	B.1938, No.6, T.1
1948-49	1948-50	Ch.5,T.7	Ch.5,p.6, Note 5	Ch.5,T.3	BS1952-50 Ch.4,Sect.1, T.XXIV	Ch.5, T.7

[1] For the special situation in these years, see Appendix G, Notes 2-4, respectively.

CUMULATIVE AND OTHER SUBJECT
ENROLLMENTS BY SEX

For many years high school education was no respecter of sex. Since girls have outnumbered boys in high school, at least since 1890, it is of some historical interest and educational importance to see what effects this fact has had on enrollments by sex in an expanding curriculum.

Although all subjects could not be included in the tables below, the list is fairly complete through 1910, and reference is made to most of the others brought in after that date. The resulting picture has two serious drawbacks; the data are based on actual enrollments for each sex, only through 1928, except in science and mathematics. These are carried through 1955; the other subjects, through 1949. Between 1934 and 1949, inclusive, total enrollments in these other subjects are known from official records, but not proportionate enrollments by sex. For lack of other evidence proportions corresponding to those of 1928 are assumed for 1934 and 1949.

In 1890, as Table 22 shows, Greek was the only one of nine subjects listed in which girls did not outnumber boys, and in every instance, by a considerable margin. In all of the subjects except Greek and geometry their numbers were proportionately greater than their numerical superiority in the entire enrollment. In 1900 the preponderance of girls except in Greek and trigonometry was again striking. The proportion of girls in high school, however, had increased slightly and was proportionately greater than their numerical superiority in 9 of the 16 (out of 18) subjects in which they led the boys. In 1910 they led the boys in 19 out of 24 subjects, and in 11 of the 19 their numerical superiority was proportionately greater than their percentage of high school enrollment, which had decreased slightly in the intervening decade. Among the sciences chemistry was the first to leave the distaff column, but physics was tottering on the brink of male dominance and by 1922 had been decidedly masculinated. In that year, the first of national woman's suffrage, although the girls held the lead in 5 out of 10 subjects in science, the number of boys in the whole field

TABLE 22[1]

PERCENTAGE OF GIRLS IN CERTAIN SUBJECTS IN THE LAST FOUR YEARS OF PUBLIC HIGH SCHOOLS IN CERTAIN YEARS BETWEEN 1889-90 AND 1954-55

	1890[2]	1900	1910[3]	1922[4]	1928[5]	1948[6]	1955[7]
Enrollment in 1000's	203	519	739	2155	2897	5653	6584
Percent of Girls	57.6	58.4	56.2	53.6	51.9	51.4	51.0
Physics	58.4	57.4	50.6	41.4	34.4	28.9	20.0
Chemistry	58.9	55.6	43.4	42.8	42.0	44.3	43.1
Biology			60.8	53.0	53.4	53.2	50.9
General Science				49.1	49.3	52.4	
Physiology		57.5	56.6	55.6	56.5		
Phys. Geography		57.9	54.1	52.8	51.5		
Geology		59.3	53.9	49.5	43.2		
Zoology			57.7	49.9	45.5		
Astronomy		62.2	57.8	52.2	48.4		
Botany			57.9	56.0	56.1		
Algebra	58.0	57.8	54.0	48.6	47.3	45.7	45.3
Geometry	57.2	58.9	53.8	48.0	45.6	40.7	38.7
Trigonometry		47.0	27.9	24.9	22.9	19.8	21.5
General Math.				56.4	50.4	48.5	47.3
Latin	59.1	61.2	59.3	56.3	58.0		
Greek	33.8	46.3	44.1	36.5	38.7		
French	65.6	64.9	62.9	58.6	56.7		
German	59.2	61.1	57.0	41.2	43.4		
Spanish			49.5	51.2	51.1		
History	58.9	60.6	56.9				
Amer. History				55.3	53.2		
Ancient History				53.2	51.3		
Med. & Mod. History				52.8	50.9		
Civil Government			55.6[8]		53.1		
Civics		57.5[8]		54.5[8]	51.7		
Rhetoric		59.5	56.1				
English Literature		61.6	56.4				
English				54.2	52.2		
Bus. & Comm. Courses		51.6	56.8				
Bookkeeping				62.7	61.1		
Shorthand				76.5	80.9		
Typing				69.9	70.9		
Home Economics			94.4	99.1	99.1		
Manual Training			36.8	4.7	1.4		

[1]Percentages not given in 1910 or before indicate that the subjects were not listed by the Office of Education in those years. Those not given after 1928 indicate that the subject had

dropped out of the curriculum or that the data were insignificant or unavailable. As noted previously arithmetic, and not general mathematics, was listed in 1922. Unless otherwise indicated, references are the same as those given in Appendix B.

[2] The percentage of girls in each subject was based on actual enrollments given in CR 1889-90, II, p. 1388. The total enrollment for each sex yielded 57.6% as the proportion of girls. This percentage, however, did not take into account 1,161 students for whom division by sex was not possible at the time of publication. This division was published in BS 1950-52, Ch. 5, Table A, and the revised figures yielded 57.7% as the proportion of girls. Although the difference was obviously negligible, the percentage of 57.6 is used in this table because it is consistent with the subject percentages by sex.

[3] The percentage of girls was based on the total enrollment given, on which the subject percentages by sex were based. The actual total enrollment was 915,000, of whom 56.4% were girls. The larger figure could not be used because many of the schools did not return usable questionnaires. See Appendix G, Note 2.

[4] The situation in this year paralleled that in 1910. The actual total enrollment was 2,230,-000, of whom 53.6% were girls. By coincidence this was exactly the same proportion of girls in the smaller enrollment figure used in the table.

[5] The actual total enrollment was 3,354,000, of whom 52.3% were girls. The smaller figure and percentage are used in the table for the reason given in the latter part of Note 2 above. For the larger figure, see BS 1926-28, p. 974; for smaller, p. 1062.

[6] In science the subject percentages by sex were calculated by the writer from data in *Bulletin 1950, No. 9*, Tables 7 and 8. In this special study by Philip G. Johnson, total enrollment in the selected schools was 164,551, of whom 53.2% were girls. The actual total enrollments in 1947-48, as given to the writer by the Office of Education, was 5,653,000, of whom 51.4% were girls. The smaller percentage is used in the table, but the subject percentages by sex are based on the special study mentioned above. The subject percentages in mathematics were calculated by the writer from data in *Bulletin 1953, No. 5*, pp. 42-43, a special study by Kenneth E. Brown. The data are for the fall of 1952.

[7] The enrollment for this year was taken from the enrollments in grades 9-12, as estimated by Foster and Hobson (*School Life*, May 1955), p. 126. The percentage of girls was estimated by the writer on the basis of the trend indicated in the table and in other actual percentages given for 1938 (51.9), 1946 (51.7), and 1952 (51.1), in BS 1950-52, Ch. 5, Table A. The percentages for physics, chemistry, biology, general mathematics, and trigonometry, were taken from Tables 6 and 14 of a special study made by Kenneth E. Brown, published by the Office of Education as *Pamphlet No. 118*, 1956. The study covered 10% of the public high schools, which contained about 10% of the total enrollment (p. 24). The schools were carefully selected and were considered fairly representative of the schools throughout the country. The percentage of girls in the selected schools could not be determined. Table 14 gave the percentage of boys in elementary and intermediate algebra, and in plane and solid geometry. By applying these percentages to the estimated actual enrollments in those courses, given in *School Life* (June 1956), p. 6, the writer calculated the percentages of girls in algebra and geometry which are shown in the table. Subject enrollments and percentages, converted into those for girls by the writer, were given in the reference as follows: elementary algebra, 1,205,000, and 47.5%; intermediate algebra, 432,000, and 39.1%; plane geometry, 664,000, and 41.0%; solid geometry, 85,000, and 21.2%. Although the figure for solid geometry probably should have been 149,000 (see Chapter VI, Table 19, Note 4), it is assumed that the percentage would not have changed.

[8] Enrollments in civics and civil government were probably combined in these years.

outnumbered girls for the first time. The same thing was true in mathematics. In that year the boys established a numerical superiority in those two fields that has never since been in doubt.

In foreign languages, social studies, and English the girls maintained a decreasing lead through 1928. From the trend shown in that period enrollments in some of the separate subjects are probably about equally divided today.

In business and commercial subjects, in addition to the three sub-

jects listed in the table for 1922 and 1928, the girls also held strong leads in all other subjects listed in the field. The striking contrast between enrollments in home economics and manual training has almost certainly been maintained in the former. With the enlargement of the manual training field to include nonvocational subjects, the disparity between the two sexes has probably become less, but boys are doubtless still in the lead.

When drawing was first listed in 1914-15 girls slightly outnumbered boys. By 1922, however, boys were ahead by a sizeable margin. In 1928, when art and drawing were combined, girls were far in the lead. During this same period there were far more girls than boys in all branches of music instruction, except in instrumental music in 1928.

Up until 1922 the only form of physical training reported statistically was military drill, in which only boys took part in relatively small numbers. In that year boys slightly outnumbered girls in physical training, which was listed for the first time. In 1928 considerably more girls than boys were enrolled in physical education, but with the help of military drill the boys maintained their lead.

As shown in the table, after 1928 the Office of Education discontinued the breakdown of enrollments by sex. Since that date a few special studies included such information for science and mathematics, or provided data from which it could be obtained. In these special studies the percentage patterns for girls after 1928, in every case except in chemistry and trigonometry, seem to bear out the trend indicated before 1928. There is no reason to think that the same thing would not be true in the other subjects.

One bit of evidence that points in that direction is the commonly accepted assumption that certain subjects are more suitable for one sex than for the other—mathematics and science for boys, almost all others for girls. Before 1910 such an assumption would have been difficult to document; by 1928 it might seem to have had reasonable validity. This in itself may have had an unconscious psychological influence on the girls or their parents and advisers, in the selection of some subjects instead of others.

A few examples will show, however, that division of subject enrollments by sex is relatively meaningless and might even be misleading. In 1890 boys constituted 66% of the students in Greek and 41% of the students in Latin. The two figures give not the slightest indication that boys in Latin outnumbered those in Greek 10 to 1, or that total enrollments in Greek were 3.1% of the high school enrollment and those in Latin, 34.7%. In 1955 boys were 55% of the total in

algebra, and 80% of the total in physics. The two figures could give no clue to the actual enrollments of boys in each subject—242,000 in physics, over 900,000 in algebra.

In recent years, when the shortage of scientists and engineers has become a problem of major proportions, it is certainly necessary to know how many boys—the main source of supply—are studying mathematics and science in high school. But to relate their number to the number of girls does not get at the heart of the problem, which is simply this: What proportion of each sex is enrolled in the basic subjects? This will show not only the actual source but what is equally important, how it compares with the potential source.

Information of this sort involves more than our national security. When it is compared with similar statistics for other subjects, it also reveals the kind of education our boys and girls—for they should be included—are receiving in high school.

It is not to be expected that all who study science and mathematics and foreign languages in high school will specialize in those or related fields in college. This has not been so in the past; it will not be so in the future. Hence no attempt is made in Table 23 to relate the proportion of boys and the proportion of girls in various subjects to their post high school plans. The table traces in chronological sequence, within the limits of available data, the changing pattern of high school studies, as reflected in the proportionate subject enrollments of each sex.

The percentages in this table follow the pattern of those in Table 1 (Mathematics), Table 2 (Foreign Languages), and Table 3 (Science), of Chapter IV. Among the individual science subjects, physics had its largest proportion of enrollments of each sex in 1890. In 1894-95 four new science subjects were listed, and in 1895-96 the number of boys enrolled in the six subjects (chemistry included) was equal to 98.3% of all boys enrolled in high school; the number of girls, to 97.3% of all girls in high school.[1] The proportion of each sex enrolled in each of these subjects, except chemistry, decreased in 1910 and each year thereafter. Between 1900 and 1922 the proportion of boys in chemistry increased slightly. After a slight setback in 1928, the proportion reached its all-time high in 1948. The proportion of girls increased slightly between 1910 and 1922, had a setback in 1928, and a good recovery in 1948. It was still, however, below its high points of 1890 and 1900.

Of the three new subjects listed in 1910 only biology increased in the proportion of students enrolled in each sex. The proportion of boys

TABLE 23 [1]

PERCENTAGE OF EACH SEX ENROLLED IN CERTAIN SUBJECTS IN THE LAST FOUR YEARS OF PUBLIC HIGH SCHOOLS IN CERTAIN YEARS BETWEEN 1889-90 AND 1954-55

	1890 [2]		1900		1910		1922		1928		1948 [3]		1955 [4]	
	B	G	B	G	B	G	B	G	B	G	B	G	B	G
In 1000's	85	116	216	303	323	415	999	1155	1391	1506	2747	2906	3226	3358
Physics	22.5	23.2	19.5	18.7	16.5	13.2	11.3	6.9	9.4	4.5	8.4	3.0	7.5	1.8
Chemistry	9.9	10.4	8.2	7.4	8.9	5.3	9.1	5.9	8.0	5.7	10.3	7.2	8.5	6.2
Biology					1.0	1.2	8.9	8.7	13.2	14.0	19.5	19.5	19.7	19.6
Gen. Science							20.1	16.7	18.5	16.6	18.8	17.9	19.0 [13]	18.5 [5]
Physiology			28.0	27.0	15.2	15.4	4.9	5.3	2.4	2.9				
Phy. Geography			23.6	23.2	20.3	18.6	4.3	4.2	2.7	2.6				
Geology			3.5	3.8	1.2	1.1	0.2	0.2	0.1	0.1				
Astronomy			2.5	3.0	0.5	0.5	0.1	0.1						
Zoology					7.7	8.3	1.7	1.4	0.9	0.7				
Botany					16.1	17.4	3.6	4.0	1.4	1.7				
TOTAL	32.4	33.6	85.3	83.1	87.4	81.0	64.2	53.4	56.6	48.8	57.0	47.6	54.7	46.1
Algebra	45.3	46.0	57.0	55.8	59.7	54.6	44.5	36.4	38.7	32.0	33.4	27.6	27.8	22.1
Geometry	21.7	21.3	27.0	27.7	32.6	29.6	25.4	20.3	22.4	17.4	19.3	15.0	15.5	9.4
Trig.			2.4	1.5	3.1	0.9	2.5	0.7	2.0	0.6	2.0	0.6	4.1	1.1
Gen. Math.							9.9	11.1	8.1	7.6	7.5	7.1	13.1	11.3
TOTAL	67.0	67.3	86.4	85.0	95.4	85.1	82.3	68.5	71.2	57.6	62.2	50.3	60.5	43.9
Latin	33.7	35.8	47.1	53.1	45.6	51.7	25.9	28.9	20.6	23.2	14.9	16.8	6.3	7.1
Greek	4.8	1.8	3.7	2.6	1.0	0.6	0.12	0.04						
French	4.8	6.7	6.6	8.7	8.4	11.1	13.8	16.9	12.6	15.3	9.8	11.9	5.0	6.1
German	10.2	10.9	13.4	15.0	23.3	24.0	0.8	0.5	2.2	1.5	2.9	2.0	0.9	0.7
Spanish					0.8	0.6	11.8	10.8	9.6	9.3	6.3	6.1	7.4	7.2
TOTAL	53.5	55.2	70.8	79.4	79.1	88.0	52.4	57.1	45.0	49.3	33.9	36.9	19.6	21.2
History	27.1	28.4	36.1	39.6	54.1	55.7								
Amer. Hist.							14.7	15.7	17.4	18.2	16.9	17.7	31.3	32.8
Ancient Hist.							17.4	17.1	10.6	10.3	6.9	6.7	1.6	1.5
Med.& Mod. Hist.							15.6	15.3	11.6	11.1	6.3	6.1	2.2	1.9
Civil Government					15.8	15.4			6.4	6.7	5.8	6.1	7.6	8.1
Civics			22.2	21.4			19.1	19.8	13.4	13.3	10.4	10.3	9.5	9.4
TOTAL	27.1	28.4	58.3	61.0	69.9	71.1	66.8	67.9	59.4	59.6	46.3	46.9	52.2	53.7
Rhetoric			37.5	39.2	57.2	57.1								
English Lit.			40.7	42.9	56.9	57.3								
English							77.6	79.4	92.6	93.5	90.0	90.8	92.3	93.2
TOTAL			78.2	82.1	114.1	114.4	77.6	79.4	92.6	93.5				

Bus.& Comm. Course	15.3	11.8	10.9	11.1							
Bookkeeping					10.1	14.7	8.2	12.9	7.6	12.0	6.7	10.5
Shorthand					4.5	12.7	3.5	13.5	3.6	13.9	3.1	12.2
Typing					8.5	17.0	9.2	20.6	10.1	22.6	19.6	30.4
TOTAL	15.3	11.8	10.9	11.1	23.1	44.4	20.9	47.0	21.3	48.5	29.4	53.1
Home Economics		0.5	6.3	0.2	26.4	0.3	29.8	0.3	30.1	0.4	43.6	
Manual Training		5.2	2.4	21.4	1.0	15.2	0.2	24.7	0.3	31.3	0.4	

[1] For references, except as indicated below, and pertinent comments, see Notes 1-8 to Table 22. The enrollment by sex is given in thousands. In 1910, 1922, and in 1928 the sums of enrollments by sex are 1,000 less than the total enrollments given in Table 22. This was caused from rounding off the figures to the nearest thousand. The total percentages, as in the tables of Chapter IV, indicate that all enrollments in the various courses of a subject-matter field equal that percentage of the total high school enrollment. Students taking more than one subject in a given field could not be eliminated.

[2] See Note 2 of Table 22 above. If the distribution of the "extra" students, made in the second reference, had been followed, boys would have numbered 86,000; girls, 117,000. Since the distribution did not extend to subject enrollments, the additional students were not included in the total enrollments by sex. The subject percentages for each sex, therefore, should be slightly lower.

[3] The percentages for science subjects were calculated by the writer from data in *Bulletin 1950, No. 9*, Tables 7 and 8 (note 6 of Table 22 above). The percentages in all other subjects in this column are for the year 1933-34 and were calculated by the writer with a proportion set up for each subject as follows: subject-percentage for boys *is to* the total subject-percentage of that year *as* X *is to* the total subject-percentage of the next year in sequence. The solution for X gives the subject-percentage for boys in the latter year. One example will illustrate. In 1927-28 the percentage of all high school students enrolled in algebra was 35.2. In 1933-34 it was 30.4. The following proportion then was set up: 38.7:35.2 *as* X:30.4. Solution for X gave 33.4 as the percentage of all boys enrolled in algebra in 1933-34. A similar proportion was set up for girls.

The use of this method meant of course that the *relationship* between the percentages for girls and boys would be the same in each of the two years. After an interval of one or two years, this would not have been strange; after an interval of six years it would have been a rare occurrence. Since subject-enrollments were not broken down by sex after 1927-28, except in special studies, the method used was the only one possible. The percentages for 1933-34 are at best, therefore, only approximate, but they do fit into the general pattern.

A comparison of the percentages based on actual enrollments and those calculated by the method of proportion, may be illustrated by another example from algebra. The percentages in the table for 1922 and 1928 are based on actual enrollments. By calculation the percentage of boys in 1928 was 38.9 as compared with 38.7; of girls, 31.8 as compared with 32.0. A similar calculation for physics in the same years gave 8.6 for boys in 1928 as compared with 9.4, and 5.3 for girls as compared with 4.5.

These comparisons show that between 1922 and 1928 enrollments in algebra decreased proportionately a little more for boys than for girls; in physics, slightly less for boys than for girls. From these and other comparisons, not given here, it seems reasonably safe to conclude that the calculated percentages for 1933-34 are less than 0.5% in error for mathematics, foreign languages, and social studies.

[4] See Note 7 of Table 22 above for mathematics and science. By applying the percentages for girls in Table 22, and for boys as derived from it, to the estimated actual enrollments given in *School Life* (June 1956), p. 6, the writer calculated the percentage of each sex enrolled in the various subjects in science and mathematics, except general science. Enrollments in foreign languages were taken from PMLA, pp. 52-56. It was assumed that the estimated percentage (51.0) of girls in high school was correct. The percentages in all other subjects were for the year 1948-49, the last year in which enrollment figures were available, and were calculated by the method described in Note 3 of this table.

[5] Since no data were collected for general science in the special study, the procedure mentioned in Note 3 could not be followed. The writer estimated the percentages on the basis of trends shown in this table and in Table 22.

in general science, first listed in 1922, after a decrease between that year and 1928, began a slow recovery which lasted through 1955. The proportion of girls, except for a slight setback in 1928, showed a gradual increase.[2]

The addition of four subjects in 1894-95, mentioned above, brought about the tremendous increase in the proportion of student concentration in science subjects, that year and the year following. The proportions for each sex declined considerably in 1900. By 1910 the proportion of boys had increased slightly over that of 1900, but that of girls had continued to decrease. This was the beginning of a steadily widening gap between the proportions of the two sexes, through 1922. After that year the difference remained remarkably constant. Throughout the entire period the proportion of girls compared very favorably with that of boys in most subjects, was larger in some, and this explains the larger number of girls in many of these subjects, as shown in Table 22. The great change in the proportion of each sex studying science came between 1910 and 1922. It may be pure coincidence that this was the period during which general science was introduced.

Although the overall developments in mathematics paralleled to a great extent those in science, there are several interesting contrasts. One of these was touched on above. The percentage peak for science, in both sexes, came in 1896; in mathematics it came in 1910. The period of real percentage decline in both subject fields, however, came after 1910. Except in 1890 and 1955, the number of different subjects in mathematics was always fewer than the number in science, if the two levels of algebra and the two geometries are counted as separate subjects. Despite this difference in numbers, the proportion of students of each sex, except of girls in 1955, was always greater in mathematics than in science. With a few exceptions—fewer in mathematics than in science—the proportion of boys was always greater than that of girls. In 1890, if trigonometry, which was in the curriculum, had been listed, boys would have exceeded girls in total percentage. As it was, the slightly larger proportion of girls in algebra overbalanced the slightly larger proportion of boys in geometry.

The continuity of subject-matter in mathematics also offers a contrast with science, in which study of a particular science is often determined by grade-level of the student. Although there are many variable factors, such as alternation of courses in smaller schools and different requirements, a comparison of the percentages in algebra and geometry shows some interesting phenomena. Between 1890 and 1910 the differences between the two percentages range from 23.6 to

30.0 to 27.1 for boys, and from 24.7 to 28.1 to 25.0 for girls. Between 1922 and 1928, they decrease from 19.1 to 16.3 for boys, and from 16.1 to 14.6 for girls. In 1955 the difference for boys was 12.3; for girls, 12.7. Except in 1890 and 1955 the differences in the corresponding years were slightly greater for boys than for girls. In all cases except two the differences in matching figures were greatest when the two figures were largest, and there were gradations in difference as the two figures became larger or smaller. These relationships undoubtedly indicate that increases or decreases in geometry, since comparable percentages represent comparable figures in each sex, are directly connected with increases or decreases in algebra. These figures also show that in the same year the difference between the percentages of algebra and geometry for boys is very close to the comparable difference for girls. This relationship also shows up in a comparison of percentages in elementary and intermediate algebra, and in elementary algebra and plane geometry. In 1928, of the boys in high school 29.2% were enrolled in elementary and 9.5% in intermediate algebra. The difference was 19.7. In that same year 25.1% and 6.9% of the girls were in the respective courses. The difference was 18.2. In plane geometry 19.1% of boys were enrolled—a difference with algebra of 10.1; the difference for girls, with 15.9% in plane geometry, was 9.2. In 1955 the percentage of boys in elementary and intermediate algebra was 19.6 and 8.2 respectively—a difference of 11.4; in plane geometry, 12.4—a difference of 7.2. For girls the comparable percentages were 17.1, 5.0, and 8.1; comparable differences, 12.1 and 9.0.[3]

No such relationships as these could be found among any of the sciences.

After 1928, as pointed out above, it was impossible to determine the percentage of subject-enrollments by sex on the basis of actual enrollments in any of the subject-matter fields except mathematics and science. The assumption that the proportions of 1928 in the other fields were maintained in 1934 and 1949 leaves much to be desired, but no other approach was possible. It is believed, without any demonstrable proof, that any errors resulting from this assumption would have been slight in 1934. During the much longer period between 1934 and 1949, however, there were many influences at work. These undoubtedly made the situation in 1949 somewhat different from the one given in Table 23, on which the analysis concerned with 1934 and 1949 is unavoidably based.

The developments in foreign languages show some interesting similarities and contrasts with those in social studies. Although the pro-

portion of girls was always slightly higher than that of boys in both fields, the differences within each field were never great, except in 1910 in foreign languages. Between 1890 and 1910 enrollments of each sex in foreign languages were considerably greater than those in social studies. The reversal of this relationship after 1910 was caused by the addition of many social studies and the simultaneous decline in the proportion of language enrollments. By 1934 boys in all social studies outnumbered those in foreign languages a little over two to one; girls, almost two to one. In 1949 the ratio was over four to one for boys, and almost exactly four to one for girls.

It is not intended to imply that the changes in foreign language enrollments were caused primarily by increased emphasis on social studies. Undoubtedly that was a factor. Another, and perhaps greater factor, was the growing interest in business and commercial subjects, home economics, and industrial or vocational training. The effects were much more pronounced on girls than on boys.

In 1922 the number of girls in foreign languages was greater than those in all business subjects, for the last time. In 1928 the ratio of girls in the latter was almost one and a half to one; in 1934, almost two to one, and in 1949, over three to one. In 1949 the ratio in home economics was a little over two to one. In this same year girls in home economics, for the first time, almost equalled the number in mathematics and in science.

The proportion of boys in all business subjects was greater than that of girls in 1900. Since that time it has been slightly more than half that of girls in each of the years listed. In 1934 the number of boys in business subjects was slightly larger than the number in foreign languages, and in 1949, over twice as large. The same thing was probably true in vocational and non-vocational subjects.

[1] The writer calculated the percentages from data in CR 1895-96, II, pp. 1566-71.

[2] These statements about developments in general science assume, whether rightly or wrongly, that the estimated percentages for 1955 are approximately correct. See Note 5 of Table 23.

[3] The computations for 1928 were based on data in CR 1926-28, II, pp. 1062 and 1065; for 1955, in *Pamphlet No. 118, 1956*, Table 14, and *School Life* (June 1956), p. 6.

HIGH SCHOOL STUDENTS AND COLLEGE

Information about high school students and their preparation for or entrance into college has varied considerably in the publications of the Office of Education. The first statistics appeared in the Commissioner's Report for 1886-87. They included the number of boys and of girls preparing for a classical course in college, the number preparing for a scientific course in college or in a scientific school, and the "total number of 1886-87 who have entered college or scientific school." [1] Presumably these last were graduates in the spring of 1887 who entered college in the fall of that year. There was no separation of enrollments by type of college or curriculum. Since the number of graduates was not given, the percentage of graduates who entered kind were not made available until some thirty-five years later—in 1921-22.

In the meantime, however, data of two kinds were collected and published. The first of these was mentioned above: the number of all high school students preparing for one of two curricula in college, and for scientific school. These statistics appeared in each of the eighteen Annual Reports published between 1889-90 and 1909-10,[2] and in 1915-16 (for the year 1914-15). Data from five of these reports and from the one in 1886-87,[3] added for the sake of comparison, are presented in Table 24.

This table contains the three familiar characteristics previously noted in many of the tables in this study. As shown in lines 3, 6, 9, and 12, these are: increase in percentages and curriculum enrollments (1887 to 1890); decrease in percentages but increase in curriculum enrollments (1890 to 1905); decrease in percentages and in curriculum enrollments (1905 to 1910).

Since the total high school enrollments increased steadily throughout the entire period, the number of students preparing for the two curricula in college also increased through 1905, although their pro-

Table 24[1]
PERCENTAGE OF TOTAL HIGH SCHOOL STUDENTS BY SEX IN
GRADES 9-12 PREPARING FOR ONE OF TWO CURRICULA IN COLLEGE
OR SCIENTIFIC SCHOOL IN CERTAIN YEARS
BETWEEN 1886-87 AND 1989-10

	1887[2]	1890[3]	1895[4]	1900[5]	1905[6]	1910[7]	LINE
Total Boys in 1000's	27	86	144	216	288	399	1
Total Girls in 1000's	42	116	206	303	391	517	2
Boys and Girls in 1000's	68	203	350	519	680	915	3
Classical Curriculum — Boys[8]	11.3	9.4	8.9	7.0	5.2	3.0	4
Classical Curriculum — Girls[8]	3.9	5.9	6.5	5.3	5.1	3.2	5
Boys and Girls[9]	6.7	7.4	7.5	6.0	5.2	3.1	6
Scientific Curriculum — Boys[8]	5.2	8.1	8.0	6.4	6.1	4.4	7
Scientific Curriculum — Girls[8]	2.2	6.3	4.9	3.7	3.0	1.1	8
Boys and Girls[9]	3.3	7.1	6.2	4.8	4.3	2.5	9
Total Boys[10]	16.5	17.5	16.9	13.4	11.3	7.4	10
Total Girls[10]	6.1	12.2	11.4	9.0	8.1	4.3	11
Boys and Girls[11]	10.0	14.5	13.7	10.8	9.5	5.6	12

[1] In 1887, 1890, 1905, and 1910 the total enrollment is 1 (for 1000) more or less than the sum of each enrollment by sex. This was caused by rounding off the figures to the nearest thousand. The figures and percentages representing both sexes are underscored for easy identification. The writer calculated the percentages. Those in line 12 are the sums of the two percentages underscored in lines 6 and 9.

[2] CR 1886-87, pp. 494-97, 512.

[3] CR 1889-90, II, pp. 1388-89.

[4] CR 1894-95, I, pp. 20-23, 38.

[5] CR 1899-1900, II, pp. 2122, 2129-30.

[6] CR 1904-05, II, pp. 816, 823-24.

[7] CR 1909-10, II, pp. 1135, 1143-45. Table A, p. 1139, is a convenient reference for the underscored percentages between 1890 and 1910, but not for enrollments. It also includes similar percentages for all other years between 1889-90 and 1909-10 except for 1906-07 to 1908-09 inclusive, when no data were collected.

[8] These percentages show the proportion of boys and the proportion of girls who were preparing for each of the two curricula in college.

[9] These percentages (underscored) were found by adding the number of boys and girls preparing for each of the two curricula in college and dividing that sum by the total enrollment of boys and girls.

[10] These two percentages show the proportion of boys and of girls preparing for both curricula in college.

[11] These percentages represent the sum of the percentages mentioned in Note 9.

portion to the total enrollment decreased after 1890 (line 12). This proportion was greatest in 1890 (line 12), when the actual number preparing for the two curricula was smallest (29,000),[4] and smallest in 1910, when the actual number was almost twice as large—51,000. The number in 1910, however, was 13,000 smaller than the number in 1905, 6,000 smaller than the number in 1900 and only 3,000 larger than the number in 1895.

These same developments also took place in the total number of
boys (line 10) and of girls (line 11). Since the girls (line 2) always
outnumbered the boys (line 1), it is not surprising that the proportion
of girls preparing for the two curricula (line 11) was always less than
the proportion of boys (line 10). Between 1890 and 1910, however,
the actual numerical difference between boys and girls was insignificant, until 1910. Before that year girls comprised about 49% of the
total preparing for both curricula. In 1910 their percentage fell to 43.
This was also the percentage of girls in 1887.

Comparison of the total percentages for each of the two curricula
shows that those for the classical (line 6) were consistently larger
than those for the scientific curriculum (line 9). Among those of both
sexes preparing for the classical curriculum, the girls consistently outnumbered the boys in actual figures, except in 1890. In that year for
the first and only time the girls in the scientific curriculum (line 8)
outnumbered the boys (line 7). Except for that year, there were
more girls in the classical curriculum (line 5) than in the scientific
(line 8). The boys in the classical curriculum (line 4) outnumbered
those in the scientific (line 7), except in 1905 and 1910.

To conclude this brief analysis, two things must be emphasized.
First, the percentages and figures just cited refer only to the high
school students who were preparing for two specific curricula in college.
These students made up only a relatively small percentage of the total
high school enrollment (lines 3 and 12). Many other students were
undoubtedly studying the same high school subjects. Although these
subjects were not specified in the tables from which these statistics
were taken, they were listed in other tables, and the number and percentage of all high school students who studied them were considerably greater in corresponding years than the figures and percentages
in this table.[5]

In the second place, the table gives no statistics on the number of
high school students who actually entered college. Information of
that kind was given for the first time in the Biennial Survey of 1920-
22. Before turning to the graduates and their college plans, however,
it may be interesting to present some of the data in Table 24, arranged
by regions rather than sex.

In 1890, as this table shows, five of the nine regions had more students preparing for the scientific curriculum in college than for the
classical. All of these, with one exception—ESC—were in the Middle
West, Southwest, and Far West. WSC had the greatest proportion of
students in the classical curriculum; PAC, the greatest proportion in

TABLE 25 [1]

PERCENTAGE OF HIGH SCHOOL STUDENTS GRADES 9-12 PREPARING FOR ONE OF TWO CURRICULA IN COLLEGE, BY REGION, IN 1890, 1900, AND 1910

	1890			1900			1910		
	CLASSICAL	SCIENTIFIC	TOT.	CLASS.	SCI.	TOT.	CLASS.	SCI.	TOT.
NE	11.7	4.9	16.6	11.5	4.7	16.2	8.0	4.1	12.1
	3	7	4	1	5	1	1	1	1
MA	6.3	6.1	12.4	5.3	3.1	8.3	2.9	3.6	6.5
	7	6	8	6	8	9	3	2	3
SA	12.1	3.1	15.2	8.9	2.4	11.4	3.6	1.2	4.8
	2	8	6	2	9	6	2	7	4
ESC	6.2	6.6	12.8	8.7	5.0	13.7	2.1	1.4	3.5
	8	5	7	3	4	4	7	6	8
WSC	12.4	7.0	19.3	6.9	4.0	10.9	2.8	1.2	4.0
	1	4	2	4	7	7	4	7	7
ENC	4.6	7.0	11.6	4.4	4.4	8.8	2.3	2.1	4.4
	9	4	9	9	6	8	6	4	6
WNC	8.4	10.2	18.6	4.9	6.7	11.6	1.6	1.4	3.0
	5	2	3	8	3	5	8	6	9
MT	7.0	8.5	15.5	5.8	9.5	15.3	2.7	1.8	4.5
	6	3	5	5	2	2	5	5	5
PAC	8.8	15.4	24.1	5.1	10.1	15.2	3.6	3.4	7.0
	4	1	1	7	1	3	2	3	2
TOT. (US)	7.4	7.1	14.5	6.0	4.8	10.8	3.1	2.5	5.6

[1] For references, see Notes 3, 5, and 7 of Table 24. Occasionally the total percentage is 0.1 less or more than the sum of two percentages. Rounding off the percentages to the nearest decimal is the reason. The writer calculated all of the regional percentages. Those in the last line are found in CR 1909-10, II, Table A, p. 1139.

For regional enrollments in 1890 and 1900, and the states in each region, see Appendix F, Table 30. In 1910 the regional percentages in the table above were based on total enrollments, rather than on enrollments in the schools that returned usable questionnaires, on which subject percentages between that year and 1934 had to be based (see Appendix F, Table 30, Note 1). These regional enrollments were as follows: NE—95,861; MA—205,300; SA—43,021; ESC—34,840; WSC—50,733; ENC—241,537; WNC—155,012; MT—25,202; PAC—62,655. Total—915,061. For the sake of ready comparison the relative rank of each region is shown by the number under each percentage in each column. They should be read by column and not by row.

the scientific. PAC's overwhelming lead in the science field gave it the largest proportion of students preparing for college.[6]

By 1900, however, that lead had passed to NE, where it remained through 1910. In 1900 the scientific curriculum was leading in only three regions—WNC, MT, and PAC, and tied with the classical in another—ENC. The classical curriculum had a decided lead in the other five regions, and this lead again put it ahead throughout the country.

Although by 1910 the number of high school students was almost

double that of 1900 (see Table 24, line 3), the total number in each of the two curricula was less in 1910 than in 1900. Enrollments in the classical curriculum were less in all regions except NE, MT, and PAC; in the scientific curriculum, except NE, MA, SA, and PAC. Percentages for each of the two curricula continued to decrease in all regions except MA. In that region alone the number and percentage in the scientific curriculum were greater than in 1900, and greater than the percentage and number in the classical curriculum in 1910.

These decreases should not be misinterpreted. They do not mean that fewer high school students were studying classical and scientific subjects in 1910 than in 1900. They are simply the reflection of changes that were taking place both in high school and in college.

Between 1886-87 and 1889-90, for example, the list of undergraduate degrees which students might obtain increased markedly. In 1886-87 and 1887-88 the two courses, classical and scientific, were set apart from "other first-degree courses" not named. In 1888-89, A.B. and B.S. courses were listed specifically for the first time. The other courses listed were for the Bachelor of Letters, Bachelor of Philosophy, and Civil Engineering. In 1889-90, in addition to these, students could work for a Bachelor of Mechanical Arts, of Engineering, Agriculture, Architecture, Music, Pedagogy, Painting, Laws, and Divinity. By 1910, some of these degrees had dropped out of sight and a few others added—Scientific Agriculture, Fine Arts, Commercial Science, and several in Engineering. Separate tabulations for enrollments in the classical and scientific courses appeared in 1909-10 for the last time. In 1914-15, the familiar "arts and sciences" designation was used for the first time.[7]

In all these years students in the college classical course outnumbered those in all other courses down to 1910. In that year students in general science—the field not the subject—and in engineering together almost equalled the number in the classical course. Recipients of the A.B. degree, however, constituted the largest single group of graduates. But the distinction between A.B. and B.S. had begun to break down as early as 1890, when some colleges conferred the A.B. on students who had completed their college work without Latin or Greek.[8] It was impossible to trace this development, but undoubtedly the increasing lack of any clear-cut distinction between the A.B. and the B.S. made such a division more and more meaningless. Since 1915, as mentioned above, college students or graduates in arts and sciences have been grouped under that heading, to distinguish them from those in engineering, education, business, law, and a few other subject-

TABLE 26[1]
HIGH SCHOOL GRADUATES BY SEX AND REGION
IN 1892-93, 1899-1900, AND 1909-10

	1893 B	G	T	1900 B	G	T	1910 B	G	T
NE	2,062	3,409	5,471	3,375	5,570	8,945	5,194	7,796	12,990
MA	2,302	3,984	6,284	4,704	7,772	12,476	9,095	13,747	22,842
SA	208	412	620	559	1,373	1,932	1,459	2,722	4,181
ESC	213	464	677	685	1,173	1,858	1,012	1.995	3,007
WSC	204	326	530	663	1,290	1,953	1,674	3,006	4,680
ENC	3,149	6,402	9,551	7,448	12,306	19,754	13,672	19,680	33,352
WNC	1,681	3,353	5,034	4,004	7,626	11,630	7,824	13,289	21,113
MT	123	267	390	388	693	1,081	1,062	1,669	2,731
PAC	314	537	851	749	1,359	2,108	2,665	3,802	6,467
TOTAL	10,256	19,154	29,410	22,575	39,162	61,737	43,657	67,706	111,363

[1] The references are as follows: CR 1892-93, I, p. 55; CR 1899-1900, II, p. 2130; CR 1909-10, II, p. 1143.

matter fields. As a result, the degree of Bachelor of Arts has become the generally accepted label in the liberal arts college, regardless of the student's undergraduate major.

Between 1890-91 and 1914-15 statistics were given on the number of high school graduates who were prepared for college. As indicated above, they did not indicate the number who actually entered. In 1909-10 and later, statistics were also given on the number prepared for higher institutions, other than college.[9] The first year in which fairly reliable figures could be arranged by sex and by geographical regions was 1892-93.

A comparison of Table 27 with Table 26 shows that the regions with the smallest numbers of graduates had the greatest proportion of students prepared for college. It is significant, perhaps, that two of the regions with the smallest percentages—NE and MA—were in the heavily industrialized area of the Upper Atlantic Seaboard. Although the other two—ENC and WNC[10]—were located in the great Farming Belt of the Middle West, they had many large industrial centers. Between 1893 and 1900 the lead in preparation for college shifted from the southern to the western part of the country. In 1910 the southern part was again in the lead. In all three years those two sections were considerably ahead of all others.

As Table 26 shows, girl graduates consistently outnumbered the

TABLE 27 [1]

PERCENTAGE OF HIGH SCHOOL GRADUATES BY SEX AND REGION PREPARED FOR COLLEGE AND OTHER HIGHER INSTITUTIONS IN 1892-93, 1899-1900, AND 1909-10

	1893 COLLEGE			1900 COLLEGE			1910 [2]/ COLLEGE			OTHER			
	B 1	G 2	T 3	B 1	G 2	T 3	B 1	G 2	T 3	B 4	G 5	T 6	GT 7
NE	33.5	17.1	23.3	34.4	21.0	26.0	39.4	15.0	24.8	9.2	19.1	17.4	42.2
	8	8	8	9	8	8	9	9	8	6	2	2	9
MA	30.7	12.7	19.3	35.5	17.4	24.2	43.1	18.3	24.8	12.1	26.7	20.9	49.0
	9	9	9	7	9	9	7	8	8	1	1	1	7
SA	46.1	39.1	41.4	42.6	25.0	30.1	60.5	44.6	50.1	7.5	10.3	9.4	59.5
	5	4	5	3	6	6	1	1	1	7	8	9	1
ESC	93.9	78.4	83.3	41.0	30.6	34.4	54.0	33.8	40.6	9.9	10.3	10.1	50.7
	1	1	1	5	5	5	4	5	5	5	8	8	5
WSC	60.3	48.8	53.2	35.3	37.4	36.7	54.2	38.9	44.4	10.4	16.1	14.0	58.4
	3	2	2	8	2	4	3	3	3	3	3	3	2
ENC	42.1	23.3	29.5	36.9	24.4	29.1	41.8	27.8	33.6	10.7	15.4	13.4	47.0
	7	7	7	6	7	7	8	7	7	2	4	4	8
WNC	43.4	33.1	36.5	42.3	34.3	37.0	44.5	31.5	36.3	10.2	14.4	12.8	49.1
	6	6	6	4	4	3	6	6	6	4	6	5	6
MT	50.4	39.7	43.1	50.0	35.5	40.7	55.7	39.7	45.9	7.2	12.1	10.2	56.1
	4	3	4	2	3	2	2	2	2	8	7	7	3
PAC	65.3	35.0	46.2	50.5	39.8	43.6	50.2	34.8	41.1	6.3	15.3	11.6	52.7
	2	5	3	1	1	1	5	4	4	9	5	6	4
TOTAL	40.4	24.4	29.9	38.1	25.8	30.3	44.5	27.2	34.0	10.2	17.9	14.9	48.9

[1] References are the same as in Table 26, except for one addition in 1892-93. The number of graduates, by sex, prepared for college that year is found in CR 1894-95, I, pp. 81-83. The same reference contained similar data for the year 1891-92, but discrepancies between two sets of figures could not be reconciled. The figures underscored indicate the three regions with the highest percentages in a given year. For ready comparison the relative rank of each region is shown by the numeral under each percentage. They should be read by columns. Columns 1 and 2 give the percentage of each sex prepared for college; column 3, of both sexes together.

[2] The grand total (GT) in column 7 is the sum of columns 3 and 6. It shows the percentage of all graduates, boys and girls, prepared for all higher institutions.

boys, and in some regions in 1893, two or more to one. With one exception, however—WSC in 1900—the proportion of boys prepared for college was consistently and considerably larger than that of girls. In MA the proportion was more than two to one in each of the three years. In NE it was almost two to one in 1893, and considerably more than two to one in 1910. These were the very regions, it is worth noting, with the greatest percentage of girls prepared for other higher institutions in 1910. In each of these two regions this percentage was more than twice as large as that for boys. In general, except for WSC and WNC, the proportion of boys and girls prepared for college was in sharp contrast with the proportion prepared for other higher

TABLE 28 [1]
HIGH SCHOOL GRADUATES BY SEX AND REGION
IN 1920-21, 1932-33, AND 1936-37

	1921			1933			1937		
	B	G	T	B	G	T	B	G	T
NE	9,300	13,318	22,618	25,447	28,379	53,826	30,450	33,778	64,228
MA	20,183	27,715	47,898	61,583	63,538	125,121	102,336	109,708	212,044
SA	4,957	8,363	13,320	27,855	37,047	64,902	30,303	40,344	70,647
ESC	3,239	5,287	8,526	17,793	22,085	39,878	20,851	25,667	46,518
WSC	6,307	9,718	16,025	31,795	37,478	69,273	38,653	45,623	84,276
ENC	27,000	36,168	63,168	85,707	89,365	175,072	99,284	106,219	205,503
WNC	16,449	26,630	43,079	51,449	61,877	113,326	56,518	64,729	121,247
MT	3,308	5,292	8,600	15,096	16,892	31,988	17,504	18,722	36,226
PAC	8,588	11,826	20,414	35,756	36,232	71,988	40,328	41,336	81,664
TOTAL	99,331	144,317	243,648	352,481	392,893	745,374	436,227	486,126	922,353

[1] References are as follows: BS 1920-22, II, pp .559-60; BS 1932-34, Ch. V, pp. 57-58; BS 1936-38, Ch. V, pp. 73-75.

institutions. If the regions are ranked in each category, given in the order just mentioned, this contrast is made clear: NE, 8-2; MA, 8-1;[11] SA, 1-9; ESC, 5-8; WSC, 3-3; ENC, 7-4; WNC, 6-5; MT, 2-7; PAC, 4-6. A similar comparison of sex with sex in the two categories follows approximately this same pattern.

Preparation for college by both sexes together and by girls alone increased throughout the seventeen-year period.[12] Between 1893 and 1900 the total percentage for boys decreased slightly. Three of the regions—ESC, WSC, and PAC—had such decided drops that the accuracy of the figures in 1893 might well be questioned, but the figures given yielded the percentages as listed. Between 1900 and 1910 the first two regions made a strong comeback; PAC was the only region out of the nine that showed a continued decrease for boys—although it was slight—in 1910. Along with WNC and NE it also showed a decrease for girls, and in all three cases that decrease brought the total percentage of each below that of 1900.

From information given in the sources it could not be determined whether the data for 1893 and 1900 included the number of graduates prepared for higher institutions other than liberal arts colleges. In 1910, when these data were specifically added, over 60% of boys were prepared for higher institutions in four regions—SA, ESC, WSC, and MT; over 50% in four other regions, and slightly under 50% in only

TABLE 29 [1]

PERCENTAGE OF HIGH SCHOOL GRADUATES BY SEX AND BY REGION ATTENDING COLLEGE AND OTHER HIGHER INSTITUTIONS IN THE FALL FOLLOWING THEIR GRADUATION IN

1920-21, 1932-33, 1936-37

	1921 [2] College			1921 Other			1933 College			1933 Other			1937 College			1937 Other		
	B 1	G 2	T 3	B 4	G 5	T 6	B 1	G 2	T 3	B 4	G 5	T 6	B 1	G 2	T 3	B 4	G 5	T 6
NE	30.7	12.8	20.2	13.5	20.6	17.7	17.1	12.9	14.9	5.3	7.5	6.5	17.8	14.0	15.8	6.7	9.5	8.2
	9	9	9	2	2		9	9	9	1	2	2	9	9	9	1	2	1
MA	42.7	18.7	28.8	15.1	26.9	21.9	24.0	18.9	21.5	4.4	9.4	7.0	26.7	20.1	23.3	5.1	9.8	7.5
	5	8	8	1	1		4	6	5	2	1	1	4	7	6	2	1	2
SA	54.5	37.8	44.0	7.3	13.6	11.3	30.0	25.2	27.3	2.0	4.4	3.4	30.7	28.1	29.2	3.2	4.8	4.1
	1	2	2	6	5		1	3	3	5	4	4	3	3	3	4	7	6
ESC	44.8	28.8	34.9	8.1	16.3	13.2	29.0	27.1	27.9	1.9	3.1	2.6	34.3	31.0	32.5	2.9	4.6	3.8
	3	5	5	5	4		2	1	1	6	8	8	2	2	2	6	8	8
WSC	.8.8	42.0	44.6	8.4	10.5	9.7	21.8	20.0	20.8	1.8	2.4	2.1	26.2	23.4	24.7	2.9	4.6	3.9
	2	1		4	8		6	5	6	7	9	9	6	5	5	6	8	7
ENC	36.4	25.9	30.4	10.7	17.4	14.5	19.1	17.0	18.1	1.9	3.6	2.8	21.5	18.9	20.2	2.6	5.2	3.9
	8	6	6	3	3		8	8	8	6	7	7	8	8	8	7	5	7
WNC	36.7	24.9	29.4	6.6	12.3	10.1	20.4	18.6	19.4	2.0	3.8	3.0	23.8	21.7	22.6	2.9	5.6	4.3
	7	7	7	7	7		7	7	7	5	6	6	7	6	7	6	4	4
MT	44.7	32.6	37.2	4.8	10.1	8.1	22.5	21.8	22.3	2.2	3.9	3.1	26.4	24.8	25.6	3.1	5.1	4.2
	4	3	3	9	9		5	4	4	4	5	5	5	4	4	5	6	5
PAC	40.8	31.1	35.2	5.6	13.4	10.1	28.9	26.3	27.6	2.6	4.7	3.9	35.0	32.3	33.6	3.5	6.1	4.8
	6	4	4	8	6		3	2	2	3	3	3	1	1	1	3	3	3
TOTAL	39.8	25.7	31.4	10.1	17.3	14.4	22.8	19.9	21.3	2.7	4.9	3.9	25.9	22.4	24.0	3.7	6.5	5.2

[1] For references, see Note 1 of Table 28. For explanation of numerals under each percentage, see Note 1 of Table 27.

[2] The total percentages in columns 2, 3, 4, 5, and 6 do not agree with comparable percentages given in BS 1932-34, Ch. V, Table G, p. 13 (repeated in BS 1936-38, Ch. V, Table H, p. 15). If the percentages in Table G were based on the figures given in BS 1920-22, II, p. 559, which the writer used, his percentages in this table are believed to be correct. The writer's total percentages for 1933 agree with those in Table G, except in column 6, which is 3.8 in Table G. For 1937, Table H (see above) has 3.6 for the writer's 3.7 (Col. 4). Regional percentages were not calculated in any of the official reports cited.

one—NE. Of girls, four regions had over 50%—SA, WSC, MT, and PAC; only one region—NE again—had under 40%. Of boys and girls, three regions—SA, WSC, and MT—had over 55%; two others over 50%—ESC and PAC; and only NE, under 45%.

None of these statistics, as was pointed out above, indicated what proportion of graduates actually entered higher institutions. That information was first given for the graduates of 1921 (Tables 28 and 29). This was undoubtedly one factor in the general decreases that took place between 1910 and 1921. Since data on preparation and performance are not really comparable, the increases shown by some of the regions in one or more of the categories are noteworthy. The increase of boys entering other higher institutions in NE and MA

raised the total percentage of boys entering both types in MA, but not in NE. The percentage of girls entering college increased in MA and WSC; of girls entering other higher institutions, in NE, MA, SA, ESC, and ENC; of girls entering both types, in MA, ESC, and ENC. Only MA, however, had an increase in the total percentage of boys and girls entering both types.[13]

The general decline between 1915 and 1921 was continued and accentuated by the depression in 1933. Between 1921 and 1933, as might have been expected, decrease in the percentage of those going to college was proportionately greater for boys than for girls. At the same rate of decrease, the percentage for girls in 1933 would have been 14.7 instead of 19.9. As also might have been expected, decrease in the percentage of those going to other higher institutions was proportionately greater than the decrease of those going to college. This decrease was proportionately greater for boys than for girls, although the difference was slight. At the same rate of decrease the percentage would have been 4.6 for the girls instead of 4.9. Among the nine regions none showed an increase in the percentage of boys going to college. Only NE and MA showed slight increases in the percentage of girls. All regions had decreases in the percentage of each sex going to other higher institutions. There were remarkably small differences in any region between the percentage of boys and of girls going to both types of institutions. In MT the percentage of girls was actually 1.0 larger than that of boys; in WNC both percentages were the same. In all other regions the percentage for boys was slightly higher. On a national scale the percentage for boys was 25.5; for girls, 24.8.

In the short span between 1933 and 1937 the national percentages increased to 29.6 and 28.9 respectively. The difference between the two was exactly the same as the comparable difference in 1933— 0.7%. Apparently the Great Depression was also the Great Equalizer of educational opportunities.

This fact is borne out also among the regions. In five regions the proportion of boys continuing education beyond high school was less than 2% larger than that of girls; in two regions the proportion of girls was slightly larger—WNC and MT; and in one—ENC—the proportion was the same for each. In still another—PAC—the proportion of boys was only 0.1% larger.

As Table 29 shows, between 1921 and 1933 the percentage of each sex attending college decreased proportionately less than the percentage attending other higher institutions. Between 1933 and 1937 the

percentage of each sex attending college increased proportionately less than the percentage attending other higher institutions.

In 1910 (Table 27) the percentage of each sex *prepared* for college was highest in SA, MT, and WSC. In 1921 (Table 29) the percentage *going* to college was highest in WSC, SA, and MT; in 1933, in ESC, PAC, and SA; in 1937, in PAC, ESC, and SA. The percentage of each sex prepared for or going to other higher institutions was highest in MA, NE, and WSC in 1910 and 1921 (with ENC in place of WSC); in MA, NE, and PAC in 1933 and 1937. In each of these years the proportion prepared for or actually entering college was less in NE than in any other region. Its greater number of private schools for both sexes was undoubtedly the primary reason.

In 1910 the actual number of boys prepared for college was for the first time slightly larger than the actual number of girls. The number of girls prepared for other higher institutions, however, was so much larger than the number of boys that in both categories combined girls outnumbered boys. This same development prevailed through 1937. Since girls have continued to outnumber boys in high school and in graduation from it, more girls than boys may have entered institutions of higher learning each year since 1937.[14] Unfortunately that was the last year in which figures on continuation beyond high school could be divided by region, sex, and types of institution. Available data indicate, however, that the percentage of high school graduates continuing their education has been rising since 1937. In 1940 the percentage was 35.2, and in 1952, 44.8, but both of these were based on statistics from all secondary schools, private and public.[15] In the fall of 1953 the number of first-time college students, exclusive of veterans, was 607,570. They constituted 50.7% of graduates of the preceding June in all public and non public secondary schools.[16] If the veterans enrolled in college for the first time had been included, the percentage would have been 55.4.

Since the percentages just cited and the figures on which they were based include part-time as well as full-time students in college, the difficulty of determining the percentage of public high school graduates attending college is clearly obvious. Nevertheless, on the basis of a comparison with the situation in 1937 and 1951, when the facts were known, a reasonable estimate may be made for 1953.

In 1937 there were 367,983 first-time college students, of which 269,631, or 73.3%, were from public high school graduates. The remaining students, 98,352, or 26.7% came from nonpublic secondary school graduates.[17] The total number of graduates from all types of

secondary schools in the preceding June was 1,067,712, of which the number from public high schools was 922,353, or 86.4%. In 1951 the public high schools graduated 1,045,588 students,[18] or 88.5% of secondary school graduates. If it is assumed that high school graduates constituted 75% of first-time college students that fall, instead of 73.3% as in 1937, then approximately 38% of their 1951 graduates entered college that fall.[19] By 1953, when the veterans in college for the first time were counted separately, that uncertainty is removed from the calculations. If the percentages used for 1951 are used for 1953, approximately 43% of the high school graduates entered college in the fall of that year. If the 1951 percentages are increased from 88.5 to 90, and from 75 to 80, approximately 45% of the public high school graduates in 1953 entered college in the following fall. Neither percentage, of course, could distinguish between full or part-time students.

According to the United States Office of Education there were 735,065 first-time college students in the fall of 1956. This was approximately 55.7% of the June graduates from all types of secondary schools.[20] If it is assumed that the public high school graduates constituted 90% of the 1,318,700 secondary school graduates, and 80% of the first-time college students cited above, 49.5% of public high school graduates in June 1956 entered college that fall. This compares favorably with the estimates made by the Office of Education: of the 1956 June graduates of public high schools, 42% enrolled in college on a full-time basis, 8% were part-time students.[21] It also suggests that the writer's estimates for 1953 were approximately correct.

The avalanche has indeed begun.

[1] CR 1886-87, p. 497. The other data mentioned are given on pp. 496 and 512.

[2] See Note 7 of Table 24.

[3] The statistics in this Report were collected primarily from city school systems and were far from being complete or representative.

[4] The number in 1887 was much smaller—6,800—but the figures for that year, as pointed out in Note 3, above, were far from complete.

[5] For a comparison, see Chapter IV, Table 2 (foreign languages), 3 (science), 1 (mathematics).

[6] As the total US percentages in columns 1 and 2 show, students in the two curricula were almost equally divided—14,969 to 14,320 in actual figures. Four regions—NE, MA, ENC, and WNC—accounted for 12,863 and 12,646 of these respectively.

[7] CR 1915-16 (for the year 1914-15), II, p. 248. References for the other years mentioned are: CR 1909-10, II, pp. 856-861; CR 1889-90, II, pp. 774-77. The last reference includes data for 1886-87 through 1888-89.

[8] CR 1889-90, II, p. 772. Most likely some colleges were doing so before 1890.

⁹ Normal schools were the only type identified in 1910 (CR 1909-10, II, p. 1131). The others undoubtedly included agricultural and mechanical colleges, sometimes referred to as schools of science; schools of medicine, law, and theology.

¹⁰ In 1900, WNC had a larger percentage of boys prepared for college than ESC and WSC; a larger proportion of girls than SA and ESC, and a larger proportion of both than SA, ESC, and WSC. This was not true in the other two years.

¹¹ MA tied with NE for eighth place in percentage prepared for college.

¹² In 1891, the percentage was 28.6 for boys and girls together (CR 1890-91, II, pp. 792-93). A breakdown by sex could not be made.

¹³ It is interesting to note that the upward trend between 1893 and 1910 continued through 1914-15. In that year the national percentage of boys prepared for college increased to 45.4; for other higher institutions, to 10.8; for both, to 56.2. The percentage of girls prepared for college reached 29.3; for other higher institutions, 19.9; for both, 49.2. The percentage of boys and girls prepared for college reached 35.9; for other higher institutions, 16.2; for both, 52.1. CR 1915-16 (for 1914-15), II, pp. 454-55.

¹⁴ The dropout rate for girls is evidently much higher than that for boys. Otherwise it is difficult to explain why men in higher educational institutions have consistently outnumbered women and by considerable margins. For a summary by decades between 1890 and 1920 and for 1922, see BS 1920-22, II, pp. 297-98. For a summary of enrollments and degrees by sex and type of institution between 1900 and 1938, see BS 1936-38, Ch. IV, pp. 43-5. For the latest figures, see *Earned Degrees* for 1955-56.

¹⁵ BS 1950-52, Ch. 1, Table 6. Percentages were calculated by the writer. In 1953-54 the percentage was 51.2 (BS 1953-54, Ch. 1, Table 6).

¹⁶ BS 1952-54, Ch. 4, Section 1, Table XXIV, p. 58.

¹⁷ *Ibid.*, and BS 1936-38, Ch. V, p. 73. These are also the references for the figures used in the calculations to follow, unless otherwise indicated.

¹⁸ BS 1950-52, Ch. 5, Table 17. The writer calculated the percentage.

¹⁹ Since the total number of first-time college students—529,950—included an indeterminable number of veterans, the percentage is undoubtedly too large.

²⁰ The figures were taken from an Associated Press report published by the *Washington Post and Times Herald* (October 28, 1956). The percentage, calculated by the writer, was based on figures published in mimeographed form by the Office of Education as of September 21, 1956. See Appendix G, Note 12.

²¹ The percentages were given to the writer by telephone on November 15, 1956. If the public high-school graduates listed for 1955-56 in Appendix G, Table 38, are used, the percentage attending college that fall would be 50.3.

SPECIAL PROBLEMS IN 1949

For 1948-49 there were certain difficulties in estimating individual subject percentages in four different subject-matter fields: vocational and nonvocational subjects, physical education, art, and music. These difficulties were caused by the nature of the subjects and by the way subject enrollments were reported to the Office of Education. Many reports did not completely break down subject enrollment by grades. Since this study deals primarily with subject enrollments in grades 9-12, it was felt that some attempt should be made to bring the 1948-49 percentages into line with those of the preceding years. The procedure used is a bit complicated, but the writer could find no other.

Explanation for Table 7, Chapter IV

In Chapter 5 of the Biennial Survey for 1948-50, Table 3 gives enrollments for each of 13 different subjects in Industrial Arts—Nonvocational. Each subject enrollment was divided by the total high school enrollment for the individual subject percentage. The addition of each subject enrollment divided by the total high school enrollment gave the percentage of the whole subject matter field. That percentage was 32.4. Duplicates, of course, could not be excluded.

Chapter 5 did not contain percentages for the 13 separate subjects. It did, however, give the total enrollment and percentage for the whole field—26.6 (Table 7). Since this percentage was smaller than the one mentioned above, it was obvious that the individual percentages, also mentioned above, were a little too large. The smaller individual percentages were determined by the following proportion: 32.4: 26.6 as A: X. For A, substitute each of the 13 individual percentages; the result would give X for each of the 13 subjects.

But it was also fairly clear that only five of the subjects would be suitable for students below grades 9-12. Accordingly the proportion was worked out for those five subjects; the percentages for the other eight were kept as they were computed originally. The 13 percentages

then added up to 27.9. The difference between 27.9 and 26.6 came from the fact that the proportion was worked out on the assumption that it would be applied to all percentages. Since it was applied to only five, the proportion was not quite accurate for those five. Although corrective adjustments would have been easy by a "seaman's eye," it was decided to let the five percentages stand as they appear in Table 7 of the text. They are marked with an asterisk.

Explanation for Table 10

Solution of a similar problem in Health, Safety, and Physical Education involved a slightly different approach from the one used above. In this case Table 3 of Chapter 5 gave enrollments in each of 6 different subjects. Table 7 gave the correct official percentage for one, physical education. The problem was to find the corrected percentage for each of the writer's subject percentages. The proportion, therefore, took this form: The writer's P.E. percentage: official percentage *as* the writer's percentage for another subject: X. Since two of the subjects, driver education and military drill, were probably not taught below grades 9-12, corrections were not applied to them. This undoubtedly threw the corrections for safety, health, and hygiene slightly off. In the case of safety education this assumption is apparently verified by the statement (Ch. 5, pp. 24-5) that almost 4% of all secondary students were studying it in 1948-49. The writer's original percentage for the subject was 4.7. His corrected percentage is a bit too small; 3.6 or 3.7 would probably be about right. The writer's original percentage for driver education, 3.8, seemingly checks with another official statement: that "almost 4% of all pupils in regular and senior high schools" received driver training (*Ibid.*, p. 25).

Explanation for Table 11

The procedure used in nonvocational subjects was also used in Music, for which only the official percentage of 30.1 was given (Ch. 5, Table 7). Corrections were applied to all subjects except harmony, theory and practice. The individual corrected percentages, plus the original percentages for those two subjects, added up to 30.1. The original percentages totaled 46.0.

Explanation for Table 12

The problem in Art was a little more complicated than that of any other subject-matter field. As in the case of nonvocational subjects and of music, only an official total percentage was given—9.0 (Ch. 5,

Table 7). This total contrasted sharply with the writer's total percentage, 24.2, which was the sum of the individual percentages derived from the subject enrollments given in Chapter 5, Table 3.

Although the corrective procedure, previously described, yielded a total of 9.0% when it was applied to all of the seven art subjects, some of the individual percentages seemed out of line with official estimates. For instance, it was stated (Ch. 5, p. 25) that freehand drawing and art appreciation each enrolled "approximately 5.5% of the pupils in all types of schools combined." The writer's percentages for these two subjects, based on enrollments given in Table 3, were 7.1 and 6.9. The corrected percentages were 2.6 and 2.5 respectively. The writer's percentage for general art, 4.7, was corrected to 1.8% Both of these figures contrasted with the official percentage of 3.7 "of the total secondary school enrollment" (p. 26) in general art. There was an even greater contrast in general service art. The writer's percentage, 1.7, was corrected to 0.6. The official percentage was 0.1 of enrollments "in all public secondary schools" (p. 26).

The percentage differences just mentioned undoubtedly resulted from the difference between enrollments in *all* public secondary schools and enrollments in the last four years of such schools. If this was the situation in Art, similar situations must have existed in the other three subject-matter fields mentioned in this Appendix. Although the writer's corrected total percentages agree with the official percentages, except in the case of nonvocational subjects—and even they could have been brought into line—his individual corrected percentages in many instances are undoubtedly wrong. Perhaps the overall picture, however, is the important thing.

CUMULATIVE SUBJECTS BY REGION

Tables 1-13 of Chapter IV show the changes that took place between 1890 and 1949 in the proportion of high school students enrolled in thirteen different subject-matter fields throughout the United States. The tables in this appendix show the corresponding changes in three of those fields—mathematics, foreign languages, and science, in each of nine geographical regions. Table 30 gives the total high school enrollments in each region, on which the subject-percentages in Tables 31-33 are based. For the sake of ready comparison, a summary table is added—No. 34—which corresponds to Tables 14 and 15 of Chapter V. A final table, No. 35, permits another kind of comparison: the correlation between regional rankings based on the proportion of high school students and college majors in the various subjects and subject-matter fields.

From these tables certain facts stand out. Although proportionate concentration in individual subjects shifted considerably, the lead in the fields of science and mathematics was in the southern part of the country between 1890 and 1934. In 1949 the lead in mathematics remained there, but in science it shifted to the Middle Atlantic Region, where it undoubtedly is today.[1] The lead in foreign languages was in the South in 1890, but after that year it was in New England, with MA next, after 1900. SA was in third place between 1910 and 1934, but had dropped to sixth in 1949.

In comparative rankings the relationships between mathematics and science are rather consistent and close in most of the regions. The glaring exceptions are in NE in 1890, MT and PAC in 1900, MA in 1910, WSC in 1934, NE and MA in 1949, and NE, MA, ENC, and WSC in 1955.[2] No such relationship as this is apparent between foreign languages and either of the other two fields.

Although many high school students go to college outside of their own regions, the great majority do not. The comparative rank of the regions in these three cumulative subject-matter fields, therefore, may

TABLE 30 [1]
HIGH SCHOOL ENROLLMENTS GRADES 9-12 IN NINE GEOGRAPHICAL
REGIONS[2] IN CERTAIN YEARS BETWEEN 1889-90 AND 1954-55

	1890	1900	1910	1922	1934	1949
NE	35,492	63,392	81,912	174,121	328,456	309,274
MA	45,551	114,452	118,575	479,673	1,114,668	1,180,016
SA	5,802	18,574	34,108	135,976	312,096	620,646
ESC	3,918	18,808	24,960	82,937	180,750	368,550
WSC	4,900	20,861	36,033	148,402	328,187	509,707
ENC	67,088	159,010	187,701	532,215	1,113,870	1,098,852
WNC	33,558	95,806	121,138	338,135	552,151	580,016
MT	1,819	10,349	20,167	82,297	164,828	207,356
PAC	4,835	17,999	49,549	181,814	401,508	525,035
TOTAL US	202,963	519,251	739,143	2,155,460	4,496,514	5,399,452

[1] References are given in Appendix B. For the special situation between 1910 and 1934 inclusive, see Appendix G, Notes 2-4. Since there has been no national curriculum survey since 1948-49, regional enrollments since then are not available. Total enrollment in 1954-55 is an estimate (see *School Life*, May 1955).

[2] States in each region are as follows—
NE (New England): Connecticut, Maine, Massachusetts, New Hampshire, Rhode Island, and Vermont.
MA (Middle Atlantic): Delaware, District of Columbia, Maryland, New Jersey, New York, and Pennsylvania. In the Commissioners' Reports the last three states were grouped with the New England States to form a North Atlantic Division. The first three states were grouped with the states in SA, to form a South Atlantic Division. The re-grouping used here conforms to the regional scholastic associations to which the schools in all these states belong.
SA (South Atlantic): Florida, Georgia, North and South Carolina, Virginia, and West Virginia.
ESC (East South Central): Alabama, Kentucky, Mississippi, and Tennessee. These states and those in WSC formed a South Central Division in the Commissioners' Reports. The grouping used here and below follows the regional boundaries of the Census Bureau.
WSC (West South Central): Arkansas, Louisiana, Oklahoma, and Texas.
ENC (East North Central): Illinois, Indiana, Michigan, Ohio, and Wisconsin. These states were combined, in the Commissioners' Reports, with those in WNC, to form a North Central Division.
WNC (West North Central): Iowa, Kansas, Minnesota, Missouri, Nebraska, North and South Dakota.
MT (Mountain): Arizona, Colorado, Idaho, Montana, Nevada, New Mexico, Utah, and Wyoming. These states were formerly included with those listed in PAC, to form a Western Division.
PAC (Pacific): California, Oregon, Washington.

have some relationship with the order of rank based on college majors in these fields. The high school graduates of 1948-49 would theoretically have finished college in 1952-53. Table 35 is for 1953-54 college graduates, but it may afford some interesting comparisons— and speculations.

TABLE 31 [1]

PERCENTAGE OF HIGH SCHOOL STUDENTS GRADES 9-12 ENROLLED IN SCIENCE BY GEOGRAPHICAL REGION IN CERTAIN YEARS BETWEEN 1889-90 AND 1953-54

	NE	MA	SA	ESC	WSC	ENC	WNC	MT	PAC	US	LINE
Enrollment	3	2	5	8	6	1	4	9	7		(1890)
Physics	23.1 (6)	19.4 (9)	34.2 (2)	21.6 (7)	43.4 (1)	21.2 (8)	24.6 (4)	28.5 (3)	24.0 (5)	22.8	1
Chem.	13.9 (3)	8.0 (8)	9.4 (6)	5.0 (9)	14.0 (2)	9.1 (7)	10.1 (4)	9.9 (5)	17.8 (1)	10.1	2
TOT.(2)[2]	37.0 (5)	27.4 (8)	43.6 (2)	26.6 (9)	57.4 (1)	30.3 (7)	34.7 (6)	38.4 (4)	41.8 (3)	32.9	5
Enrollment	4	2	7	6	5	1	3	9	8		(1900)
Physics	19.1 (7)	18.0 (8)	20.0 (4)	23.8 (2)	26.4 (1)	17.4 (9)	20.2 (3)	19.4 (5)	19.2 (6)	19.0	1
Chem.	11.1 (3)	6.8 (7)	8.0 (4)	6.2 (9)	6.6 (8)	7.0 (5)	6.9 (6)	12.6 (1)	11.6 (2)	7.7	2
TOT.(2)[2]	30.2 (4)	24.8 (8)	28.0 (6)	30.0 (5)	33.0 (1)	24.4 (9)	27.1 (7)	32.0 (2)	30.8 (3)	26.7	5
OTH.SCI.[3]	36.8 (8)	58.9 (4)	75.5 (3)	79.9 (2)	94.8 (1)	58.1 (5)	56.8 (6)	47.0 (7)	31.7 (9)	57.2	6
Enrollment	4	2	7	8	6	1	3	9	5		(1910)
Physics	16.2 (3)	14.3 (5)	14.5 (4)	18.2 (1)	17.5 (2)	14.4 (6)	14.2 (7)	14.3 (5)	11.1 (8)	14.6	1
Chem.	8.7 (1)	7.8 (3)	5.4 (7)	4.1 (9)	5.0 (8)	6.5 (6)	6.0 (5)	8.0 (2)	7.7 (4)	6.9	2
Biol.	0.2 (4)	3.6 (1)	0.2 (6)	0.6 (3)	0.0 (9)	0.2 (5)	0.1 (4)	0.8 (2)	0.6 (2)	1.1	3
TOT.(3)[2]	25.1 (2)	25.7 (1)	20.1 (8)	22.9 (4)	22.5 (5)	21.1 (6)	20.3 (7)	23.1 (3)	19.4 (9)	22.6	5
OTH.SCI.[3]	30.5 (9)	66.4 (5)	77.7 (1)	68.1 (3)	76.1 (2)	66.9 (4)	54.7 (6)	51.2 (7)	35.0 (8)	59.0	6
Enrollment	5	2	7	8	6	1	3	9	4		(1922)
Physics	8.8 (3)	8.8 (3)	7.1 (5)	9.4 (2)	7.6 (4)	9.4 (2)	11.0 (1)	7.0 (6)	7.1 (5)	8.9	1
Chem.	8.7 (2)	8.3 (3)	8.2 (4)	7.5 (6)	6.2 (8)	7.2 (7)	4.9 (9)	7.9 (5)	9.3 (1)	7.4	2
Biol.	5.8 (6)	18.6 (1)	9.9 (3)	12.8 (2)	4.3 (8)	5.5 (7)	3.3 (9)	7.6 (4)	6.9 (5)	8.8	3
Gen. Sci.	19.5 (3)	16.8 (7)	24.5 (1)	19.3 (4)	12.6 (9)	19.7 (5)	17.9 (8)	19.2 (6)	16.6 (7)	18.3	4
TOT.(4)[2]	42.8 (4)	52.5 (1)	49.7 (2)	49.0 (3)	30.7 (9)	41.8 (5)	37.1 (8)	41.7 (6)	39.9 (7)	43.4	5
OTH.SCI.[3]	6.6 (9)	7.9 (8)	14.4 (5)	17.6 (4)	27.2 (1)	20.8 (2)	18.4 (3)	10.9 (6)	8.8 (7)	14.9	6

[1] The numbers under the regions rank them by size of high school enrollments. There were six shifts in 1900, three in 1910, two in 1922 and in 1934, and none in 1949. For the

	NE	MA	SA	ESC	WSC	ENC	WNC	MT	PAC	US	LINE
Enrollment	5	1	7	8	6	2	3	9	4		(1934)
Physics	7.5 (2)	5.6 (5)	4.6 (8)	5.2 (6)	4.1 (9)	7.4 (3)	8.2 (1)	6.1 (4)	5.0 (7)	6.3	1
Chem.	10.2 (1)	7.0 (7)	7.8 (6)	8.1 (4)	6.2 (8)	8.0 (5)	5.5 (9)	9.5 (2)	8.3 (3)	7.6	2
Biol.	12.9 (8)	12.6 (9)	20.9 (1)	16.7 (2)	13.9 (6)	15.0 (5)	15.6 (4)	15.7 (3)	13.5 (7)	14.6	3
Gen. Sci.	18.5 (4)	17.9 (5)	23.3 (1)	19.7 (2)	18.9 (3)	16.9 (6)	18.9 (3)	14.3 (7)	12.8 (8)	17.8	4
TOT.(4)²	49.1 (3)	43.1 (7)	56.6 (1)	49.7 (2)	43.1 (7)	47.3 (5)	48.2 (4)	45.6 (6)	39.6 (8)	46.3	5
OTH.SCI.³	3.8 (8)	1.8 (9)	4.1 (7)	5.6 (5)	7.4 (2)	7.8 (1)	5.9 (4)	6.8 (3)	4.6 (6)	5.1	6
Enrollment	5	1	7	8	6	2	3	9	4		(1949)
Physics	7.4 (1)	7.1 (2)	3.8 (8)	3.9 (7)	2.5 (9)	6.2 (3)	5.8 (4)	4.9 (5)	4.2 (6)	5.4	1
Chem.	10.0 (1)	9.1 (2)	7.8 (5)	7.1 (6)	5.4 (9)	7.9 (4)	5.7 (8)	8.2 (3)	6.7 (7)	7.6	2
Biol.	16.6 (8)	17.2 (6)	22.5 (1)	18.9 (4)	16.8 (7)	19.4 (2)	17.9 (5)	19.0 (3)	17.2 (6)	18.4	3
Gen. Sci.	20.1 (6)	26.6 (1)	21.9 (3)	22.7 (2)	20.8 (5)	16.9 (7)	21.3 (4)	14.5 (9)	15.3 (8)	20.8	4
TOT.(4)²	54.1 (3)	60.0 (1)	56.0 (2)	52.6 (4)	45.5 (8)	50.4 (6)	50.7 (5)	46.6 (7)	43.4 (9)	52.2	5
OTH.SCI.³	2.2 (3)	1.7 (6)	0.5 (9)	1.2 (8)	1.4 (7)	1.9 (5)	2.0 (4)	3.1 (2)	3.8 (1)	1.9	6
											(1954⁴)
Physics	6.8 (1)	5.8 (3)	3.3 (7)	5.3 (4)	4.4 (6)	6.3 (2)	4.5 (5)	5.3 (4)	2.9 (8)	5.1	1
Chem.	9.4 (3)	9.6 (1)	6.5 (6)	7.9 (4)	9.5 (2)	6.9 (5)	5.1 (7)	9.4 (3)	5.0 (8)	7.1	2
Biol.	14.3 (9)	25.2 (3)	20.2 (6)	17.2 (7)	26.4 (1)	21.4 (5)	15.0 (8)	26.1 (2)	25.0 (4)	21.2	3
Gen. Sci.	13.0 (8)	16.4 (5)	15.5 (7)	27.9 (1)	17.1 (4)	25.9 (2)	19.9 (3)	11.9 (9)	16.3 (6)	19.8	4
TOT(4)	44.4 (8)	56.8 (4)	45.5 (7)	58.3 (2)	57.4 (3)	60.5 (1)	44.5 (7)	52.7 (5)	49.2 (6)	53.2	5

special situation in 1954, see Note 4 below. The numbers under the percentages rank the regions by subject-percentage size. Regions with the same percentage are given the same rank. The sequence of size, from largest to smallest, begins with number 1.

² Since the subject enrollments in each region are divided by the same high school enrollment, the percentages may be added. The resulting total percentage represents the equivalent of that many students enrolled in science, by region, and for the whole country, in a given year. Multiple enrollments—students enrolled in more than one course—could not be determined. In 1890 only two science subjects, physics and chemistry, were listed. The percentages in lines 5 and 6 were therefore the same. Biology was first listed in 1910, general science, in 1922. These four science subjects received individual treatment because after 1910 they were the four principal subjects in science.

[3] For all science subjects listed, see Ch. IV, Table 3. It will be noted that the total percentages in that table are the same in a given year as those for the US given in Line 6 of this table.

[4] The percentages for 1954 are based on data collected by the writer in the spring of that year, on the subjects listed. Although the total percentages in Line 5 give the sum of the percentages in Lines 1-4, in all conscience the additions should not have been made, and may, in good conscience, be disregarded. The reason is the writer's own fault. He admits the culpable attempt of trying to use all of the usable figures he received.

One example will illustrate the kind of problem he faced and the statistical depths to which he descended to solve it. The school systems (not individual schools) from the Pacific Region that reported physics and chemistry had a total enrollment of 80,575 students. Of these, 2,364 studied physics and 4,057, chemistry. The systems that reported biology, however, had a total enrollment of 2,266 students, of whom 566 were enrolled in biology. The latter constituted 24.97% of all students enrolled in the systems that reported the subject, but only 0.7% of enrollments in the systems that reported physics and chemistry. Although 25% was undoubtedly too large for biology enrollments throughout the region, it was most certainly more nearly accurate than 0.7%. Of the rather frequent variations of this sort, the most glaring, as it happens, were in biology and general science. Since the same reasoning was followed in each case, many of the percentages for the four subjects are based on different enrollments in the same region, and consequently should not be added.

A comparison of individual regional percentages with those in 1949 indicates that some of those in 1954 are undoubtedly inaccurate. In 1955 the US percentage for physics was 4.6%; for chemistry, 7.3%; for biology, 19.6% (*Pamphlet No. 118*, 1956, Table 2). The corresponding US percentages for 1954 may be slightly inaccurate, but they fit fairly well into the general trend between 1949 and 1955. Statistics on general science were not gathered in 1955.

The writer wishes to acknowledge with gratitude help given by the staff of the College of General Studies in sending out the questionnaires for his survey and in tabulating the data from it. His special thanks go to Mrs. Carroll Quigley and Mr. Walter H. Hayes, Jr.

A comparison of Table 35 (total) with Table 34 (1949) shows a definite correlation in mathematics and science and, to a slightly less degree, in foreign languages. In mathematics WSC, ESC, and SA ranked 1, 2, and 3 respectively in Table 34. In Table 35 ESC ranked first, WSC and SA tied for second. In 1949 MA and NE ranked 5 and 6; in 1954, both were in the first five. MT, which ranked 4 in 1949, ranked 8 in 1954.

In science the order of the first four in 1949 was MA, SA, NE, and ESC; in 1954 the order was NE, MA, ESC, and SA. The order of the next two in 1949, WNC and ENC, was reversed in 1954.

In 1954 MA nosed out NE in foreign languages, although in 1949 NE led by a small margin. PAC, which came third in 1949, was next to the bottom in 1954; MT slipped from 4 to 5; ENC went from 5 to 3, and SA from 6 to 4.

Among individual subjects correlation between two corresponding tables, 32 (1949) and 35 (1954), varied considerably. In 1949 the first five regions in algebra, for example, were WSC, ESC, SA, MT, and NE; in 1954 they were ESC, WSC and SA (tied in second place), NE, MA, and WNC (tied in third). In geometry the first five in 1949 were WSC, MT, MA, ESC, and ENC; in 1954, ENC and MT were 7 and 8; SA, NE, and WNC, which were among the first six, in 1949 were

TABLE 32 [1]

PERCENTAGE OF HIGH SCHOOL STUDENTS GRADES 9-12 ENROLLED
IN MATHEMATICS BY GEOGRAPHICAL REGION IN CERTAIN
YEARS BETWEEN 1889-90 AND 1953-54

	NE	MA	SA	ESC	WSC	ENC	WNC	MT	PAC	US	LINE
Enrollment	3	2	5	8	6	1	4	9	7		(1890)
Algebra	41.4	40.5	66.5	47.5	74.3	44.8	46.7	47.0	62.8	45.4	1
	8	9	2	4	1	7	6	5	3		
Geometry	18.3	21.5	26.7	15.8	33.7	20.7	21.0	19.1	39.3	21.3	2
	8	4	3	9	2	6	5	7	1		
TOT.(2)	59.7	62.0	93.2	63.3	108.0	65.5	67.7	66.1	102.2	66.7	5
	9	8	3	7	1	6	4	5	2		
Enrollment	4	2	7	6	5	1	3	9	8		(1900)
Algebra	48.6	52.6	74.5	68.9	74.5	53.7	58.5	61.7	62.1	56.3	1
	8	7	1	2	1	6	5	4	3		
Geometry	29.5	26.2	25.3	27.2	34.9	24.8	28.2	35.0	35.1	27.4	2
	4	7	8	6	3	9	5	2	1		
Trig.	1.2	2.4	3.7	4.9	4.7	1.3	1.0	3.7	2.5	1.9	3
	7	5	3	1	2	6	8	3	4		
TOT.(3)	79.3	81.2	103.5	101.0	114.1	79.8	87.7	100.4	99.7	85.6	5
	9	7	2	3	1	8	6	4	5		
Enrollment	4	2	7	8	6	1	3	9	5		(1910)
Algebra	47.7	54.9	81.0	71.9	76.0	52.1	61.1	57.2	48.7	56.9	1
	9	6	1	3	2	7	4	5	8		
Geometry	31.5	30.7	25.1	28.1	31.2	33.0	31.0	32.7	26.4	30.9	2
	3	6	9	7	4	1	5	2	8		
Trig.	1.5	2.5	2.5	3.1	2.4	1.2	1.3	2.2	2.2	1.9	3
	5	2	2	1	3	7	6	4	4		
TOT.(3)	80.7	88.1	108.6	103.1	109.6	86.3	93.4	92.1	77.3	89.7	5
	8	6	2	3	1	7	4	5	9		
Enrollment	5	2	7	8	6	1	3	9	4		(1922)
Algebra	31.4	40.9	53.1	52.0	50.8	39.3	36.4	34.2	34.8	40.2	1
	9	4	1	2	3	5	6	8	7		
Geometry	19.0	21.2	21.3	24.5	23.1	24.1	26.1	22.5	19.5	22.7	2
	9	7	6	2	4	3	1	5	8		
Trig.	1.6	2.1	1.2	1.2	1.9	0.9	0.7	1.2	3.4	1.5	3
	4	2	5	5	3	6	7	5	1		
Gen.Math.[2]	13.2	8.5	20.6	17.2	10.7	9.9	8.5	7.8	9.2	10.5	4
	3	7	1	2	4	5	7	8	6		
TOT.(4)	65.2	72.7	96.2	94.9	86.5	74.2	71.7	65.7	66.9	74.9	5
	9	5	1	2	3	4	6	8	7		

[1] For references, see Appendix B and Note 1 to Table 30. Line 3 is not needed until 1900 and Line 4 until 1922; Line 6 is not needed at all because in every year except 1948-49 all subjects in mathematics are included. In that year several subjects are listed, registrations in which equalled 0.3% of the total high school enrollment. The US percentages, except for that year and for 1953-54, are the same as those given in Chapter IV, Table 1.

[2] This term was not used until 1928. In that year and in 1933-34 separate statistics were also given for arithmetic, which alone was listed in 1922. In 1948-49 enrollments in both subjects were combined under general mathematics. In the summary table (No. 7) for 1948-

	NE	MA	SA	ESC	WSC	ENC	WNC	MT	PÁC	US	LINE
Enrollment	5	1	7	8	6	2	3	9	4		(1934)
Algebra	25.48	27.56	46.51	46.42	43.13	28.05	29.84	27.37	21.69	30.4	1
Geometry	13.79	14.38	16.66	21.92	22.01	18.15	19.54	20.05	14.47	17.1	2
Trig.	1.82	2.01	0.78	1.16	1.63	0.97	0.78	1.25	1.54	1.3	3
Gen.Math.	9.23	4.78	19.91	9.14	10.62	6.37	6.76	4.69	7.15	7.4	4
TOT.(4)	50.17	48.58	83.71	78.52	77.33	53.35	56.74	53.16	44.6C	56.2	5
Enrollment	5	1	7	8	6	2	3	8	4		(1949)
Algebra	25.85	24.96	34.03	36.02	36.31	22.88	24.67	26.64	18.99	26.8	1
Geometry	12.96	13.53	10.19	13.24	15.71	13.15	12.57	14.32	10.78	12.8	2
Trig.	2.62	3.51	1.17	1.17	1.36	1.93	1.45	1.74	1.74	2.0	3
Gen.Math.	11.48	12.05	18.21	13.73	12.14	11.29	11.86	11.57	16.72	13.1	4
TOT.(4)	52.76	53.95	63.43	64.02	65.41	49.08	50.37	54.14	48.09	54.7	5
											(1954[3])
Algebra	18.38	18.97	22.94	30.72	36.11	24.23	19.46	19.85	17.29	21.4	1
Geometry	13.04	13.83	11.76	10.97	11.85	15.41	10.48	13.92	9.69	12.7	2
Trig.	2.92	2.04	1.75	1.07	2.23	1.46	0.79	3.51	0.98	1.5	3
Gen.Math.	11.27	16.33	20.82	15.94	11.55	7.58	26.01	6.19	11.46	14.5	4
TOT.(4)	45.47	51.05	57.13	58.52	61.61	48.56	56.54	43.38	39.19	50.1	5

49, the total US enrollment in general mathematics for 1922 is given as 266,918, and the US percentage as 12.4. In BS 1920-22, II, p. 593 (Table 33), the total enrollment for arithmetic is 226,918, and the US percentage 10.5. This figure and the correct percentage were repeated in BS 1926-28, p. 1058 (Table 59). In *Bulletin 1938, No. 6*, Table 1, however, the number is given as 266,918, but with the same percentage—10.5. In BS 1948-50, Ch. 5, Table 7, the new figure was apparently used as the basis for changing the percentage to 12.4.

[8] The writer's survey. As in science for 1953-54, many of the regional percentages are undoubtedly inaccurate. Since they also were based on different high school enrollments (see Note 4 to Table 31 above), the total percentages may be disregarded. Among the US percentages, algebra and trigonometry are quite certainly too low, geometry, too high; general mathematics is reasonably accurate.

In 1952-53 the percentages were: algebra, 24.6; geometry, 11.6; trigonometry, 1.7, and general mathematics, 15.0 (*Bulletin 1953, No. 5*, Table 49). In 1954-55, comparable percentages were 24.8, 11.4, and 2.6 (*Pamphlet No. 118, 1956*, Table 11). On the basis of statistics in *School Life* (June 1956), p. 6, the percentage for general mathematics (not included in *Pamphlet No. 118*) was 12.7. Comparable regional percentages were not given in either of the two special studies, and the figures from which they might have been obtained could not be combined to produce them.

TABLE 33 [1]

PERCENTAGE OF HIGH SCHOOL STUDENTS GRADES 9-12 ENROLLED IN FOREIGN LANGUAGES BY GEOGRAPHICAL REGION IN CERTAIN YEARS BETWEEN 1889-90 AND 1954-55

	NE	MA	SA	ESC	WSC	ENC	WNC	MT	PAC	US	LINE
Enrollment	3	2	5	8	6	1	4	9	7		(1890)
Latin	44.8	28.1	58.0	54.4	32.9	33.3	33.5	16.2	32.1	35.1	1
	3	8	1	2	6	5	4	9	7		
French	22.3	2.2	13.8	0.7	6.3	1.6	1.8	0.0	2.8	5.8	2
	1	5	2	8	3	7	6	9	4		
German	5.8	13.8	14.9	11.0	8.2	11.9	8.9	3.1	6.2	10.5	3
	8	2	1	4	6	3	5	9	7		
Greek	8.6	2.8	3.4	1.9	4.4	1.4	1.0	0.0	2.6	3.1	4
	1	4	3	6	2	7	8	9	5		
TOT.(4)	81.5	46.9	90.1	68.0	51.8	48.2	45.2	19.3	43.7	54.5	6
	2	6	1	3	4	5	7	9	8		
Enrollment	4	2	7	6	5	1	3	9	8		(1900)
Latin	48.1	48.0	65.5	56.5	56.4	47.3	54.9	59.0	49.1	50.6	1
	7	8	1	3	4	9	5	2	6		
French	31.5	8.3	7.8	2.5	6.3	2.6	1.8	7.0	5.7	7.8	2
	1	2	3	7	5	8	9	4	6		
German	10.3	22.3	5.4	6.2	3.7	15.5	11.6	19.4	9.4	14.3	3
	5	1	8	7	9	3	4	2	6		
Greek	9.1	3.9	2.1	2.9	0.8	1.2	0.9	2.3	2.4	2.9	4
	1	2	6	3	9	7	8	5	4		
TOT.(4)	99.0	82.5	80.8	68.1	67.2	66.6	69.2	87.7	66.6	75.6	6
	1	3	4	6	7	8	5	2	8		
Enrollment	4	2	7	8	6	1	3	9	5		(1910)
Latin	38.9	50.3	73.4	67.0	60.4	45.4	51.0	46.7	36.5	49.0	1
	8	5	1	2	3	7	4	6	9		
French	42.0	12.2	6.2	5.5	2.9	2.4	2.2	3.6	8.0	9.9	2
	1	2	4	5	7	8	9	6	3		
German	18.5	36.3	7.3	11.9	7.8	24.7	20.3	24.9	18.3	23.7	3
	5	1	9	7	8	3	4	2	6		
Greek	2.9	0.7	1.0	0.9	0.2	0.3	0.3	0.3	0.5	0.7	4
	1	4	2	3	7	6	6	6	5		
Spanish	0.2	0.1	0.1	0.0	1.9	0.1	0.5	2.6	5.2	0.7	5
	5	6	6	7	3	6	4	2	1		
TOT.(5)	102.5	99.6	88.0	85.3	73.2	72.9	74.3	78.1	68.5	84.0	6
	1	2	3	4	7	8	6	5	9		
Enrollment	5	2	7	8	6	1	3	9	4		(1922)
Latin	25.3	31.6	41.8	35.4	25.2	28.6	23.8	17.8	15.2	27.5	1
	5	3	1	2	6	4	7	8	9		
French	38.3	24.6	18.1	10.3	5.1	11.6	6.4	6.3	10.5	15.5	2
	1	2	3	6	9	4	7	8	5		

[1] References, except for 1955, are found in Appendix B. Although Greek and several other languages were listed in scattered sections of the country in 1922 and later, the small number of registrants made it impractical to calculate regional percentages. In 1948-49 the addition of Italian and general language would increase the US percentage to 22.0. See Chapter V, Table 2.

	NE	MA	SA	ESC	WSC	ENC	WNC	MT	PAC	US	LINE
German	2.3 (1)	1.3 (2)	0.05 (6)	0.1 (5)	0.04 (7)	0.5 (3)	0.2 (4)	0.1 (5)	0.02 (8)	0.6	3
Greek	0.4 (1)	0.2 (2)	0.05 (3)	0.0 (6)	0.0 (6)	0.03 (4)	0.03 (4)	0.02 (5)	0.0 (6)	0.09	4
Spanish	8.9 (5)	16.2 (4)	6.0 (7)	5.3 (8)	19.7 (2)	6.5 (6)	5.0 (9)	17.2 (3)	22.9 (1)	11.3	5
TOT.(5)	75.2 (1)	73.9 (2)	66.0 (3)	51.1 (4)	50.0 (5)	47.2 (7)	35.4 (9)	41.4 (8)	48.6 (6)	55.0	6
Enrollment	5	1	7	8	6	2	3	9	4		(1934)
Latin	20.5 (1)	18.6 (2)	17.7 (4)	16.2 (5)	10.0 (8)	18.0 (3)	13.1 (6)	11.7 (7)	9.4 (9)	16.0	1
French	30.9 (1)	15.2 (3)	16.2 (2)	9.7 (4)	3.2 (8)	7.8 (6)	3.3 (7)	3.1 (9)	8.0 (5)	10.9	2
German	2.8 (3)	3.3 (2)	0.1 (8)	0.1 (8)	0.3 (7)	3.4 (1)	2.0 (5)	0.5 (6)	2.3 (4)	2.4	3
Spanish	4.0 (5)	3.5 (8)	4.6 (4)	3.7 (7)	17.8 (1)	3.9 (6)	2.5 (9)	16.4 (2)	16.1 (3)	6.2	4
TOT.(4)	58.2 (1)	40.6 (2)	38.6 (3)	29.7 (8)	31.3 (7)	33.1 (5)	20.9 (9)	31.7 (6)	35.8 (4)	35.5	6
Enrollment	5	1	7	8	6	2	3	9	4		(1949)
Latin	15.0 (1)	10.9 (2)	6.4 (4)	5.2 (7)	2.3 (9)	9.7 (3)	4.7 (8)	5.5 (5)	5.4 (6)	7.8	1
French	17.3 (1)	8.9 (2)	6.6 (3)	1.5 (6)	1.0 (8)	2.4 (5)	0.7 (9)	1.1 (7)	2.6 (4)	4.7	2
German	1.2 (2)	1.9 (1)	0.0 (9)	0.03 (7)	0.02 (8)	1.0 (3)	0.4 (5)	0.2 (6)	0.6 (4)	0.8	3
Spanish	6.8 (5)	11.0 (3)	4.9 (7)	3.8 (8)	8.4 (4)	6.7 (6)	3.7 (9)	14.0 (2)	15.7 (1)	8.2	4
TOT.(4)	40.3 (1)	32.7 (2)	17.9 (6)	10.5 (8)	11.7 (7)	19.8 (5)	9.5 (9)	20.8 (4)	34.3 (3)	21.5	5
											(1955²)
Latin	14.1 (1)	11.9 (2)	5.6 (4)	3.2 (7)	2.3 (9)	8.9 (3)	2.4 (8)	4.2 (6)	4.8 (5)	6.9	1
French	17.1 (1)	11.6 (2)	6.5 (3)	1.1 (7)	0.8 (8)	2.4 (5)	0.5 (9)	1.4 (6)	3.5 (4)	5.6	2
German	1.3 (2)	2.2 (1)	0.01 (6)	0.0 (7)	0.04 (5)	0.8 (3)	0.4 (4)	0.4 (4)	0.8 (3)	0.8	3
Spanish	5.8 (4)	12.3 (2)	4.3 (5)	2.3 (8)	2.7 (7)	4.4 (5)	2.1 (9)	10.6 (3)	15.5 (1)	7.3	4
TOT.(4)	38.3 (1)	38.0 (2)	16.4 (6)	6.6 (7)	5.8 (8)	16.5 (5)	5.4 (9)	16.6 (4)	24.6 (3)	20.6	5

²PMLA LXX 4 2 (September 1955), 52-56. Enrollment figures in each language were collected in a national survey made by the Modern Language Association of America. In the reference cited the figures were given by states. The writer obtained the total high school enrollment figures from the Modern Language Association, grouped both sets of state figures into regions and calculated the regional percentages. Although the survey covered primarily the year 1954-55, data from a few states were not obtained for that year, and were replaced

by the most recent data available. The total enrollment in the schools covered by the survey was approximately 4,521,000. Since the different regions varied in completeness, regional enrollments are not given. Some of the regional percentages are therefore only approximate, but they are undoubtdly close to the actual situation.

TABLE 34: SUMMARY [1]

TOTAL PERCENTAGE OF HIGH SCHOOL STUDENTS GRADES 9-12 ENROLLED IN SCIENCE, MATHEMATICS, AND FOREIGN LANGUAGES BY GEOGRAPHICAL REGION IN CERTAIN YEARS BETWEEN 1889-90 AND 1954-55

	NE	MA	SA	ESC	WSC	ENC	WNC	MT	PAC	U.S.
Enrollment	3	2	5	8	6	1	4	9	7	(1890)
Science	37.0(5)	27.4(8)	43.6(2)	26.6(9)	57.4(1)	30.3(7)	34.7(6)	38.4(4)	41.8(3)	32.9
Math.	59.7(9)	62.0(8)	93.2(3)	63.3(7)	108.0(1)	65.5(6)	67.7(4)	66.1(5)	102.2(2)	66.7
For.Lang.	81.5(2)	46.9(6)	90.1(1)	68.0(3)	51.8(4)	48.2(5)	45.2(7)	19.3(9)	43.7(8)	54.5
TOTAL	178.2(4)	136.3(8)	226.9(1)	157.9(5)	217.2(2)	144.0(7)	147.6(6)	123.8(9)	187.7(3)	154.1
Enrollment	4	2	7	6	5	1	3	9	8	(1900)
Science	67.0(8)	83.7(5)	103.5(3)	109.9(2)	127.8(1)	82.5(6)	83.9(4)	79.0(7)	62.5(9)	83.9
Math.	79.3(9)	81.2(7)	103.5(2)	101.0(3)	114.1(1)	79.8(8)	87.7(6)	100.4(4)	99.7(5)	85.6
For.Lang.	99.0(1)	82.5(3)	80.8(4)	68.1(6)	67.2(7)	66.6(8)	69.2(5)	87.7(2)	66.6(8)	75.6
TOTAL	245.3(6)	247.4(5)	287.8(2)	279.0(3)	309.1(1)	228.9(8)	240.8(7)	267.1(4)	228.8(9)	245.1
Enrollment	4	2	7	8	6	1	3	9	5	(1910)
Science	55.6(8)	92.1(3)	97.8(2)	91.0(4)	98.6(1)	88.0(5)	75.0(6)	74.3(7)	54.4(9)	81.6
Math.	80.7(8)	88.1(6)	108.6(2)	103.1(3)	109.6(1)	86.3(7)	93.4(4)	92.1(5)	77.3(9)	89.7
FOR.Lang.	102.5(1)	99.6(2)	88.0(3)	85.3(4)	73.2(7)	72.9(8)	74.3(6)	78.1(5)	68.5(9)	84.0
TOTAL	238.8(8)	279.8(3)	294.4(1)	279.4(4)	281.4(2)	247.2(5)	242.7(7)	244.5(6)	200.2(9)	255.3
Enrollment	5	2	7	8	6	1	3	9	4	(1922)
Science	49.4(8)	60.4(4)	64.1(2)	66.6(1)	57.9(5)	62.6(3)	55.5(6)	52.6(7)	48.7(9)	58.3
Math.	65.2(9)	72.7(5)	96.2(1)	94.9(2)	86.5(3)	74.2(4)	71.7(6)	65.7(8)	66.9(7)	74.9
For.Lang.	75.2(1)	73.9(2)	66.0(3)	51.1(4)	50.0(5)	47.2(7)	35.4(9)	41.4(8)	48.6(6)	55.0
TOTAL	189.8(5)	207.0(3)	226.3(1)	212.6(2)	194.4(4)	184.0(6)	162.6(8)	159.7(9)	164.2(7)	188.2

Enrollment	5	1	7	8	6	2	3	9	4	(1934)
Science	52.9 (5)	44.9 (8)	**60.7 (1)**	55.3 (2)	50.5 (7)	55.1 (3)	54.1 (4)	51.8 (6)	44.2 (9)	51.4
Math.	50.1 (7)	48.5 (8)	**83.7 (1)**	78.5 (2)	77.3 (3)	53.3 (5)	56.7 (4)	53.1 (6)	44.6 (9)	56.2
For.Lang.	**58.2 (1)**	40.6 (2)	38.6 (3)	29.7 (8)	31.3 (7)	33.1 (5)	20.9 (9)	31.7 (6)	35.8 (4)	35.5
TOTAL	161.2 (3)	134.0 (7)	**183.0 (1)**	163.5 (2)	159.1 (4)	141.5 (5)	131.7 (8)	136.6 (6)	124.6 (9)	143.1

Enrollment	5	1	7	8	6	2	3	9	4	(1949)
Science	56.3 (3)	**61.7 (1)**	56.5 (2)	53.8 (4)	46.9 (9)	52.3 (6)	52.7 (5)	49.7 (7)	47.2 (8)	54.1
Math.	52.7 (6)	53.9 (5)	63.4 (3)	64.0 (2)	**65.4 (1)**	49.0 (8)	50.3 (7)	54.1 (4)	48.0 (9)	54.7
For.Lang.	**40.3 (1)**	32.7 (2)	17.9 (6)	10.5 (8)	11.7 (7)	19.8 (5)	9.5 (9)	20.8 (4)	24.3 (3)	21.5
TOTAL	**149.3 (1)**	148.3 (2)	137.8 (3)	128.3 (4)	124.0 (6)	121.1 (7)	112.5 (9)	124.6 (5)	119.5 (8)	130.3

	5	1	7	8	6	2	3	9	4	(1954[2])
Science	44.4 (9)	56.8 (4)	45.5 (7)	58.3 (2)	57.4 (3)	**60.5 (1)**	44.5 (8)	52.7 (5)	49.2 (6)	53.2

	5	1	7	8	6	2	3	9	4	(1954[2])
Math.	45.4 (7)	51.0 (5)	57.1 (3)	58.5 (2)	**61.6 (1)**	48.5 (6)	56.5 (4)	43.3 (8)	39.1 (9)	50.1

	5	1	7	8	6	2	3	9	4	(1955[3])
For.Lang.	**38.3 (1)**	38.0 (2)	16.4 (6)	6.6 (7)	5.8 (8)	16.5 (5)	5.4 (9)	16.6 (4)	24.6 (3)	20.6
TOTAL	128.1 (2)	**145.8 (1)**	119.0 (6)	123.4 (5)	124.8 (4)	125.5 (3)	106.4 (9)	112.6 (8)	112.9 (7)	123.9

9, 6, and 7 respectively. There was even less correlation in trigonometry. It is quite clear, therefore, that regional rankings based on all mathematics in high school are closer to the regional rankings in college than those in high school based on individual subjects. The same thing is true in science.

Table 35 [1]

PERCENTAGE OF COLLEGE GRADUATES WITH MAJORS IN MATHEMATICS, PHYSICS, CHEMISTRY, BIOLOGY, AND ONE OF FOUR FOREIGN LANGUAGES, BY REGION, IN 1953-54

TOTAL

	Math.	Physics	Chem.	Biol.	TOT(3)	Latin	French	Spanish	German	TOT(4)
NE (25319)	1.5	1.1	2.3	2.6	6.0	0.26	0.85	0.32	0.17	1.60
MA (66633)	1.5	0.8	2.5	2.4	5.7	0.31	0.63	0.52	0.15	1.61
SA (28676)	1.6	0.4	2.1	2.3	4.8	0.09	0.55	0.39	0.04	1.07
ESC(18036)	1.8	0.5	2.4	2.6	5.5	0.11	0.18	0.37	0.05	0.71
WSC(27775)	1.6	0.6	1.5	1.6	3.7	0.13	0.19	0.43	0.05	0.80
ENC(56082)	1.3	0.7	1.8	1.8	4.3	0.27	0.36	0.40	0.14	1.17
WNC(26684)	1.5	0.5	1.8	1.8	4.1	0.19	0.24	0.28	0.15	0.86
MT (11776)	1.0	0.6	1.7	1.0	3.3	0.05	0.26	0.53	0.11	0.95
PAC(27747)	0.9	0.7	1.4	1.3	3.4	0.04	0.29	0.38	0.07	0.78
US (288728)	1.4	0.7	2.0	2.0	4.7	0.20	0.43	0.41	0.11	1.15

MEN

	Math.	Physics	Chem.	Biol.	TOT(3)	Latin	French	Spanish	German	TOT(4)
NE (16944)	1.5	1.5	2.5	3.0	7.0	0.24	0.24	0.12	0.13	0.73
MA (44191)	1.3	1.1	3.0	2.7	6.8	0.31	0.23	0.20	0.12	0.86
SA (16531)	1.5	0.7	2.8	2.5	6.0	0.06	0.27	0.20	0.04	0.57
ESC(10070)	2.0	0.79	3.7	3.0	7.49	0.10	0.14	0.14	0.07	0.35
WSC(17214)	1.9	0.9	2.0	1.9	4.8	0.18	0.10	0.20	0.05	0.53
ENC(36150)	1.5	0.97	2.3	1.8	5.07	0.31	0.10	0.18	0.12	0.71
WNC(17332)	1.8	0.80	2.3	2.0	5.1	0.22	0.09	0.16	0.13	0.60
MT (7941)	1.2	0.90	2.2	1.1	4.2	0.05	0.19	0.47	0.10	0.81
PAC(18061)	1.1	1.1	1.8	1.5	4.4	0.04	0.12	0.26	0.08	0.50
US (184434)	1.5	1.0	2.5	2.2	5.7	0.22	0.16	0.20	0.10	0.68

WOMEN

	Math.	Physics	Chem.	Biol.	TOT(3)	Latin	French	Spanish	German	TOT(4)
NE (8375)	1.6	0.12	1.7	1.8	3.62	0.30	2.10	0.72	0.24	3.36
MA (22442)	1.8	0.12	1.4	1.8	3.32	0.29	1.40	1.10	0.20	2.99
SA (12145)	1.7	0.03	1.1	2.0	3.13	0.12	0.93	0.64	0.05	1.74
ESC(7966)	1.5	0.04	0.82	2.0	2.86	0.04	0.44	0.67	0.03	1.18
WSC(10561)	1.1	0.03	0.59	1.2	1.82	0.05	0.34	0.80	0.06	1.25
ENC(19932)	0.99	0.09	0.93	1.7	2.72	0.21	0.82	0.80	0.17	2.00
WNC(9352)	0.97	0.05	0.75	1.4	2.20	0.15	0.52	0.49	0.18	1.64
MT (3835)	0.52	0.05	0.50	0.65	1.20	0.05	0.42	0.78	0.13	1.38
PAC(9686)	0.67	0.03	0.52	0.84	1.39	0.03	0.62	0.60	0.06	1.31
US (104294)	1.3	0.07	1.0	1.6	2.67	0.17	0.92	0.79	0.13	1.84

[1] All figures are taken from *Earned Degrees*, 1953-54; total number of first-level graduates, by sex, Table 10; subject enrollments, by sex, Table 11. Figures in Table 10 were given by state; those in Table 11, by individual colleges within each state. For the exceedingly tedious task of assembling the college figures by state and combining those of each state into the nine regions, the author wishes to thank his former assistant, Mrs. Carroll Quigley. The number of graduates—men, women, and total—is based on figures from the United States. In each of the three categories, therefore, the number is slightly smaller than the corresponding totals in Table 2 of the reference. The writer formed the graduates into regions and calculated the percentages. The total percentages for the United States are the same as those in Table 3 of the reference, rounded off to the nearest decimal.

In foreign languages the correlation is much closer in French and German than in Latin and Spanish. Again, however, the correlation between all languages in high school and college is closer than the correlation of individual subjects in each.

From this brief analysis it would seem reasonable to conclude that the high schools' total enrollment in each of these three cumulative subject-matter fields is a stronger factor in determining college majors in the three broad fields than the high schools' enrollment in individual subjects in the three fields.

It is interesting to note that in three of the regions, NE, MA, and SA in 1953-54, the proportion of majors in mathematics was larger for women than for men. This was not true in a single science or in total sciences, but the disparity between men and women was progressively less in chemistry and biology than in physics. In Latin the proportion of women was greater than that of men in all regions except in MA, ESC, ENC, WNC, and PAC. in MT it was the same for both. In French and Spanish the proportion of women was greater in each region, and in German, except in ESC and PAC. In all languages the percentage of women was far greater than that of men in each region.

In view of the teacher shortages in the cumulative subjects, it would be interesting to see if there is any correlation between such shortages and the regional rankings in these subjects. Comparable data on teachers unfortunately could not be obtained.

[1] This statement is based on the percentages in *Pamphlet No. 118*, 1956, Table 4. New England was a close second, with ESC and SA third and fourth, respectively. Table 13 of this reference shows that WSC is still in the lead in mathematics, with ESC, SA, and MA next in that sequence.

[2] The ranking in 1955 (Fall of 1954) was based on enrollment of students expressed as the percentage of students in the grade in which the course is usually offered. This may account for the increase in the number of exceptions.

DISTRIBUTION OF HIGH SCHOOL STUDENTS

Changes in the distribution of high school students involve several different factors. Among them are three of primary importance: increase of enrollments, progression from one grade to the next, and drop-out rates. Although the effects produced by each of the three cannot be separated, their results are plainly evident in Table 36.

TABLE 36

DISTRIBUTION OF STUDENTS BY GRADE IN PUBLIC HIGH SCHOOLS IN NUMBERS AND PERCENTAGES OF THE TOTAL HIGH SCHOOL ENROLLMENT IN CERTAIN YEARS BETWEEN 1889-90 and 1954-55

	1890[1]	1900[1]	1910[2]	1922[3]	1934[4]	1949[5]	1955[6]
Totals in 1000's	203	519	915	2230	5621	5399	6584
Grade 9 in 1000's	87	223	393	869	1827	1641	1998
" 9 percentage	43.0	43.0	42.9	39.0	32.5	30.4	30.3
" 10 in 1000's	53	135	248	608	1540	1491	1782
" 10 percentage	26.0	26.0	27.1	27.3	27.4	27.6	27.1
Percentage 9 minus 10	17.0	17.0	15.8	11.7	5.1	2.8	3.2
Grade 11 in 1000's	37	93	163	427	1231	1242	1500
" 11 percentage	18.0	18.0	17.8	19.1	21.9	22.9	22.8
Percentage 10 minus 11	8.0	8.0	9.3	8.2	5.5	4.7	4.3
Grade 12 in 1000's	26	68	111	326	1023	1026	1304
" 12 percentage	13.0	13.0	12.2	14.6	18.2	19.1	19.8
Percentage 11 minus 12	5.0	5.0	5.6	4.5	3.7	3.9	3.0
TOTAL PERCENTAGE	100.0	100.0	100.0	100.0	100.0	100.0	100.0

[1] In CR 1904-05, II, p. 822, the grade percentages for that year were calculated on the basis of grade enrollments in the high schools of a number of cities. This was the first instance found of such calculations. The writer applied these percentages to the total high school enrollment given in CR 1889-90, II, p. 1388, and in CR 1899-1900, II, p. 2129, for the grade enrollments shown in this table.

[2] CR 1909-10, II, p. 1130. These figures and percentages were based on reports from 10,213 public high schools. Subject enrollments and their percentage of the total high school enrollment, however, were based on reports from 8,097 high schools with a total enrollment

of 739,143—or 80.7% of the real total (pp. 1174-84).

³ BS 1920-22, II, pp. 534-35. These figures and percentages were based on reports from 14,056 public high schools. Subject enrollments and their percentage of the total high school enrollment were based on reports from 13,700 schools with a total enrollment of 2,155,460—or 96.6% of the total (pp. 580-601).

⁴ *Bulletin 1938, No. 6*, p. 9, Note 3, gives enrollments as follows: grade 9—1,461,367; grade 10—1,232,045; grade 11—984,737; grade 12—818,365; total—4,496,514, from 17,632 public high schools (p. 32). The reference also states that this was "nearly 80% of the total number of pupils attending high school." On the basis of this statement, corroborated in BS 1948-50, Ch. 5, pp. 5 and 27, this total enrollment was corrected for 80%, as given in the table. It was assumed that the grade distribution would be the same for the larger as for the smaller figure.

In BS 1932-34, Ch. 2, Table 2, enrollments reported by state systems were as follows: grade 9—1,855,026; grade 10—1,540,254; grade 11—1,209,180; grade 12—1,005,375; total—5,639,-835. In Ch. 5, Table 1, the number reported in 23,614 high schools was 5,340,563. Distribution by grades was not given in this table, but in Table E, as follows: grade 9—1,702,817; grade 10—1,435,636; grade 11—1,150,868; grade 12—956,011; total—5,245,322, from 17,-975 schools (p. 11). The grade percentages were exactly the same as those worked out for the enrollments given above from p. 9, which are used in this table.

⁵ BS 1948-50, Ch. 5, p. 6, Note 3. Percentages were calculated by the writer.

⁶ Grade percentages were calculated by the writer from grade enrollments estimated by Foster and Hobson in *School Life* (May 1955). See Note 11 below.

This table provides several interesting contrasts. As the figures for grade 9 increase, its percentage of the total enrollment decreases. As the figures for grades 11 and 12 increase, their percentages also increase. The figures for grade 10 increase, but its percentage remains remarkably constant.

The differences between the percentages of two consecutive grades go in a descending scale, which accelerates rapidly for grades 9 and 10 after 1922. After 1922 also, the differences between grades 10 and 11 are greater than those between grades 9 and 10. This would seem to suggest that the period for the largest percentage of drop-outs had changed from the period between grades 9-10 to that between grades 10-11. The broken sequence for some of the percentages between 1934 and 1955 is somewhat puzzling. When actual enrollments for 1954-55 become available, the numbers and therefore the percentages for that year may have slight changes, that will bring them more in line.¹

In 1889-90, as the table shows, there were approximately 26,000 students in grade 12. Of these about 22,000 graduated.² Those in grade 12 presumably entered high school in the fall of 1886, when enrollments in grade 9 were approximately 34,000.³ Four years later 76% of these had "survived" to grade 12 and approximately 65% to graduation. Approximately 85% of the seniors graduated.

These figures, by tracing the progress of students from grade 9 through grade 12, show the effects of promotion, failure, and drop-outs, in a way that could not be done in Table 36. The table below gives

additional statistics of this kind for thirteen four-year periods or quadrennia between 1890 and 1958.

TABLE 37 [1]

CONTINUATION RATES OF PUBLIC HIGH SCHOOL STUDENTS FROM GRADE 9 THROUGH 12 IN CERTAIN FOUR-YEAR PERIODS BETWEEN 1889-90 AND 1957-58

	GRADE 9	GRADE 10	COL. 1	GRADE 11	COL. 1	COL. 2	GRADE 12	COL. 1	COL. 2	COL. 3
1889-90 to 1892-93 [2]	87	55	63.2	43	78.2	49.4	33	76.7	37.9	89.1
1896-97 to 1899-00 [3]	176	117	66.5	86	73.5	48.9	68	79.1	38.1	90.8
1906-07 to 1909-10 [4]	289	209	72.3	150	71.8	51.9	111	74.6	38.7	99.9
1918-19 to 1921-22 [5]	665	490	75.0	387	77.6	58.2	326	84.2	49.0	87.4
1930-31 to 1933-34 [6]	1702	1387	81.5	1138	82.0	66.8	1005	88.3	59.0	80.2
1938-39 to 1941-42 [7]	1995	1767	88.6	1517	85.8	76.0	1273	84.0	64.0	91.2
1948-49 to 1951-52 [8]	1709	1512	88.5	1313	86.8	76.8	1111	84.6	65.0	95.3
1949-50 to 1952-53 [9]	1756	1548	88.1	1338	86.4	76.2	1132	84.6	64.5	93.6 [15]
1950-51 to 1953-54 [10]	1781	1582	89.9	1373	86.8	77.1	1190	86.6	66.8	94.7 [15]
1951-52 to 1954-55 [11]	1820	1655	90.9	1412	85.3	77.6	1240	87.8	68.1	95.0 [15]
1952-53 to 1955-56 [12]	1885	1717	91.1	1473	85.9	79.4	1300	88.1	68.9	95.0 [15]
1953-54 to 1956-57 [13]	1944	1776	91.3	1534	86.4	78.3	1353	88.2	69.6	95.0 [15]
1954-55 to 1957-58 [14]	1978	1810	91.5	1575	87.0	79.8	1390	88.3	70.2	96.0 [15]

[1] Grade 10 is the second year in each quadrennium, grade 11, the third year, grade 12, the fourth. Column 1 gives the percentage of a given grade in terms of the one immediately preceding; column 2 gives the percentage in each case in terms of grade 9. Column 3 gives the percentage of students in grade 12 who graduated. All grade enrollments are given in thousands rounded off to the nearest whole number; all percentages are rounded off to the nearest decimal. In the quadrennia ending in 1941-42 and after, certain figures are underscored to indicate that they were based on reports of actual enrollments. The other figures after that date are estimated in the manner indicated in appropriate notes below. Before that date, the figures are actual unless otherwise indicated.

[2] For this quadrennium and the next only total enrollments were available in each year. Enrollments were estimated for each grade in each of the eight years with the grade percentages used in Table 36 (Note 1) for 1890. For enrollments in years other than 1889-90, see CR 1893-94, I, p. 37. For the number of graduates in 1893, see CR 1892-93, I, p. 55.

[3] For enrollments, see CR 1899-1900, II, p. 2120; for graduates, p. 2130.

[4] BS 1920-22, II, Ch. VI, Table 2 contains enrollments by grade for each year between 1906-07 and 1915-16, and for 1917-18, 1919-20, and 1921-22. For grade and total enrollments and graduates in 1909-10, see CR 1909-10, II, pp. 1130, 1142-43.

[5] Enrollments in grade 9 for 1918-19, and in grade 11 for 1920-21 were estimated by comparing the enrollments in the corresponding grades in the year immediately preceding and following, and by noting the trend of the percentages in column 1. Enrollments in grades 10 and 12 were given in the first reference in Note 4. For graduates in 1921-22, see *Ibid.*, Tables 1 and 22.

[6] BS 1932-34, Ch. 2, Table 2, p. 48, contains enrollments by grade for each year between 1922-23 and 1933-34. Those for the years ending in even numbers, i.e. 1923-24, were based on biennial surveys; those for the other years were officially estimated from trends indicated by the surveys. All enrollments came from reports made by state rather than individual school systems. This was true also for the next two quadrennia. For graduates in 1933-34,

see *Ibid.*, Ch. 5, Table 41. The graduates were reported by individual school systems, and the percentage was based on enrollments in grade 12 (Table E, p. 9 of reference) reported by those schools. It was derived in the same way, therefore, as those for the preceding years listed.

[7] BS 1948-50, Ch. 1, Table 14. See comment on enrollments by grade in Note 6. The percentage of graduates in grade 12 was calculated from data in Table 6 of reference. This table gives the percentage of students in grade 5 who graduated seven years later, for each septennium between 1930-31 and 1942-43 and ending consecutively between 1937-38 and 1949-50. Although the figures were based on data from public and nonpublic schools—this was also true of the percentage of graduates in column 3—comparable percentages worked out by this writer were 88.5 for grade 10, column 1, 88.8 and 76.0 for grade 11, columns 1 and 2, and 83.9 and 63.8 for grade 12, columns 1 and 2. Table 17 of the reference contains a study similar to the one in Table 6, for high school grades only during the same period. Its figures verify the percentages calculated from Table 6.

[8] BS 1950-52, Ch. 1, Table 12. The enrollments by grade were based on reports by state systems or estimated from them (Note 6). Tables 6 and 14 correspond to Tables 6 and 17 in Note 7, and add two septennia and quadrennia respectively. Comparable percentages worked out by this writer also bore out the percentages in the various columns in the way indicated in Note 7.

[9] BS 1950-52, Ch. 1, Table 12, for enrollments in grades 9 to 11. The enrollment in grade 12 was estimated by Foster and Hobson (*School Life*, May 1955, p. 126) as 1,202,000. This figure yielded 89.8% for column 1 and 68.4% for column 2. Both of these seemed to vary too much from the patterns of the preceding years. Since the figures for grades 9 and 11 were actual, the estimate for grade 12 was apparently too high. A comparison of the estimates for 1953-54 (Table 12 of the reference) with the actual enrollments for that year, reported in *School Life* (May 1956, pp. 8-9), shows the following:

Grade		1952-53	1953-54	1953-54 Cor.	1954-55	1955-56
9	(1000's)	1903	1964	1944—20	1998	2073
10	"	1661	1722	1717— 5	1782	1815
11	"	1401	1439	1412—27	1500	1559
12	"	1202	1264	1190—74	1304	1364

The fifth column figures appear in reverse order of grades in Table 37, beginning with the quadrennium ending in 1953-54. The grade corrections for 1953-54 were applied, with some variations, to the estimated grade enrollments in the years between 1949-50 and 1957-58 (Table 37). The percentage patterns in columns 1, 2, and 3 were used as a guide in making the corrections.

[10] *School Life* (May 1955), p. 126, for enrollments in grades 9 through 11. *Ibid.* (May 1956), p. 9, for enrollment in grade 12. The enrollment in grade 11 was corrected as indicated in Note 9.

[11] Enrollments in grades 9, 10, and 12 from *School Life* (May 1955), p. 126, with grades 10 and 12 corrected as indicated in Note 9. Enrollment in Grade 11 from *School Life* (May 1956), p. 9.

[12] Enrollments in grades 9, 11, and 12 from first reference in Note 11, corrected as indicated in Note 9. Enrollment in grade 10 from second reference in Note 11.

[13] Enrollment in grade 9 from *School Life* (May 1956), p. 9. Other enrollments, *Ibid.* (May 1955), corrected as indicated in Note 9.

[14] All enrollments from *School Life* (May 1955), p. 126, corrected, with some variations, as indicated in Note 9.

[15] See text below for discussion of percentages in column 3.

Although many of the figures in this table after 1933-34 are based on comparative estimates, the resulting percentages in columns 1 and 2 form a reasonable pattern. If it may be assumed, in the absence of a more authentic guide, that they are approximately correct, continuation rates [4] have shown an almost constant upward trend. The slight variations are most likely caused by erroneous estimates, and show up most plainly in the progression from grade 10 to 11. It is noticeable

that between 1890 and 1934 a smaller proportion of students went from grade 9 to 10 than from 10 to 11, except in the quadrennium ending in 1910. During this period, except in the first quadrennium, the proportion going from grade 11 to 12 was larger than either of the other two progression rates. After 1933-34 the continuation rates from grade 9 to 10 were consistently larger than those of the other two. Between that date and 1953-54 the continuation from grade 10 to 11 was proportionately larger than the progression from grade 11 to 12. During this period the trend from 10 to 11 was slightly up, the trend from 11 to 12 was slightly down, but after a leveling off it had begun to climb by 1953-54. The war and the draft clearly affected the age group in grade 11. Since 1953-54 the continuation rates for grades 9 and 11 have slowly risen. The rate from grade 10 to 11 declined slightly between 1954 and 1955. The rate since then has been up, and in the current year it has inched ahead of its 1953-54 level. Although the period between grades 10 and 11 has clearly become the most critical in the high school years, since 1900 the differences among the continuation rates have had a somewhat remarkable uniformity. At the present time it is possible to say with some assurance that about 90% of the students will continue from grade 9 to grade 10. Of these about 85% will continue into grade 11, and of these about 88%, into grade 12. Of those who begin in grade 9, approximately 70% will enter grade 12 and about 65% will graduate.[5]

The proportion of students in grade 12 who graduate fluctuated considerably in the six quadrennia listed between 1889-90 and 1941-42 (T. 37, Col. 3 for grade 12). In the first two quadrennia the percentages may be somewhat low because enrollments in grade 12 could only be estimated. This may help to explain the decided contrast with an unusual situation in 1909-10 when grade 12 and the graduating class were all but identical—the first and only instance of the kind in high school history. As the table shows, there was a rapid falling off by 1921-22[6] which continued on into the low point of the entire 68-year period, during the depression in 1933-34. But by 1941-42 the reverse and upward trend was well under way, and since 1951-52 more than nine out of ten seniors stay on each year to graduate. ....

When actual figures of public high school graduates were last published, for the year 1953-54, they numbered 1,129,000—94.7% of grade 12, and 63.4% of students who entered grade 9 in 1950-51. They also constituted 88.5% of all public and nonpublic high school graduates in 1953-54. Table 38 puts these and comparable figures into historical perspective and supplementing Tables 36 and 37.

TABLE 38[1]

A COMPARISON BETWEEN THE NUMBER OF GRADUATES IN PUBLIC
AND NONPUBLIC HIGH SCHOOLS IN CERTAIN YEARS
BETWEEN 1889-90 AND 1957-58

	Public	%9	Nonpublic	Total	Public H.S. % of Total
1889-90	21,882	64.1	21,849	43,731	50.4
1899-1900	61,737	35.1	33,146	94,883	65.1
1909-10	111,363	38.5	45,066	156,429	71.2
1921-22	284,674[2]	42.8	72,326	357,000[3]	79.7
1933-34	806,510[2]	47.4	108,343	914,853[3]	88.2
1937-38	1,030,216	53.8	89,863	1,120,079[3]	91.9
1945-46	1,011,173	53.2	68,860	1,080,033[4]	93.6
1950-51	1,045,633	62.5	136,267	1,181,800[5]	88.5
1951-52	1,058,900[6]	61.9	137,600	1,196,500[7]	88.5
1952-53	1,060,500[6]	60.4	137,800	1,198,300[5]	88.5
1953-54	1,129,341[8]	63.4	146,759	1,276,100[7]	88.5
1954-55	1,178,000[6]	64.7	156,000	1,334,000[9]	88.3
1955-56	1,235,000[6]	64.4	166,000	1,401,000[9]	88.2
1956-57	1,286,000[6]	66.1	175,000	1,461,000[9]	88.2
1957-58	1,340,000[6]	67.7	186,000	1,526,000[9]	87.8

[1] Through 1950-51 public high school graduates, except as indicated, are conveniently listed in BS 1950-52, Ch. 5, Table A; total high school graduates, in Ch. 1, Table 15. Figures in second column give percentage of grade 9 who graduated. For enrollments in grade 9 in certain corresponding years, see Table 37.

[2] See Appendix B.   [4] BS 1952-54, Ch. 1, Table 15.
[3] *Bulletin, 1940, No. 2,* Ch. 1, Table 15.   [5] BS 1952-54, Ch. 4, Sect. 1, Table XXIV.
[6] Calculated from figures in total column as explained in text.
[7] BS 1952-54, Ch. 1, Table 15.   [8] BS 1952-54, Ch. 2, Table 13.
[9] From "Number of High-School Graduates From Public and Nonpublic Schools, 1939-40 to 1953-54 and Forecasts to 1960-70." This is a single, mimeographed sheet with data "As of September 21, 1956," kindly furnished to the writer by the Office of Education. A revision of these estimates was made in February 1957 and still another revision will be presented in a forthcoming publication.

In each of the fifteen years listed in this table there are two basic figures: those for the graduates of public high schools and those for the total graduates of public and nonpublic types.[7] Between 1889-90 and 1950-51 and in 1953-54 the three sets of figures and the percentages in the last column are scarcely open to doubt. In each of the last two years just mentioned public high school graduates constituted 88.5% of the total. The same percentage was therefore assumed for the two intervening years.

The pattern thus created shows that graduates from public high schools increased steadily between 1889-90 and 1957-58, except for a slight setback in 1945-46. The proportion of such graduates, after the equilibrium of 1889-90, reached its highest point in 1945-46, and since that year has hovered around 88%.

Graduates from nonpublic high schools form a much less regular pattern. Although actual figures increased steadily through 1933-34, the more rapid rate of increase in public schools caused a steady decrease in the proportion of nonpublic graduates. The effects of the Depression and of World War II, as might have been expected, were much more pronounced on schools of the nonpublic type. Between 1933-34 and 1937-38, while the nonpublic graduates decreased about 14%, those in public schools increased about 27%— their lowest rate up to that point. In the next period, ending with 1945-46, the public schools lost only a little less than 2%, but the nonpublic, a little more than 23%.

Since 1953-54, on the basis of figures given in Table 38, graduates from nonpublic schools have increased at a more rapid rate than those from public schools. This had happened once before— between 1945-46 and 1950-51—and with such propulsion that the same fundamental causes seem to have remained in operation. One was the general prosperity which enabled more parents to afford private education for their children; another was undoubtedly the growing and increasingly evident dissatisfaction with public high school education.

In this connection it should be made plain that the figures from 1954-55 through 1957-58 are derived from calculations by the writer (see Note 9 of Table 38). These assumptions guided the calculations: 1) about 95% of grade 12 in public high schools have graduated each year since 1953-54 (Col. 3, Table 37 and Col. 1 of Table 38); 2) there is a close relationship in the corresponding years between the percentage of students who continue from grade 9 into grade 12 and the percentage who continue from grade 9 to graduation (Table 37, Col. 2 of grade 12, and Col. 2 of Table 38); 3) the number of public school students in grade 12 (Table 37) is not far above or below 19.2% of the total in grades 9-12; and 4) public high school graduates constitute approximately 88% of total secondary school graduates.

Any one of these four assumptions might be used as a starting point from which appropriate calculations could be made, provided a certain figure is given—or assumed. For example, if there are 1,000,000 graduates in public and nonpublic high schools in a given year, about 880,-000 of these would be from the public high schools. This figure would be about 95% of the students in grade 12 of the public high schools, about 18% of the students in grades 9-12,[8] and about 67% of those who entered grade 9 four years earlier. The figure for grade 12

would be about 19% of the total high school enrollment and about 70% of those who entered grade 9.

A starting point could also be made of course with figures, given or assumed, for any of the grades nine through 12. The latest study shows for example, that 67% of grade 9 students enroll in general science. In the fall of 1957, out of an assumed enrollment of 2,300,000 students about 1,540,000 would be studying general science. In the fall of 1958, about 91% of grade 9 would continue into grade 10 (Table 37). Of these, according to the latest study, about 74% or 1,549,000 would study biology. In the fall of 1959, about 87% of grade 10 would continue into grade 11 (Table 37). Of these, about 34.4% or 626,000 would study chemistry.

In the fall of 1960, about 88% of grade 11 would go into grade 12 (Table 37). Of these, about 24.5% or 388,000 would study physics.[9] Of the 1,584,000 who entered grade 12, about 95% or 1,505,000 would graduate. These would constitute about 88% of all secondary school graduates (Table 38), a total of about 1,730,000. The public school graduates would also total about 18% of the total public school enrollment in grades 9-12—approximately 8,355,000. Of these about 31% would be in grade 9, 27.5% in grade 10, 22.5% in grade 11, and 19% in grade 12.[10]

From these grade percentages and from continuation and subject percentages used above, it would be easy to estimate the number of high school students in each of the four sciences in 1960-61 and in the three years following. By that time, and probably sooner, many of the percentages would have changed and new formulae would have to be worked out. Because of the numbers involved the change of only a few percentage points would make a tremendous difference in grade and subject enrollments.

An example of this can be seen in Tables 36 and 37. A comparison of the two shows discrepancies in the enrollments of certain grades in the same year: grade 12 in 1933-34 and in 1954-55; grade 9 in 1948-49, and grades 10 and 11 in 1954-55 (Table 37, quadrennia 5, 10, 7, 12, and 11 respectively).

As indicated previously (Note 6 of Table 37), after 1933-34 all figures in Table 37, except those underscored, are taken from or based on official estimates of enrollments in state systems. Although the 1949 figure for grade 9 in Table 36, based on enrollments reported by individual schools, could have been used in Table 37, it would not have fit in with other figures in quadrennium 7, which were based on state reports. The same reason prevented use of the grade 12 figure for 1933-34 (Table 36) in quadrennium 5.

When estimates for each of the four grades in 1953-54 were corrected by actual enrollment figures, it seemed appropriate to make comparable corrections for the grade enrollments of 1954-55 and 1955-56. In the first of these two years the corrections, including those for grade 9 (Table 37, quadrennium 13), totaled 113,000, as compared with 125,000 in 1953-54 and 93,000 in 1955-56, exclusive of grade 9 (compare figures for these years in Table 37 with those in Note 9 of that table). It is obvious that the reduction of grade enrollments would decrease subject enrollments in those grades. A comparison is made only of the changes that would have occurred in 1954-55.[11]

Tables 36, 37, and 38, then, illustrate better than words the staggering growth of the public high schools during the last sixty-eight years. Despite the fluctuations caused by war, depression, and the staccato spread of educational opportunities among minority groups, the long-range trend of continuation rates has been steadily up. Although nearly a third of grade 9 students still fail to graduate, it seems likely that public awareness will cause a general decrease of this unprofitable proportion. From this group alone may come several hundred thousand additional graduates each year. If only half of these enter college, by 1970-71 the number of students in college will almost equal the number in high school during the current year.[12]

[1] This happened when the estimates for 1953-54 (see reference in Note 6 of Table 36) were checked against actual enrollments for that year in *School Life* (May 1956). The estimated enrollments were 125,000 larger, and the shift in grade enrollments caused a shift in percentages: an increase in grades 9 and 10, but a decrease in grade 12. The percentage for grade 11 was the same. See also Note 9 of Table 37.

[2] BS 1920-22, II, Ch. 6, Table 1, and BS 1950-52, Ch. 5, Table A.

[3] For the total high school enrollment that year, see CR 1893-94, I, p. 37. Grade 9 was estimated as 43% of that total (Note 1 of Table 36).

[4] The writer prefers this term because it emphasizes what the students do. The more usual term, "retention rates," seems to emphasize what the schools do, and has the connotation of "holding back."

[5] In 1952 the proportion, based on data from public and nonpublic schools, was 61.6%. In 1950 it was 62.5 and in 1951, 62.3. See BS 1950-52, Ch. 1, Table 14. The comparable percentage in 1953-54 was 63.4 (BS 1952-54, Ch. 1, Table 14).

[6] The intervening stage is shown in CR 1915-16 (for 1914-15), II, pp. 448 and 454, with 94.7%.

[7] These include private academies, secondary or preparatory schools operated by public and private institutions, and schools for exceptional children. See BS 1952-54, Ch. 1, Table 13.

[8] In 1950-51 this percentage for public and nonpublic schools was 18.4; in 1946, 18.8%; in 1938, 17.5%; in 1930, 14.3; in 1920, 12.5. Those calculated by the writer for the public high schools alone were slightly lower in each of these years.

[9] These percentages are taken from *Pamphlet No. 120*, 1956, Table 7. Comparable percentages for mathematics are found in Tables 17 and 18 of reference: general mathematics, 43.1% and elementary algebra, 67% (both subjects in grade 9); plane geometry, 41.6% (grade 10); intermediate algebra, 32.2% (grade 11); plane trigonometry, 9.2% and solid geometry, 7.6% (both subjects in grade 12). These last two percentages are for the first semester only; for both semesters they would be approximately 16% and 13% respectively.

[10] The total enrollment figure is in line with the projection made by Foster and Hobson (*School Life*, May 1955). Their estimate for 1959-60 is 8,132,000. The grade percentages will differ slightly from those given in the text above.

[11] Although these revised grade enrollments and percentages were not substituted for those that appear in Table 36, which are official estimates, it is believed that the revised figures are more nearly accurate. If they are substituted for the grade enrollment figures for 1955 in Chapter VI, Table 19, the following changes would occur in that table and in the 1955 column of Table 18 in the same chapter:

	Grade 9	T. 19	T. 18		Grade 10	T. 19	T. 18
	1978	20.5			1776	19.1	
Alg. 1	1193	14.5	60.3	P. Geom.	662	10.5	37.3
Gen. Math.	793	11.2	41.1	Biol.	1289	29.5	72.6
Gen. Sci.	1444	28.7	73.0				
	Grade 11				Grade 12		
	1473	18.5			1240	20.8	
Alg. 2	420	3.9	28.5	Trig.	161	47.6	13.0
Chem.	474	15.1	32.2	S. Geom.	141	50.0	11.3
				Physics	288	—1.4	23.2

Every percentage in Table 19 changed; in Table 18, only those for general mathematics and solid geometry. All percentages are *plus*, except for physics in Table 19. Enrollments are given to the nearest thousand. Comparable changes in Table 20 of Chapter VI were not made. All the subject-enrollment figures would be smaller, and the grade percentages in foreign languages would be reduced approximately as follows: Grade 9—3.0%; grade 10—2.2; grade 11—0.3; grade 12—0.1. Grade percentages in English would change very little.

[12] "Projections of Regular Session Enrollment in Institutions of Higher Education in Continental United States: 1954-55 to 1970-71 (Projections as of March 1956)." A mimeographed sheet furnished to the writer by the Office of Education. A companion piece to this, dealing with first-time enrollments, predicted 727,000 such students for the fall of 1956. The estimated actual number was 735,065 (*School and Society*, December 8, 1956, p. 201). The estimate was based on the 37th annual survey conducted by Raymond Walters and published in the issue of the reference cited.

INDEX*

Academies, 5-8, 31-34, 58-60, 62, 115
Agriculture, 42-44, 61, 69
Algebra, 24-25, 62-63, 86
  enrollments by grade, 93-96, 101, 109-110
  percentages by grade, 82-83, 87-93, 101-102
American history, 30, 31, 37, 63, 77
  percentages by grade, 145, 149
Ancient history, 2, 31-32, 77
Astronomy, 28, 88
Art and music, 46-50, 61, 69, 72, 118, 168-169
Arts and sciences, fusion of, 133-134

Bachelor's degrees, 104-105, 108, 158-159
Barnard, Henry, 11-12
Biology, 105, 124
  college majors in, 104, 106, 109, 181
  enrollments by grade, 93-96
  high school percentages, 28-29
  percentages by grade, 91-96
  teachers of, 128-29
Botany, 28-29, 64, 90
Brown, Kenneth E., 54, 137, 146
Business and commercial subjects, 35-37, 61, 69, 73, 118, 119
  college majors in, 104-105
  distribution by sex, 146-147, 153

Chase, Mary Ellen, 130
Cheever, Ezekiel, 3
Chemistry, 95, 124, 181
  college majors in, 104, 181-182
  grade sequence, 83, 85-87, 89-92
  grade percentages, 86-88, 91, 121
  high school percentages, 27-29, 106
  new teachers of, 128-129
Classical languages, 4-5, 9, 30, 33, 58, 62, 76, 114, 118
  college majors in, 104-109, 181-182
  curriculum, 12-14, 60, 65-66, 85, 157-158
  grade enrollments and percentages, 97
  high school percentages, 26-27, 145,

149
  in elementary schools, 63
  new teachers of, 128-130
  see Foreign languages, Latin, Greek
College majors by subjects, 104-109, 181-182
Colleges
  agricultural, 42-43
  community, 6, 115
  entrance requirements, 9, 58, 62, 68
  Land Grant, 37
  mortality rate in, 133
  student enrollments in, 104-106, 164
Committee of Fifteen, 67-68, 79, 137
Committee of Ten, 62-68, 71, 79, 84-89, 118, 132, 134, 137-138
  philosophy of, 116-117
Committee on College Entrance Requirements, 67-68, 71, 137
Committee on Economy of Time, 72
Compulsory education, 9, 74-75, 115
Cumulative subjects, 68-70, 72-73, 99, 117, 119-121, 134, 170-182
Curricula
  academies and private schools, 5-8, 31, 33-34, 59, 62, 115
  agricultural, 43-44
  classical, 154-158
  college, 24
  college preparatory, 9, 62
  English, 34, 59, 67, 85
  evening schools, 4, 23-24
  grammar schools, 4
  high schools, 14-16, 24, 37, 59-62, 70-75, 84, 89, 114-118, 123, 132
  "model", 84-86
  modern languages, 12, 13, 63-66, 85
  normal school, 7, 51-53
  scientific, 154-158
  vocational, 38-40
Curriculum surveys, 11-18, 59-60
  historical summary tables, 17-19

Departments of Education, 51, 122
Department of Health, Education, and Welfare, 131
Dewey, John, 71, 73

*Prepared with the assistance of John Hill Monroe.

LEMON AND GARLIC SHRIMP

¼ cup olive oil
2 tablespoons butter
1 pound large raw shrimp, peeled and deveined
3 cloves garlic, crushed
2 tablespoons lemon juice
½ teaspoon paprika
¼ teaspoon salt
⅛ teaspoon black pepper
2 tablespoons finely chopped fresh parsley
   Italian or French bread, sliced

1. Heat oil and butter in large cast iron skillet over medium-high heat until mixture sizzles. Add shrimp and garlic; cook and stir 4 to 5 minutes until shrimp are pink and opaque.

2. Add lemon juice, paprika, salt and pepper; cook and stir 1 minute. Remove from heat; discard garlic. Spoon shrimp and skillet juices into large serving bowl; sprinkle with parsley. Serve with bread for dipping.   *Makes 6 to 8 servings*

CROQUE MONSIEUR BITES

8 thin slices firm sandwich bread
4 slices Swiss cheese, halved (about 4 ounces)
4 slices smoked ham (about 4 ounces)
   Dash grated nutmeg
2 tablespoons butter, melted

1. Cut crusts from bread. Place four bread slices on work surface. Layer each with half of slice cheese, one slice ham and remaining half of slice cheese; sprinkle with nutmeg. Top with remaining four bread slices. Brush outsides of sandwiches with melted butter.

2. Cook sandwiches in large cast iron skillet over medium heat 2 to 3 minutes per side or until golden brown and cheese is melted. Cut into quarters.   *Makes 16 pieces*

TIP: These sandwiches can be prepared ahead of time. Leave sandwiches whole after cooking and refrigerate until ready to serve. Cut into quarters and place on foil-lined baking sheet. Bake in preheated 350°F oven about 8 minutes or until sandwiches are heated through and cheese is melted.

Lemon & Garlic Shrimp

CRISPY TUNA FRITTERS

1 cup corn bread and muffin mix
¼ cup minced onion
2 tablespoons minced pimiento
¼ teaspoon salt
⅛ teaspoon ground red pepper
⅛ teaspoon black pepper
¾ cup boiling water
1 can (9 ounces) tuna packed in water, drained
Vegetable oil for frying

1. Combine corn bread mix, onion, pimiento, salt, red pepper and black pepper in small bowl; mix well. Slowly stir in water. (Mixture will be thick.) Stir in tuna until blended.

2. Pour oil into large cast iron skillet to depth of ½ inch; heat to 375°F over medium heat.

3. Drop batter by tablespoonfuls into hot oil. Cook about 1 minute per side or until golden brown. Drain on paper towel-lined plate.   *Makes 30 fritters (about 6 servings)*

SERVING SUGGESTION: Serve fritters with thousand island dressing or tartar sauce.

Make sure the oil is hot before you drop the batter into the skillet—if the fat is not hot enough, then the food will absorb too much oil and be greasy. To test the oil without a thermometer, drop a few pieces of bread or bread crumbs into the skillet. If they start to sizzle immediately, the oil is ready.

QUICK CHICKEN QUESADILLAS

4 boneless skinless chicken breast halves
3 tablespoons vegetable oil
½ teaspoon salt
1 large yellow onion, thinly sliced
8 medium flour tortillas (6 to 8 inches)
3 cups (12 ounces) shredded Cheddar or Monterey Jack cheese
   Salsa, sour cream and/or guacamole (optional)

1. Cut chicken into 1×¼-inch strips.

2. Heat 2 tablespoons oil in large cast iron skillet over high heat. Add chicken; cook and stir 3 to 4 minutes or until lightly browned and cooked through. Season with salt. Remove to plate with slotted spoon.

3. Add onion to skillet; cook and stir about 5 minutes or until translucent. Remove from skillet.

4. Heat remaining 1 tablespoon oil in skillet over medium heat. Place one tortilla in skillet; top with one quarter of chicken, onion and cheese. Place second tortilla over filling; press down lightly. Cook quesadilla about 2 minutes per side or until tortillas are browned and cheese is melted. Repeat with remaining tortillas and filling.

5. Cut into wedges; serve with desired toppings. *Makes 8 appetizer servings*

FALAFEL NUGGETS

2 cans (about 15 ounces each) chickpeas
½ cup whole wheat flour
½ cup chopped fresh parsley
1 egg, beaten
⅓ cup plus 2 tablespoons lemon juice, divided
¼ cup minced onion
2 tablespoons minced garlic
2 teaspoons ground cumin
1 teaspoon salt, divided
½ teaspoon ground red pepper or red pepper flakes
½ cup canola oil
2½ cups tomato sauce
⅓ cup tomato paste
2 teaspoons sugar
1 teaspoon onion powder

1. Preheat oven to 400°F. Spray baking sheet with nonstick cooking spray.

2. For falafel, drain chickpeas, reserving ¼ cup liquid. Combine chickpeas, reserved ¼ cup liquid, flour, parsley, ⅓ cup lemon juice, minced onion, garlic, cumin, ½ teaspoon salt and red pepper in food processor or blender; process until well blended. Shape into 36 (1-inch) balls; place 1 to 2 inches apart on prepared baking sheet. Refrigerate 15 minutes.

3. Meanwhile, for sauce, combine tomato sauce, tomato paste, remaining 2 tablespoons lemon juice, sugar, onion powder and remaining ½ teaspoon salt in medium saucepan; simmer over medium-low heat 20 minutes, stirring occasionally. Keep warm.

4. Heat oil to 350°F in large cast iron skillet over medium-high heat. Cook falafel in batches until browned. Place on prepared baking sheet; bake 8 to 10 minutes. Serve with warm sauce.

Makes 12 servings

POULTRY

LEMON GARLIC ROAST CHICKEN

4 sprigs fresh rosemary, divided

6 cloves garlic, divided

1 lemon

2 tablespoons butter, softened

2 teaspoons salt, divided

2 large russet potatoes, peeled and cut into ¾-inch pieces

2 onions, cut into 1-inch pieces

2 tablespoons olive oil

½ teaspoon black pepper

1 whole chicken (3 to 4 pounds)

1. Preheat oven to 400°F. Finely chop 2 sprigs of rosemary (about 2 tablespoons). Mince 3 cloves garlic. Grate peel from lemon; reserve lemon. Combine butter, chopped rosemary, minced garlic, lemon peel and ½ teaspoon salt in small bowl; mix well. Set aside while preparing vegetables.

2. Combine potatoes, onions, oil, 1 teaspoon salt and pepper in medium bowl; toss to coat. Spread mixture in single layer in large cast iron skillet.

3. Smash remaining 3 cloves garlic. Cut lemon into quarters. Season cavity of chicken with remaining ½ teaspoon salt. Place garlic, lemon quarters and remaining 2 sprigs of rosemary in cavity; tie legs with kitchen twine, if desired. Place chicken on top of vegetables in skillet; spread butter mixture over chicken.

4. Roast about 1 hour or until chicken is cooked through (165°F) and potatoes are tender. Let stand 10 minutes before carving. Season with additional salt and pepper to taste.   *Makes 4 servings*

CRISPY BUTTERMILK FRIED CHICKEN

2 cups buttermilk
1 tablespoon hot pepper sauce
3 pounds bone-in chicken pieces
2 cups all-purpose flour
2 teaspoons salt
2 teaspoons poultry seasoning
1 teaspoon garlic salt
1 teaspoon paprika
1 teaspoon ground red pepper
1 teaspoon black pepper
1 cup vegetable oil

1. Combine buttermilk and hot pepper sauce in large resealable food storage bag. Add chicken; turn to coat. Marinate in refrigerator 2 hours or up to 24 hours.

2. Combine flour, salt, poultry seasoning, garlic salt, paprika, red pepper and black pepper in another large food storage bag or shallow bowl; mix well. Working in batches, remove chicken from buttermilk, shaking off excess. Add to flour mixture; shake to coat.

3. Heat oil to 350°F in large cast iron skillet over medium heat. Cook chicken in batches 30 minutes or until cooked through (165°F), turning occasionally to brown all sides. Drain on paper towel-lined plate. Keep warm. *Makes 4 servings*

NOTE: Carefully monitor the temperature of the oil during cooking. It should not drop below 325°F or go higher than 350°F. The chicken can also be cooked in a deep fryer following the manufacturer's directions. Never leave hot oil unattended.

FAJITAS

⅓ cup fresh lime juice (from 2 or 3 limes)
¼ cup corn or vegetable oil
2 tablespoons Fajita Seasoning Mix (recipe follows)
1 pound chicken or pork, thinly sliced into bite-size pieces
½ white or red onion, cut lengthwise into ½-inch slices
½ green bell pepper, cut lengthwise into ½-inch slices
½ red bell pepper, cut lengthwise into ½-inch slices
  Flour tortillas, heated
  Grated cheese, fresh cilantro, sliced avocado, diced tomatoes and/or salsa (optional)

1. Combine lime juice, oil and 2 tablespoons Fajita Seasoning Mix in large bowl or resealable food storage bag; mix well. Add chicken; turn to coat. Marinate in refrigerator 1 hour.

2. Remove chicken from marinade; discard marinade. Heat large cast iron skillet over medium-high heat. Add chicken, onion and bell peppers; cook and stir over medium-high heat until chicken is cooked through and vegetables are tender.

3. Spoon mixture into warm tortillas; garnish as desired.　　　　*Makes 6 servings*

FAJITA SEASONING MIX

½ cup chili powder
3 tablespoons ground red pepper
2½ tablespoons garlic powder
2½ tablespoons celery salt
2 tablespoons lemon pepper
1 tablespoon ground cumin
2 teaspoons salt
2 teaspoons dried oregano
2 teaspoons paprika
1 teaspoon ground nutmeg
1 teaspoon firmly packed brown sugar

Whisk all ingredients in medium bowl until well blended. Store in airtight container.

Makes 1⅓ cups

ROASTED CHICKEN THIGHS WITH MUSTARD-CREAM SAUCE

8 bone-in skin-on chicken thighs
¾ teaspoon black pepper, divided
½ teaspoon salt, divided
2 teaspoons vegetable oil
2 shallots, thinly sliced
½ Granny Smith apple, peeled and cut into ¼-inch pieces
½ cup chicken broth
½ cup whipping cream
1 tablespoon spicy brown mustard
½ teaspoon chopped fresh thyme

1. Preheat oven to 400°F.

2. Sprinkle both sides of chicken with ½ teaspoon pepper and ¼ teaspoon salt. Heat oil in large cast iron skillet over medium-high heat. Add chicken, skin side down; cook 8 to 10 minutes or until skin is golden brown. Remove chicken to plate; drain excess fat from skillet.

3. Return chicken to skillet, skin side up. Transfer to oven; roast about 25 minutes or until cooked through (165°F). Remove chicken to clean plate; tent with foil to keep warm.

4. Drain all but 1 tablespoon fat from skillet; heat over medium heat. Add shallots and apple; cook and stir about 8 minutes or until tender. Stir in broth; cook over medium-high heat about 1 minute or until reduced by half, scraping up browned bits from bottom of skillet. Add cream, mustard, thyme, remaining ¼ teaspoon pepper and ¼ teaspoon salt; cook and stir about 2 minutes or until slightly thickened. Spoon sauce over chicken. Serve immediately. *Makes 4 servings*

TURKEY AND VEGGIE MEATBALLS

1 pound ground turkey
½ cup finely chopped green onions
½ cup finely chopped green bell pepper
⅓ cup old-fashioned oats
¼ cup shredded carrot
¼ cup grated Parmesan cheese
1 egg, beaten
2 cloves garlic, minced
½ teaspoon salt
½ teaspoon Italian seasoning
¼ teaspoon fennel seeds
⅛ teaspoon red pepper flakes (optional)
2 tablespoons olive oil
   Tomato-basil or marinara pasta sauce (optional)

1. Combine turkey, green onions, bell pepper, oats, carrot, cheese, egg, garlic, salt, Italian seasoning, fennel seeds and red pepper flakes, if desired, in large bowl; mix well. Shape into 36 (1-inch) balls.

2. Heat oil in large cast iron skillet over medium-high heat. Add meatballs; cook 11 minutes or until no longer pink in center, turning frequently. Use fork and spoon for easy turning. Serve immediately with sauce, if desired, or cool and freeze (see Tip).

Makes 4 servings

TIP To freeze the meatballs, cool completely and spread in a single layer on a large baking sheet. Freeze, uncovered, until solid, then place the meatballs in a large resealable food storage bag. Release any excess air from the bag; seal and freeze flat for easier storage and faster thawing. To reheat, place the meatballs in a 12x8-inch microwavable dish and cook on HIGH 20 to 30 seconds or until hot.

CHICKEN SCARPIELLO

3 tablespoons extra virgin olive oil, divided

1 pound spicy Italian sausage, cut into 1-inch pieces

1 (3-pound) chicken, cut into 10 pieces*

1 teaspoon salt, divided

1 large onion, chopped

2 red or orange bell peppers, cut into ¼-inch strips

3 cloves garlic, minced

½ cup dry white wine such as sauvignon blanc

½ cup chicken broth

½ cup coarsely chopped seeded hot cherry peppers

½ cup liquid from cherry pepper jar

1 teaspoon dried oregano

Additional salt and black pepper

¼ cup chopped fresh Italian parsley

*Or purchase 2 bone-in chicken leg quarters and 2 chicken breasts; separate drumsticks and thighs and cut breasts in half.

1. Heat 1 tablespoon oil in large cast iron skillet over medium-high heat. Add sausage; cook about 10 minutes or until well browned on all sides, stirring occasionally. Remove sausage to plate.

2. Heat 1 tablespoon oil in same skillet. Sprinkle chicken with ½ teaspoon salt; arrange skin side down in single layer in skillet (cook in batches if necessary). Cook about 6 minutes per side or until browned. Remove chicken to plate. Drain excess fat from skillet.

3. Heat remaining 1 tablespoon oil in skillet. Add onion and remaining ½ teaspoon salt; cook and stir 2 minutes or until onion is softened, scraping up browned bits from bottom of skillet. Add bell peppers and garlic; cook and stir 5 minutes. Stir in wine; cook until liquid is reduced by half. Stir in broth, cherry peppers, cherry pepper liquid, oregano and additional salt and pepper to taste; bring to a simmer.

4. Return sausage and chicken along with any accumulated juices to skillet. Partially cover skillet and simmer 10 minutes. Uncover and simmer 15 minutes or until chicken is cooked through (165°F). Sprinkle with parsley.

Makes 4 to 6 servings

TIP: If too much liquid remains in the skillet when the chicken is cooked through, remove the chicken and sausage and continue simmering the sauce to reduce it slightly.

CHICKEN PICCATA

3 tablespoons all-purpose flour
½ teaspoon salt
¼ teaspoon black pepper
4 boneless skinless chicken breasts (4 ounces each)
2 teaspoons olive oil
2 teaspoons butter
2 cloves garlic, minced
¾ cup reduced-sodium chicken broth
1 tablespoon fresh lemon juice
2 tablespoons chopped fresh Italian parsley
1 tablespoon capers, drained

1. Combine flour, salt and pepper in shallow bowl. Reserve 1 tablespoon flour mixture for sauce; set aside.

2. Pound chicken to ½-inch thickness between sheets of waxed paper with flat side of meat mallet or rolling pin. Coat chicken with remaining flour mixture, shaking off excess.

3. Heat oil and butter in large cast iron skillet over medium heat until mixture sizzles. Add chicken; cook 4 to 5 minutes per side or until no longer pink in center. Remove to plate; keep warm.

4. Add garlic to skillet; cook and stir 1 minute. Add reserved flour mixture; cook and stir 1 minute. Add broth and lemon juice; cook 2 minutes or until thickened, stirring frequently. Stir in parsley and capers. Spoon sauce over chicken.

Makes 4 servings

TIP

Capers are the deep green flower buds of a Mediterranean bush that have been preserved in a vinegary brine. They range in size from the tiny nonpareil variety from France to pistchio-size buds from Italy and Spain. Rinse them in cold water to remove any excess salt and brine before using.

BBQ CHICKEN SKILLET PIZZA

    1 pound frozen bread dough, thawed
    1 tablespoon olive oil
    2 cups shredded cooked chicken*
    ¾ cup barbecue sauce, divided
    ¼ cup (1 ounce) shredded mozzarella cheese
    ¼ cup thinly sliced red onion
    ½ cup (2 ounces) shredded smoked Gouda cheese
    Chopped fresh cilantro (optional)

*Use a rotisserie chicken for best flavor and convenience.

1. Preheat oven to 425°F. Roll out dough into 13-inch circle on lightly floured surface. Brush oil over bottom and side of large cast iron skillet; place in oven 5 minutes to preheat.

2. Combine chicken and ½ cup barbecue sauce in medium bowl; toss to coat. Remove hot skillet from oven; press dough into bottom and about 1 inch up side of skillet

3. Spread remaining ¼ cup barbecue sauce over dough. Sprinkle with mozzarella; top with chicken mixture. Sprinkle with half of onion and Gouda cheese; top with remaining onion.

4. Bake about 25 minutes or until crust is golden brown. Garnish with cilantro. *Makes 4 to 6 servings*

TUSCAN-STYLE SAUSAGE SKILLET

    1 tablespoon olive oil
    ½ cup chopped fresh fennel
    ½ cup chopped sweet or yellow onion
    3 cloves garlic, minced
    1 can (about 14 ounces) fire-roasted diced tomatoes
    1 package (9 ounces) fully cooked chicken or turkey Italian sausage, cut into ½-inch pieces
    ¾ teaspoon dried rosemary
    1 can (about 15 ounces) navy or Great Northern beans, rinsed and drained
    4 cups baby spinach or torn spinach

1. Heat oil in large cast iron skillet over medium-high heat. Add fennel, onion and garlic; cook and stir 5 minutes.

2. Stir in tomatoes, sausage and rosemary; cover and cook over low heat 10 minutes or until vegetables are tender. Stir in beans; cook over medium-high heat until heated through. Add spinach; cover and cook 2 minutes or until spinach is wilted. *Makes 4 servings*

BBQ Chicken Skillet Pizza

CHICKEN BURGERS WITH WHITE CHEDDAR

1¼ pounds ground chicken

1 cup plain dry bread crumbs

½ cup diced red bell pepper

½ cup ground walnuts

¼ cup sliced green onions

¼ cup light-colored beer

2 tablespoons chopped fresh parsley

2 tablespoons lemon juice

2 cloves garlic, minced

¾ teaspoon salt

⅛ teaspoon black pepper

1 tablespoon vegetable oil

4 slices white Cheddar cheese

4 whole wheat buns

Dijon mustard

Lettuce leaves

1. Combine chicken, bread crumbs, bell pepper, walnuts, green onions, beer, parsley, lemon juice, garlic, salt and black pepper in large bowl; mix lightly. Shape into four patties.

2. Heat oil in large cast iron skillet over medium-high heat. Cook patties 6 to 7 minutes per side or until cooked through (165°F). Place cheese on patties; cover skillet just until cheese melts.

3. Serve burgers on buns with mustard and lettuce.

Makes 4 servings

MEXICAN CASSEROLE WITH TORTILLA CHIPS

　1 tablespoon vegetable oil
12 ounces ground turkey
　1 can (about 14 ounces) stewed tomatoes
　1 package (8 ounces) frozen bell pepper stir-fry mixture, thawed
　¾ teaspoon ground cumin
　½ teaspoon salt
　½ cup (2 ounces) finely shredded sharp Cheddar cheese
　2 ounces tortilla chips, lightly crushed

1. Heat oil in large cast iron skillet over medium heat. Add turkey; cook until no longer pink, stirring to break up meat. Stir in tomatoes, bell pepper mixture and cumin; bring to a boil. Reduce heat; cover and simmer 20 minutes or until vegetables are tender. Stir in salt.

2. Sprinkle with cheese and chips.

Makes 4 servings

GREEK LEMON CHICKEN

　2 tablespoons extra virgin olive oil, divided
　2 tablespoons lemon juice
　1 teaspoon grated lemon peel
　1 teaspoon dried oregano
　1 clove garlic, minced
　¼ teaspoon salt
　⅛ teaspoon black pepper
　4 boneless skinless chicken breasts (about 4 ounces each)
　1 lemon, cut into wedges (optional)
　　Baby spinach leaves (optional)

1. Combine 1 tablespoon oil, lemon juice, lemon peel, oregano, garlic, salt and pepper in large resealable food storage bag. Add chicken; turn to coat. Marinate in refrigerator at least 30 minutes or up to 8 hours.

2. Heat remaining 1 tablespoon oil in large cast iron skillet over medium heat. Remove chicken from marinade; discard marinade. Add chicken to skillet; cook 3 minutes. Turn and cook over medium-low heat 7 minutes or until no longer pink in center.

3. Serve with lemon wedges and spinach, if desired.

Makes 4 servings

Mexican Casserole with Tortilla Chips

PAN-FRIED CHICKEN FINGERS

⅓ cup mayonnaise

1 tablespoon honey

1 tablespoon mustard

1 tablespoon packed dark brown sugar

1½ cups biscuit baking mix

1 cup buttermilk*

1 egg, beaten

12 chicken tenders (about 1½ pounds), rinsed and patted dry

Salt and black pepper to taste

¼ to ½ cup canola or vegetable oil

*Or substitute 1 tablespoon vinegar or lemon juice plus enough milk to equal 1 cup. Let stand 5 minutes.

1. Preheat oven to 200°F or "warm" setting. For dipping sauce, combine mayonnaise, honey, mustard and brown sugar in small bowl; mix well.

2. Place baking mix in shallow bowl. Whisk buttermilk and egg in another shallow bowl until well blended. Coat chicken with baking mix, then with buttermilk mixture. Roll in baking mix again to coat. Place on baking sheet; sprinkle with salt and pepper.

3. Heat ¼ cup oil in large cast iron skillet over medium-high heat. Cook chicken in batches over medium heat 5 to 6 minutes per side or until golden, adding additional oil as needed. Remove chicken to clean baking sheet; sprinkle with additional salt and pepper, if desired. Keep warm in oven.

4. Serve chicken with dipping sauce.   *Makes 4 main-dish servings or 12 appetizers*

CHICKEN FRICASSEE

   1 whole chicken (about 3 to 4 pounds), cut up
½ cup all-purpose flour
   1 teaspoon salt
¼ teaspoon black pepper
   2 to 3 tablespoons vegetable oil
   2 to 3 tablespoons butter
1½ cups chicken broth
¾ teaspoon dried thyme
1½ cups baby carrots or 1-inch carrot slices
   1 medium onion, cut into wedges
   2 stalks celery, cut into 1-inch slices

1. Remove skin from chicken, if desired. Cut large chicken breasts in half crosswise. Combine flour, salt and pepper in large resealable food storage bag. Add chicken pieces, two or three at a time; shake to coat. Reserve remaining flour mixture.

2. Heat 2 tablespoons oil and 2 tablespoons butter in large cast iron skillet over medium heat until mixture sizzles. Add chicken; cook about 8 minutes per side or until lightly browned, adding remaining 1 tablespoon oil and butter if necessary. Remove to plate.

3. Stir 2 tablespoons reserved flour mixture into skillet; cook and stir 1 minute. Gradually whisk in broth until smooth. Stir in thyme. Return chicken to skillet. Add carrots, onion and celery; bring to a boil. Reduce heat to low; cover and simmer 35 minutes or until chicken is tender.

4. Remove chicken and vegetables to large plate. Bring liquid to a boil; boil gently about 5 minutes or until sauce reaches desired thickness. Serve chicken and vegetables with sauce. *Makes 4 to 6 servings*

SPINACH AND TURKEY SKILLET

8 ounces turkey breast tenderloin or turkey strips
⅛ teaspoon salt
1 tablespoon olive oil
¼ cup chopped onion
2 cloves garlic, minced
⅓ cup uncooked rice
¾ teaspoon Italian seasoning
¼ teaspoon black pepper
1 cup reduced-sodium chicken broth, divided
2 cups packed fresh spinach
⅔ cup diced plum tomatoes
¼ cup shredded Parmesan cheese

1. Cut turkey into bite-size pieces; sprinkle with salt.

2. Heat oil in medium cast iron skillet over medium-high heat. Add turkey; cook and stir until lightly browned. Remove to plate. Add onion and garlic to skillet; cook and stir over low heat 3 minutes or until tender. Return turkey to skillet; stir in rice, Italian seasoning and pepper.

3. Reserve 2 tablespoons broth. Stir remaining broth into skillet; bring to a boil over medium-high heat. Reduce heat to low; cover and simmer 15 minutes. Stir in spinach and reserved broth; cover and cook 2 to 3 minutes or until liquid is absorbed and spinach is wilted. Stir in tomatoes; heat through. Sprinkle with Parmesan cheese.

Makes 2 servings

BALSAMIC CHICKEN

1½ teaspoons fresh rosemary leaves, minced *or* ½ teaspoon dried rosemary

  2 cloves garlic, minced

¾ teaspoon black pepper

½ teaspoon salt

  6 boneless skinless chicken breasts (about 4 ounces each)

  2 tablespoons olive oil, divided

¼ cup balsamic vinegar

1. Combine rosemary, garlic, pepper and salt in small bowl; mix well. Place chicken in large bowl; drizzle with 1 tablespoon oil and rub with spice mixture. Cover and refrigerate 1 to 3 hours.

2. Preheat oven to 450°F. Brush large cast iron skillet with remaining 1 tablespoon oil. Place chicken in skillet; bake 10 minutes. Turn chicken, stirring in 3 to 4 tablespoons water if drippings begin to stick to pan.

3. Bake about 10 minutes or until chicken is golden brown and no longer pink in center. If pan is dry, stir in additional 1 to 2 tablespoons water to loosen drippings.

4. Drizzle vinegar over chicken in skillet. Remove chicken to plates. Stir liquid in skillet, scraping up browned bits from bottom of skillet. Drizzle over chicken. *Makes 6 servings*

TIP To remove the leaves from a sprig of rosemary, hold the stem at the top and run your thumb and forefinger down the stem to strip the leaves from the stem. (This method is quicker than removing the leaves one by one.)

MEAT

HAM AND BARBECUED BEAN SKILLET

1 tablespoon vegetable oil

1 cup chopped onion

1 teaspoon minced garlic

1 can (about 15 ounces) kidney beans, rinsed and drained

1 can (about 15 ounces) cannellini or Great Northern beans, rinsed and drained

1 cup chopped green bell pepper

½ cup packed brown sugar

½ cup ketchup

2 tablespoons cider vinegar

2 teaspoons dry mustard

1 ham steak (½ inch thick, about 12 ounces)

1. Heat oil in large cast iron skillet over medium-high heat. Add onion and garlic; cook and stir 3 minutes. Stir in kidney beans, cannellini beans, bell pepper, brown sugar, ketchup, vinegar and mustard; mix well.

2. Trim fat from ham; cut ham into ½-inch pieces. Add ham to skillet. Reduce heat to low; simmer 5 minutes or until sauce thickens and mixture is heated through, stirring occasionally.

Makes 4 servings

OPEN-FACE STEAK AND BLUE CHEESE SANDWICHES

4 boneless beef top loin (strip) or tenderloin steaks, cut ¾ inch thick
   Black pepper
1 teaspoon olive oil
   Salt
4 slices ciabatta bread
8 thin slices blue cheese

1. Season steaks with pepper. Heat oil in large cast iron skillet over medium heat.

2. Add steaks to skillet; do not crowd. Cook 10 to 12 minutes or until medium-rare (145°F), turning once. Remove to cutting board. Tent with foil; let stand 5 to 10 minutes. Slice steaks; season with salt.

3. Toast bread. Place 2 slices blue cheese on each toast slice; top with steak slices. Serve immediately.

Makes 4 servings

PORK MEDALLIONS WITH MARSALA

2 tablespoons all-purpose flour
1 pound pork tenderloin, cut into ½-inch slices
2 tablespoons olive oil
1 clove garlic, minced
½ cup sweet marsala wine
2 tablespoons chopped fresh parsley

1. Place flour in shallow bowl. Coat pork slices with flour, shaking off excess.

2. Heat oil in large cast iron skillet over medium-high heat. Add pork; cook 3 minutes per side or until browned. Remove to plate.

3. Add garlic to skillet; cook and stir 1 minute over medium heat. Add marsala and pork; cook 3 minutes or until pork is barely pink in center. Remove pork to clean plate. Stir in parsley; simmer 2 to 3 minutes or until sauce is slightly thickened. Spoon sauce over pork. *Makes 4 servings*

NOTE: Marsala is a rich, smoky-flavored wine imported from the Mediterranean island of Sicily. This sweet varietal is served with dessert or used for cooking. Dry marsala is served as a before-dinner drink.

Open-Face Steak and Blue Cheese Sandwiches

PORK SCHNITZEL WITH MUSHROOM GRAVY

6 thin-cut boneless pork sirloin chops or boneless pork loin chops* (about 1¼ pounds)
    Salt and black pepper
½ cup plus 1 tablespoon all-purpose flour, divided
2 eggs
1 cup plain dry bread crumbs
2 tablespoons chopped fresh parsley *or* 1 tablespoon dried parsley flakes
¼ cup vegetable oil
4 tablespoons butter, divided
¼ cup finely chopped onion
1 package (8 ounces) sliced button mushrooms
1 cup chicken broth
2 to 3 tablespoons half-and-half

*Pork cutlets can be substituted for the boneless pork chops.

1. Pound pork chops to ⅛-inch thickness between sheets of waxed paper with meat mallet. Season with salt and pepper. Place ½ cup flour in shallow bowl. Lightly beat eggs in another shallow bowl. Combine bread crumbs and parsley in third shallow bowl.

2. Coat pork with flour, then with eggs. Roll in bread crumb mixture to coat.

3. Heat oil and 2 tablespoons butter in large cast iron skillet over medium heat until mixture sizzles. Cook pork in batches 3 minutes per side or until browned. *Do not overcook.* Remove to plate; keep warm.

4. Heat remaining 2 tablespoons butter in same skillet over medium heat. Add onion; cook and stir 1 minute. Add mushrooms; cook and stir 6 to 7 minutes or until mushrooms are lightly browned and most liquid has evaporated. Stir in remaining 1 tablespoon flour; cook 1 minute. Stir in broth; bring to a boil, stirring constantly. Boil 1 minute. Remove from heat; stir in half-and-half.

5. Spoon gravy over pork. Serve immediately.   *Makes 6 servings*

PIZZA CASSEROLE

   2 cups uncooked rotini or other spiral pasta
1½ pounds ground beef
   1 medium onion, chopped
     Salt and black pepper
   1 can (about 15 ounces) pizza sauce
   1 can (8 ounces) tomato sauce
   1 can (6 ounces) tomato paste
   ½ teaspoon sugar
   ½ teaspoon garlic salt
   ½ teaspoon dried oregano
   2 cups (8 ounces) shredded mozzarella cheese
  12 to 15 slices pepperoni

1. Preheat oven to 350°F. Cook pasta according to package directions; drain.

2. Meanwhile, cook beef and onion in large cast iron skillet over medium-high heat 6 to 8 minutes or until browned, stirring to break up meat. Drain fat. Season with salt and pepper.

3. Combine pasta, pizza sauce, tomato sauce, tomato paste, sugar, garlic salt and oregano in large bowl; mix well. Add beef mixture; stir until blended. Spread half of mixture in skillet; top with 1 cup cheese. Top with remaining beef mixture, cheese and pepperoni.

4. Bake 25 to 30 minutes or until heated through and cheese is melted.   *Makes 6 servings*

TIP When cooking pasta for a casserole, reduce the suggested cooking time by a few minutes. The pasta will continue to cook and absorb liquid in the oven.

PORK TENDERLOIN WITH CHERRY SAUCE

1 tablespoon plus 2 teaspoons olive oil, divided
¼ cup finely chopped shallots
1 pork tenderloin (about 12 ounces)
¼ teaspoon salt
⅛ teaspoon black pepper
1 cup reduced-sodium chicken broth
1 cup frozen sweet cherries, thawed
2 tablespoons finely chopped dried sour cherries (optional)
1 tablespoon balsamic vinegar
1 teaspoon butter
1 teaspoon brown sugar

1. Preheat oven to 350°F. Heat 1 tablespoon oil in large cast iron skillet over medium heat. Add shallots; cook 2 to 3 minutes or until lightly browned. Remove to plate; set aside.

2. Season pork with salt and pepper. Heat remaining 2 teaspoons oil in same skillet over medium-high heat. Add pork; cook about 10 minutes or until browned on all sides.

3. Transfer skillet to oven. Roast about 8 minutes or until 145°F. Remove pork to cutting board; tent with foil to keep warm.

4. Return skillet to stovetop. Add broth, sweet cherries, dried cherries, if desired, and vinegar; cook over medium-high heat, scraping up browned bits from bottom of skillet. Mash cherries with fork; cook 5 to 6 minutes or until liquid is reduced to about ½ cup. Reduce heat to medium; stir in butter and brown sugar until well blended.

5. Slice pork. Spoon sauce over pork; sprinkle with reserved shallots.　　　*Makes 2 servings*

EMERALD ISLE LAMB CHOPS

2 tablespoons vegetable or olive oil, divided
2 tablespoons coarse Dijon mustard
1 tablespoon Irish whiskey
1 tablespoon minced fresh rosemary leaves
2 teaspoons minced garlic
1½ pounds loin lamb chops (about 6 chops)
½ teaspoon *each* salt and black pepper
¾ cup dry white wine
2 tablespoons black currant jam
1 to 2 tablespoons butter, cut into pieces

1. Whisk 1 tablespoon oil, mustard, whiskey, rosemary and garlic in small bowl to form paste. Season lamb chops with salt and pepper; spread paste over both sides. Cover and let stand at room temperature 30 minutes or refrigerate 2 to 3 hours.

2. Heat remaining 1 tablespoon oil in large cast iron skillet over medium-high heat. Add lamb in single layer; cook 2 to 3 minutes per side or until desired doneness. Remove to plate; keep warm.

3. Drain excess fat from skillet. Add wine; cook and stir about 5 minutes, scraping up browned bits from bottom of skillet. Stir in jam until well blended. Remove from heat; stir in butter until melted. Spoon sauce over lamb. *Makes 4 to 6 servings*

PEPPER STEAK

1 tablespoon coarsely cracked black pepper
½ teaspoon dried rosemary
2 beef tenderloin or rib-eye steaks (4 to 6 ounces each)
1 tablespoon butter
1 tablespoon vegetable oil
   Salt
¼ cup brandy or dry red wine

1. Combine pepper and rosemary in bowl. Coat both sides of steaks with spice mixture.

2. Heat butter and oil in large cast iron skillet over medium heat until mixture sizzles. Add steaks; cook 5 to 7 minutes per side for medium rare to medium or until desired doneness. Remove to plate. Sprinkle with salt; keep warm.

3. Add brandy to skillet; bring to a boil over high heat, scraping up browned bits from bottom of skillet. Boil about 1 minute or until liquid is reduced by half. Spoon sauce over steaks. *Makes 2 servings*

Emerald Isle Lamb Chops

SAUSAGE AND PEPPERS

Light-colored beer or water
1 pound hot or mild Italian sausage links
2 tablespoons olive oil
3 medium onions, cut into ½-inch slices
2 red bell peppers, cut into ½-inch slices
2 green bell peppers, cut into ½-inch slices
1½ teaspoons coarse salt, divided
1 teaspoon dried oregano
Italian rolls (optional)

1. Fill medium saucepan half full with beer or water; bring to a boil over high heat. Add sausage; cook 5 minutes over medium heat. Drain and cut diagonally into 1-inch slices.

2. Heat oil in large cast iron skillet over medium-high heat. Add sausage; cook about 10 minutes or until browned, stirring occasionally. Remove to plate.

3. Add onions, bell peppers, 1 teaspoon salt and oregano to skillet; cook over medium heat about 25 minutes or until vegetables are very soft and browned in spots, stirring occasionally. Add sausage and remaining ½ teaspoon salt; cook 3 minutes or until heated through. Serve with rolls, if desired.

Makes 4 servings

PORK AND SWEET POTATO SKILLET

1½ tablespoons butter, divided
12 ounces pork tenderloin, cut into 1-inch cubes
¼ teaspoon salt
⅛ teaspoon black pepper
2 medium sweet potatoes, peeled and cut into ½-inch pieces (about 2 cups)
1 small onion, sliced
4 ounces smoked sausage, halved lengthwise and cut into ½-inch pieces
1 small apple, cut into ½-inch pieces
½ cup sweet and sour sauce

1. Melt ½ tablespoon butter in large cast iron skillet over medium-high heat. Add pork; cook and stir 2 to 3 minutes or until pork is no longer pink. Season with salt and pepper. Remove to plate.

2. Add remaining 1 tablespoon butter, sweet potatoes and onion to skillet; cover and cook over medium-low heat 8 to 10 minutes or until tender, stirring occasionally. Add pork, sausage, apple and sweet and sour sauce; cook and stir until heated through.

Makes 4 servings

Sausage and Peppers

TEPPANYAKI

⅓ cup tamari or soy sauce

2 tablespoons mirin (Japanese sweet rice wine)

1 tablespoon lemon juice

1 tablespoon orange juice

⅛ to ¼ teaspoon red pepper flakes (optional)

4 small frozen corn on the cob pieces, thawed

2 to 3 tablespoons vegetable oil

2 medium zucchini or yellow squash, cut diagonally into thin slices

4 ounces shiitake mushrooms, stemmed and cut into thick slices

8 ounces beef tenderloin or top loin steak, thinly sliced crosswise

8 ounces pork tenderloin, thinly sliced crosswise

8 ounces medium raw shrimp, peeled and deveined

1. For dipping sauce, combine tamari, mirin, lemon juice, orange juice and red pepper flakes, if desired, in small bowl; set aside.

2. Preheat oven to 200°F or "warm" setting. Microwave corn according to package directions just until heated through. Heat 2 tablespoons oil in large cast iron skillet over medium-high heat. Brown corn about 2 minutes, turning frequently. Remove to large baking pan in oven to keep warm.

3. Add zucchini to skillet; cook and stir 2 to 3 minutes or until browned and tender, adding additional oil if necessary. Remove to pan in oven to keep warm. Add mushooms to skillet; cook 2 to 3 minutes or until tender. Remove to oven.

4. Add beef to skillet; cook 2 minutes or until browned and tender, adding additional oil as needed. Remove to oven. Add pork to skillet; cook about 3 minutes. Remove to oven. Add shrimp to skillet; cook 2 to 3 minutes or until pink and opaque, stirring occasionally.

5. Serve meat and vegetables with dipping sauce.

Makes 4 servings

SERVING SUGGESTION: Teppanyaki is often served with several dipping sauces. A traditional ponzu sauce, as in this recipe, is usually one of them. You can make a quick ginger dipping sauce by adding minced fresh ginger, sake and a bit of wasabi to tamari or soy sauce.

MILANESE PORK CHOPS

    2 tablespoons all-purpose flour
    ½ teaspoon salt
    ½ teaspoon black pepper
    1 egg
    1 teaspoon water
    ¼ cup seasoned dry bread crumbs
    ¼ cup grated Parmesan cheese
    4 boneless pork loin chops, cut ¾ inch thick
    1 tablespoon olive oil
    1 tablespoon butter
        Lemon wedges

1. Preheat oven to 400°F. Combine flour, salt and pepper in shallow bowl. Beat egg and water in another shallow bowl. Combine bread crumbs and Parmesan cheese in third shallow bowl.

2. Coat pork chops with flour mixture, then with egg mixture. Roll in bread crumb mixture to coat, pressing mixture onto pork. Place on waxed paper-lined plate; refrigerate 15 minutes.

3. Heat oil and butter in large cast iron skillet over medium-high heat until mixture sizzles. Add pork; cook 4 minutes or until golden brown. Turn pork and transfer skillet to oven. Bake 6 to 8 minutes or until cooked through (145°F). Serve with lemon wedges. *Makes 4 servings*

"Milanese" is a preparation where meat is typically pounded thin, coated with egg and then with bread crumbs and Parmesan cheese, and pan-fried in butter and/or oil. It is commonly prepared with pork or veal, but it can be made with chicken as well.

BEEF TENDERLOIN WITH LEMON BUTTER

2 beef tenderloin (filet mignon) steaks (6 ounces each)
¼ teaspoon salt, divided
⅛ teaspoon black pepper
⅛ teaspoon garlic powder
3 tablespoons butter, softened, divided
1 tablespoon finely minced fresh parsley
¾ teaspoon grated lemon peel
¼ teaspoon dried tarragon
1 tablespoon canola oil

1. Sprinkle both sides of steaks with ⅛ teaspoon salt, pepper and garlic powder. Let stand 15 minutes.

2. Meanwhile, combine 2 tablespoons butter, parsley, lemon peel and tarragon in small bowl; mix well.

3. Heat remaining 1 tablespoon butter and oil in medium cast iron skillet over medium-high heat until mixture sizzles. Add steaks; cook 2 minutes per side. Reduce heat to medium; cook 3 minutes per side or until desired doneness. Top steaks with lemon butter. *Makes 2 servings*

TUSCAN LAMB SKILLET

8 lamb rib chops (1½ pounds), cut 1 inch thick
2 teaspoons olive oil
3 teaspoons minced garlic
1 can (19 ounces) cannellini beans, rinsed and drained
1 can (about 14 ounces) diced Italian-style tomatoes
1 tablespoon balsamic vinegar
2 teaspoons minced fresh rosemary leaves

1. Trim fat from lamb chops. Heat oil in large cast iron skillet over medium heat. Add lamb; cook 4 minutes per side for medium (160°F) or until desired doneness. Remove to plate; keep warm.

2. Add garlic to skillet; cook and stir 1 minute. Stir in beans, tomatoes, vinegar and rosemary; bring to a boil. Reduce heat to medium-low; simmer 5 minutes. Serve with lamb. *Makes 4 servings*

Beef Tenderloin with Lemon Butter

GRILLED PROSCIUTTO, BRIE AND FIG SANDWICHES

¼ cup fig preserves
4 slices (½ to ¾ inch thick) Italian or country bread
   Black pepper
4 to 6 ounces Brie cheese, cut into ¼-inch-thick slices
2 slices prosciutto (about half of 3-ounce package)
¼ cup baby arugula
1½ tablespoons butter

1. Spread preserves over two bread slices. Sprinkle pepper generously over preserves. Top with Brie, prosciutto, arugula and remaining bread slices.

2. Heat medium cast iron skillet over medium heat 5 minutes. Add 1 tablespoon butter; swirl to melt and coat bottom of skillet. Add sandwiches to skillet; cook over medium-low heat about 5 minutes or until bottoms of sandwiches are golden brown.

3. Turn sandwiches and add remaining ½ tablespoon butter to skillet. Tilt pan to melt butter and move sandwiches so butter flows underneath. Cover with foil; cook about 5 minutes or until cheese is melted and bread is golden brown.   *Makes 2 sandwiches*

STEAK DIANE WITH CREMINI MUSHROOMS

1½ tablespoons vegetable oil, divided
2 beef tenderloin steaks (4 ounces each), cut ¾ inch thick
¼ teaspoon black pepper
⅓ cup sliced shallots or chopped onion
4 ounces cremini mushrooms, sliced *or* 1 (4-ounce) package sliced mixed wild mushrooms
1½ tablespoons Worcestershire sauce
1 tablespoon Dijon mustard

1. Heat 1 tablespoon oil in medium cast iron skillet over medium-high heat. Add steaks; sprinkle with pepper. Cook 3 minutes per side for medium-rare or until desired doneness. Remove to plate; keep warm.

2. Add remaining ½ tablespoon oil to skillet; heat over medium heat. Add shallots; cook and stir 2 minutes. Add mushrooms; cook and stir 3 minutes. Add Worcestershire sauce and mustard; cook 1 minute, stirring frequently.

3. Return steaks and any accumulated juices to skillet; cook until heated through, turning once. Serve steaks with mushroom mixture.   *Makes 2 servings*

Grilled Prosciutto, Brie and Fig Sandwiches

MEXICAN TAMALE SKILLET CASSEROLE

1 pound ground chuck
1 cup frozen corn kernels, thawed
1 can (4 ounces) chopped green chiles
1 can (8 ounces) tomato sauce
½ cup water
1 package taco seasoning mix
½ teaspoon ground cumin
1 cup whole milk
½ cup biscuit baking mix
2 eggs
1½ cups (6 ounces) shredded Monterey Jack cheese or Mexican cheese blend
Sour cream, sliced olives, chopped tomatoes and/or chopped fresh cilantro (optional)

1. Preheat oven to 400°F. Cook beef in large cast iron skillet over medium-high heat about 6 minutes or until browned, stirring to break up meat. Drain fat. Stir in corn, chiles, tomato sauce, water, taco seasoning and cumin; mix well. Remove from heat; smooth top of mixture into even layer.

2. Combine milk, baking mix and eggs in small bowl; stir until well blended. Spread evenly over beef mixture in skillet.

3. Bake about 40 minutes or until crust is golden and knife inserted into center comes out clean. Sprinkle with cheese; let stand 5 minutes before serving. Serve with desired toppings.   *Makes 4 servings*

TIP To lighten up this casserole, substitute ground turkey or chicken for the ground chuck. Or swap out half of the beef for black beans, adding them to the skillet with the corn and chiles. (Drain and rinse canned beans before using.)

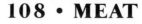

PORK CHOPS AND STUFFING SKILLET

  4 thin bone-in pork chops (4 ounces each)
¼ teaspoon dried thyme
¼ teaspoon paprika
⅛ teaspoon salt
  4 ounces bulk pork sausage
  1 tablespoon vegetable oil
  2 cups corn bread stuffing mix
  1 cup diced green bell pepper
¼ teaspoon poultry seasoning (optional)
1¼ cups water

1. Preheat oven to 350°F. Sprinkle one side of pork chops with thyme, paprika and salt.

2. Heat oil in large cast iron skillet over medium-high heat. Add pork, seasoned side down; cook 2 minutes. Remove to plate; keep warm. Add sausage to skillet; cook until no longer pink, stirring to break up meat.

3. Remove from heat; stir in stuffing mix, bell pepper, poultry seasoning, if desired, and water just until blended. Arrange pork, seasoned side up, over stuffing mixture.

4. Cover and bake 15 minutes or until pork is no longer pink in center. Let stand 5 minutes before serving.

Makes 4 servings

SEAFOOD

PAN-ROASTED PIKE WITH BUTTERY BREAD CRUMBS

6 tablespoons butter, divided
2 garlic cloves, minced
⅓ cup plain dry bread crumbs
½ teaspoon salt, divided
4 tablespoons chopped fresh parsley
4 pike or other medium-firm white fish fillets (about 6 ounces each)
⅛ teaspoon black pepper
2 tablespoons lemon juice

1. Preheat oven to 400°F.

2. Heat 2 tablespoons butter in small skillet over medium-high heat. Add garlic; cook and stir 1 minute or just until lightly browned. Stir in bread crumbs and ⅛ teaspoon salt; cook and stir 1 minute. Remove to small bowl; stir in parsley.

3. Heat 1 tablespoon butter in large cast iron skillet over medium-high heat. Sprinkle pike fillets with ¼ teaspoon salt and pepper. Add to skillet, skin side up; cook 1 minute. Remove from heat; turn fish and top with bread crumb mixture. Transfer skillet to oven; roast 8 to 10 minutes or until fish begins to flake when tested with fork.

4. Wipe out small skillet with paper towel; heat over medium heat. Add remaining 3 tablespoons butter; cook 3 to 4 minutes or until melted and lightly browned, stirring occasionally. Stir in lemon juice and remaining ⅛ teaspoon salt. Spoon mixture over fish just before serving.   *Makes 4 servings*

PAN-FRIED OYSTERS

¼ cup all-purpose flour
½ teaspoon salt
¼ teaspoon black pepper
2 eggs
½ cup plain dry bread crumbs
5 tablespoons chopped fresh parsley, divided
2 containers (8 ounces each) shucked fresh oysters, rinsed, drained and patted dry
    or 1 pound fresh oysters, shucked and patted dry
  Canola oil for frying
5 slices thick-cut bacon, crisp-cooked and chopped
  Lemon wedges

1. Combine flour, salt and pepper in shallow bowl. Beat eggs in another shallow bowl. Combine bread crumbs and 4 tablespoons parsley in third shallow bowl.

2. Coat oysters with flour mixture, then with eggs. Roll in bread crumb mixture to coat.

3. Pour oil into large cast iron skillet to depth of ½ inch; heat over medium-high heat until very hot but not smoking (about 370°F). Add one third of oysters; cook about 2 minutes per side or until golden brown. Drain on paper towel-lined plate. Repeat with remaining oysters.

4. Toss oysters with bacon and remaining 1 tablespoon parsley in large bowl. Serve immediately with lemon wedges.

Makes 4 appetizer servings

FISH TACOS WITH CILANTRO CREAM SAUCE

½ cup sour cream
¼ cup chopped fresh cilantro
1¼ teaspoons ground cumin, divided
1 pound skinless tilapia, mahimahi or other firm white fish fillets
1 teaspoon chipotle hot pepper sauce, divided
1 teaspoon garlic salt
2 teaspoons canola or vegetable oil
1 red bell pepper, cut into strips
1 green bell pepper, cut into strips
8 corn tortillas, warmed
2 limes, cut into wedges

1. For sauce, combine sour cream, cilantro and ¼ teaspoon cumin in small bowl; mix well. Refrigerate until ready to serve.

2. Cut tilapia fillets into 1-inch chunks; toss with ½ teaspoon hot pepper sauce, remaining 1 teaspoon cumin and garlic salt in medium bowl. Heat oil in large cast iron skillet over medium heat. Add fish; cook 3 to 4 minutes or until fish is opaque in center, turning once. Remove to plate.

3. Add bell peppers to skillet; cook and stir 6 to 8 minutes or until tender. Return fish to skillet with remaining ½ teaspoon hot pepper sauce; cook and stir just until heated through.

4. Spoon mixture into warm tortillas. Serve with sauce and lime wedges.   *Makes 4 servings*

TIP To warm tortillas in the microwave, wrap them loosely in a damp paper towel. Microwave for 30 seconds or until heated through.

BLACKENED SHRIMP WITH TOMATOES AND RED ONION

1½ teaspoons paprika
  1 teaspoon Italian seasoning
½ teaspoon garlic powder
¼ teaspoon black pepper
  8 ounces small raw shrimp (about 24), peeled with tails left on
  1 tablespoon canola oil
½ cup sliced red onion, separated into rings
1½ cups halved grape tomatoes
    Lime wedges (optional)

1. Combine paprika, Italian seasoning, garlic powder and pepper in large resealable food storage bag. Add shrimp; shake to coat.

2. Heat oil in large cast iron skillet over medium-high heat. Add shrimp; cook 4 minutes or until shrimp are pink and opaque, turning occasionally. Add onion and tomatoes; cook and stir 1 minute or until tomatoes are heated through and onion is slightly wilted. Serve with lime wedges, if desired.

Makes 4 servings

TUNA MONTE CRISTO SANDWICHES

  4 slices (½ ounce each) Cheddar cheese
  4 oval slices sourdough or challah (egg) bread
½ pound deli tuna salad
¼ cup milk
  1 egg, beaten
  2 tablespoons butter

1. Place one cheese slice on each of two bread slices. Top with tuna, remaining cheese and bread slices.

2. Whisk milk and egg in shallow bowl until well blended. Dip sandwiches in egg mixture, turning to coat.

3. Melt butter in large cast iron skillet over medium heat. Add sandwiches; cook 4 to 5 minutes per side or until cheese melts and sandwiches are golden brown.

Makes 2 servings

Blackened Shrimp with Tomatoes and Red Onion

CAJUN BASS

2 tablespoons all-purpose flour
1 to 1½ teaspoons Cajun or Caribbean jerk seasoning
1 egg white
2 teaspoons water
⅓ cup seasoned dry bread crumbs
2 tablespoons cornmeal
4 skinless striped bass, halibut or cod fillets (4 to 6 ounces each), thawed if frozen
1 teaspoon butter
1 teaspoon olive oil
   Chopped fresh parsley (optional)
4 lemon wedges

1. Combine flour and seasoning in shallow bowl. Beat egg white and water in another shallow bowl. Combine bread crumbs and cornmeal in third shallow bowl.

2. Coat bass fillets with flour mixture, then with egg white mixture. Roll in bread crumb mixture to coat.

3. Heat butter and oil in large cast iron skillet over medium heat until mixure sizzles. Add fish; cook 4 to 5 minutes per side or until golden brown and fish is opaque in center and begins to flake when tested with fork.

4. Sprinkle with parsley, if desired. Serve with lemon wedges.   *Makes 4 servings*

SPANISH PAELLA

6 cups chicken broth

3 tablespoons olive oil

½ pound boneless skinless chicken thighs, cut into bite-size pieces

2 to 3 links chorizo sausage (about 5 ounces), sliced

1 medium onion, chopped

1 red bell pepper, chopped

4 cloves garlic, minced

1 teaspoon saffron threads, minced

1½ cups uncooked white rice

1 can (10 ounces) diced tomatoes with chiles

3 tablespoons tomato paste

½ teaspoon salt

¼ teaspoon black pepper

1 pound large raw shrimp, peeled and deveined (with tails on)

½ pound mussels

½ cup frozen peas, thawed

1. Bring broth to a boil in medium saucepan over high heat; keep warm over low heat.

2. Heat oil in large cast iron skillet over medium-high heat. Add chicken and chorizo; cook 1 minute, stirring once. Add onion, bell pepper, garlic and saffron; cook and stir 5 minutes or until vegetables are soft and chorizo is browned.

3. Stir in rice, diced tomatoes, tomato paste, salt and black pepper; cook 5 minutes, stirring occasionally. Add warm broth, ½ to 1 cup at a time, stirring after each addition until broth is almost absorbed.

4. Reduce heat to medium. Cover skillet with foil; cook 25 to 30 minutes or until rice is tender. Remove foil; gently stir in shrimp, mussels and peas. Replace foil; cook 5 to 10 minutes or until shrimp are pink and opaque and mussels open. (Discard any mussels that do not open.)

Makes 6 to 8 servings

SALMON PATTY BURGERS

1 can (about 14 ounces) red salmon, drained
1 egg white
2 tablespoons toasted wheat germ
1 tablespoon dried onion flakes
1 tablespoon capers, drained
½ teaspoon dried thyme
¼ teaspoon black pepper
1 tablespoon vegetable oil
4 whole wheat buns, split
2 tablespoons Dijon mustard
4 tomato slices
4 thin red onion slices *or* 8 dill pickle slices
4 lettuce leaves

1. Place salmon in medium bowl; mash with fork. Add egg white, wheat germ, onion flakes, capers, thyme and pepper; mix well.

2. Shape mixture into four patties; cover and refrigerate 1 hour or until firm.

3. Heat oil in large cast iron skillet over medium heat. Add patties; cook 5 minutes per side.

4. Spread cut sides of buns with mustard. Place patties on buns; top with tomato, onion, lettuce and tops of buns. *Makes 4 servings*

NOTE: Red salmon is more expensive with a firm texture and deep red color. Pink salmon is less expensive with a light pink color.

SOUTHERN FRIED CATFISH WITH HUSH PUPPIES

Hush Puppy Batter (recipe follows)
4 catfish fillets (about 1½ pounds)
½ cup yellow cornmeal
3 tablespoons all-purpose flour
1½ teaspoons salt
¼ teaspoon ground red pepper
Vegetable oil for frying
Prepared remoulade or tartar sauce (optional)

1. Prepare Hush Puppy Batter; set aside.

2. Rinse catfish fillets; pat dry with paper towels. Combine cornmeal, flour, salt and red pepper in shallow bowl. Coat fish with cornmeal mixture.

3. Pour oil into large cast iron skillet to depth of 1 inch; heat to 375°F over medium heat. Cook fish in batches 4 to 5 minutes or until golden brown and fish begins to flake when tested with fork. Drain on paper towel-lined plate; keep warm. *Allow temperature of oil to return to 375°F between batches.*

4. Drop hush puppy batter by tablespoonfuls into hot oil (oil should be 375°F); cook in batches 2 minutes or until golden brown. Drain on paper towel-lined plate. Serve with catfish and sauce, if desired.

Makes 4 servings

HUSH PUPPY BATTER

1½ cups yellow cornmeal
½ cup all-purpose flour
2 teaspoons baking powder
½ teaspoon salt
1 cup milk
1 small onion, minced
1 egg, lightly beaten

Combine cornmeal, flour, baking powder and salt in medium bowl. Add milk, onion and egg; stir until well blended. Allow batter to stand 5 to 10 minutes.

Makes about 24 hush puppies

LEMON SESAME SCALLOPS

8 ounces uncooked whole wheat spaghetti

3 tablespoons sesame oil, divided

¼ cup chicken broth or clam juice

3 tablespoons lemon juice

2 tablespoons oyster sauce

1 tablespoon cornstarch

1 tablespoon soy sauce

½ teaspoon grated lemon peel

1 tablespoon vegetable oil

2 carrots, cut into thin strips

1 yellow bell pepper, cut into thin strips

4 slices peeled fresh ginger

1 clove garlic, minced

1 pound sea scallops

6 ounces fresh snow peas, trimmed, or frozen snow peas, thawed

2 green onions, thinly sliced

1 tablespoon sesame seeds, toasted*

*To toast sesame seeds, spread seeds in small skillet. Shake skillet over medium heat about 3 minutes or until seeds begin to pop and turn golden.

1. Cook spaghetti according to package directions; drain. Toss with 2 tablespoons sesame oil in medium bowl; keep warm.

2. Whisk broth, lemon juice, oyster sauce, cornstarch, soy sauce and lemon peel in small bowl until smooth and well blended; set aside.

3. Heat remaining 1 tablespoon sesame oil and vegetable oil in large cast iron skillet over medium heat. Add carrots and bell pepper; cook and stir 4 to 5 minutes or until crisp-tender. Remove to large bowl.

4. Add ginger and garlic to skillet; cook and stir 1 minute over medium-high heat. Add scallops; cook and stir 1 minute. Add snow peas and green onions; cook and stir 2 to 3 minutes or until scallops are opaque. Remove and discard ginger. Add scallop mixture to vegetable mixture in bowl, leaving any liquid in skillet.

5. Stir broth mixture into skillet; cook and stir 5 minutes or until thickened. Return scallop and vegetable mixture to skillet; cook 1 minute or until heated through. Serve scallops and vegetables over warm spaghetti. Sprinkle with sesame seeds. *Makes 4 servings*

PROSCIUTTO-WRAPPED SNAPPER

1 tablespoon plus 1 teaspoon olive oil, divided
2 cloves garlic, minced
4 skinless red snapper or halibut fillets (6 to 7 ounces each)
½ teaspoon salt
½ teaspoon black pepper
8 large fresh sage leaves
8 thin slices prosciutto (4 ounces)
¼ cup dry marsala wine

1. Preheat oven to 400°F.

2. Combine 1 tablespoon oil and garlic in small bowl; brush over snapper fillets. Sprinkle with salt and pepper. Place two sage leaves on each fillet. Wrap two prosciutto slices around fish to enclose sage leaves; tuck in ends of prosciutto.

3. Heat remaining 1 teaspoon oil in large cast iron skillet over medium-high heat. Add fish, sage side down; cook 3 to 4 minutes or until prosciutto is crisp. Carefully turn fish. Transfer skillet to oven; bake 8 to 10 minutes or until fish is opaque in center. Remove to plate; keep warm.

4. Add wine to skillet; cook over medium-high heat, scraping up browned bits from bottom of skillet. Stir constantly 2 to 3 minutes or until mixture has reduced by half. Drizzle over fish.   *Makes 4 servings*

NUTTY PAN-FRIED TROUT

2 tablespoons olive oil
½ cup seasoned dry bread crumbs
4 trout fillets (about 6 ounces each)
½ cup pine nuts

1. Heat oil in large cast iron skillet over medium heat. Place bread crumbs in shallow bowl. Coat pike fillets with bread crumbs.

2. Add fish to skillet; cook 4 minutes per side or until fish begins to flake when tested with fork. Remove to plate; keep warm.

3. Add pine nuts to drippings in skillet; cook and stir 3 minutes or until nuts are lightly toasted. Sprinkle over fish.   *Makes 4 servings*

Prosciutto-Wrapped Snapper

TUNA CAKES WITH CREAMY CUCUMBER SAUCE

½ cup finely chopped cucumber

½ cup plain yogurt or Greek yogurt

1½ teaspoons chopped fresh dill *or* ½ teaspoon dried dill weed

1 teaspoon lemon pepper

⅓ cup shredded carrots

¼ cup sliced green onion

¼ cup finely chopped celery

¼ cup mayonnaise

2 teaspoons spicy brown mustard

1 cup panko bread crumbs, divided

1 can (12 ounces) albacore tuna in water, drained

1½ tablespoons canola oil or olive oil, divided

Lemon wedges (optional)

1. For sauce, combine cucumber, yogurt, dill and lemon pepper in small bowl; mix well. Cover and refrigerate until ready to serve.

2. Combine carrots, green onion, celery, mayonnaise and mustard in medium bowl. Stir in ½ cup panko. Add tuna; stir until blended.

3. Place remaining ½ cup panko in shallow bowl. Shape tuna mixture into five ½-inch-thick patties. Coat patties with panko.

4. Heat 1 tablespoon oil in large cast iron skillet over medium heat. Add patties; cook 5 to 6 minutes or until golden brown, turning once and adding remaining ½ tablespoon oil to skillet when patties are turned. Serve with sauce and lemon wedges, if desired. *Makes 5 servings*

CATFISH WITH CHERRY SALSA

1 cup halved pitted fresh sweet cherries

¼ cup minced red onion

1 jalapeño pepper, seeded and minced*

1 teaspoon balsamic vinegar

¾ teaspoon salt, divided

Pinch ground allspice

¼ cup all-purpose flour

2 tablespoons cornmeal

¼ teaspoon black pepper

¼ teaspoon paprika

⅛ teaspoon garlic salt

2 tablespoons vegetable oil

4 medium catfish fillets (about 1¼ pounds)

Lime wedges (optional)

Chopped fresh cilantro (optional)

*Jalapeño peppers can sting and irritate the skin, so wear rubber gloves when handling peppers and do not touch your eyes.

1. For salsa, combine cherries, red onion, jalapeño, vinegar, ½ teaspoon salt and allspice in small bowl; mix well.

2. Combine flour, cornmeal, remaining ¼ teaspoon salt, black pepper, paprika and garlic salt in shallow bowl. Coat catfish fillets with flour mixture.

3. Heat oil in large cast iron skillet over medium-high heat. Add fish; cook 4 to 5 minutes per side or until golden brown and opaque in center.

4. Serve fish with cherry salsa, lime wedges and cilantro, if desired. *Makes 4 servings*

ALMOND-COATED SCALLOPS

¼ cup panko bread crumbs

2 tablespoons sliced almonds, chopped

1½ teaspoons grated lemon peel, divided

¼ teaspoon salt

⅛ teaspoon black pepper

8 jumbo sea scallops, cut in half horizontally (about 1 pound)

2½ tablespoons olive oil, divided

1 clove garlic, crushed

1. Combine panko, almonds, 1 teaspoon lemon peel, salt and pepper in shallow bowl. Brush scallops with ½ tablespoon oil; coat with panko mixture.

2. Heat remaining 2 tablespoons oil in large cast iron skillet over low heat. Add garlic; cook and stir 2 minutes. Discard garlic.

3. Add scallops to skillet in batches; cook over medium-high heat 2 to 3 minutes or until golden brown. Turn and cook 1 to 2 minutes. Sprinkle with remaining ½ teaspoon lemon peel. Serve immediately.

Makes 4 servings

CHILI GINGER SHRIMP

1 tablespoon plus 2 teaspoons soy sauce, divided

1½ tablespoons vegetable oil, divided

2 teaspoons grated fresh ginger

2 teaspoons lemon juice, divided

1 pound raw jumbo shrimp, peeled and deveined

2 tablespoons chili garlic sauce

⅛ teaspoon black pepper

2 tablespoons minced fresh cilantro

1. Combine 1 tablespoon soy sauce, ½ tablespoon oil, ginger and 1 teaspoon lemon juice in large bowl. Add shrimp; toss to coat. Cover and refrigerate 1 hour. Combine chili garlic sauce, remaining 2 teaspoons soy sauce, 1 teaspoon lemon juice and pepper in small bowl; set aside.

2. Heat remaining 1 tablespoon oil in large cast iron skillet over medium-high heat. Drain shrimp, reserving marinade. Add shrimp to skillet; cook and stir 6 minutes or until shrimp are pink and opaque.

3. Add reserved marinade and chili garlic sauce mixture to skillet; cook and stir 1 minute or until sauce boils and thickens slightly. Sprinkle with cilantro.

Makes 4 servings

Almond-Coated Scallops

VEGETABLES & SIDES

HAGGERTY

    8 slices bacon (about 8 ounces)
    3 onions, thinly sliced
1½ cups (6 ounces) shredded Irish Cheddar cheese, divided
    2 tablespoons butter, divided
    5 medium red potatoes (about 1¼ pounds), very thinly sliced
      Salt and black pepper

1. Preheat oven to 375°F.

2. Cook bacon in large cast iron skillet until crisp. Drain on paper towel-lined plate; crumble into medium bowl. Drain all but 1 tablespoon drippings from skillet.

3. Add onions to skillet; cook and stir over medium heat about 8 minutes or until translucent but not browned. Drain on paper towel-lined plate. Remove to bowl with bacon; mix well.

3. Reserve ¼ cup cheese; set aside. Melt 1 tablespoon butter in same skillet or 8- to 9-inch casserole. Arrange one quarter of potato slices to cover bottom of skillet. Season with salt and pepper. Top with one third of bacon-onion mixture; sprinkle with one third of remaining cheese. Repeat layers twice. Top with remaining one quarter of potato slices; dot with remaining 1 tablespoon butter.

4. Cover with foil and bake 50 minutes. Uncover and bake 10 minutes or until potatoes are tender. *Turn oven to broil.* Broil 2 to 3 minutes or until lightly browned. Sprinkle with reserved ¼ cup cheese. Serve warm.   *Makes 6 to 8 servings*

TIP: Use a mandolin to slice the potatoes very thin (about ⅛ inch). Thicker pieces may require a longer cooking time.

VEGETABLE FAJITAS WITH SPICY SALSA

3 medium tomatoes

1 small unpeeled yellow onion

1 jalapeño pepper*

6 unpeeled garlic cloves

   Juice of 1 lime

2 teaspoons salt, divided

12 flour tortillas, fajita size

1 tablespoon canola oil

4 medium bell peppers, cut into strips

1 medium red onion, peeled, cut in half vertically and thickly sliced

¼ teaspoon black pepper

1 can (16 ounces) refried beans

   Chopped fresh cilantro and sour cream (optional)

*Jalapeño peppers can sting and irritate the skin, so wear rubber gloves when handling peppers and do not touch your eyes.

1. For salsa, preheat broiler. Line baking sheet with parchment paper or foil. Place tomatoes, yellow onion, jalapeño and garlic on prepared baking sheet; broil 10 minutes. Turn vegetables and rotate pan. Broil 10 minutes or until blackened. Cool 10 minutes. Peel tomatoes, onion and garlic; peel and seed jalapeño. Place in blender or food processor with lime juice and 1 teaspoon salt; blend until desired consistency. Refrigerate until ready to serve. (Salsa can be made up to 1 week in advance.)

2. Heat large cast iron skillet over medium-high heat. Cook tortillas, one at a time, about 15 seconds per side or until blistered and browned. Keep warm.

3. Heat oil in same skillet over medium heat. Add bell peppers, red onion, remaining 1 teaspoon salt and black pepper; cook 10 minutes or until vegetables are tender, stirring occasionally.

4. Heat refried beans in small saucepan over medium heat or microwave in microwavable bowl on HIGH 1 minute, stirring occasionally. Spread 2 tablespoons beans on each tortilla; top with ⅓ cup vegetables and about 2 tablespoons salsa. Roll up tortillas; serve immediately. Garnish with cilantro and sour cream.

Makes 6 servings

CLASSIC HASH BROWNS

1 large russet potato, peeled and grated
¼ teaspoon salt
⅛ teaspoon black pepper
2 tablespoons vegetable oil

1. Squeeze liquid from potatoes in paper towels or clean kitchen towel to remove as much moisture as possible.

2. Heat medium cast iron skillet over medium heat 5 minutes. Combine potato, salt and pepper in small bowl; toss to coat.

2. Add oil to skillet; heat 30 seconds. Spread potato mixture evenly in skillet. Cook, without stirring, about 5 minutes or until bottom is browned. Turn potatoes; cook 6 to 8 minutes or until golden brown and crispy.

Makes 2 servings

CRISPY BATTERED PLANTAINS

¼ cup sugar
½ teaspoon ground cinnamon
½ cup masa harina, divided
1 egg
¼ cup cornstarch
½ cup cold water
Vegetable oil for frying
4 large black-skinned plantains, peeled and cut into quarters

1. Combine sugar and cinnamon in medium bowl; set aside.

2. Place ¼ cup masa harina in shallow bowl. Beat egg in another shalllow bowl. Add cornstarch, remaining ¼ cup masa harina and water, blending until smooth.

3. Pour oil into large cast iron skillet to depth of 1 inch; heat to 375°F over medium-high heat. Adjust heat to maintain temperature. Coat plantains with masa harina, then with batter. Add to hot oil in batches; cook until golden brown on both sides. Drain on paper towel-lined plate.

4. Roll plantains in cinnamon-sugar. Serve warm.

Makes 8 servings

Classic Hash Browns

TANGY RED CABBAGE WITH APPLES AND BACON

8 slices thick-cut bacon
1 large onion, sliced
½ small head red cabbage (1 pound), thinly sliced
1 tablespoon sugar
1 Granny Smith apple, peeled and sliced
2 tablespoons cider vinegar
½ teaspoon salt
¼ teaspoon black pepper

1. Heat large cast iron skillet over medium heat. Add bacon; cook 6 to 8 minutes or until crisp, turning occasionally. Drain on paper towel-lined plate. Coarsely chop bacon.

2. Drain all but 2 tablespoon drippings from skillet. Add onion; cook and stir over medium-high heat 2 to 3 minutes or until onion begins to soften. Add cabbage and sugar; cook and stir 4 to 5 minutes or until cabbage wilts. Stir in apple; cook 3 minutes or until crisp-tender. Stir in vinegar; cook 1 minute or until absorbed.

3. Stir in bacon, salt and pepper; cook 1 minute or until heated through. Serve warm or at room temperature. *Makes 4 servings*

MASHED POTATO CAKES

2 cups cold mashed potatoes
⅓ cup shredded Cheddar cheese
3 strips bacon, crisp-cooked and crumbled
2 egg yolks, beaten
2 tablespoons chopped fresh parsley
2 tablespoons snipped fresh chives
1 tablespoon all-purpose flour
1 teaspoon salt
⅛ teaspoon black pepper
3 tablespoons vegetable oil

1. Combine mashed potatoes, cheese, bacon, egg yolks, parsley, chives, flour, salt and pepper in large bowl, mix well.

2. Heat oil in large cast iron skillet over medium heat. Scoop ¼ cupfuls of potato mixture into skillet. Cook 8 to 10 minutes per side or until golden brown. *Makes 4 servings*

Tangy Red Cabbage with Apples and Bacon

CHARRED CORN SALAD

3 tablespoons fresh lime juice

½ teaspoon salt

¼ cup extra virgin olive oil

4 to 6 ears corn, husked

⅔ cup canned black beans, rinsed and drained

½ cup chopped fresh cilantro

2 teaspoons minced seeded chipotle pepper (1 canned chipotle pepper in adobo sauce *or* 1 dried chipotle pepper, reconstituted in boiling water)*

*Chipotle peppers can sting and irritate the skin, so wear rubber gloves when handling peppers and do not touch your eyes.

1. Whisk lime juice and salt in small bowl. Gradually whisk in oil. Set aside.

2. Heat large cast iron skillet over medium-high heat. Cook corn in single layer about 15 minutes or until browned and tender, turning frequently. Remove to plate to cool slightly. Slice kernels off ears and place in medium bowl.

3. Microwave beans in small microwavable bowl on HIGH 1 minute or until heated through. Add beans, cilantro and chipotle to corn; mix well. Pour lime juice mixture over corn mixture; toss to combine.

Makes 6 servings

NOTE: Chipotle peppers in adobo sauce are available canned in the ethnic section of most supermarkets. Since only a small amount is needed for this dish, spoon leftovers into a covered plastic container and refrigerate or freeze for another use.

CRISPY SKILLET POTATOES

2 tablespoons olive oil

4 red potatoes, cut into thin wedges

½ cup chopped onion

2 tablespoons lemon pepper

½ teaspoon coarse salt

Chopped fresh parsley

1. Heat oil in large cast iron skillet over medium heat. Add potatoes, onion, lemon pepper and salt; cover and cook 20 minutes, stirring occasionally. Uncover and cook 10 minutes or until potatoes are tender and browned.

2. Sprinkle with parsley just before serving. *Makes 4 servings*

HONG KONG FRIED RICE CAKES

1 package (about 6 ounces) chicken-flavored rice and vermicelli mix

½ cup sliced green onions

2 eggs, beaten

2 tablespoons chopped fresh parsley

1 tablespoon hoisin sauce

1 tablespoon soy sauce

1 teaspoon minced fresh ginger

1 clove garlic, minced

2 to 3 tablespoons vegetable oil, divided

1. Prepare rice according to package directions, omitting butter. Cover and refrigerate 1 hour or until cold. Add green onions, eggs, parsley, hoisin sauce, soy sauce, ginger and garlic; mix well. Shape mixture into 3-inch patties.

2. Heat 1 tablespoon oil in large cast iron skillet over medium heat. Cook four patties at a time 3 to 4 minutes per side or until golden brown, adding additional oil as needed. *Makes 4 to 6 servings*

Crispy Skillet Potatoes

HAVARTI AND ONION SANDWICHES

½ tablespoon olive oil
⅓ cup thinly sliced red onion
4 slices pumpernickel bread
6 ounces dill havarti cheese, cut into slices
½ cup prepared coleslaw

1. Heat oil in large cast iron skillet over medium heat. Add onion; cook and stir 5 minutes or until tender. Layer two bread slices with onion, cheese and coleslaw; top with remaining two bread slices.

2. Heat same skillet over medium heat. Add sandwiches; press down with spatula or weigh down with small plate. Cook 4 to 5 minutes per side or until cheese is melted and bread is crisp.

Makes 2 sandwiches

SMOKY BARBECUED THREE-BEAN SKILLET

1 cup chopped yellow onion
1 green or red bell pepper, diced
2 thick slices bacon, diced
1 jar (18 ounces) baked beans
1 can (15 ounces) no-salt-added red beans or kidney beans, undrained
1 can (15 ounces) no-salt-added navy beans, undrained
¼ cup ketchup
2 tablespoons packed brown sugar
2 tablespoons Dijon or yellow mustard
1 teaspoon hot pepper sauce or chipotle pepper sauce (optional)

1. Cook onion, bell pepper and bacon in large cast iron skillet over medium-high heat 6 minutes or until onion is translucent, stirring frequently.

2. Add baked beans, red beans with liquid, navy beans with liquid, ketchup, brown sugar, mustard and hot pepper sauce, if desired; bring to a simmer. Cook over medium-low heat about 10 minutes or until bell pepper is tender, stirring occasionally.

Makes 10 servings

NOTE: The liquid from the no-salt-added beans helps to thicken this dish. You may substitute regular canned red beans and/or navy beans; however, to reduce the sodium content, you should rinse and drain the beans. As a result, the dish will not be as thick.

Havarti and Onion Sandwiches

SKILLET MAC AND CHEESE

1 pound uncooked cavatappi or rotini pasta
8 ounces thick-cut bacon, cut into ½-inch pieces
¼ cup finely chopped onion
¼ cup all-purpose flour
3½ cups whole milk
1½ cups (6 ounces) shredded fontina cheese
1 cup (4 ounces) shredded white Cheddar cheese
1 cup (4 ounces) shredded Gruyère cheese
¾ cup grated Parmesan cheese, divided
½ teaspoon salt
½ teaspoon dry mustard
¼ teaspoon ground red pepper
¼ teaspoon black pepper
¼ cup panko bread crumbs

1. Preheat oven to 400°F. Cook pasta in large saucepan according to package directions until al dente; drain.

2. Meanwhile, cook bacon in large cast iron skillet over medium heat until crisp; drain on paper towel-lined plate. Pour drippings into glass measuring cup, leaving thin coating on bottom of skillet.

3. Heat 4 tablespoons drippings in large saucepan over medium-high heat. Add onion; cook and stir about 4 minutes or until translucent. Add flour; cook and stir 5 minutes. Slowly add milk over medium-low heat, stirring constantly. Cook and stir until slightly thickened. Stir in fontina, Cheddar, Gruyère, ½ cup Parmesan, salt, mustard, red pepper and black pepper until smooth and well blended. Add cooked pasta; stir gently until coated. Stir in bacon. Spread mixture in prepared skillet.

4. Combine panko and remaining ¼ cup Parmesan in small bowl; sprinkle over pasta. Bake about 30 minutes or until top is golden brown. *Makes 6 servings*

SUMMER SQUASH SKILLET

2 tablespoons butter

1 medium sweet or yellow onion, thinly sliced and separated into rings

2 medium zucchini or yellow squash (or one of each), sliced

¾ teaspoon salt

¼ teaspoon black pepper

1 large tomato, chopped

¼ cup chopped fresh basil

2 tablespoons grated Parmesan cheese

1. Heat butter in large cast iron skillet over medium-high heat. Add onion; stir to coat with butter. Cover and cook 3 minutes. Uncover; cook and stir over medium heat about 3 minutes or until onion is golden brown.

2. Add squash, salt and pepper; cover and cook 5 minutes, stirring once. Add tomato; cook uncovered about 2 minutes or until squash is tender. Stir in basil and sprinkle with cheese.   *Makes 4 servings*

BOXTY PANCAKES

2 medium russet potatoes (1 pound), peeled, divided

⅔ cup all-purpose flour

1 teaspoon baking powder

½ teaspoon salt

⅔ cup buttermilk

3 tablespoons butter

1. Cut one potato into 1-inch chunks; place in small saucepan and add cold water to cover by 2 inches. Bring to a boil over medium-high heat; cook 14 to 18 minutes or until tender. Drain potato; return to saucepan and mash. Remove to medium bowl.

2. Shred remaining potato on large holes of box grater; add to bowl with mashed potato. Stir in flour, baking powder and salt until blended. Stir in buttermilk.

3. Heat 1 tablespoon butter in large cast iron skillet over medium heat. Drop four slightly heaping tablespoonfuls of batter into skillet; flatten into 2½-inch circles. Cook about 4 minutes per side or until golden and puffed. Remove to plate; cover to keep warm. Repeat with remaining batter and butter. Serve immediately.   *Makes 4 servings (16 to 20 pancakes)*

SERVING SUGGESTION: Serve with melted butter, sour cream or maple syrup.

Summer Squash Skillet

SKILLET ROASTED ROOT VEGETABLES

1 sweet potato, peeled, halved lengthwise and cut crosswise into ½-inch slices
1 large red onion, cut into 1-inch wedges
2 parsnips, cut diagonally into 1-inch slices
2 carrots, cut diagonally into 1-inch slices
1 turnip, peeled, halved and cut crosswise into ½-inch slices
2½ tablespoons olive oil
1½ tablespoons honey
1½ tablespoons balsamic vinegar
1 teaspoon coarse salt
1 teaspoon dried thyme
¼ teaspoon ground red pepper
¼ teaspoon black pepper

1. Preheat oven to 400°F.

2. Combine all ingredients in large bowl; toss to coat. Spread vegetables in single layer in large cast iron skillet. Roast 1 hour or until vegetables are tender, stirring once halfway through cooking time.

Makes 4 servings

COUNTRY-STYLE CORN

4 slices bacon
1 tablespoon all-purpose flour
1 can (about 15 ounces) corn, drained
1 can (about 15 ounces) cream-style corn
1 red bell pepper, diced
½ cup sliced green onions
Salt and black pepper

1. Cook bacon in large cast iron skillet over medium heat until crisp; drain on paper towel-lined plate. Crumble bacon; set aside.

2. Whisk flour into drippings in skillet. Add corn, cream-style corn and bell pepper; bring to a boil. Reduce heat to low; cook 10 minutes or until thickened.

3. Stir green onions and bacon into corn mixture. Season with salt and black pepper.

Makes 6 to 8 servings

Skillet Roasted Root Vegetables

GRILLED MOZZARELLA AND ROASTED RED PEPPER SANDWICH

1 tablespoon olive oil vinaigrette or Italian salad dressing
2 slices Italian-style sandwich bread (2 ounces)
   Fresh basil leaves
⅓ cup roasted red peppers, rinsed, drained and patted dry
1 to 2 slices (1 ounce each) mozzarella or Swiss cheese
½ tablespoon olive oil

1. Brush dressing on one side of one bread slice; top with basil, roasted peppers, cheese and remaining bread slice.

2. Heat oil in large cast iron skillet over medium heat. Cook sandwich 4 to 5 minutes per side or until cheese melts and sandwich is golden brown. *Makes 1 sandwich*

STOVIES WITH BACON

3 medium russet potatoes (about 1½ pounds), peeled
6 slices bacon
2 large onions, halved vertically and sliced
4 teaspoons butter
½ teaspoon salt
⅛ teaspoon black pepper
⅓ cup water

1. Place potatoes in large saucepan; add cold water to cover by 2 inches. Bring to a boil over medium-high heat; cook 15 minutes or until partially cooked. Drain; let stand until cool enough to handle. Cut potatoes into ½-inch-thick slices.

2. Cook bacon in large cast iron skillet over medium-high heat 6 to 7 minutes or until crisp, turning occasionally. Drain on paper towel-lined plate. Chop bacon; set aside.

3. Drain all but 2 tablespoons drippings from skillet; heat over medium heat. Add onions; cook 8 to 9 minutes or until softened but not browned, stirring occasionally. Remove onions to small bowl.

4. Add butter to skillet; heat over medium heat until melted. Add potatoes; sprinkle with salt and pepper. Top with onions and water; cover and cook 5 minutes. Stir in bacon; cook, uncovered, 10 to 12 minutes or until potatoes are tender and browned, stirring occasionally. *Makes 4 servings*

Grilled Mozzarella & Roasted Red Pepper Sandwich

BALSAMIC BUTTERNUT SQUASH

    3 tablespoons olive oil
    2 tablespoons thinly sliced fresh sage (about 6 large leaves), divided
    1 medium butternut squash, peeled and cut into 1-inch pieces (4 to 5 cups)
    ½ red onion, halved and cut into ¼-inch slices
    1 teaspoon salt, divided
    2½ tablespoons balsamic vinegar
    ¼ teaspoon black pepper

1. Heat oil in large cast iron skillet over medium-high heat. Add 1 tablespoon sage; cook and stir 3 minutes. Add butternut squash, onion and ½ teaspoon salt; cook 6 minutes, stirring occasionally. (Squash should fit in crowded single layer in skillet.) Reduce heat to medium; cook 15 minutes without stirring.

2. Stir in vinegar, remaining ½ teaspoon salt and pepper; cook 10 minutes or until squash is tender, stirring occasionally. Stir in remaining 1 tablespoon sage; cook 1 minute.   *Makes 4 servings*

MOROCCAN CHICKPEAS

    1 cup chopped onion
    ¼ cup reduced-sodium vegetable broth
    2 cloves garlic, minced
    2 cans (about 15 ounces each) chickpeas, rinsed and drained
    1 can (28 ounces) diced tomatoes
    ½ cup sliced red bell pepper
    ½ cup sliced yellow bell pepper
    ½ cup sliced green bell pepper
    2 tablespoons oil-cured olives, pitted and chopped
    1 teaspoon ground cumin
    1 teaspoon ground ginger
    1 teaspoon ground turmeric
    1 bay leaf
    2 tablespoons lemon juice

1. Combine onion, broth and garlic in large cast iron skillet. Cook and stir over medium heat 3 minutes or until onion softens.

2. Stir in chickpeas, tomatoes, bell peppers, olives, cumin, ginger, turmeric and bay leaf; simmer 10 minutes or until bell peppers are tender. Remove and discard bay leaf. Stir in lemon juice; adjust seasonings.
          Makes 6 servings

Balsamic Butternut Squash

SKILLET SUCCOTASH

1 tablespoon canola oil
½ cup diced onion
½ cup diced green bell pepper
½ cup diced celery
½ teaspoon paprika
¾ cup frozen white or yellow corn
¾ cup frozen lima beans
½ cup canned diced tomatoes
1 tablespoon minced fresh parsley
½ teaspoon salt
¼ teaspoon black pepper

1. Heat oil in large cast iron skillet over medium heat. Add onion, bell pepper and celery; cook and stir 5 minutes or until onion is translucent and bell pepper and celery are crisp-tender. Stir in paprika.

2. Add corn, lima beans and tomatoes. Reduce heat to low; cover and simmer 20 minutes or until beans are tender. Stir in parsley, salt and black pepper just before serving.   *Makes 4 servings*

TIP: For additional flavor, add 1 clove minced garlic and 1 bay leaf. Remove and discard bay leaf before serving.

SWISS ROSTI POTATOES

4 large russet potatoes (about 6 ounces each)
4 tablespoons butter
Salt and black pepper

1. Preheat oven to 400°F. Scrub potatoes and pierce in several places with fork. Bake 1 hour or until fork-tender. Cool completely, then refrigerate until cold.*

2. When potatoes are cold, peel with paring knife. Grate potatoes on large holes of box grater or with large grating disk of food processor.

3. Heat butter in large cast iron skillet over medium-high heat until melted and bubbly. Press grated potatoes evenly into skillet. (Do not stir or turn potatoes.) Season with salt and pepper to taste. Cook 10 to 12 minutes until golden brown.

4. Cover skillet with serving plate; invert potatoes onto plate. Serve immediately.   *Makes 4 servings*

*Prepare potatoes several hours or up to 1 day in advance.

Skillet Succotash

BREADS & DESSERTS

SAUSAGE AND CHEDDAR CORN BREAD

1 tablespoon vegetable oil
½ pound bulk pork sausage
1 medium onion, diced
1 jalapeño pepper,* diced
1 package (8 ounces) corn bread and muffin mix
1 cup (4 ounces) shredded Cheddar cheese, divided
⅓ cup milk
1 egg

*Jalapeño peppers can sting and irritate the skin, so wear rubber gloves when handling peppers and do not touch your eyes.

1. Heat oil in large cast iron skillet over medium heat. Add sausage; cook until browned, stirring to break up meat. Add onion and jalapeño; cook and stir 5 minutes or until vegetables are softened. Remove to medium bowl.

2. Preheat oven to 350°F. Combine corn bread mix, ½ cup cheese, milk and egg in separate medium bowl. Pour batter into skillet. Spread sausage mixture over batter; sprinkle with remaining ½ cup cheese.

3. Bake 20 to 25 minutes or until edges are lightly browned. Cut into wedges. Refrigerate leftovers.

Makes 10 servings

CHAPATIS

2 cups whole wheat flour (or a combination of whole wheat and all-purpose flour)
1 tablespoon vegetable oil
1 teaspoon salt
¾ to 1 cup warm water

1. Combine flour, oil and salt in food processor. With motor running, drizzle ¾ cup water through feed tube until dough forms a ball that cleans side of bowl. Let dough stand 1 to 2 minutes.

2. Turn on processor and slowly add additional water until dough is soft but not sticky. If dough is hard or dry, cut into quarters and sprinkle water over quarters. Process until dough forms a soft ball, gradually adding additional water if dough will absorb it. Let dough stand in work bowl 5 minutes.

3. Turn dough onto lightly greased surface; shape into a ball. Cover and let stand at room temperature about 1 hour.

4. Divide dough into 16 equal pieces. Roll out each piece into 6- to 8-inch thin circle on lightly floured surface.

5. Heat large cast iron skillet over medium heat until hot enough to sizzle a drop of water. Cook each chapati about 1 minute per side or until golden. (Press down dough with wide spatula to cook evenly.) Serve hot.

Makes 16 chapatis

Chapati, also known as roti, is an unleavened flatbread common in northern India and Pakistan. Chaptis are often served with meals; pieces are torn off and used to scoop up small amounts of meat or vegetable dishes.

CINNAMON PECAN ROLLS

¼ cup (½ stick) butter, melted, divided
1 loaf (1 pound) frozen bread dough, thawed
½ cup packed dark brown sugar
2 teaspoons ground cinnamon
½ cup chopped pecans

1. Brush large cast iron skillet with ½ tablespoon melted butter. Roll out dough into 18×8-inch rectangle on lightly floured surface.

2. Combine brown sugar, 3 tablespoons butter and cinnamon in medium bowl; mix well. Brush mixture evenly over dough; sprinkle with pecans. Starting with long side, roll up tightly jelly-roll style. Pinch seam to seal.

3. Cut crosswise into 1-inch slices; arrange slices cut side down in prepared skillet. Cover loosely with plastic wrap. Let rise in warm place about 30 minutes or until doubled in bulk.

4. Preheat oven to 350°F. Brush tops of rolls with remaining ½ tablespoon butter. Bake 20 to 25 minutes or until golden brown. Serve warm. *Makes 18 rolls*

VARIATIONS: If desired, sprinkle ½ cup raisins over the dough instead of or in addition to the pecans before rolling it up. For an extra rich treat, sprinkle with ½ cup semisweet chocolate chips.

TIP: For a quick and easy icing, whisk ½ cup powdered sugar and 1 tablespoon milk in a small bowl until smooth. Drizzle over warm rolls.

CONFETTI CORN BREAD

3½ tablespoons vegetable oil, divided
1½ cups all-purpose flour
¾ cup yellow cornmeal
2 tablespoons sugar
1 tablespoon baking powder
1 teaspoon baking soda
¾ teaspoon salt
½ teaspoon black pepper
1⅓ cups buttermilk
½ cup finely chopped red bell pepper
1 tablespoon dried chives or dried onion flakes
1 cup corn
¾ cup (3 ounces) shredded Cheddar cheese

1. Preheat oven to 425°F. Brush 10-inch deep cast iron skillet with ½ tablespoon oil. Place in oven to heat.

2. Combine flour, cornmeal, sugar, baking powder, baking soda, salt and black pepper in large bowl; mix well. Combine buttermilk, bell pepper, remaining 3 tablespoons oil and chives in 2-cup glass measure.

3. Make well in center of flour mixture; add buttermilk mixture and stir just until dry ingredients are moistened. *Do not overmix.* Fold in corn and cheese. Spoon batter into hot skillet.

4. Bake 20 to 25 minutes or until toothpick inserted into center comes out clean. Cut into wedges; serve immediately.

Makes 12 servings

BASIL BISCUITS

2 cups all-purpose flour
4 tablespoons grated Parmesan cheese, divided
1 tablespoon baking powder
½ teaspoon baking soda
¼ teaspoon salt
4 tablespoons cream cheese
2½ tablespoons butter, divided
6 ounces plain yogurt
⅓ cup slivered fresh basil leaves

1. Preheat oven to 375°F.

2. Combine flour, 2 tablespoons Parmesan, baking powder, baking soda and salt in large bowl. Cut in cream cheese and 1 tablespoon butter with pastry blender or two knives until mixture resembles coarse crumbs. Stir in yogurt and basil, mixing just until dough clings together. Turn dough out onto lightly floured surface and gently pat into a ball. Knead just until dough holds together. Pat and roll dough into 7-inch log. Cut into 7 (1-inch-thick) slices.

3. Melt remaining 1½ tablespoons butter. Brush 10-inch cast iron skillet with ½ tablespoon butter. Arrange biscuits in single layer in skillet; brush with 1 tablespoon melted butter. Sprinkle with remaining 2 tablespoons Parmesan.

4. Bake 20 to 30 minutes or until golden and firm. *Makes 7 biscuits*

WARM MIXED BERRY PIE

2 packages (12 ounces each) frozen mixed berries, thawed and drained
⅓ cup sugar
3 tablespoons cornstarch
2 teaspoons grated orange peel
¼ teaspoon ground ginger
1 refrigerated pie crust (half of 14-ounce package)

1. Preheat oven to 350°F.

2. Combine berries, sugar, cornstarch, orange peel and ginger in large bowl; toss to coat. Spoon into large cast iron skillet. Place crust over filling; crimp edge as desired.

3. Bake 1 hour or until crust is golden brown. Let stand 1 hour before serving.   *Makes 8 servings*

BANANAS FLAMBÉ

2 tablespoons butter
½ teaspoon ground cinnamon
2 small firm ripe bananas, peeled and cut in half crosswise
2 tablespoons frozen unsweetened apple juice concentrate
2 tablespoons brandy or cognac

1. Heat butter in large cast iron skillet over medium heat. Stir in cinnamon. Add bananas; cook about 1 minute per side or until heated through. Add apple juice concentrate; cook 1 minute, stirring occasionally. Drizzle with brandy; remove from heat. Carefully ignite with lighted match; shake skillet until flames are extinguished.

2. Transfer bananas to individual dessert dishes, reserving liquid in skillet. Cook liquid over medium-high heat about 1 minute or until thickened and bubbly. Pour over bananas; serve immediately.

Makes 2 servings

Warm Mixed Berry Pie

CHOCOLATE-STUFFED DOUGHNUTS

½ cup semisweet chocolate chips
2 tablespoons whipping cream
1 package (7½ ounces) refrigerated buttermilk biscuits (10 count)
½ cup granulated or powdered sugar
¾ cup vegetable oil

1. Combine chocolate chips and cream in small microwavable bowl. Microwave on HIGH 20 seconds; stir until smooth. Cover and refrigerate 1 hour or until firm.

2. Separate dough into individual biscuits. Using melon baller or small teaspoon, scoop out 1 rounded teaspoon chocolate mixture; place in center of each biscuit. Press dough around chocolate and pinch to form a ball. Roll pinched end on work surface to seal dough and flatten ball slightly.

3. Place sugar in shallow bowl. Heat oil in medium cast iron skillet until hot but not smoking. Cook doughnuts in small batches about 30 seconds per side or until golden brown. Drain on paper towel-lined plate.

4. Roll warm doughnuts in sugar to coat. Serve warm or at room temperature. (Doughnuts are best within a few hours of cooking.) *Makes 10 doughnuts*

TIP: For a quicker chocolate filling, use chocolate chips instead of the chocolate-cream mixture. Place 6 to 8 chips in the center of each biscuit; proceed with shaping and cooking doughnuts as directed.

INDIVIDUAL FRIED APPLE CRANBERRY PIES

- 3 tablespoons butter
- 3 Gala apples (about 12 ounces), peeled and diced
- 3 tablespoons dried cranberries
- 3 tablespoons packed brown sugar
- 1½ tablespoons lemon juice
- ¾ teaspoon ground cinnamon
- ¼ teaspoon ground nutmeg
- ⅛ teaspoon salt
- 1 package (about 14 ounces) refrigerated pie crusts
- Vegetable oil for frying
- Powdered sugar

1. Heat butter in large cast iron skillet over medium heat. Add apples; cook 8 minutes, stirring frequently. Add cranberries, brown sugar, lemon juice, cinnamon, nutmeg and salt; cook and stir 4 minutes or until apples are tender. Remove to medium bowl; cool 15 minutes. Wipe out skillet.

2. Let crusts stand at room temperature 15 minutes. Heat 2 cups oil to 350°F in same skillet over medium heat.

3. Roll out each crust into 12½-inch circle on floured surface; cut out seven 4-inch circles from each crust. Place generous tablespoon apple mixture on half of one dough circle, leaving ¼-inch border. Dip finger in water and moisten edge of dough circle. Fold dough over filling, pressing lightly. Dip fork in flour and crimp edge of dough to seal completely. Repeat with remaining dough and filling.

4. Working in batches, cook pies 1 minute. Turn and cook 1 minute or until lightly browned. Remove to paper-towel lined baking sheet. Allow oil temperature to return to 350°F between batches.

5. Sprinkle with powdered sugar; serve warm or at room temperature.   *Makes 14 pies*

NOTE: Granny Smith apples can be substituted for Gala apples. Increase brown sugar to 4 tablespoons and replace lemon juice with water.

CHOCOLATE CHIP SKILLET COOKIE

1¾ cups all-purpose flour
1 teaspoon baking soda
1 teaspoon salt
¾ cup (1½ sticks) butter, softened
¾ cup packed brown sugar
½ cup granulated sugar
2 eggs
1 teaspoon vanilla
1 package (12 ounces) semisweet chocolate chips
Sea salt (optional)
Ice cream (optional)

1. Preheat oven to 350°F.

2. Combine flour, baking soda and 1 teaspoon salt in medium bowl. Beat butter, brown sugar and granulated sugar in large bowl with electric mixer at medium speed until creamy. Beat in eggs and vanilla until well blended. Gradually beat in flour mixture at low speed just until blended. Stir in chocolate chips. Press dough evenly into well-seasoned* 10-inch cast iron skillet. Sprinkle lightly with sea salt, if desired.

3. Bake about 35 minutes or until top and edges are golden brown but cookie is still soft in center. Cool on wire rack 10 minutes before cutting into wedges. Serve warm with ice cream, if desired.

Makes 8 servings

*If skillet is not well seasoned, brush with 1 tablespoon melted butter.

TIP Even better than a warm wedge of skillet cookie is a personal skillet cookie! You can find small (4- to 6-inch) cast iron skillets at kitchenware and home goods stores—they are inexpensive and perfect for making individual servings. You can use them for other desserts such as mini pies and crisps; they can also be used for single servings of casseroles and pot pies.

GINGER PLUM TART

    1 refrigerated pie crust (half of 14-ounce package)
1¾ pounds plums, cut into ½-inch slices
    ½ cup plus 1 teaspoon sugar, divided
1½ tablespoons all-purpose flour
1½ teaspoons ground ginger
    ¼ teaspoon ground cinnamon
    ⅛ teaspoon salt
    1 egg
    2 teaspoons water

1. Preheat oven to 400°F. Let crust stand at room temperature 10 minutes. Combine plums, ½ cup sugar, flour, ginger, cinnamon and salt in large bowl; toss to coat.

2. Roll out crust into 14-inch circle on lightly floured surface. Transfer to 10-inch cast iron skillet. Mound plum mixture in center of crust, leaving 2-inch border around fruit. Fold crust up over filling, pleating as necessary and gently pressing crust into fruit.

3. Beat egg and water in small bowl; brush over crust. Sprinkle with remaining 1 teaspoon sugar.

4. Bake about 45 minutes or until crust is golden brown.   *Makes 6 to 8 servings*

CHERRY CLAFOUTI

    1 tablespoon butter, softened
    1 cup whole milk
    4 eggs
    ½ cup all-purpose flour
    ½ cup packed brown sugar
    1 teaspoon vanilla
    ¼ teaspoon salt
    1 package (1 pound) frozen dark sweet cherries, thawed, drained and patted dry

1. Preheat oven to 350°F. Grease 10-inch cast iron skillet with butter.

2. Combine milk, eggs, flour, brown sugar, vanilla and salt in blender; blend until smooth. Pour batter into prepared skillet; sprinkle cherries over batter.

3. Bake about 35 minutes or until set, puffed and golden brown and toothpick inserted into center comes out clean.   *Makes 8 servings*

Ginger Plum Tart

HONEY SOPAIPILLAS

¼ cup plus 2 teaspoons sugar, divided
½ teaspoon ground cinnamon
2 cups all-purpose flour
½ teaspoon salt
2 teaspoons baking powder
2 tablespoons shortening
¾ cup warm water
  Vegetable oil for frying
  Honey

1. Combine ¼ cup sugar and cinnamon in small bowl; set aside. Combine remaining 2 teaspoons sugar, flour, salt and baking powder in large bowl. Cut in shortening with pastry blender or two knives until mixture resembles fine crumbs. Gradually add water; stir with fork until mixture forms dough. Turn out onto lightly floured surface; knead 2 minutes or until smooth. Shape into a ball; cover with bowl and let rest 30 minutes.

2. Divide dough into four equal pieces; shape each into a ball. Flatten each ball into 8-inch circle about ⅛ inch thick. Cut each round into four wedges.

3. Pour oil into large cast iron skillet to depth of 1½ inches; heat to 360°F over medium-high heat. Adjust heat to maintain temperature. Cook two pieces of dough at a time 2 minutes or until puffed and golden brown, turning once. Remove with slotted spoon; drain on paper towel-lined plate. Sprinkle with cinnamon-sugar mixture. Serve hot with honey. *Makes 16 sopaipillas*

NOTE: Sopaipillas are a New Mexican specialty, originating in Albuquerque more than 200 years ago. These deep-fried pockets of dough may be served with meals instead of bread or used as a pocket for stuffing with taco fillings. (Omit the cinnamon-sugar and honey.) The most popular way to enjoy sopaipillas is for dessert, served with honey.

APPLE CRANBERRY CRUMBLE

4 large apples (about 1⅓ pounds), peeled and cut into ¼-inch slices
2 cups fresh or frozen cranberries
⅓ cup granulated sugar
6 tablespoons all-purpose flour, divided
1 teaspoon apple pie spice, divided
¼ teaspoon salt, divided
½ cup chopped walnuts
¼ cup old-fashioned oats
2 tablespoons packed brown sugar
¼ cup (½ stick) butter, cut into small pieces

1. Preheat oven to 375°F.

2. Combine apples, cranberries, granulated sugar, 2 tablespoons flour, ½ teaspoon apple pie spice and ⅛ teaspoon salt in large bowl; toss to coat. Transfer to medium cast iron skillet.

3. For topping, combine remaining ¼ cup flour, walnuts, oats, brown sugar, remaining ½ teaspoon apple pie spice and ⅛ teaspoon salt in medium bowl; mix well. Cut in butter with pastry blender or two knives until mixture resembles coarse crumbs. Spread over fruit in skillet.

4. Bake 50 to 60 minutes or until filling is bubbly and topping is lightly browned.   *Makes 4 servings*

TIP This crumble can be also made with pears or a combination of apples and pears.

METRIC CONVERSION CHART

VOLUME MEASUREMENTS (dry)

$\frac{1}{8}$ teaspoon = 0.5 mL
$\frac{1}{4}$ teaspoon = 1 mL
$\frac{1}{2}$ teaspoon = 2 mL
$\frac{3}{4}$ teaspoon = 4 mL
1 teaspoon = 5 mL
1 tablespoon = 15 mL
2 tablespoons = 30 mL
$\frac{1}{4}$ cup = 60 mL
$\frac{1}{3}$ cup = 75 mL
$\frac{1}{2}$ cup = 125 mL
$\frac{2}{3}$ cup = 150 mL
$\frac{3}{4}$ cup = 175 mL
1 cup = 250 mL
2 cups = 1 pint = 500 mL
3 cups = 750 mL
4 cups = 1 quart = 1 L

VOLUME MEASUREMENTS (fluid)

1 fluid ounce (2 tablespoons) = 30 mL
4 fluid ounces ($\frac{1}{2}$ cup) = 125 mL
8 fluid ounces (1 cup) = 250 mL
12 fluid ounces (1$\frac{1}{2}$ cups) = 375 mL
16 fluid ounces (2 cups) = 500 mL

WEIGHTS (mass)

$\frac{1}{2}$ ounce = 15 g
1 ounce = 30 g
3 ounces = 90 g
4 ounces = 120 g
8 ounces = 225 g
10 ounces = 285 g
12 ounces = 360 g
16 ounces = 1 pound = 450 g

DIMENSIONS

$\frac{1}{16}$ inch = 2 mm
$\frac{1}{8}$ inch = 3 mm
$\frac{1}{4}$ inch = 6 mm
$\frac{1}{2}$ inch = 1.5 cm
$\frac{3}{4}$ inch = 2 cm
1 inch = 2.5 cm

OVEN TEMPERATURES

250°F = 120°C
275°F = 140°C
300°F = 150°C
325°F = 160°C
350°F = 180°C
375°F = 190°C
400°F = 200°C
425°F = 220°C
450°F = 230°C

BAKING PAN SIZES

Utensil	Size in Inches/Quarts	Metric Volume	Size in Centimeters
Baking or Cake Pan (square or rectangular)	8×8×2	2 L	20×20×5
	9×9×2	2.5 L	23×23×5
	12×8×2	3 L	30×20×5
	13×9×2	3.5 L	33×23×5
Loaf Pan	8×4×3	1.5 L	20×10×7
	9×5×3	2 L	23×13×7
Round Layer Cake Pan	8×1½	1.2 L	20×4
	9×1½	1.5 L	23×4
Pie Plate	8×1¼	750 mL	20×3
	9×1¼	1 L	23×3
Baking Dish or Casserole	1 quart	1 L	—
	1½ quart	1.5 L	—
	2 quart	2 L	—